The Acting Biz

A Career Guide
to the Twin Cities

Beth Chaplin

Kirk House Publishers
Minneapolis, Minnesota

The Acting Biz:
A Career Guide to the Twin Cities

by Beth Chaplin

Library of Congress Cataloging-in-Publication Data
Chaplin, Beth.
  The acting biz: a career guide to the Twin Cities / Beth Chaplin.
    p. cm.
  Includes bibliographical references and index.
  ISBN-13: 978-1-933794-17-4 (alk. paper)
  ISBN-10: 1-933794-17-8 (alk. paper)
  1. Acting--Vocational guidance--Minnesota--Minneapolis. 2. Acting--Vocational guidance--Minnesota--St. Paul. I. Title.
  PN2055.C385 2010
  792.02'8--dc22
                                        2009037395

Kirk House Publishers, PO Box 390759, Minneapolis, Minnesota 55439
www.kirkhouse.com
Manufactured in the United States of America

Contents

APPENDICES:

Dedication

In fond memory of Roger Klemmer, founder of Voice Plus.
Rog was a true professional in front of a microphone and as an agent.
He was one of the first people in the business
to take the time to answer my questions and offer valuable advice.
It is in that same spirit that I offer this book.
Thanks, Rog.
We miss you.

In loving memory of Maureen Dunham,
my dear aunt, who shared her wisdom, sharp wit,
and humor in abundance.

Preface

"It takes a lot of courage
to show your dreams to someone else."

Erma Bombeck

Just about everyone who wants to be an actor is pursuing some kind of dream. Actually diving in takes courage. Congratulations for taking the plunge! (Or at least congratulations for thinking about it!) Whether you are already working as an actor or your "inner actor" has yet to make a public appearance, I'm glad you have found this book.

When I left my full-time teaching job in 1990, I auditioned all over town and sent my headshot and resume to agents, trying to get a foot in the door—any door. Some doors opened to interesting opportunities, some doors led nowhere, some simply slammed shut, and still other doors led to people who wanted only my money. However, I found no one who would or could answer all the questions I had about the acting world in the Twin Cities. My learning was strictly by trial and error.

I swore to myself that if I ever figured it all out, I would share what I had learned with whoever needed it. That vow of eighteen years ago has finally resulted in this book.

Lots of folks in town could have written this book. I am not the only expert; however, I am writing from a unique vantage. In the past eighteen years, I have learned all about this business from a variety of perspectives:

- As an actor in hundreds of commercials, industrials, and voice-overs.

- As an actor on a handful of Twin Cities' stages and in a few independent films.

- As an acting student with over a dozen local acting teachers.

- As an agent interviewing and auditioning new talent, directing on-camera and voice auditions, and booking actors for jobs.

- As a teacher and coach in classes on the business of acting, on-camera acting, ear prompting and voice-overs.
- As a documentary video director and producer.

I have also answered thousands of questions from new actors. It is amazing to me that I can now answer the same questions I was asking almost two decades ago.

In New York, Chicago, and Los Angeles, it is easy to find resources with all kinds of information for actors. Some of that information will apply to the Twin Cities; much of it does not. This is a thriving market, but it is quite different from the acting world in the three biggest markets. That is what makes this book unique. There never has been one single reference book that will answer questions about how the business really works here in the Twin Cities. I hope this book will do that for you.

As you read, I hope you will feel free to contact me with any questions that I have neglected to answer. I also welcome differing opinions and perspectives. I will try to include them in subsequent versions. I welcome any and all feedback! (beth@actingbiztc.com)

I wish someone had written this book decades ago. It would have saved me time, frustration, and money. I know that some lessons must be learned the hard way in this business—being an actor is not easy. There is no instant road to success, but there are definitely some paths to avoid! I offer no guarantees, only suggestions. I hope this book will illuminate your path and help you avoid some of the unnecessary obstacles. Chase your dream, and let this book help you plan the chase.

Break a leg!

Introduction

How to read this book

It may help you to view this as a reference book. Feel free to read from beginning to end, or simply skim the sub-headings to find the answers to your particular questions. Each chapter contains numerous sub-headings in a short topic or question-and-answer format. It has been shaped by hundreds of questions from past students. Where you are in your acting journey will determine the most useful information for you.

The appendices contain some of the most important information in the book. It is a listing of who's who, what's what, where they are, and how to find them. If I have left any question unanswered in the text of the book, someone listed in the appendices can certainly provide an answer.

This book is about the business side of the acting world, not the artistic side. It is about where the work is and how to best go about getting it. While there is no overall emphasis on stage acting, Chapter 10 discusses theater in the Twin Cities, and Chapters 7 and 9 discuss auditions and training for the stage. The primary emphasis of this book is the *business* of acting in the broadest sense—in other words, getting work: agents, auditions, unions, commercials, industrials, voice-overs, video shoots, finances, etc.

One of my editors suggested that I occasionally take a negative tone in the book, while another editor complained that I occasionally use too many superlatives. ("It is *so* great, *so* wonderful. . . .") They are both absolutely right. I am attempting to walk a tightrope between encouragement and reality. Rather than thinking of me as acting coach or cheerleader, consider me a business advisor. I will not present a view of the acting world through rose-colored glasses, but I will try to encourage you to pursue your dreams despite some of the challenging realities. My goal is to give sound, honest advice.

Colleges and universities generally teach the art of acting and the history of the theater; however, too many neglect to teach an actor how to actually get work. This book fills that void in an actor's preparation. There is work for actors in the Twin Cities, if you know where and how to look for it.

CHAPTER 1

The Biz in the Twin Cities

Los Angeles, New York, Chicago, and then us!

Are there really a lot of acting opportunities in the Twin Cities?

Yes! The Twin Cities market is said to be the fourth largest video production market in the country, trailing only Los Angeles, New York, and Chicago. Thousands of actors have made money in commercials and industrials (non-broadcast programs) in the Twin Cities. Some have made good money. And thousands of actors work on stage here—some are paid, many are not—but the opportunities are abundant.

This is a great place for actors!

Before I begin searching for acting opportunities in the Twin Cities, what should I know first?

A note of caution: You do not need to spend a lot of money to try your hand at acting! However, you do need to know the following truths about the industry:

- Do not give money to anyone who promises you work. No one can guarantee that you will get legitimate work as an actor.
- Do not give money to anyone who promises they can help you "be discovered."
- Do not pay an agency to represent you. Agents get paid when you get work.
- Do not pay anyone to put your photo in a book or on a website until you know that they have lots of clients who hire actors.
- If any person or organization wants a check from you the first time you ever meet them, rest assured they are far more interested in your checkbook than your acting career.

Be careful about paying anyone for anything in this business! Ask around and do some research first. Trust me on this. People who want to be actors and models (adults and children alike) are often too eager to launch their careers, so they will often believe anyone who tells them they are talented because they want it so badly.

I put this statement front and center so that even if you are skimming this book and you are about to put it back on the shelf, you will at least be warned!

To those who plan to keep reading, I am glad you found this book. I want you to enjoy your acting pursuit in the Twin Cities and to avoid being cheated in the process. This book is a great place to begin your journey.

> New actors will often jump at the first opportunity that they think will help them become an actor. Unscrupulous people know this and will prey on you if you do not do your homework first! Those people exist, even here in Minnesota-nice-land.

What kinds of work can an actor find in the Twin Cities?

- Stage work for both professional and amateur actors.
- Student films, low-budget independent films, and the rare major motion picture or made-for-TV movie. (The leading roles in major movies are almost always cast in the bigger markets. Smaller roles are sometimes available for local actors.)
- Commercials for radio, TV, and the internet, to broadcast locally, regionally, and nationally.
- Industrials (the commonly used term for any video or audio production that is not for broadcast, typically for training, marketing, or educational purposes).
- Voice-overs for radio and TV commercials as well as industrials. (See Chapter 12 for details.)
- Live industrials. (Companies hire actors to present their products and messages at trade shows and corporate events or to entertain at conventions.)
- Modeling and print advertising. (See Chapter 14 for details.)
- Jingle singing (though this work primarily goes to established vocal performers).
- Every possible variation and combination of any of the above.

What exactly do you mean by "actor"?

We all define the word actor in different ways. In this book, the term describes every kind of actor—from trained, experienced stage actors to total beginners who yearn to give acting a try.

You may be training to be a serious stage actor. Or you may have your sights set on New York or L.A. to chase the dream of working in TV and film. (You may even be here to *escape* from New York or L.A.!) Perhaps you are already a seasoned stage actor trying to figure out how to get into the world of commercials and industrials. Or you may be brand new to acting, and may simply want to act in community theater or make some money on the side doing a commercial or two.

Whatever your goals may be, welcome to the art and craft of acting. Please recognize, however, that others may define the term "actor" quite differently. Acting can only be mastered with a lifetime of dedication and commitment. I have twenty years of experience, and I know how the business of acting functions here in the Twin Cities; however, when it comes to the art of acting, I feel more like a novice than a master. My level of experience and dedication pales in comparison to the most experienced and talented actors in the Twin Cities. I am proud to call myself a professional actor; yet, to those more experienced and gifted actors, I tip my hat in respect.

In the Twin Cities, opportunities are available for beginning and experienced actors alike, but to be successful you will need to be dedicated. You eventually will be competing with and working with incredibly talented actors who have been working and training for years. Regardless of your level of experience and training, welcome to the profession.

"I wanna be a star!"

Sorry, you are in the wrong town. There are no million-dollar contracts here. No names in lights, no press clippings that will launch your career. This is a great place to be an actor, and it is a great place to gain some experience and training before moving on to a bigger market; however, star-making vehicles do not travel by way of I-35W and I-94.

On the other hand, if you are an accomplished stage actor, you can certainly earn tremendous respect from the acting community. That is the closest thing to stardom you will find in this town. There are a lot of very talented, experienced, highly-trained actors who work on stage here. Many of these actors could compete in the bigger markets, but have chosen to forego the more "glamorous" acting opportunities in order to retain the quality of life they have here in the Twin Cities.

You really will not find any stardom being a commercial/industrial actor—except perhaps a little respect from a few of your peers and agents. It is professional, well-paid work, but you will receive no big kudos for it.

If you are certain you are already a big star, this is not where you need to be. A "diva" attitude does not go over very well here—I doubt it goes over well anywhere. Successful actors here are working actors. If you waltz in with a big ego and starry eyes, you will stick out like a sore thumb!

On the other hand, team players get along really well in this business—both on stage and in the commercial world. If you are not worried about your own spotlight and you are ready to collaborate with fun, creative people, you will be welcomed with open arms.

Stage work vs. commercials and industrials

Let's make a quick distinction. Stage work is quite different from commercial/industrial work. Stage acting involves the art and craft of acting. Commercials and industrials have less to do with art; they have everything to do with marketing, sales, and business. When you work in a commercial or industrial, you will be using your acting talent and skill, but the ultimate goals of the work are to sell a product or to train employees.

Some actors do both commercial and stage work, and do them well. Some actors do only one or the other. If you are a trained stage actor, you may be able to easily make the jump to commercial work. The pay is a good way to support or supplement your stage habit. (Stage actors are rarely highly-compensated, to say the least!) You may need specific training in order to make the transition to the camera, but your stage acting knowledge and skill will serve you well.

If your only experience is in commercials and industrials, you will probably need some work and training to make the leap from commercials to stage. Stage acting requires very different skills. It all depends on your goals in the biz. The concepts in this book apply to all actors, no matter what your pursuit.

A good portion of this book will apply to commercials and industrial work; however, particular attention is given to stage work in Chapters 7 and 10.

The term "talent"

For commercial and industrial work, you will commonly hear actors referred to as "talent." Talent is the term that names the function of the actor on the commercial set. "Actor" refers to your profession and your art; "talent" refers to your function in the commercial world. The term "talent" simply refers to the human(s) who will be seen or heard in the spot or program. You do not necessarily have to *have* talent to *be* talent—but often that's the case!

What exactly is an "industrial"?

An industrial is just about anything in the biz that is not for commercial broadcast. It can be a training DVD or CD, an interactive computer program, an internet or intranet corporate training program, or anything on any format for training or marketing purposes. Actors are hired to be the "on-camera talent" or "voice talent." The purpose of most industrials is to train, teach, or inform; however, the variety is unbelievable. Here is a short list of industrial topics I have done, just to give you an idea. If you are hired to do an industrial, you might be the face, the body or body part, the voice, or all of the above:

- Programs for schools, DVDs to accompany textbooks.

- Programs for school teachers.

- New-employee orientation or explanations of benefits packages.

- Safety procedures for countless processes: proper handling of chemicals, emergency evacuation procedures, glass installation in cars as well as high-rise buildings, proper techniques to deal with infectious substances in medical settings.

- Sales techniques for insurance policies, retail products, computer equipment.

- New product introductions for health spas, recycling companies, toys.

- Phone systems or on-hold messages.

- Kiosks at retail locations and trade shows—any display where you see a person on screen or hear a voice telling you about a product.

- Product demonstrations—from vacuum cleaners to games, tractor repair to craft products.

- Business ethics discussions or demonstrations: sexual harassment situations, ethical conduct for management, understanding cultural differences.

- Medical procedure demonstrations for doctors, nurses, or patients.

- Substance abuse or domestic violence counseling dramatizations.

An actor has been hired to talk about or demonstrate almost any product or process you can name.

What's a live industrial?

Often when you are booked for a live industrial, you will be the presenter at a trade show. A trade show is usually held in a huge convention center. Companies rent space on the convention center floor to set up a booth. Actors are hired to give the same presentation at regular intervals throughout the day. Normally, it is an eight to fifteen minute show you repeat every twenty to thirty minutes. If you are lucky, it is an entertaining presentation that you get to do with other fun actors. Sometimes it is just you. The purpose is sometimes to entertain, sometimes to inform, sometimes to simply project the company's image, and often to draw people into the booth so the salespeople can get leads.

Other live industrials involve entertaining in some way at a corporate function. Some actors are hired to emcee corporate events. I once portrayed a ditsy legal secretary in a murder mystery sketch for a convention of attorneys. There were four actors in full costume and make-up. Our scenes occurred at different times throughout the three-day conference. The scenes served both as comic relief and as a way of introducing different segments of the program. That particular live industrial was great fun.

Whatever form a live industrial takes, it should pay well: $500 to $1000 per day or more.

The subject matter for live industrials varies. No matter what the message, you rarely need prior knowledge or training in the subject; you simply need to learn or ear prompt the script. (See Chapter 3 for ear prompter information.)

The good news and the bad news.

The Twin Cities area offers an abundance of opportunities for actors: on stage, in commercials, and in industrials. Just as in any city, there are no guarantees that you will achieve great financial success as an actor, but this is a great place to give acting a try. You will work with creative, interesting people. You will be challenged and rarely be bored. And many actors can and do make money along the way.

The bad news is that there are far more actors than acting opportunities. Lots of folks want to get into this game. Even the folks who are already in the game want more playing time. Thus, it can be very difficult to get a foot in the door and even more difficult to stay in. This book will give you both the good news (the opportunities and where to find them) and the bad news (the potential roadblocks and frustrations you may encounter along the way). Perseverance is important!

"There's nothing else I want to do as badly as I want to keep trying to make it. So, I say yes to everything, keep my expenses low, and every few months ask myself if I'm still happy. And, if you do decide to take a break for a while, that's okay. This business isn't going anywhere—and if it is truly what you want to do, you will be back."
—Greta Grosch, Plymouth Playhouse, Comedysportz, Hey City

Can I make a living as an actor?

It is tough to count on acting as a living. Some Twin Cities' actors make a comfortable living, but those actors comprise a minority of all actors here. Even for those actors, it may have taken a while, perhaps years, to build a stage network or commercial client base large enough to sustain a living. Still others who have made their living for a period of years may experience slow times and drops in income.

On the brighter side, there are indeed actors who make a living in the biz. Some are successful stage actors. Others are professional voice and/or on-camera talent. Many who make their living work all sides of the business.

When you are starting out, you will definitely need to have another income stream. In other words,

> "Every day is different. I don't just act. I work part time in the box office selling tickets and doing accounting work. I direct and choreograph. I do commercial work. I teach at drama camps. And if I have to, I temp to supplement my income."
>
> —Megan Kelly, Actor's Theater of Minnesota, Bloomington Civic Theater, Theatre L'Homme Dieu, Chanhassen Dinner Theatres

don't quit your day job! The majority of local actors have a "real job," or at least some kind of supplemental income. However, it is possible to make your living as an actor. Professional actors do not just sit home waiting for the phone to ring, they work at it.

Successful actors have to be diligent and creative in their art and in their business. If you want a shot at making a living as an actor, you cannot wait for the business to come to you. You have to go out and get it.

What are my chances of getting commercial/industrial work?

You are entering a business in which you will be selling yourself as a commodity. The demand for your particular product is nearly impossible to predict. Once you are established and clients know who you are and what you can do, there might be more demand for your product. However, when you are starting out (depending on your look and personality), the demand for you is low to moderate at best.

There are hundreds, even thousands of actors trying to get work here. Headshots and resumes pour into agency offices every week. Your headshot can become lost in a sea of new faces for quite some time; you may become frustrated and give up long before anyone even notices that you exist.

However, there is a constant need for fresh faces. Actors who have been around for a while can become over-exposed, so clients need to select new talent. Further, when an actor leaves the biz—to get a "real" job, move to the coast, raise children, etc.—new opportunities open up.

Here are a few suggestions to help you determine what your chances might be here in the Twin Cities. On stage, the better your talent and training, the better your chances will be.

For commercial and industrial work:

- If you have a non-Caucasian, ethnic look, you may have slightly better odds of getting work. It is the simple law of supply and demand here in Minnesota.

- If you are male instead of female, your odds are slightly better. Just listen to the radio and watch TV. How many male faces and voices do you see and hear as opposed to female faces and voices? Though it is changing, it is still a man's world. Sadly for women, the acting biz reflects that world.

- If you have either an attractive or an interesting face, your odds are better. This business is all about your "look."

- If you are age twenty to forty, you are in slightly higher demand. (However, there are so many twenty-somethings trying to get into acting, the odds may not be as favorable as you would like!)

> "Having a side job, another way to make income is imperative. Over the years, I developed my seamstress skills and am now able to be an independent contractor working from home. This is ideal because I can arrange a full load of projects when I know I'm not getting a lot of acting income — and where I do have an acting gig--say a steady theater job--I can scale down my sewing time. In addition, working from home allows me to be able to set my own hours, which means I am available for any and all commercial or voice-over auditions/gigs."
>
> —Seri Johnson, AEA, Old Log Theater, Chanhassen Dinner Theatres

- If you are a well-trained, experienced actor, your odds are better.

During my first few years in this business, after auditioning for one of the biggest agencies in town, I asked the agent that very question: "What are my chances?" Her response: "If you're good, you'll work." I wanted a more specific answer! The truth is, no one can answer that question. They can theorize based on your look and current skill level, but any one person's opinion is totally subjective. Some very talented, experienced actors can go out on twenty-five commercial and industrial auditions and get nothing. Some new, totally green actor can show up and be booked on a job right away. Training and experience can definitely increase your odds of getting work, but there are no guarantees. If you ask an agent about your potential, you want to hear a wonderful, positive answer. You can still ask the question, but they may not be able to tell you what you want to hear.

So how do I know if I have talent?

Do not worry about it! If acting is your passion, just do it. Your talent will emerge.

Acting "talent" is difficult to define. I believe acting talent is the same as musical talent, artistic talent, and athletic talent. To be blunt, some have it, some do not. For example, I could take voice lessons for the rest of my life and still never be able to belt out a Broadway tune or sing opera (outside of the shower). I could run and train for years and never run a six-minute mile. I just do not have that kind of talent.

The same is true for acting. There are actors who are simply gifted; their work seems effortless. There are others with a little talent who work hard to maximize what they have. There are some with little talent but loads of personality, charm, and charisma to carry them through. It is impossible to know where you fall in that spectrum. We actors are not very good at being objective about ourselves.

You cannot define or quantify acting talent, nor can you control how much talent you may or may not have. If you have the desire to act, simply dive in and try it. Follow your passion, bring your unique talent forth, and make the most of it through training.

> "I started acting because it was a childhood dream. I loved the idea of being somebody else and escaping into the great beyond. I stick with acting because I am getting better at it and am able to truly create that imaginary world my characters exist in. (Plus, my reviews are getting better and better, and my ego likes that!)"
>
> —Lori Neal, Penumbra, Jungle Theater, Frank Theatre, Mixed Blood, Theatre Unbound, Children's Theatre, Pillsbury House

Cold hard facts: Will I find work?

A dose of reality is often a healthy thing. If you understand what you are up against as you enter the acting world, your ego may better survive some of the harsh blows of reality.

Many people enter this business with wide-eyed optimism. A few experience relatively speedy success. For most, it is tough to get a foot in the door. As the months pass, the rejection—or worse, total lack of response—can quickly turn optimism into frustration, anger, and defeat. The best thing to do is arm yourself with as much knowledge as possible, combine the optimism with realism, gather your patience, and dive in!

Some of the realities:

- Like every actor in town, you will be rejected more often than you will be cast. Compare it to the feelings you had in grade school physical education class, lining up and picking teams. You may often feel like the last kid, standing alone, still waiting to be picked. Prepare yourself for this reality.

- You may never make a consistent living in the biz.

- A significant proportion of the work, particularly in industrials and voice-overs, goes to the same small circle of actors. If clients find an actor they like, they use that actor over and over. It is possible to break into that circle, but it may take a while.

What are the other "down sides" to being an actor?

> "My husband says I became an actor in my 40s—10 years ago this year—because 'I had something to say.' And I have never found a better answer. And now that I have found my theatrical voice and am not yet tired of sharing it, I still do it. . . . I work not for the pay (so I'm unusual in that regard) but for the exhilaration of performing . . . . We humans all need to tell stories to one another to talk about our place in the world . . . some of us do it with painting and sculpture, some of us dress up in clothes and pretend to be other people."
> —Linda Sue Anderson, Torch Theater, Theatre in the Round, Workhouse Theatre

Being an actor provides: No paid days off. No paid vacation. No paid maternity leave. No paid bereavement leave. No 401k plan. No employer-provided health insurance (unless you are a successful union actor). And the worst possible job security you can imagine. It is not an easy business!

How many actors make money in the biz? How much?

It is nearly impossible to know the statistics for the Twin Cities. To my knowledge, no one keeps stats. To get a vague idea, let's look at some nationwide statistics from the Screen Actor's Guild (SAG):

Only six percent of the almost 120,000 actors who are already in the union make what SAG speaks of as "middle class" earnings of $30,000 to $70,000 a year, and only two percent make over $100,000 annually." (*How to Sell Yourself as an Actor*, K. Callan, page 20. Sweden Press, 2008. This is a must-read for any aspiring professional actor.)

A simple interpretation of these statistics? Fewer than ten percent make a living acting. These stats for union actors nationwide are probably consistent with percentages here in the Twin Cities, union and non-union—except for the six figure incomes. That percentage would likely be far less than 1 percent. There are a few local actors who earn over $100,000 in any given year, but these actors are the rare exception.

> "The thing I love is that you NEVER stop learning new skills. No two auditions or gigs are the same and the networking and friend expansion that happens once you have been around for a little while is very rewarding, refreshing and entertaining."
> —Seri Johnson

On stage, the only way to make a living is to work consistently as an Equity actor (a union member). Local stage actors can make several hundred dollars per week—perhaps a thousand dollars a week at the largest venues—but it is rare that a stage actor works all the time. For most, the work is sporadic at best.

Hundreds of actors make money in the Twin Cities. The amount of money varies widely. You likely will never hear the phrase "wealthy actor." The moral of the story? Do not plan to get rich as an actor.

I live outside of the Twin Cities. Is there work in St. Cloud? Rochester? Duluth?

There are theaters everywhere. There may not be large venues for professional actors, but if you want to act on stage, you will find opportunities in most towns.

I have worked in commercials and industrials with production companies and ad agencies located in Duluth, St. Cloud, Rochester, Fargo, Bismarck, Des Moines, Ames, and Omaha, among others. The business is out there! Much of the advice in this book will apply to professional opportunities anywhere; you just have to dig a little deeper to find opportunities in your area.

So why on earth would anyone want to be an actor?

Why would I choose a life with all of this insecurity? Simple. Because I love acting, I love the biz, and I cannot imagine doing anything else!

Acting is not for everyone. Anything worth doing comes with challenges. If you can see yourself happily following a different path, then choose it. Those who anticipate speedy success and easy money along the road are destined for disappointment. Those who possess a sense of adventure and the perseverance to handle the occasional potholes and ditches will enjoy the ride!

"I feel that being just one person and living one life is incredibly limiting. When I'm acting I feel like I'm the most connected to the world and all the people in it. I think we're all more alike than different, and acting allows me to express that philosophy. It follows that if we can practice putting ourselves in other people's situations, with their histories, we should be able to identify with anyone and not judge them. . . . That's my philosophy."
—Heidi Fellner

Still want to be an actor?

You now have a passing acquaintance with the challenges and types of work that you may find in the Twin Cities. If you really want to be an actor, do not be discouraged by the odds. Simply look before you leap and know the realities before you dive in.

If you find yourself still intrigued by all of this, then keep reading and join the rest of us who have decided to ignore the odds and continue to pursue acting as a profession.

CHAPTER 2

Your Product and Your Survival in the Biz

Just say no to angst!

While the art of acting is most definitely exciting and challenging, it can be a difficult profession. When it is done well, it looks easy; however, it is rarely as glamorous and fast-paced as it may appear. As Sir Laurence suggests, acting can be a bit masochistic.

> "Acting is a masochistic form of exhibitionism. It is not quite the occupation of an adult."
>
> —Sir Laurence Olivier, from laurenceolivier.com

This chapter is a survival guide of sorts. While it will not give you specific directions for your personal acting path; it will help to smooth some of the emotional and psychological bumps in the road.

Look, personality, skill. What are you selling?

Acting may be the only profession in which it is legal to hire strictly based on looks: hair, weight, height, skin color, age, etc.

When I first started, I took an on-camera workshop with a casting director who said: "Look, personality, and skill—in that order." Your look will be the first thing that will include or exclude you for a particular job. Your personality on camera and the skill with which you perform will be secondary factors. All three are important, but look is the primary factor.

Understand that your look and personality largely determine what you will do or not do in the biz. (This is true to a greater degree on camera than on stage. On stage, your talent and skill will carry a little more weight.) For commercial and industrial work, your look is particularly important.

Do you have to look like a model to get work?

Absolutely not. The term "look" is commonly used: "He has a great commercial look." "She has a comic look." "She has a sophisticated, corporate look." "He's got a quirky look." The common expression "your look" is in no way synonymous with "good-looking." There are many different "looks." Yours will strongly influence the roles for which you will be considered. You do not need to be a gorgeous model to be a successful actor.

Separate your self and your self-esteem from the product you are marketing.

You are a businessperson with a product to sell—your look, your personality, your skill, and sometimes your voice. You are a commodity: "actor," "talent," "spokesperson," or, as I once heard us called, "meat-puppet." (Sadly funny, but true.)

As you sell this commodity, you will be constantly judged and critiqued unfairly—a reality of the industry. Try to keep in mind that you are selling a package of your look and personality, not your soul and your self-worth.

> "What I hate about this business is our perpetual inclination to see ourselves through others' eyes . . . it is easy to lose our sense of self-worth."
> —Lynn Musgrave

The constant blows of rejection can definitely put a chink in the armor of even the most talented actor. Confidence and self-esteem suffer if you do not build up your defenses. Many of us feel good when we are working and depressed when we are not. It is a great ego boost to be in demand and demoralizing to be ignored.

Protect your self-esteem. Begin to see your "image" objectively as a product you sell. You have little control over how you are perceived by clients and directors. They will see you audition and establish an instant judgment of you that may have little to do with who you really are; however, this instant perception is the product you are selling on that day. Your real self is how your friends and family know you and how you feel about yourself; your business self and image is how you are perceived by the biz. Build your life, self-esteem, and support network on the foundation of your real self. See your "image" as simply the product you are selling.

If an agency does not want to represent you, it is not *you* that they do not like; they may simply have enough of your kind of product on their store shelf right now. If a director does not see you in a specific role, it is not *you* that she does not like; your product simply is not the right fit for this customer's needs.

Rejection: Maintaining objectivity in a subjective business.

In baseball, if you bat .300 over your entire career, you may be in the Hall of Fame. In acting, if you get one of every three auditions you do, you are amazing. For every audition you book, there will be several you do not get. It can get very discouraging to show up for audition after audition and book nothing.

Some rejections are easy to take; others sting. If you allow each rejection to sting you, you will be miserable. I try to do an audition and promptly forget about it.

Occasionally, you will be able to see—either on stage or in a commercial—which actor was cast instead of you. If you are able to be objective, you will often understand the casting decision. Examine it: look, personality, choices the actor made, etc. There is a factor that influenced the decision. Look for what that might be, and learn from it.

> "Every audition is a job in itself. Treat it as such and if you do not get the gig, it will not be as personal for you. Go in, do the audition, walk away satisfied you did a good job, and forget about it. It makes getting the jobs more exciting and not getting them less devastating."
> —Patty Mathews

In fact, stop thinking of it as rejection; it is not about you. It is about which product the client or director pulled off the shelf. They simply selected a different product because of some miscellaneous product feature.

Enjoy each audition and worry less about the outcome. (See Chapter 7 for much more about auditioning.)

What's your type? Seeing your "product" objectively is easier said than done.

When examining and attempting to define your "product," you might not always like what you see, but it is imperative that you see it.

We actors are not good at seeing ourselves objectively. Try to see "your product" the way clients and directors see it. What is your type? Into which niche do you fit? To answer these questions, begin to listen objectively to what others tell you. Observe how you are cast, and discern the "type" by which an agent seems to define you. If you consistently receive the same message from folks in the biz, then this is how you are perceived. Perception is everything. Do not fight against it; learn from it and use it.

In order to define your type, start looking at the common "products" being used in commercials. For example: young mom or dad, wholesome Midwest grandparents, freckle-faced kids, sexy model, beer-drinking football fan, everyday Joe or Jane who works in the next cubicle, friendly next-door neighbor, confident corporate executive, stuffy CEO, office nerd, rubber-faced class clown/life of the party, overbearing and pushy neighbor, office gossip, etc.

Where do you fit? This is a business in which you can view and evaluate your competition twenty-four hours per day. When commercials come on, put down the remote! Look at the actor and ask:

- Why was he/she cast?
- What does he/she represent? What "type"?
- Who is the target market?
- Would I have sent myself to that audition?
- Could I have been cast in that? Why or why not?

If you always answer, "Yes, I could be cast in that," you are not being objective. Look for a very specific type for yourself. Define it specifically, not broadly.

Another indicator of your type will be the other actors sent to the same auditions with you. Observe especially carefully if you attend a callback. Those who are called back for the same role along with you are likely your type. When you start attending auditions, look around the waiting room. Who else is there? Are there other people there in your age range? Take a look at them, and you will likely see the type into which you are being categorized. Do not object to the categorization—learn from it.

Typecasting can be a good thing! (If you know what your type is!)

Typecasting is often discussed as a negative in this business; however, when you are starting out it can be a very good thing. If you fit perfectly into a specific category—young mom or dad, CEO, sweet grandma, hip skateboard dude—the agents and casting directors will know immediately how to use you. Do not fight against your type in the name of proving your versatility. Work your type and get your feet firmly planted in that "niche" in the biz. Worry about your versatility later. (This advice comes from Jane Brody, former Chicago casting director and current DePaul University theater professor.)

Too many people try to be something they are not in hopes of fitting into a type they would like to be. You are who you are, especially on camera. If you are not glamorous, do not waste your time and headshot dollars trying project glamour. Most of us do not possess commercialized society's image of pretty or handsome, so why lament it? If you spend your time trying to project an image that really is not you, you will only confuse agents and casting directors. If they do not know *how* to use you, they *will not* use you.

It is common for us to think that we can be lots of types. We want our agents to send us for everything that comes across their desks. Some of us spent our high school and college theater careers playing all kinds of characters. We leave school thinking we can play it all.

On stage, there is a little more latitude to expand our type and play different roles, but not nearly as much as we had in school. The camera is another story; you have very little latitude, if any, to play something other than your type.

Yes, some actors are versatile and can cross over other categories and types. Most of us are not as versatile as we think. You will save yourself time and frustration if you can discover your niche as quickly as possible. Be the best of that type, get a foot firmly in the door, and establish yourself. There will be time to work on versatility later.

"But I'm an actor, I can play other things!"

Yes, you probably can. So can I. But the significant business question is, who will they cast?

Especially on-camera, they will not cast just any actor who can play a certain role, they will cast the person who *is* that role. Your agent's job is to send the people to the audition who are most like what the client requests.

Pay attention to how the biz perceives you. Learn who you are in the market, and be the best of that type that you can possibly be. Again, be specific now; be versatile later.

Is there a demand for your particular product? Are you "marketable?"

Sales of any product depend on demand. Is your product one that is used in every household and company across the country? Or is it a product that has a very specific use and a limited target audience? Further, what is the quality of the product?

Translate those questions to actor terms:

- Is your product one that is used in every household and company across the country?

  Translation: Do you have a "mainstream" look? Would you appear to be a natural fit in many different settings: around the neighborhood, at the office, or at home with the kids? (An everyman Tom Hanks or Cuba Gooding Jr., or girl-next-door Kirsten Dunst or Sally Field.)

- Is it a product that has a very specific use and a limited target audience?

  Translation: Do you have an unusual or quirky look? (Forest Whitaker, Danny DeVito, Kathy Bates, Steve Buscemi.)

- What is the quality of the product?

  Translation: Are you highly trained and versatile? Can you take direction well and deliver all kinds of copy smoothly, truthfully and consistently? Are you skilled with both comedy and drama?

Objective answers to these questions will help you determine your marketability. Your talent and training will help increase the demand for your product, and that demand will be enhanced or limited by your look.

Focus on what you are, not what you are not.

We can waste so much time and energy lamenting what we're not: "I wish I could sing, I wish I was twenty pounds lighter, I wish I was taller so I could do print work, I wish I was funnier, I wish I did not have freckles, I wish I were more extroverted." Throughout the past twenty years, these have been on my personal lamentation list; you can insert your own. During the slow times when we are not booking much work, these lamentations can ring loudly in our ears.

Be realistic. I will never be a great singer (except in the shower), so it is time to let go of that dream. I could be twenty pounds lighter, but I simply *really* like to eat. So be it; at 5'4" I'll never be a fashion model, anyway. I cannot be taller, and I cannot lose the freckles. Oh, well. I am not a comedian. I am perceived as warm, straightforward, and trustworthy. Those are my casting strengths, so why worry about being funny? I am a natural introvert, so I have taken improvisation classes to be more spontaneous, but I have accepted that I will never perform on the Brave New Workshop stage, much less on *Saturday Night Live*. I am not saying these things for therapeutic purposes; I am simply suggesting that we all have our own frustrations about our "type." We can expend a great deal of energy fighting against it, or we can accept it.

> "Figure out who you are, what you do, and do it better than anyone. There are a lot of folks who may be better singers, dancers, actors. The only thing you do better than anyone is BE YOU. So figure out who that is, and be that."
>
> —Greta Grosch

Stop lamenting what you are not, and focus on the positive. Find your strengths, and build on them. Work to improve what you can, and let go of the rest. Discover your "type," and play it well!

"Do I need to lose weight?"

I hear so many actors, especially women, say: "I cannot get new headshots done until I lose weight," or "I have to lose weight before I start auditioning again." Sigh. What society has done to our self-esteem is a crime. The industry we are in is the worst offender.

If you are a model, male or female, I guess you gotta do what you gotta do. If you are young and gorgeous and planning to move to L.A. or New York, research your competition and do what you feel you have to do in order to compete. There are sad realities in this business.

Most of us are not gorgeous glamour-types, so this whole ultra-thin thing does not apply to us anyway. What is most important is that we are healthy and we feel good.

In response to the weight question from a particularly talented actress, Jane Brody replied, "Do not change that which makes you unique!" If you want to lose weight for yourself, then do it. Do not do it for the business.

If you want to change yourself for your own happiness, then make the changes you want to make. Do not do unhealthy diets and waste time and energy beating yourself up about your weight. If you feel you are over-weight, then that is your type for the time being. If you can act, there is work for you in the Twin Cities.

God bless Kathy Bates, Oprah Winfrey, and Queen Latifah, among others. (I love it that Queen Latifah is modeling for Cover Girl cosmetics. What a breath of fresh air to see a real woman in this type of advertising, rather than an ultra skinny waif! She looks fabulous!) The biz is changing, even if change is happening too slowly.

"I'm balding. Do I need a toupee?"

I have heard this question several times. Guys, see the answers above. If you are a gorgeous model type, again, you gotta do what you gotta do. For most guys my answer is, "Be real." Lots of guys are balding or have beer bellies—or both. It is a great look for national beer commercials.

If you want to be able to change your look for various stage or commercial jobs, perhaps you will want to investigate getting a hairpiece. However, it is certainly not a must. I would not worry about it.

The dreaded age-range transition.

You may experience several good years of work, during which you will be in demand. Then, the work may seem to slow to a crawl for a year or more. It might be the economy. It might be your competition. It might be many things, but it is just as likely to be an age-range transition.

If you stick around long enough, you will feel it. As you age, your look changes; thus, your type changes. You have been playing young dad roles for as long as you can remember. You have been playing the good employee, the sales guy, the young nurse, the receptionist, etc. Suddenly, you are not getting as many calls as you used to. It is probably not your talent that is hampering you; you are simply moving out of that age range. They are going with the younger actors.

> First it is: "Beth who?"
> Then: "Get me that new girl—Beth something?"
> Then: "Be sure to send Beth."
> Then: "Send someone like Beth, only younger."
> And finally: "Beth who?"

In your thirties and forties, you may move into more corporate roles, doctors, parents of teenagers, blue-collar employees, etc. In your forties and fifties, the mom and dad roles start to disappear. More upper management and doctor auditions come your way. In your fifties and sixties, it will be doctors, CEOs, the wise sales guy, etc. Sixty-plus will be a time of more grandparent roles, and you will transition from doctor to patient in those medical programs.

The in-between times are tough: Too old to be a high school student, too young to be a mom; too old to be a dad, too young to be grandpa; too old to be the sales trainee, too young to be the CEO. You are no longer the type you have been, but you have not reached the next type yet.

Do not lament this transition time; just know that it will happen. When it comes, do your best to transition gracefully. Face lifts and hair dye will not stem the inevitable tide.

Control what you can, let go of the rest.

You cannot control your look, so work at the things you can control. It seems to me that the following list is filled with "no-brainers;" however, you would be amazed at the actors who sabotage their careers by not controlling the following essentials:

- Availability and accessibility. Can your agents find you easily when they need you? Are you available for auditions and jobs when they call? For stage work, are you available for evening rehearsals five or six days per week?

- Professionalism and work ethic. I have seen all of the following: Actors who show up to auditions, rehearsals, or jobs unprepared, hung-over, openly complaining about the shoot circumstances, or resistant to taking direction. Be professional.

- Health. Rarely are they looking for that tired, sickly look. Take care of your instrument. You cannot look and perform your best if you are not as healthy as you can be. Who wants to buy a product that is not 100 percent?

> "Get your ego out of the way and concentrate on the business. . . . ALWAYS demonstrate a positive attitude at auditions and on the job."
> —Walt Weaver

- Training and preparation. Just do it. This market is certainly not as competitive as New York or L.A; however, do not underestimate the talent and quality of the actors here. There are hundreds, perhaps thousands of actors in town with degrees in theater, acting, communications, and broadcasting. Many have years of stage experience. Though you can certainly have success without a degree in acting, you will need good training and experience to truly be successful over the long haul. Be objective about your strengths and weaknesses, and constantly work to improve your product. (But shop carefully for training. See Chapter 9.)

Those are things you *can* control. Be sure to take care of business when it comes to reliability and preparation.

Be the easiest actor in town to work with!

Always be the kind of person people want to work with! I often hear stories about difficult actors who were passed over in casting decisions. I know lots of actors who work, not because they are the most talented actors around, but because they are just so nice to work with. I hear comments like this in all areas of the biz.

Never give them a reason *not* to cast you!

Self-sabotage and bad habits.

Actors are notorious for self-sabotage. Actors with great talent sometimes have bad habits that can limit their success.

It is time to correct your habits if you tend to:

- be chronically late (my personal Achilles heel).

- be disorganized; you run out of headshots, forget to take them to auditions, miss auditions, or forget audition details because you do not write everything down.

- be impatient with agents, directors, or office staff at various auditions and jobs.

- procrastinate; you wait until the last minute to memorize copy, wait to rehearse a monologue until you do not have time to prepare properly, miss deadlines for submitting headshots, etc.

- "chicken-out" and cancel auditions because of self-doubt; you do not feel prepared or adequate (been there, done that, too).

- be lazy about your work and your craft.

We actors have no corporate manager who is trained and responsible for shaping our work habits and behaviors. We are on our own. Other than an occasional agent or director who may be honest, no one will discuss our bad habits or mistakes with us. If we become too difficult to deal with, they will simply stop calling or casting us without ever telling us why. It is not their job to correct our behavior. We have to manage our own careers.

Be honest with yourself, and change any self-sabotaging behaviors.

> "Network, network, network. Talk to people at auditions, be friendly, ask questions, and be polite to everyone. Your dresser backstage one day may be the director who will cast you in the next show. Remember, if you are easy to work with, you will get cast again and again. If you are a diva, people may think twice before handing you that job!"
> —Seri Johnson

Ethics and integrity.

Above all, carry yourself with integrity and honesty. Conflicts happen. You will avoid a lot of hassles if you are honest in all of your business relationships. If you sign agreements and contracts with agents or clients, honor them. If you find yourself in conflict, deal with those involved honestly and openly.

Honor your own sense of what is right. If you are offered an audition or job that conflicts with your moral compass, turn it down. Do not worry that your career will be over if you refuse a job, a role, or an audition.

The show must go on; Calling in sick? Hah!

Life gets in the way sometimes. There will be occasional circumstances that are completely out of your control. Try as we may to stay healthy, once in a while a bug will bite. There is no such thing as paid sick leave if you are an actor. If you have a "real job" you can often use a sick day and still be paid; not so for actors. The larger theaters will have understudies; many theaters will not. I once shot a commercial in Fargo, North Dakota, when I had the stomach flu, praying to the porcelain gods between shots, trying not to muss my make-up. There was no way I could call in sick or be replaced; the shoot had to go on. A friend of mine once worked a shoot two days after hernia surgery; he needed the work. I imagine that would make my flu day seem like a walk in the park. I had a cortisone shot in my injured back and did an audition two hours later, trying not to limp on a completely numb left leg. I could not afford to turn down even an audition. If you get laryngitis on a day you are booked for a gig, they will rarely re-schedule. Most likely, they will replace you.

I am sure there are hundreds of stories to add to this list, and we have not even touched on trying to go on stage with the flu or bronchitis. (Been there, done both.) The show must go on, and sometimes it is not easy!

Do not expect this business to be fair.

This is a totally subjective business. You will be judged unfairly. The work will never be evenly distributed. The work will not always go to those who have worked the hardest to earn it. It is not about who is a good person, or who is the most talented, intelligent, committed, and honest. Those qualities will help to build your reputation over the long haul, but they will not help you book every audition.

It is just not fair; it is as simple as that.

Do not expect great recognition.

Recognition is rare. If you do receive some form of recognition, it is short-lived. On stage, the appreciation of your co-actors and director, the applause from the audience, and an occasional good review are nice, but you start all over again after the show closes.

In the commercial/industrial business, an occasional, "Thanks, good job!" at the end of a shoot or session is about it. You are expected to function well, just as the lights and microphone are expected to function well. When your part of the job is done, they are on to the next shot or already thinking about editing. Do not hold your breath waiting for some kind of praise. Your friends might think it is cool that you are an actor, but the biz will not. The best compliment is a booking from a client or director with whom you have worked before. If they want you back, it means you did a good job the last time. The talented actor who functions effectively on the job will eventually earn respect in the biz.

Competition: Camaraderie or cut-throat?

You can go to auditions and evaluate other actors as your competition, or you can choose to view them as teammates, colleagues, and friends. Which sounds like more fun?

How do actors cope with the down times? What do I do when I am not working?

As I launched my acting career, my goal was to have something acting-related scheduled into my calendar at least five days per week. Rehearsal, audition, class, job—it did not matter if it was a professional opportunity or not. I would work my "real job" during the day, then I would take a class or meet with another actor to work on scenes or monologues. I knew if I wanted to be a full-time actor, I needed to work it every day. I did not always reach my five days per week goal, but it was incredibly motivating to look at my calendar and know that I had acting-related appointments every day in any given week.

During the slow times, do not give in to frustration. Just keep working.

> "If I'm not working because I cannot get cast, I volunteer at theaters near and dear to my heart—Theatre in the Round, Torch, and Workhouse—and work on my monologues or learn new ones."
>
> —Linda Sue Anderson

How will you know when you have arrived?

In acting, as in life, there is no destination; there is only the journey.

If you are entering this profession in order to achieve great stardom or wealth, switch to a profession with better odds. If you are really determined to reach a goal like this, then go for it. I do not want to squelch anyone's dream, but very few people ever arrive at any grand destination in this business. As soon as you feel you have arrived, the show closes and you are right back at the beginning—searching for your next audition, your next elusive job, and your next paycheck. If you really want to be an actor, perseverance will be essential.

Enjoy the audition process and all of the small mileposts along the way. Better yet, celebrate each and every one of them!

Chase your dream, but plan the chase.

Luck is where preparation meets opportunity. You need to prepare so that you can seize the opportunities that come along. Set goals and deadlines, rehearse diligently, give the work your undivided attention, and always be professional and reliable. As you plan for this new career, an excellent resource is K. Callan's book, *How to Sell Yourself As an Actor*. The book has a terrific discussion of an actor's "five-year plan." Be sure to check it out.

If ever you find yourself lost and frustrated by the business side of acting, remember that those details are merely a means to an end. The ultimate goal is to act. Cling to your passion for acting, remember what first attracted you it, and then use the business knowledge as a practical route to gain more opportunities—perhaps even some financial reward. While this book deals primarily with the business side of acting, I hope you will be able to read between the lines and sense my love of acting and actors. Congratulations for having the courage to chase your dream! Plan carefully while you chase it.

> "When you are frustrated, you need to reinvent your skills and how you market yourself. Acting is an incredibly diverse field. So if drama is burning you out, try comedy. Try sketch, try cabaret, try standup. Try voice-over. Try anything. Write something for yourself. Write a one-person show. Just keep trying. One of those things will lead to something that will inspire you or get you money."
> —Heidi Fellner

Now, what do you really need to get started in the biz? Let's move on to the nuts and bolts of the biz.

CHAPTER 3

The Tools to Support and Enhance Your Product

What are you selling?

There are certain things you will need in order to pursue acting. Here are the basic tools and concepts to help you. Your needs will vary depending upon your interests--stage, commercials, industrials, and/or voice-overs.

- A flexible schedule
- Reliable transportation
- Voice-mail, cell phone
- Headshot
- Resume
- Wardrobe and makeup
- Audio and video demos
- Ear prompter
- Self-promotion: business cards, websites, etc.

AVAILABILITY AND SCHEDULE

All the tools in the world will not help you if you are not available to do the work! Being available for auditions, rehearsals, performances, and jobs is essential.

Many theaters in town schedule evening rehearsals so they do not interfere with actors' day jobs. Theaters that pay their actors will sometimes be the exception to this rule and schedule daytime rehearsals.

Commercials and industrials most often shoot on weekdays. To work in the commercial/industrial market, you will need to find a way to be available and flexible during the week. You simply have to be available when agents call you. Sometimes an agent can work auditions into your lunch hour, but not always. Video shoots, voice-overs, and auditions are often scheduled with little advance notice. ("Shoot" is the commonly used term for an on-camera job.) Sometimes you get a few weeks notice, but that is rare. On average lead time is two or three days and occasionally as little as an hour. I have had calls asking, "How quickly can you be downtown?" I was in the studio thirty minutes later. Flexibility in your schedule is a must.

Agents understand that sometimes you just are not available. Actors have to make a living; most have to have a day job. The more flexible it is, the better; but occasionally you just cannot find someone to cover your shift, you are up against a project deadline, or you are committed to a stage rehearsal. Agents will understand these things, though they will not have patience if you are unavailable ten calls in a row. They will stop calling. You may need to creatively adjust your schedule to be available for work as an actor.

> "I swear to God, waiting tables takes the cake—especially if you can get into fine dining. Work your way up; it is very worth it."
> —Carol Butler

What "day jobs" are compatible with an actor's schedule?

Some "day jobs" work well for actors:

- Teaching music and theater to kids
- Summer camps
- Substitute teaching
- Agency or casting office work
- Temp services
- Waiting tables
- Receptionist at a small office
- Job sharing with another actor
- Caterer
- Box office at theaters (at least they have some understanding of actors)
- Any job where you can explain that you are an actor, and they will allow you to make up the hours you miss for auditions, shoots, and sessions

I do know a couple of schoolteachers who are represented by my agent. (There is little flexibility in a teacher's schedule.) The agent calls them for auditions and jobs that happen outside of school hours, whenever possible.

If an agent loves you and has confidence in you, they may make accommodations for your schedule. However, this is the exception, not the rule.

Will doing stage work interfere with commercial work?

Sometimes it does, but it is worth it. When you commit to do stage or an independent film—paid or unpaid—you should keep that commitment, even if it means turning down a big commercial day rate because of a rehearsal. If you have an understudy or the rehearsal schedule is flexible, perhaps you can discuss options with your director or stage manager, but be careful. Honor your first commitment.

Several years ago, I was cast in an unpaid independent film. I had not done much commercial work yet, so I was thrilled when my agent called with a two-day shoot: $700 plus. One of the days conflicted with the first day of the film shoot. She said, "Well how much are they paying you? You should really go with the money!" I knew the film director had arranged the entire cast, crew, and location. If I backed out, he stood to lose far more. I hated to give up the money, but I had to honor my commitment. Many actors have to turn down commercial/industrial jobs because of stage rehearsals or matinees. Agents will understand such conflicts.

Request an "evening release" when you have a stage commitment. If you are scheduled for an evening stage rehearsal or performance and your agent calls with a daytime shoot, be sure to say you need an "evening release." This is common, and it is usually no problem for you to leave by 5:00 or 6:00 p.m. However, sometimes it *is* a problem, and they will need to cast someone else; big commercial shoots often go into overtime. Actors and crew have to be at the shoot for as long as the director and client need you. If you have to turn down a job because of a stage commitment, know that it happens to actors all the time.

When you audition for a job for which you will need an evening release, you must let them know about your scheduling conflicts *before* you are booked for the job. Be sure to mention it on the audition form, then confirm it with your agent at the time of the booking, and be sure to confirm it again with the powers that be at the shoot. Communication breakdowns happen from your agent to the client to the director, etc.—5:00 p.m. is NOT the time to remind them that you have a 6:00 p.m. release. Be sure it is confirmed early in the day.

TRANSPORTATION

I know actors who have gotten by without a car, but it is difficult. Commercial and industrial auditions will take you to a wide variety of locations. Theater rehearsals often last late into the evening. If you do not have a car, learn the bus routes well, and enlist the support of friends and family for occasional rides.

A good map

Invest $20 in a good map book, the kind with an index of street names and detailed map pages. (Or invest a little more in a GPS system.) You never know where you will end up for an audition or a job. Internet maps and directions are often flawed. They can help you find a new location, but you should probably have a good local map book in your car. Mine has saved me on many occasions.

COMMUNICATION

Do I need a cell phone?

Your agent has to be able to find you and find you quickly. Even if you go for weeks or months and never get a call from your agent, keep your cell phone handy and keep checking your messages. You never know. Sometimes she will get a call for a last minute gig, she will leave messages with two or three actors, and the first one to return her call gets the gig. I have seen it happen.

With a cell phone, your agent can always find you. Further, you will always have a phone available if you are lost on the way to an audition or you are stranded at an odd location shoot. You never want to lose a job because your agent could not find you!

Keep your voice-mail message short!

If you want to be a professional actor, your home or cell phone lines are now your business lines, too. Your friends may want to hear that fuzzy, distorted music (though I doubt it), but agents and casting directors certainly do not!

Gigi Jensen, local actor and former casting associate at the Playwright's Center, seconds that

> "Don't put 'Stairway to Heaven' on your answering machine message!"
> —Kelly Gallagher of JR Casting

notion: "Yes! After making seven million calls for the Playwright's Center, I hope all actors in the Twin Cities see this!"

I've heard this complaint over and over again from agents: Keep your message short and professional!

HEADSHOTS ARE AN ESSENTIAL TOOL

Almost every actor in the country has a headshot: an 8 x 10 professional photo of yourself. A good headshot (or a three-quarter shot--more on that later) is the one absolutely necessary expense for adults who wish to be professional actors. Your headshot is your most important tool. Casting people and agents pour through stacks of headshots. You need a professional headshot that gets you noticed, not one that gets tossed in the trash.

What is the process to get headshots?

- Find a photographer that you like or one that your agent recommends. Be sure the photographer is experienced with actors' headshots. (See the list of headshot photographers in Appendix D.)

- Schedule the session. Try to schedule it for your best time of day. If you are a morning person, do it then. If you hate mornings, schedule later. You want the headshot to show you at your best.

- Do not get a haircut right before your session. Give it a couple weeks.

- Arrange for a makeup artist. Guys, this perhaps may not be necessary; ask your photographer. Women, a makeup artist is a must for you. Do not skimp here. Many photographers have makeup artists with whom they are comfortable. I have always gone with their recommendations and have never been disappointed. If you know a makeup artist and want to bring your own, that is fine; however, be sure this person knows how to do makeup for photography—not just the gal who sells at the local department store.

- Be sure to communicate to your photographer and makeup artist how you wish to market yourself. In other words, if you are not a glamorous model, you do not want dramatic makeup. Be aware that the makeup for photography will probably be heavier than you use for your everyday look, but be sure the makeup artist knows not to go for a high fashion look.

- Plan your wardrobe. Take several wardrobe options to the shoot. In most cases, go conservative—especially for this market. Clean, crisp, pressed clothes are best. Do not choose suggestive and low cut—unless you want that look to drive the way you are cast. Jeans with holes in them are too casual for most of us. (Pants matter only in a three-quarter shot; they will not show in a headshot.) Wear something in which you are comfortable, something that suggests your niche (how you are likely to be cast in the commercial market). For black and white photography, wardrobe color is not as important as neckline and textures. Tiny prints and stripes are always a bad choice—for color as well as black and white.

- Go to the session rested and relaxed. Arrive early so you are not stressed.

- Relax during the session. Do not just allow the camera to see you; be "active" during the session—communicate with the camera. (See "What makes a headshot good?")

- After the session, your photographer will either hand you a disk or call later to say that your proof-sheet is ready. Pick it up and get opinions (and not just from your mother).

- Choose a good commercial shot and perhaps a different theatrical shot, and order those prints from your photographer. (See below for commercial vs. theatrical shots.)

- Take them to a printer to typeset your name on the shot and duplicate them. You *must* have your name on the shot. They will also ask you if you want matte or glossy. Printers are listed in Appendix D.

- Pick up your shots. They are usually ready in a few days.

How much do I need to spend on headshots?

Headshots will cost from $100 to $500 (or more). These two figures are about the low end and high end in this market, and you will find every price in between. Occasionally photographers will advertise in the paper for $75 headshot packages. I have no idea if you will get quality for that price. The $500 range is what you will spend for the very best in town.

For the total photographer's fee, they will typically take twenty to fifty shots. Some will give you a disk with all of the digital shots included in the fee. Others may give you a contact sheet with all of the options printed. You will choose one shot, and they will print one 8 x 10 master for you. You may also pay $20 to $30 each for 8 x 10 prints of a different shot.

See Appendix D for a list of agency-recommended photographers. Before you choose a photographer, you may want to visit the website or call to see a sampling of the photographer's work. The busiest photographers may not be willing to do this, but it may help you decide whether you will be comfortable with that photographer or whether you should shop around.

Color? Black and white? Matte? Glossy?

You will see both color and black and white shots on agency walls. Most local agencies now prefer color, but they will accept either. If yours is still black and white, you are fine for now. When it is time to get new shots, get them done in color.

Some agencies prefer a matte finish, others prefer glossy. I prefer matte because a glossy finish can cause the glare of reflected light, making headshots a little more difficult to see. This is a minor detail. If you sign exclusive with an agency, ask for their preference.

Headshot or three-quarter shot?

A headshot is typically a head and shoulders shot of you. A three-quarter shot will show more of you, typically from your feet up, or at least waist up. This will vary from shot to shot.

Most photographers will do both in a sitting. If you have an agent interested in you or already representing you, ask what his/her preference is. If you cannot afford to do both, choose the one with which you are more comfortable. Either will work fine for this market.

Can I save money and have Uncle Bernie take my headshots? He has a really good camera!

Yes, but do you want to present yourself as professionally as possible, or do you want to suggest that you are a bargain brand? Do the headshots right. The headshot is your most important tool. I am not saying that you have to pay top dollar for headshots, but I strongly recommend a professional photographer who knows headshots. Good photographers can help you relax and bring your personality to the session. They also know what the industry expects.

> "Anyone who's been around the business can tell if a headshot is professional."
> —Gigi Jensen, former casting associate, Playwright's Center

Your uncle may be a talented photographer, but you are taking a risk by having him do your headshots for free. Agents and casting directors will sometimes toss unprofessional headshots into the trash. Your talent may not be able to rescue you from a mediocre headshot.

I have heard I should have a composite card or a portfolio . . .

Anyone who tells an actor that he or she needs a composite (or "comp card") may be someone who reaps financial profits from such things. Actors need only a headshot or three-quarter shot. Experienced, professional models will eventually have a portfolio and maybe a composite, but modeling is another subject entirely! (See Chapter 14.)

> Actors: Never, ever spend your hard-earned money on a composite! Get a good headshot. That's all you need.

Professional models have legitimate comp cards to show different styles and looks. I have seen lots of comp cards submitted by actors. They often contain three to six photos of the actor: smiling, then smiling and wearing a hat, being serious, being serious wearing glasses, smiling and wearing glasses and a hat, in a suit being all corporate and serious, etc. (Yes, they are often ridiculous.) Really, trust me on this one: Do not bother with a composite. If someone advises you to get one, get better advice.

What makes a headshot good?

- A good headshot must look like you. Do not do glamour if you are not naturally glamorous. Do not try to look studly with shirt unbuttoned to your navel. Do not give your best seductive look to the camera if you are not going to be cast in seductive roles. The shot should look like you, complete with your personality. When you walk in the door to the audition, they should instantly recognize you from your headshot.

- Do not go too trendy. Most commercial and industrial clients play it safe and conservative, especially here in the Midwest. They cannot risk offending their customers. Unless you are in the young, hip age range, you should not have a cutting-edge, trendy shot, or clients may skip over your headshot.

> A good headshot is "an interesting shot that tells me something about the actor."
> —Lynn Blumenthal, casting director

- In general, a **commercial/industrial headshot** is you at your next-door-neighbor friendliest. However, friendly does not mean dull. The shot should have life and spark in your eyes and expression.

- A **theatrical or film and TV headshot** can be less "commercial." It does not need to be friendly. It can be more serious, mysterious, dark and edgy, or it can be quirky and fun. However, it still must look like you.

- Do not wear a costume. If you really look like Santa Claus, then maybe. Otherwise, be you at your everyday, simplest self.

- No props, please. We just want to see you.

- Easy on the jewelry. You do not want anything in the shot to be more interesting than your face!

- A great headshot makes it clear what your type is, as well as who you really are. Be sure your wardrobe and your expression all help to enhance your niche in the market. (See Chapter 2.)

- Finally, and this is the most important: It is *in the eyes*. Lots of headshots have nice faces and smiles, but they say: "Look at me. I'm nice. I'm kind of pretty. I'm glad you are looking at me." The actor was simply smiling for the camera. These shots are self-conscious with "deer in the headlights" eyes.

Good headshots grab your attention. A good headshot means the casting person flips through a stack of 200 shots, then stops and looks at yours. (And I do not mean because the actor is gorgeous.) You stop and look at a headshot because there is something going on in the brain behind those eyes. The good ones make you curious about the person—they are full of fun, mischief, flirtation, deep in thought, *something*. How do you get that in your headshot? Apply your acting skills to the headshot session. Be "in relationship" with the camera. Keep in mind someone you know, and in your imagination see his or her eyes inside the camera lens. Have a running dialogue with that person, or different people—not necessarily a verbal dialogue, but a stream of actions and intentions. Flirt, tease, share a secret, laugh at, draw in, toy with, comfort, challenge. The camera will grab that something in your eyes, and your proof sheet will contain some interesting shots, not just you with a repeated, empty-headed, frozen grin. (Most actors' first headshots have that grin. Mine did. Do not worry if you already have a headshot that is not fabulous, your next shot will be better. You will have several headshots done over the course of your career.)

> What makes a headshot good? "The eyes."
> —Jean Rohn, JR casting

Do I need two different headshots? A commercial shot and a theatrical shot?

Not for this market. In larger markets, actors may have a few different headshots: commercial, theatrical, soap opera, etc. There is simply no need for that here, though go ahead and get different shots if you can afford it.

Again, a commercial shot is friendlier; a theatrical shot can be quirkier or darker. It is nice to have a contrast if you are going to audition for both commercials and stage, but not essential. If you are just starting out, get one good shot and use it for everything.

> "Headshots are the most important tool they have! Make it look professional."
> —Wehmann Models and Talent

Can I save money on photo duplication?

Perhaps. Just remember that professional headshots need to be professional—down to the photo quality paper they are printed on. Flimsy photocopy paper is not industry standard. When casting decisions are made, do you want your shot to be a cheap copy on flimsy paper sitting next to your competition's professionally printed shots? Get them printed professionally. See Appendix D for a short list of photo duplication shops.

How often should I get a new headshot?

As often as your look changes: New hairstyle, new headshot. Five years older, new headshot. New moustache, new headshot. (Unless the change is a temporary look for a stage role. Then, just make sure your agent knows about your different look, and tell your agent when you go back to "normal.") If you do not change anything, adults might be able to go five years or so without a new shot.

Do not trust yourself to decide when you need new shots. You cannot be objective about how you look. Ask for opinions. As long as it still looks like you at your current age, it will still work.

RESUMES

Your headshot and resume are what get you in the door of an audition or an agent's office. Once you are in the door, your talent and skill will keep you there.

Are acting resumes the same as business resumes?

No. Business resumes list your employment history, educational background, awards and honors, etc. In the acting world, these do not matter much unless they relate to acting.

I spent my high school and college years collecting stuff that "would look good on a resume"—things that would suggest that I am a hard-working, reliable, intelligent person. The acting biz does not care about all that. What matters? "What do you look like?" and "Can you act?" After they see the product, then they will find out if you are reliable. What kind of person you are is important, but it is of secondary importance.

Though acting resumes have important differences, some business resume rules apply: Clear, concise, correct. No typos. No misspellings. Take the time to figure out how to spell the names of local teachers, directors, and casting directors. (Do not rely on spell-check. It will not fix proper names!) Bad spelling will not kill your career; however, it is a notch off of your credibility. Your headshot and resume are a very important first impression. Make every effort to be professional.

Finally, just like corporate folks, agents and directors want to be able to scan the resume in fifteen seconds or less to get an idea of your experience and training. Concise columns and categories are good. Narrative paragraphs detailing your experience are bad.

Do I need two resumes? One for stage and one for commercial work?

There are many possible resume formats. Commercial resumes and theatrical resumes have some important differences.

- **Theatrical resumes** feature your stage work, and may leave off commercial/industrial experience entirely. (Stage directors do not care if you can sell dishwashing detergent.)

- Your **commercial/industrial resume** will still lead with your "real acting" (stage or film) credits if you have them, followed by commercial/industrial and voice-over credits. Commercial casting directors and agents will want to know your entire acting background.

Note that for other markets, actors may have several different resumes: one for stage, one for film, another for TV, and yet another for commercial work. That's not necessary here. If you are just starting out, it is fine to use only one resume for everything. Once you gain more experience to add to the resume, you may wish to differentiate your stage and commercial resumes.

What do agents look for in a resume?

Agents pour through dozens of headshots and resumes from new talent. They notice experience: stage, film, TV, where you have acted, roles you have played, directors who have cast you. They also look for training: it is an indicator of work ethic, dedication, and commitment.

Commercial and industrial experience is important on a resume, but not as important as "real acting" experience. A list of commercial and industrial gigs simply says you've been working and may be a bit more knowledgeable and less "green" than some others. Commercial/industrial credits on your resume tell an agent, casting director, or stage director little about your acting ability. By all means list them, but they are not the meat and potatoes of the resume.

Here are some comments from local agencies about what they look for on actors' resumes:

- Agency Models and Talent: "We like to see a variety of training and experience. We like flexibility!"

- Meredith: "Previous work—not filled with only 'extra' spots."*

---

* Working as an "extra" means that you are hired to be in the background of a scene for stage, commercial, or film. Essentially, you are a warm body helping to create the atmosphere for the scene. Agents and directors do not care about "extra" work on a resume because it says absolutely nothing about your talent or skill. Work as an extra to observe and learn what happens on a set or for the paycheck—however small it may be—but do not do extra work thinking it will flesh out your resume.

ear prompter
class @ NUTS

- Moore Creative: "Taking classes, *still* taking classes. Any on-camera experience. Union work!"
- NUTS, ltd: "A solid acting background."
- Talent Poole: "Stage experience/film experience. Do not need a resume filled with extra work."
- Wehmann Models and Talent: "Unions, ear prompter, languages, theater, casting director classes, improv training."

RESUME CATEGORIES

Union status

List any or all actors' unions to which you belong: SAG, AFTRA, and/or Equity. If you are not a member of any unions, leave this area blank. (See Chapter 5 for more union information.)

Height, weight, hair color, eye color.

These are standard on actor resumes. Do not lie.

Clothing sizes

Sizes do not need to be listed unless you do a fair amount of modeling. If they need sizes, they will ask for them on the casting form at the audition.

Theater

Title of show, role, theater—in three neat columns. Occasionally actors will list the director's name as well, especially if the director is well known either locally or nationally.

Film and TV

Title of film or show, role, production company, or network. Again, you may wish to list the director's name if he or she is well known.

The TV category on a resume does not mean television commercials or infomercials. It means television shows on network or cable.

If you have a significant amount of film and television experience, you may wish to separate film and television into two categories. That is not common for local actors.

Commercial

There are conflicting ideas about how to list commercial work. I have often heard, "Do not list the product name, list the production company." For example, if you list TCF Bank, Bremer Bank might not even consider using you; the same may be true with McDonald's and Burger King, Coke and Pepsi, etc.

This makes sense, but if you hide the fact you have got a spot running for certain products, you may end up with some sticky problems. For the Twin Cities' market, you are safe to list commercial credits either way. I prefer to list specific product names or clients' company names instead of the production company name. Resumes are done both ways.

Some actors list "conflicts available upon request." This suggests to the client that you have done other commercials that are not listed. I use "representative listing" at the beginning of my commercial and industrial sections on the resume. Again, it tells the client that you have done other things. If they need to know about specific conflicts, they will ask.

Infomercials are not important enough to list in a separate category. I simply lump them in with the commercial section of the resume. Unless your goal is to be an infomercial star, do not highlight them. (If your goal is to be an infomercial star, um . . . don't tell anyone, OK?)

Industrial

Simply list the client's company name. No need to list role played, etc.

You may also choose to lump your commercial and industrial work into one large category: commercial/industrial/voice-over. This is what I have done on my most recent resume. You may wish to do this when you have only a handful of credits, grouping them together to make the list appear substantial, rather than list one or two items in each of several categories.

Voice-over

List the product or client name. There is no need to worry about conflicts. Voices are not as recognizable as faces on the screen. If you do a lot of voice work or only voice work, you may want to eventually list two sections, commercial voice work and industrial voice work. Most actors will have no need to separate these.

Print/Runway

Simply list the client's name. I do one or two print gigs per year at the most but I do not list them on my resume. I am not specifically looking for modeling work, so I do not feature it. If you want to model, by all means list print and runway credits. ("Print work" means modeling jobs for newspaper or magazine ads, catalogs, corporate brochures, etc.) For further discussion of modeling, see Chapter 14.

Training and Education

Training usually comes near the end of a resume. If you have a degree in theater, of course highlight that. List any other classes, seminars, and training you have had: local classes, university courses, voice coaching, etc. List the specific classes: scene study, monologue coaching, Meisner technique, voice work, camera training, etc. Any training related to acting goes in this section of your resume. Once you have enough other credits to list on your resume, you may want to begin reducing the number of listings in this section. But until your resume begins to become crowded, feature the fact that you are training. Training suggests dedication, perseverance, and willingness to take direction.

Special skills

You never know what a client will be looking for. Agents and casting directors get some pretty strange requests. List any odd skill that you can do well. You never know.

Caution: Do not list a skill that you cannot do well on demand. Do not lie to try to pad this portion of your resume. If you cannot do the skill on a day's notice, do not list it. You will never have enough advance notice to re-learn a skill before the gig. Your agent cannot audition every skill, they have to trust you. If they tell the client you can juggle, then you arrive barely able to keep three balls in the air for twenty seconds, both you and your agent look very bad.

The most common skills listed are:

- **Ear prompter:** You must be able to ear prompt extremely smoothly, without the deer in the headlights glaze in your eyes. (Information about ear prompting follows later in this chapter.)

- **Teleprompter** is not that tough for a decent actor, but do not list it until you are sure you are good at it.

- **Dialects:** Almost every actor in the country lists dialects. Just because you did a British accent in a high school or college show does not mean you can do a good Brit. Actors' resumes with dialects listed are a dime a dozen. If you learn dialects easily, you may want to keep a mention about dialects on the resume for stage work, but be sure you are really good before you list it.

- **Foreign languages:** If you are fluent (a native or near-native speaker), be sure to list the words "fluent" or "native-speaker" on the resume in parentheses. If you are not fluent, you should list something like "limited" or "conversant." There is a big difference. I have a degree in French, but I was never fluent, especially now that I'm twenty-five years beyond college French courses! If you are not fairly proficient in the language, do not list it at all.

- **Dance**: If you are a trained dancer, be sure to highlight your dance experience and training on your resume. Include it in special skills or list it as a separate section on the resume. Lots of dance training suggests discipline and commitment. Those of us with a little bit of dance training may list it as a special skill, but not feature it on the resume.

- **Sports:** List any sport you play reasonably well—a sport for which you have had some coaching or training. I'm a sports fanatic, so perhaps I am a bit biased here. Playing pick-up basketball once in a while does not mean you have a credible jump shot.

> In 18 years, I've been called upon to do three different skills from my resume: golf, speaking French, and robot—strange, but true. (The client bought me a silver suit and metallic makeup to be a human statue at the State Fair.)

If you "throw like a girl," you shouldn't necessarily list softball or baseball as a skill. If you've played a few rounds of golf, but triple bogeys are the norm not the exception, take some lessons before you list it on your resume. I ran hurdles in high school, but I took hurdles off my resume quite a while ago. I think I would rip every muscle in my thigh if I tried to run hurdles now. If you cannot do it well for a shoot tomorrow, do not list it. List anything sports-related that you do well: water skiing, jet skiing, cross country or downhill skiing, snow shoeing, hunting/shooting, boxing, football, roller-blading, mountain-biking, discus and shot put, soccer goal keeping, hockey, etc.

- **Other skills**: Musical instruments, juggling, magic tricks, unicycle riding, impressions (they had better be great), license to drive

> "I can recite all fifty states in one breath in less than twenty seconds. I am often asked to do this. It has helped me with many auditions and allowed me to relax, be myself, and be funny all at the same time. The auditors got to see a bit of me as a person which helped me to stand out from the crowd. I have gotten several jobs because of this skill."
> —Seri Johnson

a truck (a big one, not a pick-up), demolition derby driving (yes, I have seen it on a resume), knowledge of medical terminology (or any other specific technical field), knitting, weaving on a loom, construction, carpentry, plumbing, mime, etc. The list is endless, but do not list it if you do not do it very well.

What if I do not have a lot of experience to put on my resume?

If you are very new to acting, you will not have much to put on a resume. Don't sweat it. Start your resume with whatever you have and add to it as you go. List the experience you do have: public speaking experience, dance experience, any experience in front of a camera or a microphone, and any kind of performance. If you need more, add a category called "related experience" and list stage-managing, directing, anything that is industry related.

> "If they're new, they're new. That's okay!"
> —Geanette Poole, Talent Poole talent agency

I started with a pretty sparse resume: about six high school and college plays, a handful of classes, and a few skills. I used a really big font to fill up the page. Do not feel bad about a sparse resume. Everyone has to start somewhere. Make the resume clean, concise, and professional. Then, keep adding experience! Take classes, do community theater—anything to keep fleshing out that resume.

Should I list my high school and college credits?

Depends on how old you are. If you are only a few years out of college, absolutely leave it all on there, especially if you need it to fill up the resume. My first resume at age twenty-six or twenty-seven still listed most of the roles I played in high school and college because it was all I had. As soon as I had more recent credits to add, I dropped the high school stuff, and, within a few years, I dropped the college stuff, too. Use the older credits as long as you need them, and drop them when you have more recent credits to add.

Should my credits be listed in chronological order?

Not necessarily. This is one way that an actor's resume is different from a corporate resume. Chronological order does not matter. Lead with your best credits: featured or leading roles first.

What category should I list first?

For this market, I recommend that you feature your best acting credits first—usually theater. Most local agents and casting directors will take special notice of theater credits. If you have substantial film and TV work, you may wish to lead with that. Commercial, industrial, and voice-over should follow in any order. Lead with your personal strengths.

If you do not have a lot of acting credits, lead with whatever public performance credits you have, and follow with any related training you may have. Agents, directors, and casting directors will notice the fact that you are training with good acting teachers.

Do I put my phone number on my resume, or my agent's number?

Even experienced actors are often confused about this. The overall rules:

- Your headshot must *always* have your name professionally printed on it.

- Any and all resumes must always have your name along with a phone number, either yours or your agent's.

- When you are seeking representation and sending your stuff *to an agent*, always include all of your personal phone numbers on the resume: work, home, and cell—whatever you have. An agent must know how to reach you. You may wish to include your e-mail address on a resume to agents, though this is not necessary. If they need information other than your phone numbers, they will request it at your interview.

- Anytime you audition for stage, film, or other work *for which an agent does not represent you*, include your personal phone numbers—work, home, or cell. You do not need to include a home address. List only your phone numbers.

- Anytime *your agent sends you* for an audition, list your agent's name and number, not your personal numbers. When an agent represents you, that client should deal with your agent, not directly with you.

Other resume basics.

- Always securely attach your resume to your headshot! *Not attaching them is a big pet peeve of agents and casting directors!*

  Headshots and resumes are most commonly attached with staples at all four corners. When you send out your headshot, it almost always ends up in a big stack somewhere: the bigger the stack the more likely the headshot and resume are to be separated. If they are not securely attached, they may love your headshot but not know how to contact you.

Do not show up at auditions without a resume, or with headshot and resume unattached, or attached with only a paper clip! It is a pain in the neck for the person who has to keep it all straight for the client, and it is annoying for the client!

> "Do not list your home address, only phone numbers. No one needs to know where you live— unless they are mailing you a check!"
>
> —Jean Rohn, casting director

- Do not attach an 8.5 x 11 resume to an 8 x 10 photo. Take the time to trim it. The resume should not have extra paper hanging over the edges.

- Some actors have their resumes printed directly onto the back of the headshot. This is fine; just be sure you can easily update the resume.

- The only exception to the "securely attached" rule is if your agent specifically requests headshots without staples. Some agents fax or scan your headshot into the computer, so they want copies without staples. Your agent should tell you if this is the case.

- Never print a resume that has no contact information; either your phone number or your agent's number must be listed. You want them to be able to find you!

Sample resumes.

There is no single right way to do an acting resume. What follows are a couple of sample resumes—my first resume from eighteen years ago and a more recent version. Feel free to use this format or alter it to meet your own needs. Again, there are no strict rules; use a format that works for you, following the guidelines outlined.

Last word about resumes.

As you compose or refine your resume, use these sample formats as a model or create your own style. There is no right or wrong in actor resume formats, as long as you are concise and accurate. Be sure to proofread carefully!

Beth Chaplin

(Union status and phone number here.)

Eyes: Blue

Hair: Brown

Weight: 125

Height: 5'4"

Theater

(representative listing)

Major Barbara	Barbara Undershaft	St. Olaf College
Design for Living	Helen	St. Olaf College
The Cherry Orchard	Anya	St. Olaf College
Instant Enlightenment Including Sales Tax	Carmen	St. Olaf College
You Can't Take it With You	Alice	Thompson Theater, Wheaton, Illinois
Forty Carats	Ann	Thompson Theater
Carousel	Chorus	Thompson Theater
The King and I	Chorus, Choreographer	Thompson Theater

Training

Commercial Acting	Jay Reilly
Auditioning for the Camera	Curt Akerlind
Improvisation	Ellen Heck
B.A. - Speech & Theater	St. Olaf College

Special Skills

Various Dialects/Accents	Softball
Track: hurdles, sprints	Tennis
Clarinet	French (conversant, not fluent)
Soccer	Modern Dance

BETH CHAPLIN
(Union status and phone number here)

Eyes: Blue   Height: 5'4"
Hair: Salt and pepper   Weight: 145

STAGE
(Representative listing)

The Dresser	Madge	Theatre in the Round
The Miracle Worker	Annie Sullivan	Park Square Theatre
A Few Good Men	Lt. Cmdr. Joanne Galloway	Theatre in the Round
A Piece of My Heart	Martha	Theatre Unbound
The Man Who Came to Dinner	Maggie Cutler	Theatre in the Round
Hobson's Choice	Maggie Hobson	Park Square Theatre
The Constant Wife	Constance	Park Square Theatre
Humble Boy	Rosie Pye	Theatre in the Round
The Winter's Tale	Lady Emilia	Theatre in the Round
The Women	Sylvia (understudy)	Lakeshore Players
Graceland	Bev Davies	Irelene Theater

FILM

The Hymen's Parable	Psychologist	Jon Springer
Acid Snow	Kate	Acid Snow Productions
Something Borrowed, Something New	Serene	Itman Pictures

VOICE-OVER/ INDUSTRIAL/ COMMERCIAL
(Representative listing – conflicts available upon request)

Best Buy	Target	Jani-King
US Bank	General Electric	Toro
Northwest Airlines	Hazelden	Prudential
American Airlines	Play It Again Sports	Minnesota Twins
Gillette Children's Hospital	National Camera	Cargill
Mayo Clinic	IDS	St. Paul Companies
3M	Coldwell Banker	Rosemount
Sears	Verizon	Deluxe Check
General Mills	Jostens	United Health Group
Blue Cross	Boston Scientific	Schwann Foods

TRAINING

Cold Reading, Monologue, Film and TV	Jane Brody
Advanced Meisner	Sandra K. Horner
Auditioning for the Camera - master class	Curt Akerlind, Cheryl Moore Brinkley
	Stephen Pelinski
Advanced Acting	Brave New Workshop
Improvisation	St. Olaf College
B.A. – Speech & Theater	

OTHER SKILLS

Ear prompter proficient	Clarinet
Mechanical human/robot (with silver metallic suit)	Soccer (goalkeeper)
Various dialects/accents	Softball / Baseball
Adept with medical terminology	Golf
French and Spanish (not fluent)	Hockey goalie

WARDROBE

You will need to provide your own wardrobe for auditions and shoots. Do not run out and shop for new clothes and accessories. Just know that if agents begin calling, you may need to supplement what you already have.

Do I have to provide my own wardrobe for stage work?

Usually not. For the stage, costumes are often provided. Most local theaters will have a costumer for the show. You may have to provide your own incidentals—socks, undergarments, etc. Theaters with lower budgets may ask for your help in providing costume pieces.

Do I have to provide my own wardrobe for commercial/industrial work?

Usually, yes. You will certainly need your own clothes for auditions; however, you will not need specific costumes.

For big commercial shoots, the production company will often provide wardrobe; for smaller budget projects and industrials, they will rarely provide it (unless the role calls for specific uniforms or protective equipment). If you are a union actor, you will be modestly compensated for this. If you are non-union, it is simply part of the job. Your agent will tell you what the client wants you to bring to the shoot—usually business or casual attire. It is best to bring at least three to five options for shirts, blouses and ties, and three options for slacks.

Wardrobe terminology

If you want to see what the typical attire is for this business, watch commercials and sitcoms and pick out the people who are your type.

When your agent calls for an audition or gig, she will use certain wardrobe terms. (The most common are listed below.) It is important to remember that these are just guidelines. It rarely matters much what you wear to an audition. It is more important that you feel good about how you look. I will often go to my closet with an idea of what I should wear, but a different outfit strikes me—even if it is not exactly what they requested. I go with my feelings and whims, as long as it is in the same ballpark.

Your agent will occasionally translate wardrobe information to you incorrectly. If you show up to an audition and think you are dressed all wrong for it, do not let it worry you. If you give a good audition, they will not hold your wardrobe against you. The worst thing you can do is get flustered by it and do a distracted, apologetic audition. Shake it off and do your work. Your look and personality are far more important than your wardrobe.

Clients play it safe. They rarely want trendy, unless they specifically request it. When choosing wardrobe, lean to the conservative side. However, you have some latitude to allow your personality to influence your choices. The following examples are loose guidelines.

- Corporate: Suits (for women, pants are just fine).

- Business, not corporate: Professional attire, yet somewhat less formal than a suit. For men: A sport coat, slacks, and a dress shirt; or maybe a shirt and tie without the jacket. For women: A dress, pants suit, skirt and blouse; or slacks and blouse.

- Business casual: Similar to the above description, but more relaxed—shirt or sweater and slacks.

- Upscale casual: I like to call this one "shopping and lunch at the Galleria." (For those new to Minnesota, the Galleria is an expensive, upscale shopping mall, very fashionably conservative.) For men: khakis or slacks and a nice shirt—perhaps a polo shirt in the summer or a nice sweater in the winter. For women: a comfortable dress, or slacks and a blouse or sweater. It is similar to business casual, but it can be a little more trendy or stylish.

- At-home casual: In reality, I wear sweats or old jeans at home, but not for "at-home casual" commercials. In the commercial world, think more along the lines of casual pants and a nice shirt or sweater. Adapt that to your own style. Jeans can be okay for this, but be sure they are nice jeans.

- Blue collar: Can be jeans and a work shirt or flannel shirt—very casual, yet still neat.

Your agent may give other variations from the list above, but these cover the most common wardrobe requests.

What colors are bad on camera?

The general rule is: no black, white, bright red, tiny prints, and stripes. Very shiny fabrics can also be problematic. Silks are fine, but glittery or shiny satin garments may not be.

I could go into detail about why all of the above are bad, but the whys and wherefores are unimportant. Suffice it to say that it has to do with how the camera responds to these colors. Directors will not want you to wear them; further, if you do wear them, you will not look your best. A small splash of black or white (in a collar, for example) is just fine if it is combined with a "good" camera color.

What colors are good on camera?

Wear the colors that are generally good on you (as long as you stay away from the above bad colors). If you do not know what your good colors are, start asking your friends. Personally, I know that I'm a "cool, winter/spring." (Mom took me to one of those nifty color analysis parties, so very popular in the 1970s.) Solids are always safer than prints, though prints that contain similar color intensities without tiny patterns can often work just fine.

In general, solid pastels and solid rich colors are great. Layers with different solid colors can be quite nice. Textured fabrics are also nice, as long as they do not have a tiny print or stripe to them.

What if I do not have a suit?

Business wardrobe is often requested, particularly for industrials. If you do not own a suit, talk to your agent and do the best you can. If you cannot borrow suits, be sure to communicate this to the client through your agent. Perhaps they will be willing to work something out.

If you start getting requests for "corporate" gigs, it is time to find a way to get a suit or two. I borrowed a couple of suits from friends during my first year in the biz. If you have friends who wear the same size, this may work. Visit consignment shops to look for corporate attire at a more reasonable price.

What if they request wardrobe that I do not have?

Occasionally a client will be quite particular about wardrobe. In those cases, tell your agent what you have on hand and try to borrow what you need. However, if a client has something very specific in mind, they may need to provide it. A frantic last-minute shopping trip all over town is definitely not part of the job.

I once had a client specifically request "a powder blue sweater set, pearls, matching pearl earrings, a khaki skirt, and a French manicure." I knocked myself out trying to make it all happen (begging, borrowing, and buying) when really I should have told my agent, "I do not have most of it. I'll do the best I can with no guarantees as to the specifics."

Another client asked if I would be able to provide a white lab coat. I did not have one, but knew I could easily rent one from a local costume rental source and the client willingly covered the cost. (See Appendix J.)

Another project (construction safety training) required a hard hat, heavy work jacket, work boots, etc. The client provided the hard hat; I borrowed a Carhartt jacket from a friend who works in construction and beat-up hiking boots from another friend.

If it is easily doable to satisfy a client's wardrobe requests, then do it. If it will cost you too much time or stress, do not hesitate to let your agent know what you can and cannot do. It will be up to the client to decide how badly they want their exact requests. They will need to provide specifics or pay you to shop for them. Just be sure the arrangement is clearly communicated ahead of time.

What if the client requests that I get a haircut or a manicure?

If it is just a trim and I am due for a haircut, I pay for it myself. If they want a big change in your look, it is your decision. Remember, you need to look like your headshot. If you change your hair dramatically, it may be a problem for other auditions and gigs. If the change requires that you spend money for it, be sure to talk with your agent about the possibility of being reimbursed.

I have had a few clients request that I get a manicure when my hands will be in the shot (for close-ups where I will be handling product or pointing to items on a computer screen, etc.). Keeping your hands and nails neat and trimmed is part of your job, but a specific style of manicure is a special request. Talk to your agent, and then save your receipts. You may be reimbursed for these specific requests, or you may be able to take the expense as a tax deduction.

MAKEUP

Some clients will hire a makeup artist for the shoot. That is nice when it happens. The beauty of having a makeup artist is that you are not responsible for how you look, other than not messing up the makeup artist's work! You show up with a clean face and simply styled hair and let the makeup artist do the rest.

Often, you will not have a makeup artist at a shoot, and you will certainly have to do your own makeup for auditions. I just do the basics: foundation, concealer, liner, eye shadow, mascara, blush, lips, and powder. Women, if you really do not know makeup, head to the nearest department store and have your makeup done for free. Watch carefully and ask a lot of questions. Better yet, watch the makeup artist at your headshot session. Begin to notice what you like and do not like. If you would like a private lesson about camera makeup, consult Appendix J for information about local makeup artists who may be willing to teach you. You will have to ask about pricing.

Do I need to supply my own makeup?

Often, yes. The bigger the budget for a project, the more likely you are to have a makeup artist. Low budget commercials and industrials will almost always cut the makeup artist from the budget. No makeup artist means that you will have to provide your own makeup supplies.

Men simply need to have translucent powder with a brush or powder puffs, perhaps some kind of blemish concealer, and hair care items: comb or brush and perhaps hair spray. (If you are a guy who does not have hair to spray, then you will really need powder to cut the shine!) You can get inexpensive translucent powder at most any store that sells makeup. Norcostco in Plymouth, a costume and theatrical supply house, also sells powder. (See Appendix J.)

Women will need the works: hair-styling products, foundation, eyes, lips, cheeks, and powder. Be sure to have a few different lip color options.

To be honest, I get most of my makeup at drug stores. Simple and natural is just fine. My logic tells me that if a client is particular about makeup, they should hire a makeup artist. (My makeup artist friends would second that notion.)

Do I need to supply my own makeup for stage work?

Yes, but you do not need to run out and get anything fancy. You will often just bring in your own basic makeup supplies. (Providing your own is more sanitary than using something from a theater's stock.) If you do not know anything about makeup, then talk with your costumer or director. Often other cast members are willing to help you. If you are a character actor, you may need to be a little more extravagant, but do not go out and get anything until you are cast in a role that demands it. Then discuss options with your costumer.

If you are in a lower budget production and there is no costumer, the folks at Norcostco can be very helpful.

Camera makeup basics.

- Commercial/industrial makeup is not fashion makeup. What you see in fashion magazines is often more dramatic and very different from what you will need as an actor. Commercials and industrials feature "real people."

- Matte, not frost, for eyes and lips.

- Eyes are the most important. Accentuate, but do not overdo it.

- Always carry translucent powder for eliminating shine.

- Special blotting tissues are good for soaking up oils and perspiration, as an alternative to piling on too much powder. (They are available at most makeup counters.)

- Do not panic about occasional blemishes. Real people get zits, too. They can be concealed. (If my face were to be shown in close-up on a thirty-foot movie screen, I would panic. On most televisions screens, no one will know the difference.)
- Hydration is critical for your skin. Drink plenty of water and consistently use a good moisturizer.
- Avoid the sun and use sunscreen. Sunburn and peeling skin are difficult to hide. (Skin cancer surgery and scars are even more difficult to hide.)

How about wigs?

I have had to wear wigs for several shows. Most of the time the costumer has supplied them. On two occasions, I have gone shopping for my own wig. If you are particular, you may want to do the same. Many theaters have limited budgets. What they can afford to supply is not always the best. On one occasion I rented a wig from the Guthrie Theater. For another show I purchased a hair extension, and then had it and my hair dyed to match. It was a lot of trouble and a bit expensive, but it was worth it to feel confident in my appearance on stage.

For women, long hair may be more flexible if you are going to do a lot of stage work. If you have short hair, you may have to deal with wigs more often.

Moustaches and beards for men.

Commercial clients sometimes prefer talent to be clean-shaven; thus, men will occasionally be asked to shave a beard or moustache for camera work. Your response to their request is up to you; just know that your answer may affect their casting decision. On the other hand, you may occasionally want to grow a beard or moustache for a stage role. If that is the case, just be sure your commercial agent knows about the temporary change.

Coloring your hair.

I have been asked to color out the gray many times. (I started turning gray at age twenty.) There's a great temporary hair dye called "Fanciful." It covers my gray quite well and comes out completely in one or two washings. Find it at Walgreen's and give it a try.

The choice of permanent hair color is up to you. Simply remember that for the camera it should appear natural, and you must look like your headshot.

AUDIO AND VIDEO DEMOS

It is not essential that you have an audio or video demo. Demos are simply a quick sampling of your work: quick clips edited together as a one- to five-minute demonstration of what you can do.

Audio demos.

An audio demo is essential if you want to try to break into voice work. (For voice-over information, see Chapter 12.)

Video/DVD demos.

Video demos are not used often in the Twin Cities (and are totally unnecessary for beginning actors), but they can be nice marketing tools. Video demos are also referred to as "reels"—as in "that's a nice clip for my reel" or "send me your reel." Video demos can include samples of film, television, commercial, or industrial work. For this market, you can have one demo with examples of all of the above. However, if you are targeting a specific type of work, you will eventually want to have separate demos— one for film and TV, another for commercials and industrials.

If you are seeking film and television work, do not include commercial and industrial work on your demo. This will not impress anyone in film or TV.

When you have several samples of your work, contact a video produc-tion company for pricing information to edit an actor's demo or reel. You will likely get an hourly rate of $100 per hour and up. When it comes time to edit, be sure you know exactly which moments of your work you want to include. Do not pay for editing time while you decide what you want. (See Appendix H for information about those who may be willing to edit actors' demos.)

When will I need to use a video demo?

Once in a great while, a client will ask your agent for demos. It is nice to be able to supply your agent with several copies of a demo. If you do not have a demo, you will have to send a video/DVD of any project you have. There is no guarantee you will get the original back.

Independent film producers may use actors' reels more often than agents and commercial clients do. If you begin to do independent film work, you may want to produce a reel to post on a website or send to pro-ducers and directors when casting opportunities happen.

Should I go to a studio and make a video demo from scratch?

There is no need for this in the Twin Cities; the majority of actors here do not have them. Some actors will choose copy, rehearse scenes, and monologues, and record them to submit to agents. That may be worth doing for bigger markets, but not here. If you are a good actor, your resume will get you in the agent's door and your audition will speak for itself. Do not mock up a demo tape. It will be expensive, and it will not do you much good. Once you have several clips of real work, you can decide if there is value in compiling a demo.

How can I get video/DVD copies of my work?

A good demo cannot be compiled until you have done several jobs and have copies of the video. Most production companies are happy to provide you with a copy, but they are very busy folks and it is difficult for them to remember to do it.

So, here is a nearly foolproof way to get copies of your work. During a convenient time at the shoot, ask someone (the production assistant, the director, the client—depending on who is most available and with whom you are most comfortable) if it is possible to get a copy and whom you need to contact. Occasionally there are confidentiality issues, and they will not be able to give you one.

After the shoot is done, send a self-addressed, padded mailing envelope with enough postage to cover the weight of a DVD to the attention of the contact person from the shoot along with a note thanking them for the opportunity to work with them, yada, yada, yada. Ask if it is possible for them to send a copy of the finished project in the envelope provided. Add, "Be sure to enclose an invoice for any costs involved." Rarely will you get a bill. If you do, it is in the area of $10 to $30 for editing time.

When you make it easy for them to pop it in the mail, you increase your chances of getting copies of your work. When I send requests this way, I get the copies almost every time.

Many producers will now send you a digital file of your work via e-mail. To request a copy this way, skip the self-addressed envelope and just send a professional letter with your e-mail address. (You may also send an e-mail request, but e-mails are more easily ignored and deleted. An old-fashioned business letter might catch their attention.)

If you are an extra in the shoot, do not bug them for copies. Save your requests for when you have done more substantial work. No agent is going to be able to see what you can do as an extra; it is of no use to show a DVD with you in the background.

When you are doing an independent film, it is often an unpaid gig. It is standard procedure that if you are not paid, you at least get a good copy of the finished project. Be aware that the editing process for film is much longer than for most industrials. Some commercial and industrial projects are edited within days; others sit on the shelf for weeks or months; film projects can take months or even years. Be patient.

EAR PROMPTER

An ear prompter is a wonderful tool, but it is not for everyone. Ear prompters are used primarily for industrial projects, either live or on-camera, when there is too much text to memorize easily. An actor who uses an ear prompter can save a client the cost of renting teleprompter equipment. Further, the ear prompter gives the actor and camera more flexibility in movement as opposed to a teleprompter.

A good industrial spokesperson has a "corporate" look, possesses a clear, easy-on-the-ears voice, great diction, and an engaging, smooth communication style. Ask your agent if it is something you should look into. When you begin to hear the question, "Are you ear prompted?" It is time to look into getting one.

You may have seen newscasters with earpieces and tubes coiling out of their ears—same concept, but very different use. Newscasters hear direction through the earpiece. Actors are hearing their own voice delivering the given text as recorded into a micro-cassette or digital recorder. The sound comes through a wire connection and earpiece, into the ear, through the brain, and out the mouth. It is a skill that is easy for some to learn, more difficult for others. Good actors who are comfortable in front of the camera can pick up the skill fairly easily.

> If you are not the spokesperson type, you may not want to spend the money on ear prompter equipment and training.

An ear prompter consists of an earpiece, a tube and wire connector or an "induction neck loop," and a micro-cassette or digital recorder. The cost to get fitted with the entire set-up can range from around $100 to over $1000. To get started, you only need the $100 package. If you start to work with your prompter often, you may want to upgrade to the more expensive packages.

See Appendix K for a listing of ear prompter classes and businesses that sell prompter equipment. If you have an actor friend who uses an ear prompter, he or she may be willing to show you the basics. If in doubt, consider taking a class to learn to use it properly. A shoot is the wrong place to learn that you are not yet proficient with the prompter.

Please note: If you are a beginning actor, do not rush right out and do this. Save yourself time, money, and frustration; get some training and experience on camera first.

MISCELLANEOUS SELF PROMOTION

Postcard headshots.

Occasionally you will hear the recommendation: "Get your headshot printed as postcards, then mail them to agents, casting directors, etc."

It makes sense to send these to people in the biz so they will begin to connect your name with your face. If you feel comfortable sending them, go ahead and do it, but do not spend a lot of money on it. Most photocopy places have high-quality duplication equipment that can print on "card stock." If you want to spend a little extra, Digigraphics (the company that prints many local actors' headshots) will print these for you from your headshot master.

I have always felt more comfortable sending another headshot and updated resume with a brief, friendly cover letter. Once a casting director or agent knows me, I prefer to send thank you notes in the form a fun postcard rather than just another picture of me. We actors are self-centered enough without reinforcing that stereotype by mailing our little smiling selves all over town!

> I once got these photo postcards of me printed, but I always felt odd about mailing my little photo to people. Most of my mini-headshots ended up as doodle material—an amusing way to pass the time during long phone conversations.

Business cards.

It is not a bad idea to have a business card printed, though not necessary. If you do, list your name, agent's contact info, and/or your personal information. (If you give home contact information to clients, be sure to honor your relationship with your agent. See Chapter 4.) If you are a professional actor, it is good to have professional business cards.

Some actors have their headshot printed on the business card. I have never wanted to do this, but for some actors it is a nice touch. It depends on your comfort level and personality.

Websites and social networking.

A website is not essential. Most local actors do not have one. Some actors use websites to showcase voice-over demos or video demos. Other actors who also do corporate speaking engagements and event entertaining use the website as an essential marketing tool for that side of the business. Voice-over clients sometimes hire voices via the internet. (More on this in Chapter 12.) Producers and directors may narrow their casting choices by viewing actors' reels. If you have demos or reels to post on a website, this can be a good idea, but only if you have a clear business and marketing strategy. A website is a useful business investment only if you can drive traffic to it.

Facebook, Linked In, and other websites may offer some valuable networking opportunities. Many local actors and theaters are on Facebook. Some actors post photos and videos on their Facebook pages as well as notices about current theater projects. It can be a great supplemental marketing tool—and much less expensive than a website.

The average actor does not need a website to showcase acting ability. Most directors and clients will still need to see you audition in person.

What do I really need to get started?

You can start auditioning for community theater right now. Just get out there and go for it.

You cannot get started in the business side of things until you have a good headshot and resume. When directors are doing the work of casting a project, they need to be able to clearly remember the actors they are considering. Agents must have your headshot before they will call you. Headshots are an essential tool. Once you have that and a resume, start sending them to agents.

> "At the Playwright's Center, if I don't have a headshot, there's very little chance that I'll remember the actor."
>
> —Gigi Jensen, actor and former casting associate, Playwright's Center

That is all you really need to get started. If you want to become a professional actor, you will need to pursue further training and experience to build your resume, but the professional headshot and resume are what you really need to be on your way!

CHAPTER 4

Agents

Doorway to the commercial/industrial world

An agent is the best doorway into the world of commercial/industrial work, but it is sometimes the toughest door to open. Eighteen years ago, I was on the outside looking in as the interviewee with many of the agents in town. In the past several years, I have been inside on the interviewing side of the table, and I have met with at least a few hundred "new talent" at the largest non-union agency in town (NUTS, ltd.). I've spent quite a bit of time working in the agency office, so I will spend much of this chapter with my "agency hat" on. It is a unique perspective that may help you. I wish I had known twenty years ago what I know now!

Most of the agents in the Twin Cities are truly nice folks who are very supportive of actors. However, the maddening subjectivity in this business often manifests itself in the worst way in the relationship between actors and agents. One agent will be totally uninterested, while the next agent will think you are absolutely terrific. An agent will insist you cannot possibly do comedy when you just got great reviews on stage in an uproarious comedy. An agent will think you can only do quirky comedy when some of your best work is straightforward and honest drama.

For new actors, the toughest part of this business is getting an agent to call you and let you into the game. The advice in this chapter will not guarantee that you will find an agent; or that, if you find an agent, they will call you frequently; or that, if they call you frequently, you will have a wonderful working relationship for years to come. The advice that follows will help you navigate the agent game with some sensible strategies. If you understand how an agency works and why they make the decisions they do, your agent–actor relationship will be much simpler.

To help you sort it all out, I have divided this chapter into three sections:

- Getting an agent
- The actor/agent relationship
- Building and maintaining the relationship: Relationship counseling

GETTING AN AGENT

Why do I need an agent?

If you want to do commercial and industrial work of any kind—on-camera or voice-over—your best bet is to be listed with one or more agencies. (Yes, in the Twin Cities market, it is perfectly acceptable to be with more than one agent—more on that later.) You may be able to hustle a little bit of work without an agent, but that is tough to do. A few local actors have tried with limited success. Most of the professional commercial/industrial work in town will be booked through an agency.

What is the difference between a union-franchised talent agency, and a non-union talent agency? What kind of agency should I seek?

In Chapter 5, I discuss the unions in detail. For now, here are the basics.

First, if you are a new actor, I recommend that you explore non-union work while you get your feet wet in the Twin Cities acting world. Do not worry about the details of the unions for now. There are plenty of avenues to pursue without traveling the union paths. Once you gain a little experience, you will be ready to investigate union membership.

In this market, the lines between union and non-union agencies used to be firmly drawn—the established agencies were either union or non-union. More recently, a few talent agencies have decided to represent both union and non-union actors for non-union work. This is a great development for some, troubling for others.

> If your passion is the stage and only the stage, you do not need to bother with an agent. Twin Cities' agents will do little for your stage career. (See Chapter 10 for more theater information.)

The basic difference between union franchised agencies and non-union agencies is that franchised agencies are held to professional standards based on established union rules; for example, they must uphold established union pay rates and keep agency commissions at ten percent. If you are curious, the complete contract can be found on the AFTRA website (www.AFTRA.com).

Non-union agencies are not governed by any standards other than the conscience and ethics of the people in charge. In my experience, these standards have been quite high, though there are no guarantees. If you ever have a conflict with a non-union agent, you will not have the power of a union contract to back you.

See Chapter 5 for much more information about the actors' unions, and see Appendix A for specifics about local talent agencies. This chapter will cover issues common to all talent agencies.

Will an agent represent me for theater gigs?

This is a commonly asked question from those who are new to the game. The answer? No; not in the Twin Cities. The bigger markets—New York, Los Angeles and Chicago—have separate theatrical, commercial, and film/TV agencies. That is simply not the case here. There are a few agents with ties to the theater community who will occasionally get calls from directors for recommendations and ideas. However, in most cases, do not count on an agent here in town to find theater gigs for you.

What are some of the ways to get a foot in the door?

The first step to get into the agent's game is to send your headshot and resume with a simple, professional cover letter. (See the following pages for details about cover letters.)

Do not count on that alone to get the response you want. Sending the headshot and resume is just the first step. Agents receive stacks and stacks of headshots from new talent. What causes you to rise to the top of the stack and not end up in the trash?

- A great headshot. (See Chapter 3.)
- A great "look" (a look that's good for a specific niche in the market).
- Ethnicity. Clients need diversity in their projects, thus agents need good ethnic actors on their team.
- Good experience on the resume (especially theater experience).
- Good training.
- Any combination of the above.

What do I send to an agent?

- **Headshot and resume**. First and foremost send these two things. *Always* include your phone number on the resume *and* cover letter. (Do not send a resume or headshot to an agent with a different agent's phone number on it! An agent will not contact a competing agent in order to find you!) Include *your own* contact information in every submission to an agent!
- **Voice or video demos** if you have them. As discussed in Chapter 3, demos are not necessary. Sometimes more experienced commer-

cial/industrial/film and TV actors have demos. If you do not have a demo, don't worry about it.

- **Cover letter**. Cover letters for this business are the same as in any business: short, simple, concise, correct, and professional. If you have any information that might catch the agent's attention, include such details in the cover letter, but do not elaborate too much—save it for the interview.

Details to mention:

- Names of people who have recommended you: actors, directors, casting directors. Name-dropping is fine, as long as you truly know the person. For example: "I worked with Joe Actor on show XYZ at Theater ABC, and he suggested I send my headshot to you." Or, "I just finished a class with Mary Casting Director. She suggested that you might want to see me for an interview."
- A show you have done recently or a current show.
- A class you have completed recently.
- Another market from which you have just arrived. (For example, "I have recently relocated from Chicago where I was training at Second City," or "I just moved here from Omaha where I shot a few local commercials.")

Details to leave out:

- "I am such a great and versatile actor that I am sure you will want to represent me, and I can make a lot of money for you, yada, yada, yada." Let your resume speak for itself.
- Jokes, clever witticisms, etc. Include it only if you know it is funny. When in doubt, simply be professional.
- Typos, misspellings, etc. Professionalism is important in any business. Spelling and typing are not indicators of talent, but they do suggest your level of professionalism and accountability. Be sure to proofread your cover letter and resume carefully.

If I do not hear anything from an agent, should I give up?

No. Keep sending your materials every three to six months. If you do not get an interview after your first mailing, don't despair. New talent headshots often sit in stacks for weeks or months before anyone calls for an interview. Many new talent headshots end up in the trash. That is harsh, but true.

Some agents interview new talent regularly. Some schedule interviews more sporadically. When you send your materials and hear nothing, your envelope could be still sitting unopened in a stack somewhere. It could be that they are just terribly behind in the interview process. It could be that they already have too many of your type, and they do not need you right now. It is not uncommon to submit your things and then hear nothing from an agent.

Keep in mind that acting careers do not happen overnight. A career, even in the commercial/industrial business, can take years to build. Do not be in a hurry. Just keep working. Be patient and persistent.

What if the agents still ignore me, even though I have sent my stuff to them several times? How can I get an agent's attention?

You never know what might finally catch their eye. A few ideas may help jump-start the relationship:

- Get a better headshot. If you have a cheap headshot or a headshot that does not work for you, do it again. (Ask for professional advice from commercial teachers and casting directors.)

- Invite them to any show you do. They may not attend, but at least you will be sending the signal that you are working at your craft, and that someone thought enough of you to cast you. If the agent does attend the show, they will know to watch for you. Or, they may know the director or other actors in the show and they will ask about you.

- Take a class from a casting director that may result in calls directly from the casting director. Then let agents know that the casting director is calling you directly. If the casting director likes you, the agent will have good reason to take another look at you. (See Chapter 6 for information about casting directors.)

- Ask a casting director to put in a good word for you.

- Build your resume. Go out and get more training and resubmit your materials, briefly noting in your cover letter your increased experience and training.

- If you know an actor that the agent currently represents, include that name in your cover letter and ask the actor to put in a good word for you.

- Send your materials anytime you have something new to add: a new show, a new class, an updated resume, etc.

Be persistent. Keep gaining experience and training. You never know what might catch their attention. On the flip side, do not be so persistent that you harass the agent! Daily or weekly e-mails and calls will only irritate the office personnel. Be persistent, but be professional.

The agent interview: Do not sell yourself, be yourself.

Agents interview new talent in many different ways. If you get an interview, it is a good step—something about your headshot and resume caught their eye. If they have seen you on stage and called you in, all the better. Go with confidence.

Most agency auditions will involve a brief interview and an opportunity for you to read on camera. Most often you will read commercial copy; less often you will be asked to read something more dramatic or perform a monologue. (If they require any such preparation, they will tell you in advance.) An experienced agent can very quickly assess your look and talent in a minute or less on camera. They can quickly assess your experience with a brief perusal of your resume: seventy-five percent of what they need to know, they will see in that short time; however, the other twenty-five percent can tip the scales either way. Your look and your talent will speak for themselves. Beyond that, they want to know who you are. Are you interesting, poised, reliable, flexible, and personable? Can they confidently send you to a client, knowing you can do the job?

Actors can get so caught up in being self-conscious—looking right and sounding right—that they forget to simply communicate when they interview and audition. In a typical job interview, you need to sell yourself. In the agency interview, let your look and talent do the selling; you simply need to relax and communicate. I cannot tell you what every agent is looking for, but I can tell you what has turned me off about some actors, and what interested me about others.

Intriguing qualities:

- Good communicators: people with whom I have enjoyed talking. Real people. (Clients tend to like working with these people, too.)

- People with a sense of self, people who are comfortable and easy to be with.

- Those who knows their niche (or type) and understand where they fit in the market.

- Those with truthful instincts on-camera, even if they are new actors with no training. Real people with a gift for honesty are sometimes just as good on-camera as experienced actors. If you are a new actor with little experience, trust your instincts and let your personality shine through.

- Talented actors (regardless of experience) who know instinctively what to do with a script.

Turnoffs:

- Just a pretty face; all look, little acting skill or personality on camera.

- Those who are extremely self-conscious on camera, as if it is all about getting the smile just right. Again, try to relax. Sure, you want to look good, but it is about your personality and ability to communicate, not about your hair and your teeth.

- Over-confidence. It is one thing for a really gifted, experienced actor to be confident; confidence is an attractive quality. However, I have auditioned actors who exude overbearing confidence, even arrogance, who then could not live up to their own billing. There is no need to over-sell yourself. If you have it, we will see it on camera.

- Those with no clue about the biz. Professional people would never interview for a corporate job not knowing what the company does. It is amazing how many actors try to get into this business having done no homework about the business. (Reading this book will help!)

- People who are "too big" for the camera. If you are a good stage actor, it might behoove you to learn how to translate that to the camera before you do many camera auditions.

- Those who are totally uninterested in what the agent has to say. "Just put me on camera and let me get on with my day" is the sense I get from some actors. When an agent or client or casting director wants to talk to you, at least feign interest! An actor who finds it difficult to focus and listen in an interview may also have difficulty listening to the director on a shoot—a red flag for an agent.

- If the interviewer/agent says, "Tell me about yourself," do not just recite your resume. They likely want to know more about you, not just that you are dying to be an actor. An interesting conversation will mean more to the agent than trying to impress with a recitation of your credentials.

- People who are "playing in the wrong sandbox," for example, those who read a commercial script as if it were a dramatic soap opera scene. Do not be so desperate to "show your range" that you misinterpret the script! My agent tells the story of an actor who read a light commercial about holiday gift-giving as if he was doing DiNiro and Pacino all rolled into one. It became an odd little commercial with lots of angst. Because he did not understand the game, the agent was not interested in inviting him to play.

As with any audition or acting gig, you are not trying to impress anyone. You want to reveal yourself at your truthful best.

How do I prepare for the agency's on-camera audition?

If you have never had on-camera training, the best advice I can give you is to deliver the commercial copy as if you are talking to your best friend over a cup of coffee—casual, conversational, and relaxed. That is an over-simplification, but it will help if you think of it that way.

I have seen many talented stage actors struggle with their first on-camera experiences. Agents may not be interested in representing you if you are not yet "camera ready," no matter how impressive your stage resume may be. It is a different medium that requires a specific set of skills and a certain level of comfort. You would be wise to get some kind of camera training before you audition for an agency. If you have already auditioned without much success, a camera acting class might help you get a foot in the door next time.

Further, agents may give you direction at the audition. Do your best to listen and execute their direction.

What should I wear to interview with an agent?

If you know what your niche is, dress that way. Are you corporate or blue collar? Young mom or dad? College student? Kindly grandparent?

> "During a recent new talent audition I gave direction to the talent prior to him reading the script on camera. The talent began his audition, stopped, groaned, apologized, and said, 'I think your preamble screwed me up.'
>
> "When a talent agent, casting director, client, etc. gives you direction at an audition, they are not doing it because they think you've done something wrong. Often, they've seen something they liked—and want to see you take your read even further in that direction."
> —Laura McDonnell, actor, agent, NUTS, ltd.

Most importantly, wear whatever makes you feel confident and comfortable. Anything from a suit to casual pants and a shirt will do. Be comfortable, casually professional, and relaxed.

Won't the agent see my potential?

Maybe, but that is not their top priority. They do not see you as an actor with a future. The agent's relevant questions are: "How does this actor fit into my roster right now? Will he work? Will she compete well with my current roster?" Their job is not to help you build a career. They send you out to get work. They may see all kinds of potential, but if you are not marketable right now, they may pass on you this time around. Do not be easily discouraged. It is just part of the game.

Should I call or "stop by" to meet the agent?

No. Do not call and do not drop in unless an agent specifically invites you to do so. Agents are very busy folks. I have yet to talk with an agent (or casting director) who wants new actors to stop by to drop off headshots and resumes.

> Many of us had to send our "stuff" to agents repeatedly before we got even a nibble. I heard a veritable chorus of rejections and "do not call us, we'll call you, sweetie" before I was "in" with an agent.

Send your headshot and resume to them through the mail. If you drop it off in person, you may risk annoying them. That is not the impression you want to make.

Most local agencies interview new talent on a regular basis. Mail your submissions, and they will call if they want to see you.

Should I list with out-of-town agents? ("I live in Milwaukee. Should I pursue Minneapolis agents?" Or, "I live in the Twin Cities. Should I pursue Chicago or L.A. agents?")

Generally, no. If you are an hour or two away, St. Cloud for example, then go ahead and pursue Twin Cities agents. Farther than that, and you probably should not bother. When it comes to logistics of auditions and gigs, you really need to be somewhat near your places of employment. There are exceptions to every rule, of course. You can try to get "in" with an agent via long distance, but this may require some great marketing skills on your part.

Most agents here have a talented stable of local actors. You are going to have to be extraordinarily good to assume an agent wants to go through long distance hassles to work with you. If they have local folks who are much like you, your odds are very slim. The only exception might be if you are an established name with impeccable references and credentials on your resume. Then maybe you may pursue out of town representation.

I realize that with the advent of now commonplace digital technology, voice-overs can be done in a studio here and patched through to a studio on the coast with instantly perfect sound quality. This is done all the time; sadly it is often done by local clients to get L.A. or New York talent, less often the other way around.

Some local agencies represent voice-over artists who live in other states. This is the exception to the rule. For most actors, you will likely have to move to the Twin Cities area to work this market.

As for living here and shopping yourself to Chicago, New York, or L.A. agents, if you want to try it, good luck to you. You can certainly work on contacts in those markets while preparing to move. However, those markets have thousands of great actors; there is little need for clients and casting directors to search for actors here. Again, if you are more resourceful and determined than I am, then go for it. If you have success, I would love to hear about it! For most actors, if you want to play in those markets, you will need to relocate. (See Chapter 12 for details about shopping your voice-over services to out of town clients via the internet.)

I have tried everything, and none of the agents will call me.

Do not despair if you cannot even get an interview or if your interview does not result in instant success. Remember, for new actors the toughest part of this business is getting an agent to call you and let you into the game. If you have this problem, you are not the first.

Some actors have tried to market themselves directly to clients and production companies. This takes a lot of time, expense, and legwork, but it has been done. A couple of my friends have had some success at this type of marketing. One actress in particular developed professional marketing materials that caught the attention of a few local production companies and recording studios. That type of marketing is a gamble, but if you are determined, you might give it a whirl. I wish you luck, and I admire your perseverance.

Remember, you are trying to sell a product for which there is very little demand. My best advice is to create more demand by constantly improving your product: Improve your skills, work on your craft, audition for everything, and build your experience. A quality product will eventually find a market. If you do not catch their eye the first time, interview or no interview, just keep working.

Again, send your materials every three to six months to the agents with whom you would like to work. Be sure to point out in your cover letter what you have done since your interview or last mailing. Agents want to represent "working" actors. If you are serious about your craft, they will eventually want to see you.

If you reach the point of total despair, then acting may not be the right career for you. (See Chapter 2 for advice about coping with the ups and downs of the business.)

Can I stop by to get their opinion on my new headshots, voice demo, etc.?

There are books and classes that suggest you get an opinion from an agent before you choose your headshot. If you already have a relationship with the agent, then yes, call and ask if they have time to take a look. (You may have to drop it off and pick it up later if they are really busy.) However, if you are brand new and the agent does not know you at all, they are rarely going to have the time to help you. If every new actor in town stopped by the agency to get opinions, they would have to spend hours a week just looking at headshot proofs. Get opinions from friends, fellow actors, and teachers.

Other actors will make a voice-over "scratch" demo to play for an agent to get opinions. Again, unless you already have a relationship with an agent, do not count on getting feedback. Agencies receive lots of voice demos and most do not have time to call each actor with advice. If you are going to spend the time and money on a voice demo, get good coaching, prepare well, and make a professional demo. A practice or "scratch" demo is great preparation, but do not send anything to agencies until you have a finished, professional demo. The voice-over business is very competitive; your best bet is to send high quality work to the agent from the start. (See Chapter 12 for more about voice-overs.) Some agents may call with feedback, but do not count on it. Again, get advice from teachers and other actors.

What if an agent wants money in advance for representation?

Just say no! Reputable agents ask for no money up front. Agents make their money from the ten to fifteen percent commissions they take from your paycheck when they get you a job! They make money when you make money.

The only time you should pay an agent for anything (other than a ten to fifteen percent commission) is a fee for the agency website or the agency voice demo. The fee for a website will be in the $50 to $100 range (often less, sometimes free). A slot on a voice CD will cost you $200 to $350. These are rough estimates, but fairly consistent in this market. *However, never pay these fees unless you know the agent is reputable!*

Every book I have ever read about the biz of acting in any market in the country will tell you the same thing: Never pay for agency representation. Of course the agents will tell you they love you and think you have great potential. As long as they think they can get money from you, why would they tell you anything else? If every actor to walk in the door were a potential $100 check, why would they turn anyone away?

The best agencies do not sell classes, headshot packages, photography packages, makeup consultations, or anything else. Period. If you show up for an interview and they try to sell you something, walk away.

In Appendix A the agencies that I know to be reputable are listed. Start with that list, and you will avoid many of the common actor rip-offs.

THE ACTOR/AGENT RELATIONSHIP

Okay, you are in. The agent has agreed to represent you. I hate to break it to you, but this is only the first step. It is a good first step, but you have not really arrived anywhere yet!

Even if an agent is interested in you, the likely scenario is that the agent will think about you for a while and then promptly forget you. There are so many actors in town, it is easy to get lost in the shuffle.

Welcome to the agent game. I cannot give you a rulebook, but I can present varying perspectives about how the game works. Develop your personal strategy accordingly.

What does the agent do, exactly?

The best way to understand what an agent does is to first look at the agent's role from a client's perspective. We actors tend to see an agent only from a "What have you done for me lately?" viewpoint. If you fixate on that viewpoint, you are bound to be frustrated much of the time.

Too often, actors think that an agent's primary job is to represent the actor. That is true in part, but look at the bottom line: The agent's job is to make money. An agent is a businessperson who wants the business to thrive. If you want a business to thrive, you go after the money. Who has the money? Certainly not the actors! The clients have the money. The actors are the product the agent sells. The savvy agent, a.k.a. business owner, wants to serve the customer—the client. Yes, the agent wants to please the actor as well, but that is the secondary function. (Yes, egocentric actors, we are not always first on our agents' minds! Tough for our egos to swallow, but swallow it we must if we want to maintain our sanity.)

So, how does a good businessperson serve the customer? By providing a high-quality product and a good variety of high-quality product. The product must be in stock, flexible, and immediately functional.

To translate:

- High quality product = good actor, good look (or both).
- Good variety = all kinds of looks, types, and sounds.

- In stock, flexible, and immediately functional = actors who are available, who take direction well, and who know the job and can do what the client asks without wasting time.

Thus, an agent's primary job is to provide products to satisfy clients' needs. If you begin to see the agent as a clearinghouse for actors, you will understand them better, and they will disappoint you less often.

This description of the actor/agent relationship does not sound supportive, collaborative, and creative, does it? When things are going well, the relationship can be all of that. When things are not going well, it will ease your frustration if you think like a businessperson and not take it personally.

What can I expect from an agent?

Do not expect your agent to be your friend. Do not expect your agent to be your biggest fan. Do not expect your agent to manage your career or sell you or find you work. The agent helps to satisfy clients' needs by assessing talent as objectively as possible and recommending talent to their clients. Your agent will never think that you are as good an actor as your mother thinks you are. They will never think you are as good looking as your girlfriend/boyfriend/spouse/partner thinks you are! They will never think you are as capable and versatile an actor as you think you are. Sooner or later, this will disappoint you!

An agent is your connection to opportunities. Expect the agent to call you when she thinks you are right for a particular client's project. Expect the agent to relay all the pertinent details about a gig that you get. Expect the agent to bill the client for your services. Expect the agent to work to be sure you get paid for the job.

Once you have proven yourself to be a profitable product, the agent may do even more to represent you well. It is great if that happens. There

> "Legitimate talent agencies do not charge a fee payable in advance for registering you, for resumes, for public relations services, for screen tests, for photographs, for acting lessons, or for many other services used to separate you from your money. If you are signed as a client by a legitimate talent agency, you will pay such agency nothing until you work—and then ten percent of your earnings as a performer—but nothing in advance. Legitimate talent agencies normally do not advertise for clients in newspaper classified columns, nor do they solicit through the mail."
>
> —Screen Actor's Guild website

is often a friendly relationship between actor and agent. Successes are mutually beneficial. An agent represents you, often cares about you, and wants to do right by you, but know that you are a single actor among many in an agent's stable of talent. You are part of the agent's team. Only a select few ever become star players. For your own sanity, be careful not to expect too much.

Thus, an agent serves as your connection to opportunities, your communications department, and your billing and collections department. The business will drive their decisions about representing you. Enjoy your friendship with an agent, but separate it from the business relationship. Again, do not take things too personally.

Can I be with more than one agency?

Yes. Apparently this is not the case in some other markets. In the Twin Cities, many actors are listed with several agencies, and that is just fine.

Some agents and casting directors would prefer if every actor in town would choose an agency and be exclusive. That would greatly simplify things from their perspective. In many ways, it simplifies things for the actor, too.

On the other hand, more agents may mean potential for more opportunities. This is what you want when you are starting out. Get out there and shop yourself around. This is the established norm here, especially in the non-union market.

As you gain experience, exclusivity with one agent may be a great option for you. Details about the pros and cons of exclusivity are coming up.

Can I list with both union and non-union agencies?

Yes. Once you join the union, you may be off-limits to the non-union agents. Until then, you can test the waters everywhere. (Be sure to read Chapter 5 for more information about listing with both union and non-union agencies. The complete answer to this question can be complicated.)

If I am listed with multiple agents, which do I list on my resume?

For each audition you do, list the agency that sent you to that particular audition. If you have a computer and printer, this will be easy. If you do not have a printer at your fingertips, you will need to prepare and copy resumes for each agency that represents you.

But I do not work for the agent, the agent works for me!

True, but you are walking a tightrope here. Technically you pay your agent a certain percentage of your work so that they will represent you.

However, the reality is that the agent (along with the union) makes the rules about how you will pay them and how much. The agent makes most of the rules in your business relationship. They also decide whether the relationship should even exist. Sadly, you have limited decision-making power. Yes, the agent works for you, but they have quite a bit of power in the relationship.

Most actors have differences with an agent sooner or later. Just as in your relationship with your spouse, it is important to pick your battles carefully. Do not give an agent too much power. Empower yourself. It is your career.

Agents make the rules for your relationship, but if you do not like the rules, you do not have to play for that agent's team. Pick your battles carefully, but do not compromise your principles and integrity to bow to an agent's wishes.

Agents are a necessary cog in the wheel, but they do not drive the business. They only act like they do sometimes!

Too many actors enter the biz thinking that an agent is the most important person for their career. Not true. You are the most important person for your career. There are many agents. There are many years in an acting career. There is no rush.

If clients like your work, if you are landing stage roles and you are in demand, agents will want to work with you.

Once I have an agent, I do not have to worry about the business side of things, right?

That statement could not be more wrong. Your agent will represent you for specific jobs. They cannot and will not manage your career; that is your job!

If you want to be a professional actor, you have to be professional. You are entering into a business—a very competitive business at that. You have to market yourself, keep payroll records for yourself, network for yourself, etc. Your agent plays an important, but limited, role in your career.

Agency websites: What are they for?

Most agency websites contain a listing of actors, links to headshots and resumes, and links to voice demos, where available. (Eventually as the technology becomes less expensive, there will likely be links to video demos, too.) Some agencies will charge a fee ($50 to $100) to list you on the agency website; others will charge you nothing. They will usually use your existing headshot for the website. More and more agencies these days are absorbing the cost of websites, not charging the actor a fee. Be sure to ask about this when you interview.

Clients can easily search the website to shop for actors. Before the days of websites, agents would produce expensive books of headshots or fax or mail packets of headshots to clients. They still send such packets, but not as often. Now, when the client calls with a specific need, the agents simply list names for the client to view on the website. It is quick and easy. The client can then narrow his or her search, or even cast the project from the website. An agency website is an essential marketing tool.

See Appendix A for various agency web addresses. Look at the websites for yourself.

Do I have to be on the website?

It is a good idea to be on your agency's website, but weigh this decision as you would any other business decision. What are the odds that you will get a return on your investment? There are many factors to consider before you invest.

- If the website is free and the agency is reputable, do it. The website is an essential marketing tool.

- Before you agree to pay, check out the agent's existing product. How many actors in your "type" and age range do they list? If they list fifty-plus in your age range and type, your odds are not very good. If they list only ten to fifteen (or fewer) in your type, your odds are better.

- Do you really want to be with this agency? Are you certain that they are a reputable agency? If the answers are both yes, then do it.

- If you have a good relationship with the agent and they have represented you well so far, then do the website. It will help them market you better.

As always, agents understand that actors often do not have a lot of money. If you just cannot afford it, ask them to consider you next time around. Further, there is no guarantee of a return on your investment. More exposure with clients is a good thing, but only you can decide whether to roll the dice with your money.

If you are a voice talent on your agent's demo, you absolutely should be on the website.

This is the one instance when I would say you cannot afford not to be on your agent's website. It is easy for clients to hear your voice-over demo on the agency website. You would be crazy not to pay the fee to have your demo on the site. CDs are becoming a thing of the past. Voice clips on the website are the marketing tool of choice.

Should I be on a "general" website? (A site that has no agency affiliation.)

Probably not.

There are perhaps two exceptions:

- If you have a fabulous voice-over demo and a clear marketing plan, you may wish to list on various national websites to sell your voice-over services. (Details are in Chapter 12.)
- If you are seeking local stage work, there are a couple of local websites serving the theater community. You may choose to join these for the networking opportunities these may offer. (Details are in Chapter 10.)

Aside from those two exceptions, a general talent website is of no use whatsoever for work in this market. Some actors pay to be listed on websites for Hollywood talent or "national" talent. I have no idea if this is useful to Hollywood actors or not, but for this market you are likely wasting your money. Any general or national website that charges you a fee is creating a profit for someone, but I bet it is not for us actors. If you have a good agent, you should be on the agent's website. Do not pay to be on other talent sites. If you are planning to move soon to a different market, you will need to research that particular market and the websites used there.

BUILDING AND MAINTAINING THE RELATIONSHIP: RELATIONSHIP COUNSELING

You have established the relationship, now how do you maintain it?

Ideally, you want a long, happy relationship with your agent. Some actors have a "honeymoon" period, and then the relationship fades. You quickly become the hot new talent, and then, just as quickly, you disappear from the radar. Here are a few strategies for "playing the agent game."

How do I get my agent to remember me when clients call?

On a typical busy day at your agent's office, the phones ring like crazy. A call comes in from ACME client, "I need to see ten actors tomorrow for an audition, thirty to forty years old with a corporate look." Agents often do not have time to thumb through the files to search for the right people. They often scribble a quick list of the ten to fifteen actors who are the first to come to mind. You may be perfect for it, but those ten calls go out there sits your little headshot in a file, silently waiting to be noticed. . not count on your headshot to do your work for you. You have to do it.

Every time you have an opportunity to make your face and name flash across your agent's mind, make it happen. (In other words, be your own marketing department!) Make sure your name is one of the first ten your agent recalls when those calls come in. Send cards and notes to your agent whenever you have a reason to do so. Send a card when you are cast in a show. Send a card when it opens. Send a card when you start a new class. Send a card when you complete a class. Send a card with your out-of-town dates before a trip. Send a postcard from your trip. If a card at the gift shop makes you laugh, buy it and send it to your agent just to say hi. If you send something three times a week, they will assume you need to get a life. If you send something once in a while—every month or so—that is good marketing.

You might even want to toot your own horn a bit. If you book a gig through one agent, tell your other agents that you booked it: "I just booked a commercial for Product X; watch for it! I'd love to hear from you!" They need to know you are working. They will not necessarily know that you are a "hot commodity" unless you tell them you are.

What can I do to get more calls and opportunities from my agent?

There are no guarantees, but these are important:

- Be quick and easy on the phone: If you are a pain in the neck every time the agent calls—with a million questions for more detail, complaints, problems, confusing schedule—they are not going to want to call you very often. Always have pen and paper near the phone. Ask for the details you need, but do not be needy and demanding. Always have your schedule or calendar nearby. When an agent is making fifty calls for an audition, they do not have time to mess around. Quickly write down the details you need to know, and let them get on with their work.

> Be the easiest actor in town to work with. I cannot stress this enough. Keep it simple, positive, and efficient—on the phone, at auditions, and at your jobs.

- Get them more headshots as soon as they ask for them. Better yet, simply make it a habit to send them a dozen every six months or so.

- If you are a union member, keep your union status current. Pay dues on time.

- Be available as much as possible. I have been called to be at a gig with as little as fifteen minutes notice. My agent knows that if they need an emergency actor, I am there. I am not too proud to be someone's fill-in when they just need a body or a voice. If your agent knows you are flexible and easy, you may get more calls.

- Keep your cell phone handy and check your messages frequently.

- Be totally and completely reliable and professional. Leave no room for criticism. Your acting and your look may be criticized, but do not give them reason to criticize your professionalism. It is the one thing you can control.

> A phone call can be an intrusion into an already busy day; a card in the mail is a better way to remind the agent you are still alive. A card can be read during a stress-free moment, sipping coffee at the end of the day.

- Constantly improve your product. The agent will call you when you are right for a job and they are confident you can do the job. The only way to convince an agent of this is to be the best actor you can be.

How do I choose the best agent for me?

Your best agent is the one who calls you the most often. It takes time to figure this out. List with several agents and give it time to find out who truly believes in you. It also takes time to determine which agent sends you for the most appropriate auditions for your type. If they have paid attention and they know what you can do, they are representing you well. Be loyal to the agents who treat you well.

What if two agents call me for the same audition? (Torn between two agents . . .)

The unwritten rule is "go with the first call." Most agents will tell you the same thing. Occasionally there are problems with this approach, however. When you are multiply listed, you may occasionally find yourself in some sticky conflicts. Some non-union agents will negotiate higher rates for you than others. If you choose to be listed with multiple agents, you need to honor the first call, even if the rate is higher with the second agent who calls. You can call to cancel with the first agent, but be prepared to potentially lose that agent. (If that agent's rates are consistently lower, you may want to lose them anyway.)

What are the advantages of having several agents?

Agents' opinions of you are subjective. One agent may see you differently than another agent. One may reject you for an opportunity while the other may put you first on the list. When you are new, you need to take any opportunity you can get. More agents may equal more opportunities.

The evils of listing with multiple agents.

Most non-union actors list with several different agents at first. Many choose to stay with multiple agents, thus potentially increasing their opportunities. (AFTRA and SAG union actors are typically exclusive with one agency, so the following considerations may not apply to them.) There are drawbacks to being with multiple agencies:

- Rate cutting. Agents are competitive. They compete for the good talent, and they compete for clients. In order to snare the clients, some non-union agencies will "lowball" their prices for jobs. If you are with multiple agents, clients may be buying you for the lowest price. It only takes a day or so of working next to an actor who is making $100 more than you are for the same work before you get pretty frustrated with your agent. On the other hand, some agents never cut rates; they hold the actors' rates steady so you always know what you will get. Once you reach a level of experience and training, you may wish to divorce yourself from "bargain basement" agents. (Union actors do not have to worry about this. The union establishes minimum rates, so they do not have to worry about being cheated—one of the advantages of membership. See Chapter 5 for more union information.)

- Conflicts. Because agents are competitive, you may occasionally find yourself in the middle of a conflict. I know of many such incidents, and they are stressful. If you are going to list with lots of agents, conflicts do happen. Simply hold your integrity together and deal openly and honestly. If you are honest, you will not burn any bridges.

- Confusion. When you are listed with several agents, clients are sometimes confused as to where to find you. Or worse, clients can find themselves feeling the pressure of a conflict between agents. This should never happen, but it does.

Should I be exclusive? What are the pros and cons?

"Going exclusive" means you commit to work through only one agent. This usually means signing some kind of written agreement. If you have previously listed with multiple agents, you should notify them of your decision to go exclusive—as a professional courtesy.

If you are a union member and you sign exclusively with a union-franchised agency, you must sign a standard exclusive contract, one that protects both the actor and the agency. It will detail the actor/agent relationship. Examples of these contracts are available on the AFTRA website, www.aftra.org.

One advantage to exclusivity is that, in exchange for pledging your loyalty and excluding all other agents, you receive a preferred status within the agency. Unfortunately, an agent can never guarantee work, but they can guarantee that you will be first on the list for any opportunities for your type. This can be a big advantage.

I have seen this many times at my agent's office. A call comes in for an audition for a certain type. (For example, "We want to see ten women—young moms in their twenties.") The agent goes straight to the exclusives list to fill in those audition slots. If there are leftover audition slots, then non-exclusive actors are considered. If your agent has hundreds of actors, exclusivity can be a big "leg up" to being sure you get a shot in that agency.

Another advantage to exclusivity is avoiding all of the "torn between two agents" hassles. There are no "Who called first?" games, no rate cutting, no confusion about who is representing you. It cleans things up significantly.

Some agents also offer a lower commission to exclusive talent; they take ten percent from your pay rather than fifteen percent. See Appendix A for details. (Again, union-franchised agencies take only ten percent commission, as regulated by the union.)

A disadvantage to exclusivity is the occasional missed opportunity. Some clients use several agents, while other clients use only one. If you are exclusive, there may be clients that you never meet and auditions that you never get. During the slow times, hearing from other actors about auditions you did not get can be frustrating.

All actors have to weigh their own pros and cons about exclusivity. Consider the following:

- If you have an agent who has been good to you—much better than all the others—you should consider exclusivity with that agent.

- If you are tired of the hassle of multiple agent calls, trying to discern rates, quibbling over who called first, etc., then go exclusive.

- If you are a very specific character type, you may have limited opportunities at the start. Narrowing your opportunities to only those from one agent may be a bad idea for you.

- If you are quite content to act part-time and you have a busy full-time life, you may want to simplify things and go exclusive. An occasional missed opportunity may not matter as much to you.

- If you are a type who is in demand, you may get ample opportunities through one agent. Particularly once clients know you, they will know where to find you when they need you.

- If you are with several agents, still waiting for the phone to ring, you are not in high demand. You probably still do not know who your best agent might be. Maximize your opportunities with multiple agencies.

Exclusivity can be a very good thing, but it is a relationship that should be entered into cautiously. Be sure the agent has a proven track record before you sign anything. Talk to other exclusives to see how it has worked for them. Be sure they are a big agency—"big" meaning a good volume of work for actors.

If you do agree to be exclusive, always honor that agreement. Sneaking in occasional work on the side and circumventing your agent is a very bad move. Be ethical and honest. No paycheck is worth the ethical hot water in which you may find yourself. If you decide to dissolve your exclusive agreement, be sure to put it in writing before you take that other gig.

Some successful actors never go exclusive; others are happily exclusive and would not have it any other way. You will have to weigh the decision for yourself.

When the agent game results in conflict, oh, the stress!

When it comes to conflict with your agent, pick your battles carefully. In any business relationship there are disagreements, so it goes with agents and talent. You would be wise to consider when to stand your ground and when to just let it go.

If you have a complaint, ask yourself, "What good will it do to bring it up?" If you feel it will change things for the better, then voice your concern. If it will solve nothing other than to make you feel better, you may want to sleep on it before you blow up. If they label you as a "complainer," you may get fewer calls. Not fair, you say? Agents can call whomever they please, unless a client has a specific request. If you are perceived as difficult, they may avoid calling you.

Further, remember that you are a team along with your agent. You and the agent need to keep clients happy. If there is a conflict with a client, you want to be as diplomatic as possible to work toward resolution. Make things easier, not more difficult.

Finally, never badmouth your agent to a client. If the agent screwed up, just cover and move on. If your agent gives you bad wardrobe information, do the audition anyway. You can act well no matter what you are wearing. Do not let it throw you, and do not publicly flog your agent for it. They are working so many phones that they screw up sometimes. Let them know of the error, but avoid being irate with them. Several of us once showed up in corporate suits for an audition for a paint product—in which we actually had to paint. Roll up your sleeves, take off the tie, and try not to get paint on the suit!

If you have a legitimate complaint, raise the issue diplomatically. If they want you to attend an audition for a product that ruffles your ethical feathers, say no. If there is a conflict over money, get your facts straight and present your case. If they put you in the middle of a difficult situation, be honest and hold your ground. Those are the types of battles that may be worth fighting; but do so as diplomatically as possible.

Should I call to check in with my agent weekly? Should I drop in to say "hi"?

No. Once you are listed with an agent, you can ask if they want you to call, but usually the answer will be a resounding "no!" Same goes for dropping in to say hello. Actors who call to check in too often can be irritating. Their typical answer will be, "Don't call us; we'll call when we have something for you." Agents get too many phone calls as it is.

If you have a specific, important question, by all means call. If you just want to check in, do it with a note in the mail.

If every actor dropped in for a weekly visit, the agent would not be able to do his or her job. Some actors do drop in for a visit if they know the agent well, but I recommend you do this sparingly. Some agencies may invite you to drop in any time, but this is a rare invitation. Depending on the day, agents may be swamped with work. If you choose to drop in, be sure to read the mood of the room. If they are chatty, relaxed, and friendly, then stay and chat. However, if they are polite but

"Early on I experienced a problem because I genuinely did not know that you had to be exclusive with one agency for voice-over. This rule isn't written down anywhere! So when I got a double audition for the same voice over I had to have a very serious conversation with BOTH agents. What ended up happening was that I had to CHOOSE who I wanted to represent me at that point. The lesson that I learned was that honesty and integrity can go a long way. It may feel awkward to tell the truth and express yourself but it will pay off in the long run."

—Seri Johnson

strained, they may not know how to get rid of you. Do not overstay your welcome.

Should I call after every audition to see if I booked the gig?

No. Can you imagine the number of calls an agent would get if every actor did this after every audition? If you book the job, they will call you. Otherwise, just do the audition and forget it. If you get the call, you will be pleasantly surprised.

The only exceptions might be if you have difficult scheduling issues and you really need an answer. For example, if the gig involves travel or if your other job obligations require an answer, then you may need to call your agent a day or so after the audition. If an agent wants you to routinely call and check in after every audition, they will inform you of their policy. Otherwise, do not bug your agent with questions after every audition.

Should I call my agent after every job in order to report in?

Agents have different methods of keeping track of your work in order to bill appropriately. Check with each agent if you do not know the preferred method. Some will provide you with "vouchers" to send in with all details along with a client or producer's signature. Other agents will rely on a phone call. Others will simply assume all went well, and they will bill for the usual job details unless you tell them otherwise.

Regardless of the agent's preferred method, be sure to call in right away after a job if there was anything unusual (for example, overtime, extra scripts, if you were upgraded to a speaking role from an extra, etc.). If you are ever in doubt, call and ask your agent. It is rare that a client will try to slip something by you; however, occasionally a client does not understand that if they take "stills" to use in a brochure to go with the video, that should be an extra "print" fee. If you are there to be an extra, and they give you a line or two, you have been upgraded and should receive more money.

Do not assume the client will tell your agent these things; it is your job to report anything unusual or unexpected. If there's something really unusual, you may want to call your agent during the shoot, but there is rarely a need for this.

Talking money with the client at the shoot.

You should never discuss fees with the client. It is your agent's job to respond to changes in the job and bill appropriately. If the client asks you about rates and money, simply refer them to your agent. Do not ask the client about parking reimbursement or travel costs; ask your agent. If the client hands you additional scripts or begins photographing still shots, smile, follow direction, and call your agent after the shoot. You pay your agent to take care of the money issues with a client. You are there to provide the acting.

Should I ever bring my agent gifts?

Sure, but only bring gifts if you are the type who brings gifts. If you've always brought apples to the teacher, candy for the boss, cookies for the department at work, then bring cookies for your agent, too. However, agents know that actors are often broke; they certainly do not want you to spend money that you do not have. A simple, sincere thank-you note will always do nicely.

I have given little gifts to agents, casting directors, and even a studio engineer in the past—when they've stood up for me with a particularly difficult client, when I have asked for a favor, or when they have recommended me for a really great gig. However, there are plenty of actors who never do anything of the sort. It is not necessary. Just do it if it feels right. (Though, a casting director who shall remain nameless once told me, "Freshly baked chocolate chip cookies are always appreciated!")

New phone numbers, addresses, out-of-town dates.

Always notify your agent(s) when you move, change your phone number, add a phone number, or leave town for more than a weekend.

Murphy's Law dictates that, even if you have not heard from an agent in over a year, the day you leave town is the day they finally call. Avoid the problem by routinely dropping a card in the mail or e-mailing whenever you leave town. If you do not do this, then at least check your messages frequently.

Always be sure your agent has plenty of your headshots and resumes.

Your agent should always have a dozen of your headshots and resumes on file. They may need to send them to clients. You do not want to miss out on an opportunity because your file was empty! Further, it is a pain for an agent to constantly call actors to request more headshots. Send a half-dozen every six months or so. (Of course, these must be neatly trimmed and stapled.)

That headshot and resume is your most important marketing tool. Make sure your agent has plenty of them on hand!

Sure ways to make your agent (and clients) angry.

- **Pay your union dues late.** If a client hires you, and you are not "in good standing" or "active standing" with the union, the signatory (union client, production company, or ad agency who has a contract with the union) may have to pay penalties for hiring you. It is not the agent's responsibility to keep after you to pay dues, and it is certainly not the client's. If you do not keep track of this, clients may have to pay for it. (See Chapter 5 for more union information.)

> A sincere expression of gratitude to an agent who works hard on your behalf (or anyone else in the business who's been good to you) is always a good thing.

- **Be unreliable.** If you show up late for auditions and gigs, do not return phone calls, skip an audition here and there when you do not feel like going that day, delay payment to your agent for any commissions you owe, make them remind you constantly about details they have already given you, then your relationship with your agent will be badly tarnished.

- **Complain often.** When your agent calls about an audition, you might want to think twice before complaining about the audition you had last week or saying things like, "I'm so busy that day, can't they see me on a different day?" or "I never book anything when I go there!" If you have an important issue, discuss it with your agent. Otherwise, just smile, take the information, and say thank you.

- **Betray their trust.** If you agree to be exclusive, honor that agreement. Do not assume that "they will never know." If you decide to end your exclusivity and list with other agents, notify your exclusive agent first.

- **Break written and unwritten rules of confidentiality**. Keep your agent's clients' names confidential. Do not tell other actors and agents what clients you have seen through a particular agent. Even though everyone in town may know about a particular client or gig, you are safer to not name names. Conversations such as the following are sure to ensue: "Who sent you for that?" "Why didn't my agent send me for that?" "I'm going to call my agent and complain that I wasn't included on that one!" Avoid these types of conversations. Competition between agents is often tougher than competition between actors. When in doubt, assume information is confidential.

How do I recognize if an agent is not right for me?

Unscrupulous people exist in every business. Watch for red flags:

- Pressure to sign contracts.
- Pressure to take classes. (Agents make money by booking actors for work, not by selling classes.)

- Pressure to pay money in advance of actual bookings.

- Pressure to have headshots done by a particular photographer. (Reputable agencies may make photography recommendations, but be suspicious of pressure tactics.)

- Guarantees of work or success as an actor. (No one can guarantee this.)

- Big searches or "cattle-calls" for which you need to pay to be seen.

- Pressure sales pitches for trips, photo packages, websites, etc. (When enthusiasm about representing you crosses over into a sales pitch, be wary.)

When I was starting out, I was gullible. I wanted to get into the biz so badly that I trusted and believed just about everything I was told. Fortunately, I didn't run into too much trouble. My trusting nature cost me only a couple hundred dollars and a wasted, miserable month working at less than minimum wage in exchange for promised opportunities that never materialized. For some aspiring actors, it can be (and often is) far worse.

Those are long stories, not worth sharing all the gory details. In all cases, I did not ask around and I did not trust my gut feeling. I am embarrassed and amused to admit that I was a typical "wannabe," caught up in a starry-eyed desire to be an actor. Learn from my mistakes, and you will avoid some of the frustration I and many others have experienced.

I will repeat this mantra again: Before you pay a dime or sign anything, be *sure it is* a legitimate investment of your time and money!

I am not a union member. To which agencies should I submit my headshot and resume?

The answers to questions about the union/non-union distinction are so complicated that I have devoted an entire chapter to the topic. Chapter 5 contains great detail about actors' unions. Non-union actors can be listed with any agency regardless of union affiliation. Send your headshot, resume, and cover letter to all of the agencies on the list. Depending upon your level of experience, you may wish to note in your cover letter or interview that you wish to focus solely on non-union work for a while.

If you are a union member, of course, only submit to the union franchised agencies.

If you have "financial core" status, know that some of the agencies will not represent you. Focus your search on agencies that represent both union and non-union talent.

That is the short answer. For more detail, turn to Chapter 5.

Even the best agents will frustrate you once in a while!

Just because you hear an isolated complaint about an agency, do not write them off. Every actor is frustrated once in a while. Here are some general "pet peeves" from local actors about agents. (The statements are anonymous; many actors have requested that I withhold their names.) Know that if you ever encounter any of these situations, you are not the first.

- "Not taking time to go see actors perform; not knowing who is good or not."
- "When you have a question or concern, it's an imposition on them to take time to speak with you. "
- "Agents who forget that we have a symbiotic relationship."
- "In the Twin Cities, our agents don't back talent enough or fight for our rights for fear of alienating producers/clients."
- "Agents sometimes get the information wrong! The information is rushed when conveyed to the actor."
- "They often rush me through auditions at their office. We can't do our best work when we're rushed."

Will my agent relationship really be that difficult?

Not necessarily. Most actors and agents get along just great. However, it can sometimes be a harsh business. I have listened to countless actors complain about agents. Sometimes these complaints are legitimate. However, sometimes the bitterest complaints happen because the actor expects too much from the relationship with the agent, or because the actor has not done his or her homework.

Separate the business from the personal. Understand the realities of the industry. Enjoy any friendship that you might gain with an agent, but always remember that business is business. If you keep that in mind, you will avoid the bitterness that some actors feel.

Good luck playing the "agent game"!

If you want to do commercial and industrial work, finding an agent is your best bet. Building a relationship with agents is a necessary, sometimes frustrating, part of the job, but there are lots of truly nice folks who work at the local agencies. Getting in the door can be a challenge. Staying inside can also be tough; but when you are in, you will enjoy working with them!

CHAPTER 5

Union or Non-Union?

The grass is always greener . . .

Many actors struggle with the question, "to join, or not to join?" I have wrestled with that question many times over the past decade. There are tremendous advantages to union membership. For some of us, there are disadvantages as well.

This chapter will deal more with SAG and AFTRA. For more about Equity, the union for stage actors and stage managers, see Chapter 10.

I am not a member of any of the three actors' unions, but I have seriously considered membership on several occasions. Joining is a very difficult question for many of us non-union folks; likewise, some union ac-

> **The three unions:**
> - Actor's Equity Association (AEA)
> - American Federation of Television and Radio Artists (AFTRA)
> - Screen Actors' Guild (SAG)

tors contemplate leaving the union and occasionally some do. Is the grass greener on the other side of the fence? No one can give you the definitive answer. While there are many "fence-sitters" considering the greener grass on the other side, there are just as many actors who contentedly stay on their own side of the union/non-union fence. I cannot tell you where you fit; however, in this chapter I will try to provide some of the facts, as well as various scenarios to consider.

Professional, non-union actor? Is there such a thing?

In the Twin Cities there certainly is.

In 1995, a union agent told me that the truly professional actors are in the union. That statement has some truth to it, yet it is misleading. Yes, there are many truly professional actors in the unions here—indeed, truly fabulous actors who are among the very best that the Twin Cities have to offer. However, not all of the finest actors are in the union. There are many truly professional actors who remain non-union.

This market is quite different from many other markets. We have a strong non-union market, which seems quite unusual to folks who come from New York, Chicago, or L.A. People in the industry are sometimes surprised to discover that there are non-union actors who make a fine living here. In many markets, non-union work is merely a training ground for actors who will eventually join the union. This scenario does exist here. Many non-union actors do gain experience and then move on to join the unions. I had always assumed that would be my path, but it has not happened that way. Many of us remain non-union by choice.

Why do actors need unions?

To put it simply, some clients may try to take advantage of actors. While I have encountered very few unethical clients, I have worked for a couple. There have been more than a handful of times that I wished I had the power of a union behind me.

Successful union actors are eligible for benefits and a pension. While this is not a guarantee when you join one of the actors' unions, you at least have the possibility of earning professional benefits.

The unions enforce minimum pay rates that are higher than non-union rates. For radio and television spots, the rates can be exponentially higher. The unions have worked hard to establish minimum wages for work.

Union actors are eligible for unemployment insurance. (Remember, no one said you would have job security as an actor!)

Further, actors sometimes have to work under less than favorable conditions. Union rules ensure reasonable conditions, breaks, and hours.

Read on for more detail on the advantages of union membership.

Why have I not joined the unions?

If you are a union member reading this, perhaps the fact that I am non-union has raised serious credibility issues for you, or perhaps you see me as the enemy. The fact is, I am neither pro-union nor anti-union; I am pragmatic. I now make my living in the non-union market, so non-union is what is working best for me.

Years ago, I was represented by a couple of the union-franchised agencies in town. I have no complaint with them or the union. It is simply a numbers game. There is not enough room for all of us on the union agencies' rosters, and there is not enough work to keep everyone happy. Early on, I developed a strong relationship with a non-union agency. They called most frequently for auditions, booked me on a significant number of jobs, and it ultimately lead to a loyal client base (and regular work). To join the union now would be a big transition for me, and possibly a significant drop in income. For me, it has been a simple matter of "if it ain't broke, don't fix it."

If you were to ask ten non-union actors their reasons for staying non-union, you would hear ten different answers. My story is just one among many. And while staunch union supporters may not agree with our reasonings, I hope there is not too much animosity.

THE UNIONS

Each union (Equity, AFTRA, and SAG) has different guidelines, rules, membership requirements, etc. Many details are available on each union's website as well as in various books about the business of acting. I will include only the very basics as to how the unions function in the Twin Cities. You will find the web addresses below, as well as union office numbers for those who have further questions.

(There are other related artists' and performers' unions and associations. Links to many of them are on the Equity, AFTRA and SAG websites.)

With so many new technologies and mediums, the line between AFTRA and SAG seems somewhat blurred. A very basic distinction is that anything shot on film falls under SAG's exclusive jurisdiction; anything shot on tape falls under AFTRA's exclusive jurisdiction. Both unions cover work produced digitally. For the Twin Cities, feature films and national TV commercials typically fall under SAG jurisdiction. Other broadcast media and non-broadcast industrials fall under the AFTRA umbrella. That is a simplification of the difference between the two.

In the past several years, there have been attempts at the national level to unite SAG and AFTRA, but that has yet to happen.

Actors' Equity Association (www.actorsequity.com).

Actors' Equity: The Union of American Theatrical Actors and Stage Managers is the union that governs stage work. Joining this union involves being signed to an Equity contract by a producer or registering for candidacy to join and then working a certain number of weeks in an accredited theater before gaining membership. (That is a very basic explanation; check out the website for more detailed information.)

The Minneapolis/St. Paul area Equity hotline: 612 924-4044

Initiation fees are approximately $1,100 (as of 2009), plus yearly dues that vary based on your pay under Equity contracts. If you are experienced enough to be cast in an "Equity house," then you probably already know the basics. If you are new to acting, you probably do not need to worry about this union for quite a while. If you want to know more, go to the website. The site has a very detailed FAQ section.

The hotline has a recorded message about auditions and union information. If you are not a member or a candidate, this hotline information will be of very little use to you. The regional office for Actors' Equity is in Chicago.

For further information about Actors' Equity Association and stage work, see Chapter 10. The remainder of Chapter 4 deals specifically with commercial/industrial and film work, and AFTRA and SAG.

AFTRA (www.aftra.com)

AFTRA is the American Federation of Television and Radio Artists. From AFTRA's website: "AFTRA represents actors and other professional performers and broadcasters in television, radio, sound recordings, non-broadcast/industrial programming, and new technologies such as interactive programming and CD ROMs." The website contains a lot of detail, as well as rate information for all kinds of job categories.

AFTRA is the easiest of the three unions to join. From the website: "Any person who has performed or intends to perform professional work in any one of AFTRA's jurisdictions is eligible for membership." You pay your initiation fee plus dues, and you are in. According to the AFTRA website, the initiation fee is $1300 (as of 2009). Minimum annual dues are $63.90, and can be more based on AFTRA earnings during the preceding calendar year.

The local AFTRA office is in St. Paul. See Appendix E for specific contact information.

SAG (www.sag.com)

SAG is the Screen Actors' Guild. Joining SAG is more difficult than joining AFTRA. According to the website: "You need to have proof of SAG employment or employment under an affiliated performers' union." (The website goes into great detail about eligibility.) Initiation costs $1708 (as of 2008) plus dues that are based on earnings. (The initiation fee is higher if you work in Hollywood.) The website offers answers to frequently asked questions, advice for beginning actors, and lots of other specifics about the union.

The regional SAG office is in Chicago. See Appendix E for contact information.

What's a Taft-Hartley waiver?

An oft-confusing concept for new actors is the "Taft-Hartley Waiver." A federal law called the Taft-Hartley Act applies to most states, including Minnesota. Essentially, this means that an actor who is not a member of SAG or AFTRA may work a union job without actually joining the union. This permission lasts for a period of thirty days. When you are cast in your first SAG or AFTRA gig, you go to the AFTRA office and sign a "Taft-Hartley Waiver," registering the date, category of employment, and employer for your first union job. (Note that even if you do not sign the waiver, the union records your first date of union employment, by means of the employer's report when you are paid for the job.) This "starts the clock ticking" on your thirty-day period, during which you can continue to work union without actually joining the union. (For most of us, this means we get only that one job, because for the following thirty days, the phone does not ring!) Once that thirty-day period is up, you are then on a "must-join status." This status lasts for your entire life. You can do all the non-union work you want and you can go on union auditions, however, must-join status means that when you book your next union job, you must join the union in order to do the job.

In a nutshell, if you sign the waiver you can work a union gig without joining the union. Then, once thirty days pass, you must join before you can do any further union work.

Is there a good or bad time to sign the waiver?

The answer to this varies. Signing the waiver is no big deal. However, there are some of us who booked our first union job and signed our waivers very early on in our careers, only to regret it. Personally, I would give all the money back from that first union job (and then some) in order to have the waiver back.

At that time, I was not ready to compete with union actors. I was new, and I erroneously assumed that since I booked that one job, the agent would now be very interested in me. The job itself was fine. I was paid union scale, and I was paid promptly. The problem was that I was clueless. I had no idea about the ramifications of my new must-join status, and there was no one who cared enough to explain it to me. It was my own fault, but frustrating nonetheless.

Why do I regret it? After nearly two decades with tons of experience and training, I now feel ready to compete with union talent. I would love to start going on union auditions to see how I would fare. However, my must-join status continues for life. I cannot test the union waters until I am really ready to join, and I will not know if I am really ready to join until I have had the opportunity to test the waters.

The moral of the story? If you are really new and inexperienced, you may wish to learn from my mistake and wait to pursue the union agents until you have a bit of experience under your belt. Or, you may wish to pursue all of the agents, union and non-union, to see who is interested. If you have a great look, you might be very successful in the union market despite your inexperience. You will need to make your own decision.

Can I be a member of only one union, without joining all three?

In the Twin Cities this is common. I know several working Equity members who have remained non-union for years in commercials and industrials. There are also SAG/AFTRA members who do not join Equity. The unions may frown on the practice, but it is commonplace here.

Once I join the union, can I still do non-union work?

Once you have joined AFTRA or SAG, union rules dictate that you cannot do any non-union commercials or industrials as long as you are a member. There are exceptions to this, however.

If you have not joined a union yet, you may audition for everything you can find—union or non-union. Once you book a union job, the Taft-Hartley Waiver applies. You may then still audition for everything, but you must join before you do any additional union work. That is the simple answer for those who have not joined a union.

Filmmakers with lower budgets may be able to hire union talent at reduced rates by arranging a special contract with the union. (See the SAG website for information about low budget and student film agreements with the union.)

Another, more complicated exception is "Financial Core" status.

Can I do both AFTRA/SAG work and non-union work?

More and more often during the past few years, union actors are re-signing from the union and requesting to be put on what is called Financial Core, or "fi-core" status. Performers with fi-core status may then work both union and non-union jobs.

For actors who may consider going fi-core, this is actually a legal status under labor law. Union members actually resign from their union(s) when exercising this legal status, but continue to pay what are called "representation fees" to their unions. (These fees are usually equivalent to nearly the full amount of union dues.) Financial core status performers must remain current on their representation fees, just as union members must remain current on their union dues. Performers who opt for financial core status are by definition no longer members of the union from which they resigned. This is true for SAG, AFTRA, and AEA.

This trend has been quite controversial. Staunch union members are not thrilled with this new environment, to say the least. They argue that fi-core actors undermine the strength of the union, compromising many of the reasons the actor joined the union in the first place. On the other hand, fi-core actors say they are simply trying to earn a living and find whatever work they can.

First, refer to the SAG website to read their "Facts about Financial Core." SAG considers fi-core actors "fee paying non-members." They put it quite bluntly: "Fi-core means you are quitting SAG and giving up your SAG card and membership." Once you resign from the union, joining a second time may not be a simple task. Consult the website and call the SAG membership office for advice.

You may also wish to call the local chapter of AFTRA to get their advice. According to Colleen Aho, executive director of the local AFTRA office, financial core status under AFTRA is also a resignation of membership, and those who leave the union this way must reapply to the union and appeal for permission to rejoin.

Finally, consult Appendix A to find the agencies that represent both union and non-union actors. They will likely be able to answer many of your financial core questions from a talent agency perspective.

Union agencies representing non-union actors?

Yes, this is common, though the circumstances can be confusing.

- As I just mentioned, some union-franchised agencies represent financial core talent. Thus, they send both union fi-core talent and non-union talent to compete for non-union auditions and jobs.

- For modeling and print work there is no union. Union and non-union agencies represent actors and models for all kinds of print and live modeling jobs.

- Live industrial performances (trade shows, conventions, etc.) may be covered by an Equity contract; however, many live industrial performances are not governed by a union at all. Both union and non-union agencies represent actors for "live industrials."

- Union franchised agencies may send non-union actors for union auditions. If a non-union actor is cast, he or she must sign the Taft-Hartley waiver in order to do this first union job.

To join, or not to join?

Joining the union is a big step, and for many a very good step. However, joining means you agree to follow all union rules. Therefore, you should understand the basics before you join. This is a tough question for some; easy for others.

When you join one of the unions, you are joining some of the best actors in town. If you are not really ready to "swim with the big fish," you may want to wait to pursue union work.

How To Be a Working Actor is an excellent resource. Similar to several of the books about the business of acting, its emphasis is really New York and L.A. It gives only a brief mention of other markets (as if there is nothing but a vast acting desert in between the coasts), but it has some excellent information for all of us. The chapter about unions is extremely informative.

Before I get into more specifics about joining the unions, here is a short answer: If you plan to eventually move to New York or L.A. to pursue a film and TV career, then you will definitely want to join AFTRA and SAG sooner or later.

If you plan to stay in the Twin Cities and pursue work here, the answer is a bit more complicated. Though I am usually a contented non-union actor, once every few years I hop up onto the fence to look curiously to the seemingly greener grass on the union side. I've also talked with a few AFTRA/SAG actors who have peered over to my side at the seemingly greener grass over here.

"We cannot overemphasize the fact that being a member of Equity, AFTRA, or SAG will not automatically get you a job. Your only guarantee is that, as union member, when you work you will enjoy the same benefits and protections as received by all other union members, , , ,

A discerning casting person will be able to tell from your resume whether you have merely purchased that union card or have earned it. If you are really new to The Business, have not had a great deal of experience in any area, and have few contacts among professional people, you should question whether it is essential or even advisable for you to attempt to join any of the unions at this time. As a union member you will be prohibited from working with nonprofessionals, and amateur groups, community theaters, or school groups may be the very places you should be looking to for the experience you need."

—**How To Be a Working Actor**, Mari Lyn Henry and Lynne Rogers, Back Stage Books, 2008, pages 205-206

I have explored this question (to join or not to join) with many actors and several agents. I have no definite answers. I will simply present some pros and cons.

Why is the non-union market strong?

These are only theories, with no definitive answers.

- Good non-union pay. The non-union rates shadow the union scale. The good non-union agents are careful to keep rates lower than union rates, but still respectable. The steadfastness of certain non-union agents at holding these rates solid helps to keep non-union actors satisfied with their wages.

- Some local producers dislike the perceived red tape of union regulations; I have heard this directly from some of my clients. Further, many producers prefer the lower non-union rates.

- Some actors dislike the constrictions of union rules, preferring to deal with clients their own way with more flexibility. While the protections and benefits of union membership can be great, the regulations can be occasionally frustrating for some.

- There is an abundance of talent here. There is simply not enough work to go around, and there is not enough room for all of us in the union agents' stables. Rarely will you hear an actor say, "Oh, I simply have too much work right now!" The good agents already have a team of excellent union talent, with very little room for more. Thus, many talented folks remain in the non-union pool.

Those are simply theories. Some may have differing explanations about the strength of the non-union market. No matter what the reasons, the non-union market continues to be a viable option for actors.

Advantages of union membership and drawbacks to being non-union.

While I have chosen not to join the unions, I recognize some of the drawbacks of staying non-union, as well as some advantages of joining the unions.

- The unions uphold minimum pay standards. For union members, the established union scale ensures a decent minimum rate for your services. No such protection exists outside the union. Some non-union agents lower talent rates so that they can win over clients. Thus, talent is sold at a bargain price.

- Union talent are paid significantly more for broadcast commercial work than non-union talent. When a broadcast spot continues to air, union talent are paid residuals. Residuals are rarely paid to non-union actors. The discrepancy in pay for union and non-union commercial work can be enormous.

- If you are non-union, you rarely have a shot at the big commercial gigs that audition here. (A non-union national buyout averages between $1000 and $2000. A union national can be much more, plus residuals.)

- Union members may be able to earn benefits and a pension. Outside the union, you are on your own to find health insurance and fund your retirement. (Though not all union members receive benefits. Details follow.)

- Union talent have the legal protection of union contracts when they have to battle unscrupulous clients. Non-union talent are more easily cheated. While it has not happened often, clients have neglected to pay me four times in my career. With the power of the union behind us, this may never have happened. My agents did their best, but they do not pack as much power as the union.

- In the non-union world, a client can play your spot in other markets and not tell your agent. (Thus, you receive no compensation.) Further, a client may keep playing a spot for longer than the agreed buyout period. If the commercial runs in an out-of-state market, it can be difficult to detect and collect fees. This does not happen often because most clients are ethical. However, if you are not in the union, you do not have the power of the union to discover and combat such abuse.

- If you are hurt on the job, non-union talent may have no protection. Union talent are covered by worker's compensation, etc.

- If union talent provide their own wardrobe for a shoot, they are paid a modest fee. Providing wardrobe and never being paid for it is a drag. I spend quite a bit of money on wardrobe, dry-cleaning, etc. Clients get the benefit of this without paying extra for it.

- Most of the calls for the few film and TV opportunities that come through town go to the union talent. If you are non-union, you rarely have a shot at these.

- Union contracts require employers to pay wages promptly, usually within two weeks. For non-union talent, paychecks can be slow to arrive. Sometimes it takes a month or two to be paid, at times even longer than that.

- Taxes are deducted from union paychecks. I know that does not sound like an advantage, but when you are a non-union independent contractor, there can be great confusion at tax time. Sometimes non-union actors are hired as employees and taxes are withheld; more often they are hired as independent contractors and have to pay their own taxes. This can be difficult to budget. (See Chapter 16 for more detail about taxes.)

Advantages of staying non-union and drawbacks to union membership.

- Non-union actors can find and negotiate with clients on their own. If you have a buddy who is a producer, you can cut him a deal on the side. If you are a union actor, you are supposed to abide by union rules.

- Competition tends to be tougher in the union market. Non-union competition can be tough enough. Some of the union talent here are major-league professionals. Newer actors may want to stay out of the "big leagues."

- Cost to join: You will spend well over $1000 in initiation fees, plus yearly dues.

- If you are a union actor, you may not be eligible for many of the low budget films shot here. If it is not a union gig, you cannot do it. (Again, occasionally some exceptions are made.)

- Opportunities in industrials (non-broadcast training or educational programs) more often go to non-union actors. Working in industrials is no one's "dream job." We did not decide to be actors in order to star in industrials. However, there is a lot of well-paying work in industrials for non-union actors; there are fewer opportunities in industrials for union actors.

How will I know if the audition is for a union job or a non-union job?

It is your agent's responsibility to tell you, and your responsibility to ask. If you are working through a non-union agency, you can be sure it is a non-union job. If a union-franchised agency calls you for the audition, be sure to ask about the union status of the job.

All of this may seem confusing to newer actors. If you are a non-union actor who is represented by a union agency, be sure to ask questions when the agent calls you for an audition or job. (Agents do not always convey information as carefully as we would like.) Ask if it is a SAG or AFTRA job. If you feel ready to join the union, simply accept the audition or job. If you are not ready to join, do not be shy about letting your agent know that you are not interested in doing union work yet.

You may wish to think twice before taking your first union job and signing the waiver. However, if it is a big national commercial, it may pay well enough to be worth doing, even if you are not ready to join! Ask your agent for the information you need.

The union status of a job is critical information for your career.

Union vs. non-union — point by point.

What follows is a table of simple, side-by-side comparisons. There are many other issues to consider, but this may help you to see the big picture.

	AFTRA/SAG	Non-Union
Employment status	Employee	Almost always hired as an independent contractor.
Taxes withheld	Yes	Rarely. Only when hired as an employee.
Benefits (Insurance, retirement contributions, Worker's Comp, legal protection, etc.)	Yes, for some actors, but you must earn your eligibility. Eligibility is based on your union earnings. You must make a significant portion of your income ($10,000 annually under AFTRA) in order to be eligible for health coverage, and you will need to pay quarterly premiums for this coverage. Pension benefits accrue on all union-covered earnings. Details may be found in the Pension and Health section of SAG.com, or the member benefits section of AFTRA.com.	None
Job security	None	None
Pay rates	Union scale or more. All minimum rates are established and published.	Negotiable—some agents have strict rates; others negotiate lower rates and sell you at bargain prices.

Pay schedule	Approximately two weeks to thirty days, depending on the contract. (Late fees can be assessed to the client on the actor's behalf.)	Unpredictable: two to three weeks to several months.
Residuals	Yes. Reuse and supplemental use rates and terms are established in the various union contracts.	Seldom, if ever. "Buyouts" are paid for regional or national spots and longer terms of use. Buyouts are much less than union scale. Residuals are rare for non-union talent.
Overtime pay	Yes. The amount depends on the type of job. (And if an audition runs past the one-hour mark, you should be paid.)	Yes, depending on the agent. Generally $50 per hour or more. (No pay for auditions that run long.)
Agent commissions	Ten percent (enforced by the unions)	Usually ten to fifteen percent, but sometimes as much as twenty to twenty-five percent. Ask the agent when you interview.
AFTRA/SAG film and TV opportunities	Union agents are called when these opportunities (infrequently) come through town.	Non-union actors are rarely included in these auditions.
Low budget independent film opportunities	Union actors must clear with the union any work on low budget, student or non-paying independent films. See the SAG website for details on special contracts to cover low budget, independent films.	Non-union actors are free to do whatever low-budget or unpaid work they can get.

Rates: Point-by-point comparison.

On the following page is a sampling of rates for some of the typical job categories. Variations of these categories are almost endless. Even non-union rate charts are complicated. The examples below will give you a very general overview for comparison purposes only.

Rates for commercial usage vary widely in both the union and non-union markets. Union broadcast rates will vary greatly depending upon the number of markets and the length of usage. The union has a very specific and complicated rate schedule for multiple markets and lengths of usage. For non-union broadcast spots, a "buyout" gives the client the right to use the spot for one year, two years, or forever. Each agent negotiates this differently. "Buyouts" are nice, but the amount is usually much less than the residuals a union actor would receive for a comparable spot.

Also, fees for modeling and live industrials are not governed by AFTRA/SAG, thus are not included in this comparison. Currently, the going rate for live industrials is in the area of $500 to $1000 per day, depending on the agent who represents you. (For modeling information, see Chapter 14.)

A note about non-union commercial and industrial rates.

The following rates are approximations and reflect the best rates available in the Twin Cities non-union market. The non-union has no established rates; thus, you cannot count on these rates to be consistent with every non-union agent. The union has well-established minimum pay rates. (You may find a much more complete listing of union rates at www.sag.com and www.aftra.com.) If you are new to the biz, you may need to be with any agent who will give you a chance, no matter what their rates are. However, when you have gained some experience and you are with an agent who is getting significantly less than the rates listed below, you may want to consider finding a better agent.

All of these rates are subject to change.

You cannot assume that any of the rates below will be the rates you will receive. You need to consult your agent for the rates for any job you do. AFTRA/SAG listed rates are based on information from the AFTRA and SAG websites. Amounts will change based on contract negotiation cycles. Non-union rates are based on personal experience, and will vary from agent to agent. Remember, agents will deduct their commission from the figures below.

NON-BROADCAST	AFTRA/SAG	Non-Union
Industrial spokesperson, full day.	$857-1015 depending on project category	$700
Industrial day player, full day.	$471-586 depending on project category	$400
Industrial voice-over, one-hour session.	$385.50 - $429 (first hour) depending on project category. Rate applies to principal. If you perform as part of a group with one or more other actors, rate could be less.	$225 (first hour)
BROADCAST*		
TV commercial, on-camera, single market.	$567 minimum session fee	$375 minimum
TV commercial, voice-over, single market.	$426 minimum session fee	$250 minimum
Radio commercial, single market.	$249.50 minimum session fee	$175 minimum
Commercials for use in multiple markets.	Union rates vary based on type and length of use, from "Class A Network" to "Wildspot" to "Dealer" use, etc. Rates correspond to market size, viewership, and type of use. Use payments can reach up to thousands.	Regional or national spots may double, triple or quadruple the above rates.
Typical length of use for commercials.	Thirteen weeks. After this, the client will pay "residuals."	Six months. If a client wants to use a spot longer, they will have to pay a "buyout." Occasionally a client will decide to re-use a spot and then pay a small residual to the non-union talent.
MISCELLANEOUS		
Providing own wardrobe. (If a client wants something specific, they will provide wardrobe.)	$19 or more per outfit worn.	Zip, zero, nada. You almost always provide your own wardrobe with no compensation.

* *Based on Twin Cities market*

How will I know when it is time to join the union?

As I said at the beginning of this chapter, many actors struggle with this question. If you are new to the acting world and all of this union/non-union talk is confusing to you, join the club! These are the most commonly asked questions when I teach classes and seminars on the business of acting. My suggestion is that you apply to only non-union agencies at first until you feel a little more comfortable. If the union/non-union issues do not intimidate you, then apply to all of the agencies for representation. Just be familiar with the guidelines in this chapter so you understand the situation when an agency calls.

Attend a coffee talk with local union performers.

If you have more questions, go to a coffee talk. Local AFTRA and Equity actors hold informal coffee talks, and all are welcome, especially those considering union membership. A recent ad on Minnesotaplaylist.com suggests that you can "get advice and information and ask questions about all aspects of working in the biz and about working union (AFTRA and Equity) from local union performers." To confirm date, time, and location, visit Minnesotaplaylist.com and search for the word AFTRA.

Final thoughts on greener pastures.

No one can tell you whether you should be a union actor or a non-union actor. Take all advice willingly, and then weigh it carefully. Talk to other actors and agents as you weigh these issues. Hopefully, some of the scenarios above will help as you contemplate the greener grass on either side of the fence.

CHAPTER 6

Casting Directors

No "casting couches" in this town!

When you are new to the commercial acting game, the casting directors are often the first people you meet. Knowing local casting directors can really help you. This chapter contains information specific to auditions with casting directors, but be sure to read Chapter 7 for more detail about all kinds of auditions.

Casting directors are not agents. What's the difference?

You will hear the term "casting agent," but it is inaccurate. There are agents and there are casting directors. They do different things. They both serve the overall function of connecting actors with clients, but their jobs are very different.

Agents represent actors. An agency is a central clearinghouse for actors for many types of projects. Agencies represent lots of actors, and they make their money by taking a percentage of the work they help actors get. Once an actor gets a gig, the agent looks out for the actor's interests and ensures that the actor is paid.

Casting directors work for the clients. They get paid by the clients to find, direct, and help cast just the right actors for a particular project. We do not pay them a dime; the client pays them a fee for the casting sessions. Casting directors have little to do with representing actors' interests or collecting actors' pay. (They are often in our corner, but their primary function is to serve the client, not to represent us.)

What does a casting director do?

In general terms, the process goes something like this: The client has a product to sell. They hire an advertising agency to create an ad campaign. The advertising agency hires a production company to produce the spot, and then sometimes they hire a casting director to help cast it. They send the script to the casting director, along with accompanying details. It is the casting director's job to identify actors and hold a casting session to find the right people to bring the script to life. The casting director then directs the audition and records it for the client. (Sometimes the clients, directors, or ad agency folks are present in the casting session. More often, they do not attend until the callback.)

The DVD or digital file that the casting director sends to the client or ad agency is the casting director's product. The casting director wants to offer the client as many great options as possible, thus providing a higher-quality product. The better the performances, the better the casting director looks to the client.

Casting directors need to know actors, they need a keen eye to find just the right people (which is more difficult and subtle than you might think), and they need to know how to work with actors to get the "right stuff" out of them.

Casting directors are also hired to help cast feature films, television shows, reality shows, and industrials. However, in the Twin Cities, commercial castings are far more common than film or TV auditions.

Will all of my auditions be held at a casting director's office?

No. While many big budget projects often are cast through a casting director, many projects in the Twin Cities are cast without the aid of a casting director. Producers and clients with smaller budgets often conduct their own auditions, or they ask the talent agencies to hold auditions at the agency office.

I have sent my stuff to my agent, why do I need to send it to the casting director?

Some of the casting directors keep a file of actors. You want them, first, to know that you exist, and then you want them to have your current headshot and resume. You never know when they may be searching their files for a particular type.

If you are new, send a headshot and resume (stapled together) to all the casting directors and include a simple cover letter. (Barbara Shelton of Bab's Casting tells me that she does not keep a file, so save your postage and do not send to her. She relies on the agencies to keep track of all of us.) Let them know you are new to this market, and you hope to have the opportunity to audition for them sometime. Be sure to include where they can find you, either through your agent or include your own phone number if you do not yet have an agent. (Contact information for the casting directors is available in Appendix B.)

Casting directors are neither powerful, nor intimidating, nor scary.

New actors often get uptight when auditioning for casting directors. When I was starting out, I was often more nervous auditioning for the casting directors than for others.

The casting director is not there to be critical of you or to judge you. They want you to be good so that their product will be good. If you do a good audition, the casting director has another good option to offer to the client. They want every actor who walks in the door to be "the right one" for the job. At every audition, the casting director is rooting for you.

In the audition, the casting director may be your best friend.

Casting directors have a lot of experience directing actors. Clients usually do not. You will get much better direction at an audition with a casting director than at most other commercial/industrial auditions.

Once a casting director knows you and your work, he or she becomes even better at drawing the right stuff out of you.

What if a casting director calls me directly and does not go through my agent?

This happens occasionally, for several possible reasons. The casting director may not know which agent you are with; or if you are multiply listed, they may not know which agent you prefer. When you show up for the audition, you can always fill out the audition form with your agent of choice. If you are not with an agent, you can represent yourself with the client, though I recommend you list an agent so that you have someone to go to bat for you in case of trouble with the client.

The casting director may be casting something that is lower budget than your agent would accept. In this case (if you are non-union) it is up to you and/or your agent whether to accept it or not. If you have an agreement with your agent about such things, simply explain this to the casting director and honor your agreement.

If you are non-union, you can accept whatever rate you want. That is an advantage and a drawback to being non-union. You have the freedom to make your own decisions, but be careful. Clients are already getting a pretty good rate reduction by going non-union. Further nickel and diming by a client searching for cheap talent hurts the business. If it is a creative project for a lower-budget film, certainly do the project for little or no pay for the experience. If it is a commercial client who is trying to pinch pennies on talent rates, think twice before accepting. Talent costs are a drop in the bucket compared to overall production and advertising costs.

If in doubt, ask the casting director further questions and consult your agent.

Why do they ask for all that info on the audition form?

The form you fill out is used not only for the audition and callback process, but also for the actual job. If you do not get the gig, the form ends up in the trash. If you do book the job, that form becomes important.

The casting forms all ask for basically the same stuff: name, address, phone numbers (yours and/or your agent's), birth date, union status, conflicts with posted shoot dates, and your stats—height, weight, eyes, hair, and sometimes clothing sizes and measurements.

When you book a gig and show up on the set, you will likely see how that form is used every step of the way. The wardrobe people will have it for your sizes and measurements at the wardrobe fitting. (Never lie about sizes and weight!) The makeup artist will have it to plan his/her makeup needs. The director may refer to all of the actor forms prior to the shoot so he/she knows who's who.

It is easier for them to gather all of this info in advance; that is why you put it on the form every time you audition at a casting office.

Why do they take a picture of me at the audition?

They need to know what you look like in color, on that day. While your headshot is your calling card and should always look like you, you do sometimes look a little different. The digital photo or Polaroid is a current, living color record of you for everyone involved in the process. This photo is attached to your audition form. If you book the job, it travels from the casting director to the ad agency to the client to the wardrobe folks to the makeup artist on set.

Why you should not give your age—and why you should.

Some actors worry about giving their age or birth date. This is a purely personal decision. Your actual age is usually irrelevant. As discussed earlier, what is important is not really who you are, but how you are perceived. Giving your real age may create bias in a client's mind—you appear to be in the right age range for the spot, but then the client reads your actual age and you are suddenly removed from consideration.

Many actors give "age range" instead of age or birth date. An age range helps to avoid giving clients a pre-conceived notion about your exact age that could eliminate you from consideration.

> For the purposes of the business, you are not as old as you feel; you are as old as you look!

I have stopped worrying about it, and I give my actual age or birth date. I figure if they like what I do, they will consider casting me. If they do not like what I do, my age makes absolutely no difference.

Further, some agents want to know your actual age. They often get requests for actors of a certain age. When clients are specific, the agency wants to be able to respond accurately to the client's request. If you make the agent guess, they may decide not to bother with you. It is simpler to tell the truth; but do what feels most comfortable to you.

Do I have to give my Social Security number? Why do they need it?

Some forms ask for your social security number for possible payment and tax purposes. You should always think twice before giving your social security number to anyone. The client or production company can get it if you book the job.

> "If you audition and you are not cast, your forms may end up in the trash; thus you should never fill in your social security number."
> —Jean Rohn, casting director

Why do they ask if I have done work for "competing products"?

For a broadcast commercial, the casting director's audition form will ask if you have "any spots currently running that would conflict" with the given product. If you are in a Cub Foods commercial, Rainbow will not want you in their spot. If you are in a Penn Cycle spot, Eric's Bike Shop will not want you in theirs. Always reveal when you've done a spot for a competing product. Be honest and potentially lose the job rather than lie to get the gig and face huge stress later. (Trust me, I have been there, and I have seen other actors in this kind of hot water. The agent and the casting director will be in hot water with you, and the stress is not worth it.)

Why do they need my home phone number? Shouldn't they just call my agent?

Agents keep regular business hours, while other folks in the industry often keep crazy hours! Commercials in particular are often shot at odd times. Sometimes clients and directors need to reach you when they cannot reach your agent (for scheduling changes, etc.). They will need to have all of your numbers just in case.

If a client or casting director calls you with changes, be sure to keep your agent informed. If they call you for anything other than last-minute changes, be sure to refer them to your agent.

"The casting director must not like me, because I never book those auditions."

This is a common, but erroneous statement. Casting directors have little to do with who ultimately books a job. The clients make these decisions, not the casting director. The casting director often controls who gets to attend the audition, and they can make recommendations, but rarely do they have control over the final casting decisions.

If you are attending auditions at the casting director's office, that means the casting director wants you to be on the audition DVD or digital file that she submits to the client. If you have been to a casting director's office before, and later you are asked to come for other auditions, you are doing something right.

Booking the job or not booking the job has nothing to do with whether or not a casting director likes you. Do not stress yourself out unnecessarily!

When the mood is tense . . .

It has nothing to do with you.

Sometimes you will enter the casting director's office and the mood will be relaxed and friendly. Sometimes it will be tense and hurried.

When you walk in, always be professional. Fill out your audition form right away. Then gauge the emotional temperature of the room. If the casting director and other personnel seem on edge, it is probably because the client, ad agency types or commercial director have come to the session and upset the apple cart. Your job remains the same no matter what is going on in the office. Just do your work with focus and professionalism. Anything else is not your concern.

When the casting session is behind schedule . . .

This is the number one complaint from actors about casting directors. It is an occasional reality of our business. Sometimes they are behind because the client arrived late. Sometimes the client, ad agency folks, or director wants to take a lot of time with each actor—despite the casting director's attempts to hurry things along. If this is the case, the casting director is just as frustrated as the rest of us.

If there are tons of actors waiting, you are not the only one who is frustrated. If you are in the union, they can only keep you for an hour, or they have to pay you for your time. If you are non-union, you are stuck. If you really need to keep to a tight schedule—you have other auditions, jobs, day-care or a day-job—be sure to politely say something to the person who is taking your form and headshot. They may be able to squeeze you in, or you may have to wait with the rest. If you really cannot wait, let them know that you will have to skip this audition because of other pressing obligations. Do not just leave without letting them know.

I almost always bring something to read to any audition. If you are not under any serious time constraints, it is easier to wait your turn and not stress out about it. If I am not on a tight schedule, I will try to let the stressed-out actors go ahead of me, in hopes that someone will return the favor when I need it. What goes around comes around.

Sure ways to irritate a casting director.

- **Blow off your audition.** You are messing with the casting director's product if you miss your audition. If you absolutely have to miss it, call your agent ASAP to let them know.

- **Treat their office as if it is a coffee lounge or a cast reunion.** Casting offices are offices. People work there. Coffee shops have coffee. People chat there. Greet your friends at auditions, sure, but keep it simple and quiet. Do your work, and make plans to meet for coffee after the audition. When I first started auditioning, I thought, "I hardly know any other actors. I would never do that!" Well, eighteen years later I know lots of actors, and I love to chat with them. I have broken this rule many times, I am ashamed to say. Keep it professional and quiet when you are in someone else's office.

- **Do not bring a headshot and resume; assume the casting director can pull it from their files**. The file copy is for the casting director's file; the one you bring to the audition is for the client. You want everyone to have your headshot and resume. ALWAYS bring a headshot and resume to EVERY audition you ever do. It is a good idea to carry extras, just in case.

- **Repeatedly ask the casting director for all of the details that you should have gotten from your agent.** It is your agent's job to relay the details, and your job to keep track of them. You pay your agent to give you all the details; the client pays the casting director to get a good performance out of you. The roles are very different. If you need hand holding, do not ask the casting director to do it! They can help you bring the best out in your work, but they will not hold your hand.

- **Be rude to the office staff.** This should go without saying, but it happens. The folks who work at the casting office are typically a tightly knit team—some of them are actors and directors themselves. If you are an actor with an attitude to anyone in the office, the whole office will soon know it. The client has the final decision for casting you for the current gig, but the casting director can decide whether or not to invite you to the next audition. Competition is tough enough in this business. Do not risk losing opportunities because you offend someone. Treat everyone in the office with professional respect and courtesy.

Should I give gifts to the casting directors?

Same answer applies to casting directors as to agents. It is not necessary, but if you booked a gig from an audition at their office—particularly if they helped you with good direction or a recommendation—a thank-you note is a nice touch. If you are the kind to give gifts and it feels right to you, then sure, give a gift or drop off cookies if you want. (Drop them off and chat briefly, but do not linger.) Do not drop off something just to meet the casting director; only do this as a gesture of gratitude.

Should I take classes from the casting directors?

Absolutely. Get all the feedback and experience you can get. I've taken classes with casting directors on a few different occasions; it was time and money well spent.

Getting feedback and coaching from a casting director's perspective is very valuable. Having the opportunity to work and get comfortable in their studios is a bonus. Also, this kind of opportunity is great professional networking.

> Casting directors have a client's eye view of you and can give you great feedback about where you fit in the market.

Some of the classes are geared for beginners and others for more experienced actors. When the casting directors advertise a class, call to find out if it is right for you. (See Chapter 9 and Appendix F for more information about classes, including offerings from casting directors.)

Should I drop in to say hi? Should I call to introduce myself or to check in?

No. If every actor in town dropped in to say hi, they would have to install revolving doors. If every actor called to check in, they would have to hire a receptionist. Jean Rohn of JR Casting suggests that you refrain from making follow-up calls to the casting directors. If you mailed your stuff, they have it and they will keep you on file. They will call you if they would like to see you.

The casting directors are supportive of actors. Their business is to know us, to know what we can do, and to bring out our best in the audition whenever possible. If you happen to catch them on a less-busy day, they are occasionally willing to offer advice and give feedback. (Again, do not call them to ask questions unless they know you already and your question is specific.) Once you become comfortable with them and comfortable in their offices, you will find that they can really be your allies.

Who are casting directors in the Twin Cities?

We currently have four established casting directors in town and two relatively new ones.

The contact information for each of the casting directors is available in Appendix B. By all means, send your headshot and resume to casting directors so that they begin to know who you are. Include a simple, professional cover letter, just as you do with a mailing to agents.

Auditioning for the casting directors is not all that different from auditioning elsewhere. Much of the information that follows in Chapter 7 also applies to auditioning for a casting director. Read on for much more detail about the auditioning process. If you are determined to be an actor, you are going to do a lot of auditions in your lifetime—with casting directors and many other folks.

CHAPTER 7

Auditioning

Learn to love it!

Auditioning can be both exciting and stressful at the same time. The sooner you are able to relax, the better you will audition. If you are determined to be an actor, you will do hundreds, even thousands of auditions in your lifetime. We actors often put too much emphasis on each individual audition—as if one audition will make or break a career. Auditioning is an important part of an actor's job, but each individual audition is just one tiny step along the way.

This chapter is divided into three sections:

- Auditions of all kinds—general auditioning advice.
- Auditioning for stage, film, and TV.
- Auditioning for commercials and industrials.

Either just do it, or just enjoy it.

- Just do it and do not give each audition so much importance. It is a simple, routine part of the job. Do the audition as if it were just another business errand, and then forget about it.

- Or, enjoy each audition as another new step in the journey of your career. Try to look at it this way: Sometimes an audition is the only time you get to act for an audience all month. Someone actually wants to watch you act for a minute or two. Revel in it!

Avoid irrational thoughts like these:

"I'm not prepared; I know will not be cast."

"I'm not right for this; why did my agent send me?"

"I have to improvise? I'm terrible at improv!"

"Oh, my gosh, so-and-so is here? I don't have a chance."

"This script is stupid; who could possibly deliver these lines?"

Either of these outlooks will help to reduce some of the stress. Do not give yourself added pressure. Do not allow your concentration to be sidetracked by negative thoughts. Take the script you are given, do your best work, enjoy this step in your journey, and move on to the next.

Further, remember that the director and/or clients are not there to evaluate and critique you. They are searching for the right actor. You will either be right for the role or not. When you walk in the door, they are hoping you will be the one. If you are not right, their thoughts have already turned to the next actor. Do not worry about the outcome of the audition, just do your best and let it go.

> "You're not auditioning for a job; you're auditioning for a career."
> —Jane Brody, casting director, acting instructor

I know, that is easier said than done. I still get uptight for an audition now and again; but more and more I am learning to relax, give it my best shot, and enjoy the experience. The information in this chapter can help you do the same.

AUDITIONS OF ALL KINDS: Commercial, Industrial, Stage, Film, TV

Often you will not be cast the first time you audition for a director. He or she may already have someone in mind or may not want to take a risk on someone who is still so new to them. However, the first time you audition, you introduce yourself and make a first impression. With each subsequent audition you establish your reputation and credibility. If you begin to establish a good reputation, the director, casting director, or client will eventually request you for auditions. Better yet, you will occasionally be requested for jobs without an audition. If you stick around long enough, each individual job for which you audition is not that important. It is your body of work and your reliable reputation over the course of many auditions that builds your career.

> "Remember it takes time. I believe that it is only after directors have seen you on an audition tape five or six times that they even think of using you. If you are serious about it, go for the long haul."
> —Carolyn Pool

Auditioning is networking. All business people need to network, and auditioning is the actor's most significant pathway. Auditioning for clients and directors is your first way to become known in the industry.

This networking applies to stage as well as commercial and industrial work. Once a stage director has worked with you or has seen you audition several times, he or she may invite you to an audition or callback. Directors call each other for ideas if they are having difficulties casting a particular role. It is a great feeling to walk into an audition knowing they have specifically requested to see you.

Do not sweat over each and every audition, and certainly do not despair every time you are not cast. You are simply building your career one audition at a time.

Where do I find out about auditions?

Consult Appendix C for a listing of the main sources for audition information. Be sure to check them regularly—particularly MinnesotaPlaylist.com and Callboard.org.

Know that there are many auditions that may not be advertised. Some theater directors work via word of mouth, choosing to cast actors they already know. There is nothing you can do about finding these opportunities until you build a body of work of your own and gain some networking connections.

Commercial, industrial, and modeling auditions almost always happen via the various talent agencies and casting directors in town, though occasionally some opportunities do appear in the want ads.

Model and talent "searches." Be very careful and keep a tight grip on your wallet!

Pardon me while I step up onto my soapbox for a moment. This subject makes me ornery.

Often you will see a "search" advertised. There are several different kinds; some are legit, some are questionable, and a few are complete and utter rip-offs.

Agents and casting directors in town will say exactly what I am saying. Why are these organizations constantly "searching" for lots of new models and actors, when the reality is that there is not enough work in town to go around? Do they do this as a favor to you—allowing you the opportunity to audition? Do they really have that many jobs to fill that they need to search for all these new actors? (If they had lots of jobs, the experienced actors would be flocking to them; I would be first in line.) Or, do they get you in their doors and eventually charge you a fee for something? Headshots? Websites? "Who's Who" books? Classes? Follow the money, folks.

Why do they spend all this money on advertising? It is because one way or another they are making money from these searches.

Now, some of the entities that sponsor these searches are legitimate. They are not necessarily doing anything illegal. They have a right to make money and be in business, and I'm sure some of them have actual job opportunities for some of the new talent who show up to be seen. However, I am also sure that some of them are not searching for you in order to make you a star. *Many are searching for your wallet, not you.*

Some of these things are run by actual criminals. Recently I talked with an actress who attended a "national search." It was advertised on a local radio station and conducted at a large hotel conference room. The sales pitch was slick and professional: business cards, full-color brochures, and fancy books of professional-looking photos. She interviewed, attended the photo session, had photos taken for her new comp card, paid $1000, and was told to look for her photos and further instructions in the mail in four to six weeks. Well, eight weeks later the phone number of this organization had been disconnected and no further information was available. She's out $1000, and is grasping at straws to find her money and photos.

Geanette Poole (agent) suggests that you be wary of any search that claims "no experience necessary." Established commercial clients and feature film directors are not likely to risk their big money investments by hiring some new talent with no experience.

The local entities who conduct "searches" are not criminals as in the previous story. Ads searching for talent appear in the paper nearly every week, as well as on the radio or cable TV. They may actually be searching for new talent, but they may also be trying to funnel you into their "school."

Feel free to go to these things. You might learn something, and you might make some good contacts. Who knows? They may be interested in you for reasons other than your money; some talent may actually be booked for work. However, when you hear a request for money, also hear my voice in the back of your head saying, "I told you so!" Attend if it sounds interesting; just leave your checkbook and credit card at home! Carry a healthy dose of skepticism along with you. Do not allow yourself to be a victim.

Outright scams: Learn to recognize red flags!

There's no way to know which advertised opportunities are legitimate and which are scams. Trust your instincts and recognize some red flags:

- If it seems too good to be true, it is.

- If your "interview" is at a rented space—hotel suite or conference room—this may be a transient company that does not really exist. Tell-tale signs: fancy business cards, out-of-town headquarters, a long-distance or toll-free phone number, expensive photo sessions, photos that will be sent to you in the mail in two weeks, listings in some national database, guarantees of work, flattery about how wonderful and talented you are, etc.

- If someone wants to cast you without ever seeing you audition, it is probably not for real.

- If an "agent" asks for money for signing fees, publicity fees, expensive photo package costs, you would be wise to think twice before paying.

- If you attend an audition and are surprised by a request for nudity—or any other request that makes you uncomfortable—leave immediately. (I have not heard of this type of scam in the Twin Cities yet.) If an audition or job requires you to dress in a revealing way, your agent (or the stage director) will let you know in advance. You can accept or decline the audition based on your comfort level.

- If someone wants money to put your headshot on a national website or in a book that is not affiliated with a real, local agency, it is likely a rip-off. Few, if any local jobs are booked from a national book or website. No New York, L.A., or Chicago clients are going to search for a Minnesota guy or gal on a national directory. When clients are really searching for someone here, they will work through the reputable local agencies or casting directors.

- If someone insists that you make a decision and pay now, walk away. Any reputable organization will allow you to take paperwork home with you and spend some time thinking about it before you write a check.

These types of scams are not common, but they do happen here. These folks can be masterful sales people; they appear to be slick, professional, and intelligent. When you go to an interview or audition with any unknown entity, trust your gut feeling and be prepared to walk away. Do not be the next victim.

Let's get back to the fun of auditioning.

Auditioning is a unique skill; you can improve.

Jane Brody's quote (right) is especially true of beginning actors. As you gain experience, your IQ in front of the camera will return to normal (most of the time). If you walk away from some early auditions feeling simply awful, kicking yourself for every stupid thing you did or did not do, welcome to the club! We can all tell "worst audition" stories. You will improve as you become more comfortable.

> "When the camera rolls, an actor loses 30 IQ points right off the top!"
> —Jane Brody

Great advice for all auditions: Take time to take a deep breath.

When they give you direction, it is okay to take a few seconds to absorb what they have said and decide how you want to incorporate that direction into your audition piece. If you did not understand the direction, it is okay to ask for clarification or confirmation. Do not be in a huge hurry. Breathe and listen.

> "I get nervous, and I forget to breathe, and then I don't listen. Many times they're telling me what they want, and I'm so busy thinking about myself that I don't listen. Then I'm embarrassed when I don't do what they just asked. Breathe and listen."
> —Greta Grosch

"Go out and get your fifty nos."

Most actors will have a string of rejections at the beginning of their auditioning life. Don't let it get you down. I was once told that a new actor has to go out and get the first fifty rejections out of the way before you are cast in anything. Fifty might be an exaggeration, but we all have to strike out several times before we learn how to hit. When you are starting out, be very happy if you get anything in your first several auditions.

For most of us, it is inevitable that we will be nervous and tight for our first auditions. It's as if you do not really start to succeed until you think, "Whatever; it's just another audition." That is when you begin to really relax and do good work.

Always, always, always take a headshot and resume, neatly trimmed and stapled, to every audition you ever do.

Never go to an audition without a headshot and resume. Do not forget it. Do not leave it in the car. Do not spill coffee on it. Do not assume they have you on file. Do not run out of headshots. Always take your headshot and resume to all auditions. Always.

The casting director has your headshot and resume on file, but you need to bring a headshot and resume for the client. The theater may have you on file, but you need to give a headshot and resume to the director. The agent has lots of your headshots on file, but she needs a headshot and resume to give to the client along with the audition DVD.

Agents and casting directors do not have time after every audition session is over to dig through their files to pull headshots and resumes of all the forgetful actors who did not bring their headshots with them. I hate going through files at the end of a casting session. If I have just directed forty different actors for the last five hours, I do not want to spend another hour digging through files and pulling headshots. I always say, "Oh, no problem!" But I am lying! It is so much easier for agents, casting directors, and clients if you just bring one with you.

Also, be sure that the resume is neatly trimmed and stapled to the headshot, with staples at all four corners. (Casting directors have stressed this point!) Do not leave it loose, and do not use a paperclip. In stacks of headshots and resumes, things tend to get messed up and separated. Make sure your stuff stays together.

At the risk of being excessively redundant and repeating myself repeatedly and reiterating over and over again (sigh): Never go to any kind of an audition without your headshot and resume.

The lingo:

There's a certain vocabulary that goes along with auditioning. This is just a short list.

- **Copy:** A commercial or industrial script is often referred to as "copy."

- **Side:** At a film, TV, or stage audition, a few pages of the script given to the actor is sometimes referred to as a "side."

- **Storyboard:** A series of diagrams, usually hand-drawn pictures in squares on the page showing what the camera will "see" when a commercial is shot. You will sometimes see storyboards at commercial auditions. It gives you clues as to how the role for which you are auditioning will be shown in the spot: close-ups, wide shots, your action, and to what you are reacting in the spot.

- **Slate:** You will be asked to "slate" for just about every audition you ever do on camera. You say your name and sometimes your agency's name. It is the client's first impression of you.

- **Availability:** Agents check your availability, as in, "What's your availability next week for a two-day shoot in Duluth?" They want to know if you are free and if you have any conflicts with the dates in question.

- **Book:** If you are "booked" for something, that is solid. The client has you for that gig, and you cannot accept other opportunities that may conflict with it.

- **Hold:** A hold is less solid. The client would like you to keep that day open for them, but they are not certain that they want to book you yet. If you are "on hold" and you get another offer, the first client then has to make up his/her mind to book you or "release" you.

- **Right of first refusal:** This is essentially the same as a hold. If you are put on "right of first refusal" for a shoot next Tuesday, you must hold it open. However, if you get another offer, you must first check with the client who has you on "right of first refusal."

- **Buyout:** A buyout is payment in advance to use a commercial for a longer period than the normal, specified time. (Generally this is thirteen weeks for union spots, six months for non-union.) A buyout a non-union term. The details vary depending upon the type of spot and where it will air. (Union actors are paid "residuals" if clients air a spot beyond the thirteen-week period, while non-union actors will receive a buyout up front.)

- **Cancellation:** Generally, clients can book you and cancel you with no penalty. However, if they cancel you less than forty-eight hours prior to the job, they must pay you a portion of the fee (if you have a good agent). If they cancel the same day, you generally get a full cancellation fee. This will vary from agent to agent.

- **Early release:** If you are involved in theater, you will have to specify (at the time of the audition) when you will need an "early release" for rehearsals and shows. Shoots can, and often do, go long. For example, if you rehearse at 7:00 p.m., specify that you will need a 6:00 p.m. release. If they cast you, they are agreeing that they will be done with you by 6:00 p.m. If you do not tell them in advance about an early release, do not expect to leave the set until they are done with you.

- **Monologue:** A monologue is a scene (generally about one minute long) delivered by one character, commonly used for stage auditions. Look for details later in this chapter.

- **Cold reading:** Cold readings are commonly done in all kinds of auditions. When you "cold read," you generally do not have much time to study the script or side. For stage auditions, you often may be able to get the script in advance, so it is not completely "cold."

For film and TV, you may have as much as a day or two to prepare. For commercials and industrials, you often have only a few minutes to prepare. All of these situations can be classified as a "cold reading." Cold reading is a skill you can improve dramatically with class work and experience.

- **Callback:** A callback is a good thing. They liked you at the first audition, and they want to see you again. It means they have narrowed their choices, and you are still in the running.

Why can I not get scripts ahead of time? I would be so much better!

Agents, casting directors and directors simply do not have time to get all scripts to all the actors. Often you will be able to get your hands on a script for a stage audition ahead of time. For film auditions, your agent will sometimes provide a "side," but for most commercial and industrial auditions you will get nothing in advance.

Cold reading is a common part of an actor's job. Cold reading is a skill you can improve upon with time and experience. Your goal is not necessarily to be smooth and polished. Directors do not expect perfection in a cold read, nor do they expect quick memorization. The goal is to be in the moment, truthfully communicating the message or the essence of the copy and truthfully communicating and connecting with your scene partner.

If you feel you do not cold read well, then begin by practicing as often as you can. Read aloud every chance you get: the newspaper, magazines, novels, scripts, etc. The more you read aloud, the more comfortable and skilled you will be. Further, get into the habit of arriving early to the audition; more time with the script will help.

There are classes to help you improve. See Chapter 9 and Appendix F for more details about training options.

"What do they want?"

At auditions, you sometimes get basic direction about the character or the style. Many actors ask, "What do they want?" Even if you get a decent answer to the question, it will rarely help you. Simply assume they want *you*. Give your best interpretation of the copy, communicate truthfully, and trust your instincts!

> "You are a far more interesting and complex individual than any character you can create in a few minutes."
> —Jane Brody

For most of us, creating a character is the stuff of a rehearsal process. For the audition process, begin with yourself and your own truthful, honest, and unique way of communicating. If they want you to do something different, try a different attitude but do not try to be a wildly different character (unless they insist).

Further, they often do not know exactly what they want until they see it! Simply enter the audition assuming it is *you* that they want.

When they tell you what they want, it often will confuse you anyway.

Trust your instincts. Listen to what they want, but do not dismiss your gut feeling. Once in a while their direction will help you, especially if the person directing is a skilled director.

Often, the person "directing" the audition simply does not know acting. Worse yet, a very helpful writer or client will try to give the actor a specific idea of what they want. This will often serve to confuse rather than help. Here is an example from a casting session I directed a few years ago. It is verbatim from typed character descriptions given by the client. Would this be helpful to you as an actor?

> Announcer: Youthful. Tries to sound sort of official. Some personality. Male.
>
> Moderator: Male or female. Dry. Like he or she is working off a script. Sort of professorial when asking questions and probing.
>
> Customer: Regular guy. Not dumb. Laid back.
>
> Female customer: Regular gal. Helpful, but a woman of few words. Not overly enthusiastic, though not stunningly indifferent either.
>
> With the customers and moderator, when two are auditioning together the timing will be really important. Do not cast for the "cue."

Hmmm . . . Uh, yeah. Okay. I can act that.

If you ask what they want, you might get something like that. Trust your instincts instead!

When you are the only funny looking person at the audition . . .

Often, we enter the audition waiting room and see lots of other actors auditioning for the same thing. The internal dialog begins: "Why did my agent send me for this? I'm not right for it!" "This is a room full of models, I'm not a glamour-type!" "My agent told me to wear a suit, why are they all in jeans?" "I must be at the wrong audition!" Do not do that to yourself.

You never really know what they want. Just be yourself, trust your instincts, and enjoy the opportunity.

Auditioning ethics—or "why you shouldn't over-sleep or blow off the audition."

Audition slots are valuable. Treat them as such. For each commercial/industrial audition you get, there are dozens of actors who would like to have it. If you skip it or over-sleep, you are not only building a reputation for being unreliable (a kiss of death for an actor), you are being incredibly inconsiderate to all of the actors who would like to have that opportunity.

Not only are you messing with your career, you are messing with your agent's reputation and perhaps with a casting director's reputation. Many times, stage or casting people have a limited number of time slots for auditions. Casting directors often call agents and say, "Send me five actors of such and such a type." The agents often want to send more, but the casting director or clients do not want to see a million actors. They want to see the agent's five best of that type. Further, you may even have been specifically requested! Never over-sleep or blow it off!

Jenni Lilledahl (improv teacher and co-owner of the Brave New Workshop) told me one of the best examples I have heard. Jenni got a call to audition for a casino commercial—a 20-something gal in a swim suit, parasailing. Now Jenni is thin, but she would be the first to tell you she's not a glamorous model; she's a great improv actor and teacher. Her best on-camera stuff is a bit quirky and fun. She arrived at this audition only to find a casting room full of models with their portfolios. Now, instead of being intimidated and playing all kinds of self-doubt, self-conscious games, she decided, "Oh, what the heck. I'll just go in there and have fun and be silly. That's what I do." Sure enough, she booked the gig, and it was a great spot (despite the sea-sickness she experienced on the boat all day at the shoot). My bet is that most of the models auditioned by posing for the camera. Jenni simply whooped it up as if she were on her first-ever parasail ride. She could have assumed the agent screwed up and she was at the wrong audition. Instead she trusted her instincts, auditioned truthfully and playfully, and booked the job.

If you are legitimately ill, or you really are having car trouble, or you really do have another gig that is going overtime, call your agent as soon as you even think it is a possibility you could miss the audition. Occasionally life happens; but do whatever it takes to get there—within reason.

If they give me direction and ask me to read again, does that mean I was bad?

No. If they want to see more, it is probably a good thing. They liked what you did; now they want to see how you take direction.

If they do not give me any direction and do not ask me to read again, does that mean I was bad?

No. It probably just means they have seen enough. They either like you and want to bring you to the callback, or they do not think you are right for the part.

Do not get into the habit of second guessing the meaning of their reactions or lack thereof. You will make yourself crazy. Do your best work, feel good about it, and then forget about it.

Just like at a job interview, I should ask a lot of questions at the audition, right?

Wrong. You are at an audition to be seen, not necessarily heard (except for the lines in the script). An audition is not like a job interview. They have dozens, perhaps hundreds of actors to see. They do not have time to answer the same questions over and over again. Once you know they are really interested in you, then they may want to chat more. Follow their lead.

> Also, say thank-you when you are given direction at an audition. The director is trying to help you and also see how it would be to work with you. Don't get frustrated or feel insulted. The direction is not intended as an insult. It's to try to help you be the best you can be."
>
> —Heidi Fellner

If there is something you really need to know, ask your agent. If it is a stage audition, ask the stage manager or receptionist at the table where you sign in.

Otherwise, the rule at an audition is to keep it simple and efficient. I do not mean that you should clam up and be silent; they want to see your personality. But read the feeling in the room. When in doubt, less is more. Let your acting do the talking and leave them wanting to see more of you.

Just like at a job interview, I should shake hands and introduce myself, right?

No. Sometimes you will enter the audition space, and there will be a panel of people there. If they audition fifty actors or more, imagine how much time they would spend shaking everyone's hand. Follow their lead. If they do not stand to shake your hand, do not initiate it. If the casting director introduces everyone, acknowledge them in a way that feels comfortable to you. If no specific introductions are made, say a brief hello as you walk in, smile, take your mark, take a deep breath, and be ready to work.

The callback.

If you are called back for a second or third audition, it means you are being considered for the job or the role. Consider a callback to be a compliment; you are in the running! They want to see more, or they want to see you with other actors in the same scene. Go to the callback confidently knowing that you did some good work at the audition.

It is often suggested that you wear the same wardrobe to the callback that you wore to the original audition. It will help them to remember you.

Also, the callback is not the time to do something wildly different in order to show them your range. Do what you did at the first audition, and then follow the direction they give you.

Usually, for stage and commercial work, there will be only one callback. Occasionally there is a second or even a third callback, but generally these are for a director who simply cannot make up his or her mind!

AUDITIONING FOR STAGE, FILM, and TV

Acting on stage is the most challenging and rewarding acting there is. Acting for film and TV is a different challenge—equally exciting and rewarding in its own way—though there is less of that kind of work here in the Twin Cities.

If you are a new, inexperienced actor, you may have some success in commercial and industrial work without a lot of training. If you really want to be a stage or film actor, get started auditioning for any stage work you can find and get some training as soon as you can.

Shurtleff's *Audition* and the guideposts

I will give you some auditioning basics on the following few pages, but Michael Shurtleff's book, *Audition*, is a must-read. It will help you better understand the audition process, and his "guideposts" will help you audition more effectively.

What should I wear to an audition?

Be comfortable and confident. Wear whatever helps you to move easily and feel your best. Your wardrobe is not nearly as important as how you feel. Be professional, yet comfortable.

High-heeled shoes are not a good idea, unless the character or setting of the play calls for heels. If the script specifically calls for heels, then wear them; otherwise, wear comfortable shoes that enable you to move.

If you are auditioning for a classical or period piece, feel free to dress in a style that is compatible with the period or style of the show. For example, if you are auditioning for a turn of the century comedy, you may wish to dress a little more formally: perhaps slacks and a jacket for men, a comfortable skirt ("rehearsal skirt") and pumps or dress shoes for women. What you wear will affect how you move and carry yourself.

> "Dress conservatively and age appropriately. If you dress provocatively or dramatically, all you are saying is, 'look at what I'm wearing.' Dress so that the director concentrates on your work, not your wardrobe."
>
> —Jan Hilton, founder of NUTS, ltd. talent agency

Cold reading.

Many local theaters will ask you to cold read. There's a lot more to a cold reading audition than you might think.

As a beginning actor, I often entered a cold reading audition with a smooth, clear reading of the scene, and then waited for the director to tell me what he or she wanted. Big, dull mistake. If you do not know what it means to make strong choices and connect with your scene partner, then get some training (and read *Audition* by Michael Shurtleff).

When you cold read, the idea is not to read every line smoothly. The idea is to show the director who you are and how you connect with another actor. Even if you do not have training yet, enter a cold reading confidently. Do not be timid; make bold choices and go with your instincts!

Monologues.

The alternative to cold reading is a monologue. Monologues are one- to two-minute, single-character scenes from a play. Monologues are not easy, and many of us even cringe at the word. Choosing a monologue can be challenging, and rehearsing in solitude can be even more so.

Again, entire classes are devoted to monologues. Some books discuss the art of monologues. Actors frequently hire monologue coaches. When you find a monologue you like, it is fun to work on it at first. After a time of solitary work, it can start to feel stale and old. Fresh eyes and new ideas will really help you. When I first started auditioning around town, I used a monologue that I worked on during my freshman year of college. I thought it was pretty good at the time. Hindsight tells me it was pretty dreadful. I should have gotten some coaching then!

You will need to search through monologue books and scripts in order to find a monologue. Here are a few suggestions as you begin your search.

Choosing and preparing a monologue:

> I once totally forgot that my monologue had a bit of profanity at the end, and I was halfway through an audition at the Children's Theatre when I thought it through. It really made me nervous and took me out of the piece. The lesson: Really think through your choice of monologue and its appropriateness not only to the show and the character, but also to the theater and its management."
>
> —Heidi Fellner

1. Shorter is better. Leave them wanting to see more of you, not less! If they give a time limit, never go longer. The most common time limits are one to two minutes for a single monologue, two to four minutes for two contrasting monologues. Most directors can discern whether or not you can act and if you are right for the part within a sentence or two. More time will not help you. The big emotional finish will not help you if you lost them in the first twenty seconds! Less is more.

2. Vulgarity and shock value will not help you. A director who has to watch monologue after monologue for hours on end may grow tired of vulgarity and shocking subjects. You do not need to avoid all vulgarity, just do not use it for shock value. This will not help you get a director's attention. Your great acting will get you noticed.

3. As beginning actors, many of us chose monologues thinking that big, tragic emotions in a monologue would help us make strong acting choices. It would help us "show our range." Not necessarily. Big and dramatic emotions are only good if they are truthful and honest.

4. Active monologues are usually better than memory monologues. Do not just go through play scripts looking for long speeches. Often,

these are "speeches" by characters who are reminiscing about something or telling a story. They are interesting within the context of the play, but difficult to bring to life out of context. Be sure that the material you choose is "active." I do not mean active as in lots of movement. I mean actively engaged in communication—actually trying to affect someone in the scene with you. In the case of the monologue, this someone is your imaginary scene partner. Active means listening, responding, affecting the other person in the scene, being affected by the other person. A good monologue is really a scene, not a soliloquy.

5. If you find a particularly good scene, turn it into a monologue. Leave a brief pause for the other character's line. As long as there are not too many pauses and the scene still makes sense, you can come up with a great monologue from a two-person scene. (Do not do both characters, thinking that you are showing your range! Jan Hilton says: "You'd be surprised how many times I have seen this and, of course, it is laughable." Please, leave Oral Interpretation behind when you graduate from your high school or college speech team!)

6. No dialects, please, unless they are specifically requested. It does not matter how good your dialect is. If you have several monologues ready, go ahead and have one or two in dialect, but do not use them unless dialect is requested.

7. You will eventually want to have several monologues, and keep them fresh and ready to go. There is nothing worse than seeing an ad for an audition in two days, and not having a monologue ready. If you are committed to being an actor, commit to being ready all the time. Have at least two contrasting monologues ready to go. Keep looking for new monologues, and then work on them when you are not under pressure. Working, professional actors will have several monologues at their disposal.

8. Jane Brody advises that your first monologue should be a "signature" monologue. It should be very much like you and your personality. Subsequent monologues can help you show your range, but your main monologue should show them who you are. That is what they want to see first.

9. If you find an acting teacher you like, ask if they do monologue coaching. Call when you need to brush up a monologue for an audition. A brush-up rehearsal with fresh eyes and ideas can really energize you for an audition. Or, get together with a couple of other actors and work your monologues together.

10. Do not choose a new monologue and audition with it two or three days later. Give it time to sink in and to really work it properly.

Musical auditions.

I would love to do musical theater, but my voice and stage fright just will not cooperate. (My stage fright allows me to talk just fine, but it makes my voice so tight, I sing everything dreadfully sharp!) So, here is some advice from musical theater artists who know better than I. I live vicariously through them!

> Develop a rep book with several songs you know like the back of your hand, so you always have something ready. My college professors taught me that, but I didn't get it 'til I was in the real world trying to do this for a living. It makes it so much easier! A rep book is a binder with sheet music of songs you know and are ready to perform--often 8, 16, 32 bar cuts already marked just in case someone asks for something specific or you need to change your piece length. The book may include up-tempo, ballad, character song, contemporary, belt, classical musical theater, or songs by specific composers—Rogers and Hart, Rogers and Hammerstien, Bock and Harnick, Cole Porter, etc. (Megan Kelly, Actors' Theater of Minnesota, Theatre L'Homme Dieu, Bloomington Civic Theatre, Chanhassen Dinner Theatres).

Just as actors need to have monologues ready to go, singers need to have their songs ready to go.

> Do your research! Don't show up for an audition for *Oklahoma* in a mini skirt and sing a song from *Rent*. It just isn't appropriate. You Tube and Google are amazing resources. Look up musicals you are planning to audition for and choose music that is similar to the show you want to do. Learn your music ahead of time. Do not learn a song the night before, because nerves will take over, and you will forget your lyrics. Go to shows and see who is out there working!" (Seri Johnson, AEA, Chanhassen Dinner Theatre, Old Log).

Don't get mad if they cut you off before you are done.

Either you are simply not the right type, or they have already decided to call you back. Either way, they have seen enough. As I said before, a director can often discern whether or not you are right for the part when you walk into the room. Do not be offended if they do not let you do everything you wanted to do in the audition. I know that you have probably prepared like crazy for the audition and it is a big deal to you, but you are just one actor in a long busy day for them. Do not take it personally.

I have also heard complaints such as: "They were eating lunch while I was auditioning!" "They weren't even listening!" "I don't think he ever even looked at me!" So be it. Try not to obsess about it. Directors see hundreds of actors. If they behave rudely to you, you are not the first. Do your work, smile, say thank you, and leave with all the poise in the world. Sure, you have a right to be annoyed, but getting frustrated and showing it will not do you any good. Chalk it up to one of your "first fifty nos," and show up for the next audition hoping for a better opportunity. Most directors are lovely and courteous; you will have more good experiences than bad!

What if my audition scene partner has no talent?

How do you know that your partner is not asking the same question? (Just kidding.)

It is a delight to work with a great scene partner—one who is connected, giving, and free to play with you in the moment. Often for newer actors, you will be auditioning with other inexperienced actors. Sometimes you get lucky, sometimes not. It is simply not your job to judge your scene partner. Try to connect in the scene, and play with whatever you get in return. If you spend your energy in the scene being frustrated, that is what the director will see. Be professional and do your best to play the scene with what you are given. The director will usually be able to tell. This may be the only scene partner you get that night and the only opportunity you will have to show the director what you can do. Do your work, connect with your partner as best you can, and trust that the director will see it. If you are right for the role, you will get to work with a different scene partner at the callback.

Miscellaneous stage audition advice for beginners . . .

Actor/director Dann Peterson (Theatre in the Round, Heritage, Off-Broadway Musical Theatre, Lyric Arts, Park Square) directs at several community theaters and has seen hundreds of actors audition. He offers the following advice—things they do not necessarily teach you in acting classes.

- I like to see enthusiasm that does not broach into odd behavior, crazy antics, and bizarre movements like crawling on the floor or rapid pacing of the floor. The director is most interested in your interpretation; if he/she wants to see some specific movement, he/she will ask you to demonstrate.

- Watch your behavior in the reception area, do not act too smug or too eccentric, and do not be loud and obnoxious. Greet your friends quietly and be friendly and polite to the staff greeting you, whether stage manager or not.

- Respect your fellow auditioners; practice with your assigned partner without advising them on what they should do in the scene.

- If you are auditioning with a prepared piece, be firm in your memorization; keep your explanation of background to a minimum.

- Be realistic in your expectations: Do not expect to play the ingénue if you are nearing middle age.

AUDITIONING FOR COMMERCIAL AND INDUSTRIAL WORK

Acting for the Camera 101.

For many, the first time we ever act for the camera is our first audition, and it shows. Here are a few small tips to get started. These tips apply to brand new actors as well as to trained actors who are new to the camera.

There are very specific skills used when acting for the camera. Good actor training is the foundation. Many of the acting tools that work for you on stage will also work for you on camera. It may take you a while to find the right feel for camera, but good actors can make this adjustment well. However, to be really good on-camera requires not only a good look, talent, and training, but also some very specific skills. (There are a few good local teachers that teach those skills. See Appendix F for further information.)

Problem? "Commercial and industrial scripts feel so artificial."

Solution: Who are you talking to? When you talk to the camera, talk to one person whom you know well. Cast a friend as your imaginary scene partner and talk to him or her. For example, if the industrial program's purpose is to train retail cashiers, cast your best friend as a new trainee. Talk to that friend when you deliver the copy to camera. (Do not change the text, but adjust your tone and attitude.)

Problem? "The subject matter seems so unimportant to me."

Solution: Why is it important to communicate this message? What are the stakes? If it is important enough for the client to spend thousands of dollars to produce the program, you need to find why it is important to you personally to communicate their message. Using the scenario above as an example, your new cashier trainee is your best friend. You want him to be successful at this new job so he gets promoted, your job will be more fun, his success will enhance your job status, etc. Use whatever will personalize it for you.

Problem? "I'm always told that I act 'too big' for camera."

Solution: Keep it simple. Less is definitely more on camera. Do the least necessary to sincerely communicate the thought; you do not need to sell it to the back row. (For experienced stage actors, this sometimes takes practice in class.)

Problem? Scripts seem so "announcery."

Solution: Do not "do a commercial." Many actors get a commercial or industrial script, and then read it like they think it is supposed to sound. They have heard so many mediocre or bad spokespeople in commercials that they throw out all they know about communication and good acting, and simply mimic what they have heard. Many commercials and training videos are "announcer-like" and stilted, but this does not make them good. It simply means the producer or director and actor did not know any better. (The worst are the local spots that use the car dealer's daughter or the furniture store owner's nephew or the Jacuzzi store owner's girlfriend; to us they are just annoying.)

Use your actor training in commercials and industrials to communicate truthfully. Who are you talking to? What is your relationship? What are you fighting for? Find the humor and discoveries. For commercials and particularly industrials, the stakes are often much lower than for "real" acting, but these good actor concepts can still be there, and your read will be more truthful and interesting.

Problem? "I blank and forget lines in front of the camera."

Solution: Never attempt to memorize the copy for a cold read, unless you can memorize perfectly and quickly every time. Remember, an actor's IQ tends to drop as soon as the camera rolls. Even if you do not blank, you will often be working so hard to remember that the only communication coming through your eyes will be the intense effort of memory (in other words, the telltale "deer in the headlights gaze"). Always take the script with you in front of the camera and use it whenever you need to. Try to memorize the first and last sentences, then use the copy as needed for the rest; this way you can begin and end with your eyes looking into the camera.

The best way to learn to act for the camera is with a good coach. If the preceding concepts make sense to you, try to apply them to your work. If all of that made little or no sense, seek some training. (Again, see Appendix F.) The fundamentals of good acting apply to all media—stage, camera and voice, However, there are distinct skills when it comes to acting for the camera. A good teacher can help.

Types of auditions: cattle calls, go-sees, castings, industrials, non-speaking auditions, and industrial spokesperson auditions.

Cattle calls can be frustrating. The client wants to see everybody and their dog for the role. The clients do not know what they want so they have to see lots and lots of us. Long lines and long waits are the norm. Some actors just will not go to cattle calls because the odds are too low. I usually do not mind them as long as I know it is a cattle call before I arrive. I just take a good book or magazine, and hope there will be an actor friend there with whom I can chat (quietly).

Go-sees are a bit bizarre for actors. They are mostly for print media. You will get all dressed up and in makeup, you will find the place, you will pay for parking, they will snap a picture of you and say, "Thank you very much," and you will go home. Just think of it as the easiest, fastest audition in the world. If they like your look, they will take more time with you at a callback.

Casting sessions at either your agent's office or at a casting director's office are often for commercial work. (For more detail, see Chapter 6.) Casting sessions can vary greatly, but some aspects are similar at every casting. You will sign in, fill out a form, sometimes have your picture taken, and give them your headshot and resume. This is all for the packet they give to the client with the audition DVD. When you arrive, you will get the copy and perhaps a storyboard. You will generally have a few minutes to look things over before you are brought into the audition room.

Sometimes only the casting person will be in the room; sometimes the clients will be there as well. Your job is the same regardless of who is there. The good thing about an audition with a casting director is that you will generally get better direction than at other auditions. Casting directors are usually great at giving you direction and explaining the shot they are trying to get.

Non-speaking auditions sound simple, but they can be challenging. If there is no script, they are generally looking for "reaction" shots. Experienced improv actors are often good at these. They are looking for creativity from you, ideas that they do not have to give you. Simply take the given circumstances and allow yourself to play.

A good commercial audition class and/or improv training will help you with this type of audition. Until you take a commercial class or an improv class, try to do the following in non-speaking auditions: Use your imagination to take you to a real place in your mind. (Go to your "where" as they say in improv.) The more specifically you can set the scene in your mind, the better chance you have to react truthfully, not self-consciously. Never try to plan your facial expressions; do not rehearse in the mirror. The camera can see phony acting even in a wide shot. Visualize the situation and react in the moment to whatever comes.

If you don't understand, take some classes.

Industrial auditions can vary widely. You may go to a production company studio, your agent's office, or the client's location in a conference room. Most often you will be role-playing some corporate or blue-collar situation. You may be paired with another actor, or you may be reading opposite some office staff person.

There is nothing worse than over-acting in an industrial scene. Under-play everything. Begin to see industrial auditions as an acting challenge. How can you make this stilted, corporate script into something real and human? It can be done, and I suggest that perhaps there is even an art to it. (Okay, maybe it is not really an art, but actors who can master the skills of real-life industrial scenes can earn some nice paychecks.)

Industrial spokesperson auditions will be common for you if you have a corporate or mainstream look. If you do not know if you fit this type, ask your agent. If you are a spokesperson type, you will need to be good on a teleprompter and you may want to get an ear prompter and training. A good spokesperson can rattle off a lot of copy smoothly, intelligently, and credibly—directly into the camera. It is not always exciting work, and it may be tiring depending on the length of the shoot day. If the copy is long, you may be on your feet in front of the camera all day. However, the pay is great ($600 or more for a full day, $800 or more if you are an AFTRA member).

It is not difficult to work with a teleprompter. There are classes that teach teleprompter, but if you read well and you can talk to a camera credibly, you can teleprompt easily. There is no big trick to it. If you cannot cold read well and you are not comfortable in front of the camera, you will not be getting much spokesperson work anyway.

Ear prompters take a little more effort to learn, though good actors who are already comfortable in front of the camera can often teach themselves to ear prompt. (See Chapter 3 and the listing of classes in Appendix F for more detail about ear prompting.)

The commercial/industrial script.

The commercial and industrial copy (script) given to you at auditions is often printed in a standard format. What the viewer will eventually see is printed in the left (video) column. What the viewer will hear is printed in the right (audio) column. When reading copy for an audition, actors often go right to their lines, bypassing the rest of the words on the page. Big mistake! There can be many clues given to you in both columns that will help you make better choices. Use all of the clues you are given!

Camera script terminology.

- O-C – On-camera. This will be your cue as to when you will be seen in the shot.

- V-O – Voice-over. The actor's voice will be heard, but the actor will not be seen.

- CU – Close-up.

- MCU – Medium close-up.

- ECU – Extreme close-up. (Perhaps just your face, or even just your eyes.)

- Wide – A wide shot often shows the full scene: your full body or multiple people.

- SFX – Sound effects.

- MOS – Without sound. You will hear this term at a shoot when they will be using the video, but not the audio. (For example, there will be music or narration over the shot.)

- Cutaway – In the finished video, there will be a shot inserted and the video will cutaway to a different shot.

- Diss. – Dissolve. In the edit, they will use a dissolve effect to fade out of the shot. For the actor, this means you have to maintain what you are doing in order to allow the video editor a few seconds to make this effect work.

- Alt. – Alternate. Sometimes they will want an alternate take or an alternate read. You will need to do the shot both ways, and they will decide in edit which to use, or they will need two different versions for different audiences.

- 2-shot – A shot in which you see two people on screen.

Who's watching the audition?

Sometimes just the casting director or agent directing the session will watch the audition. Sometimes it is the commercial or industrial director. Sometimes it is the ad agency people, and other times it is a table full of all of the above!

You will rarely know who they are, and you do not need to know. Listen carefully to whomever is giving you direction. Smile at the rest when you enter and exit, say thank you, and be professional.

Information from your agent: What do you need to know?

When your agent calls with an audition, know that they are often putting out dozens of other calls for this audition. They are busy. Be efficient, but be sure to get all the information you need. The essentials are:

- Client or production company name.
- Date.
- Time.
- Location.
- Wardrobe.
- Shoot date (as well as callback date, if there will be a callback).

We might like to know more detail than that: What kind of a shoot is it? How much does it pay? Who will be at the audition? Who is my scene partner? What are they looking for? What do they want? However, if you have a good agent you trust, you do not need all of this infomation.

If you have a good agent, you will usually know the approximate pay—either union scale or your non-union agent's standard rate for that kind of gig. I simply trust my agent to bill appropriately. If you are unsure about pay, ask. (See Chapter 4 for more information about agents and Chapter 5 for some standard pay rates.)

If your agent does not seem rushed, ask more questions, but be very sensitive to their stress level and time.

Be sure to get a shoot date if you have any potential schedule conflicts. If your calendar is wide open for months and you can take any work that comes along, you do not necessarily need to know the shoot date. However, if you have any conflicts at all, you need to ask the date. Here is why: I once showed up for an audition at Lynn Blumenthal Casting. Little did I know that she was seeing only ten women for the spot. We were not given a shoot date by our agent, and few of us thought to ask. I showed up, filled out my audition form, and then realized that I had a conflict with the posted shoot date. I was simply unavailable for the shoot, as were two of the other actors present. We screwed up, and the agent screwed up. Lynn needed ten good auditions to show her client. Now she was down to seven, and maybe worse. We were messing up her product, and to say she was not pleased is an understatement. It was a problem for the casting director, it was a waste of everyone's time and it was an audition opportunity that another actor should have had.

Was this the agent's fault? Perhaps, but it was also my fault. I knew I had some conflicts in my calendar; I simply took the audition and forgot to ask about the shoot date. Your agent should always ask the client, and you should always ask your agent. Always ask for the date, time, location, wardrobe, and shoot date.

A slate is not a mug shot!

You will almost always need to slate at the beginning of your audition. To slate means that you state your name and sometimes your agent's name before you begin the audition take. (The casting directors will often want you to slate without your agent's name.)

In on-camera classes you will practice your slate; but for now, just a few details: A slate is not a prison mug shot. Reveal your personality. The slate is your first impression; make it a good one. State your name as if you were saying, "It is really nice to meet you." Keep it simple and professional, consistent with your personality, and consistent with the tone of the copy you are about to read.

Contacts and glasses?

Glasses can sometimes reflect glare from the lights. Glasses can be a great part of your look, but be ready to read with or without them. If you need glasses in order to read copy, slate without them and then put them on when you begin to read. That way the client can see you both ways. Most often clients will want you without glasses, because it is easier to shoot without fighting the glare. You may wish to opt for contacts or Lasik surgery if you will be reading a teleprompter very often.

Showing your profiles after the slate.

At auditions we sometimes see beginning actors slate with their name, and then they turn to one side and the other to give the camera each profile. Apparently, someone (probably one of the modeling schools) is teaching actors to do this for every camera audition. There is no need for this unless the director specifically asks. It is a dead giveaway that you are somewhat new and most of your experience has been acquired in a classroom. The director or casting director will let you know when you need to do this.

Should I dress up in a clown suit if they want a clown?

Not unless you want them to think you are really a clown.

For most auditions, let your acting do the talking. Keep the wardrobe simple. If you are asked to attend an audition for a specific character or type—farmer or painter for example—the general rule is to wear wardrobe that "suggests" this type. Do not go all out to be that role or, worse yet, a bad stereotype (overalls, a straw hat, a red bandana and a toothpick in your mouth might be a bit over the top). Jeans and flannel are more like it. If they want a painter, wear khakis or jeans and a denim shirt, and leave your paintbrush at home. If they want a construction worker, leave the hard hat and hammer at home. If you need props for the audition, they will be provided.

If they specifically request a certain wardrobe, go for it. Then you pull out your clown suit. Otherwise, keep it simple.

Do not expect the director to direct you well—if at all!

Directors for commercials and especially for industrials are often clueless about acting. There are a few exceptions to this rule, but very few. They are usually technical people, marketing people, or corporate trainers. Do not expect them to know much about acting.

We actors often go into an audition assuming they will tell us what they want. Those assumptions could not be more wrong. Assume they know nothing about acting and directing, and you will usually be right. Use your acting instincts and give them a read that is truthful for you. Give them your interpretation of the copy. Once they have seen what you bring to it, they may have some good suggestions for you.

If they ask for something different, try to distinguish whether they want drastically different or subtly different. If they want something drastically different, give it to them. Though, as Jane Brody teaches, do not lose what was good about your first take. If they want to see more from you, it probably means they liked something about your first take. Take the suggestion and layer it on top of what was already good.

What if the copy is terrible?

You will sometimes think the copy is simply awful, but it just does not matter. It is not your job to judge the copy; it is your job to deliver the copy. Sometimes the actor who books the gig is the actor who makes the worst copy in the world sound good. Just try to make it your own and deliver it truthfully.

Can I change the words if I do not like the script?

Usually not—unless they offer you permission to do so. Sometimes they will say, "Feel free to make it more conversational." That is your cue to make little changes if you would like. This is more likely to happen with industrial copy. Commercial copy is often very carefully crafted; stick to the copy. Theater, film, and TV scripts are the creative art of the writer.

Again, it is not your job to suggest re-writes. Respect their work and deliver what is given.

Further, the copy you are reading may have received final approval from multiple committees, the marketing department, the legal department and the CEO. Once all of those people have scrutinized every last word, you would be wise to deliver every last word!

Why won't they let me do two or three takes so I can really show them my range?

Many of us think we can dramatically alter our characterization in an audition. (There are actors who can, but generally these are the more experienced actors.) Your personality will determine your interpretation of each commercial situation you are given. Even if you feel your two reads were drastically different, your audience will often perceive them as quite similar. When actors record for an audition, many will ask if they can try something different for the second take. If they do, more often than not both takes are similar. In fact, the first take is usually better because it is the more truthful, instinctive take.

Put your best stuff in the first take. Make truthful, strong choices. If they want to see more, that is probably a good thing. If they do not ask to see more, your second or third take usually would not make much difference.

Why was I not cast?

You were too tall for the guy they cast. You were too short for the gal they cast. You do not look like the son or daughter they cast. The ad agency loved you, but the client did not. Your nose is too small. Your eyes are too big. Your voice is too low. Your hairline is too high. You are too pretty. You are too quirky. You are too Midwest. You are too Scandinavian. You are too ethnic. Who knows? You will rarely get an answer to this question, and if you do, the answer is often silly. Do not ask, just move on!

When will I know the results of the audition?

Hours, days, weeks, months. You never know. They may tell you as you leave the audition when they expect to make a decision. Often they tell you nothing. When the shoot date has passed it is the clearest indication that you did not get the gig!

Will they call me either way?

Usually not. Most of the time you will not get a call if you did not get the gig. This is frustrating at first, because your auditions feel like big deal.

Once you have been at it a while, you become accustomed to forgetting about the audition as soon as you walk out the door. It is very time consuming for an agent or a director or stage manager to call everyone who auditioned to say, "Thanks, but no thanks." Do not expect those calls; they rarely happen.

The final word on auditioning.

Learn to enjoy auditioning. It is part of the job. As with any job, you will have good days and bad. Every actor has nightmare stories about auditions. Just chalk it up to experience and move on to the next one. You will do lots of good auditions, too.

If you are an inexperienced, green actor, know that you are not the only one. There are hundreds like you in the Twin Cities. Directors understand inexperience; they will at least be curious about the new face in front of them. Get out there and get some auditions under your belt.

> "Remember—and I was told this over and over but didn't believe it until I was sitting on the other side of the table—the folks running the audition want you to do well. They hope that you are the answer to their prayers. They look forward to hearing what you have to show them. They are on your side."
> —Greta Grosch

Auditions are a big part of an actor's job. Learn to love them!

CHAPTER 8

At the Shoot

Hurry up and wait!

An acting gig on camera is commonly referred to as "a shoot." The word "shoot" can be a noun or a verb in this biz. You will hear actors say: "I have a shoot tomorrow." Or, "No, I'm not available, I'm shooting that day." Or, "The shoot went long."

Working on stage often does not pay well. Working on camera often does. Even experienced stage actors can feel like a fish out of water on a commercial or industrial shoot. This chapter is for those who have never done a shoot before—commercial, industrial, TV, or film. Most experienced commercial and industrial actors have learned much of this information through on-the-job training. Hopefully this will give you a little training before you are on your first job!

> **"I am an actor. I am paid to act. Sometimes I am paid well."**
>
> —Sir Laurence Olivier (**Acting in Television Commercials for Fun and Profit**, p. 78, Three Rivers Press, New York, 1986).

Who's who at the commercial or industrial shoot.

I have been on shoots with just a cameraman and me, and I have been on sets with crews of fifty or more. Industrials tend to have smaller crews (as few as two or three people), while big budget commercials have crews of thirty more. I cannot even count the number of folks on feature film sets! There is a long list of the various jobs on a set, but you really only need to know a few. If you are interested in the details, read the book, *Gaffers, Grips and Best Boys* by Eric Taub. (St. Martin's Press, New York, 1994.) Each chapter is a description of a different film production job, written by the folks who do the job. (John Lithgow wrote the chapter on "The Actor.")

- **Director.** You will easily find out who the director is—the one who is ultimately in charge of what the actors do. Even if the client is on the set offering advice or another actor is trying to tell you what to do, always look to the director.

- **The P.A.** (Production Assistant). On a big shoot, a P.A. will be coordinating details and herding the actors to the set when needed. Often, you can direct your questions to the P.A., and he or she will be able to help you. P.A.s can be very busy and frazzled at times, so be patient.

- **Makeup artist.** If you have a makeup artist, he or she will often be your best resource. The good ones not only make you look good, but they also try to help you stay fresh all day. They sometimes bring you beverages, check on you, and ask what you need. Treat them well, and they will usually do the same for you. If you get a good makeup artist, consider it a gift!

  You may not like the style of every makeup artist you have. Most are terrific, but their style may not always suit your personal taste. If you are on a gig and you do not like your makeup, it is best to keep it to yourself. You do your job and let them do theirs. First, you probably look just fine; you simply cannot be objective about yourself. Second, if you really do not look good, it is the director's job to say so. I will sometimes let them know how I usually do my hair before they start to style it, but then I let them do what they want. Ultimately how I look is the makeup artist's responsibility.

  Sadly, makeup is often one of the first things to go if the client has to cut the budget. Especially on industrial shoots, you will often have to do your own makeup. You will then have to pay attention to when you need to powder and touch up. Often no one else on the set is paying attention to how you look; they are more focused on the shot and lighting. Appreciate makeup artists when you are lucky enough to have them.

- **The client and/or ad agency people.** Often one of the clients is at the shoot. If it is a big commercial shoot, reps from the client as well as the ad agency may be there. Some clients get involved and offer more opinions than we might want. Of course, be polite and receptive to the client; but again, always look to the director for the final word. Usually the client and director are on the same page, though every once in a while there may be some tension. You can make it worse by getting in the middle. Your boss is the director. If clients are on the set, they usually trust the director. (They are often just glad to be out of the office for the day!)

- **D.P. (director of photography), A.D. (assistant director), gaffers (electricians), grips (lighting techs), boom ops (sound guys), etc.** It is not essential that you know what each of them does, just know that they are often the most fun people on the set. They also work as hard as anyone there.

- **The sound technician** will handle your microphone and monitor the audio quality throughout the shoot. Keep in mind that when you are wearing a microphone, the audio person can likely hear everything you say. If the audio person is wearing headphones and your mic is on, know that everything you whisper will be heard! (And be sure to turn your microphone transmitter off when you head to the restroom!)

- **The writer**. Occasionally the writer of the script will be on set. (Never criticize the script; you never know who may hear you!) Your job is to deliver, not to edit!

I was once on a big shoot with three clients on the set watching the monitor. (All three of them were attorneys. Enough said.) I did no fewer than forty-eight takes on the same five lines. After several takes, the director whispered in my ear, "The clients disagree about every take. If one loves it, the other hates it. You are doing fine." All I could do was keep my cool and keep doing what the director told me. Eventually, the director convinced the clients that I had given them every conceivable variation of that scene, and that they had to make a decision during editing. Thanks to the director, I was able to simply do what I was told and not become neurotic.

Terminology (Also see the audition terminology in Chapter 7; much of it applies here.)

Most of us are familiar with stage directions—upstage, downstage, etc. Working on camera has a language of its own. These are a few of the terms that will apply to you, the actor.

- **Hit your mark**. Your "mark" is where they want you to position yourself for the shot. For close-ups, this means hitting your mark within an inch or less. Sometimes you will remain on your mark for the entire shot, or you may "walk into frame" or "out of frame." (Here, frame means the parameters of what the camera sees.) Hitting your mark exactly can be important because the lights, background, and camera may have been set up specifically for this spot. If you miss your mark, you will have to do the shot again.

- **Camera left, camera right.** When the director asks you to move left or right, he usually means camera left or right, based on what the director sees on screen. For you, this means the opposite direction. "Move camera left" means the actor moves to his or her right. Confused? Even after eighteen years I mess this up all the time.

- **Back to one**. You have completed one take, and now you are on to another take of the same shot. The director will often call, "Back to one," especially if there is a lot of movement or activity in the shot. All actors, extras, and props must go back to their original spot to start the shot again.

- **Key light**. When you work on camera, particularly if you are a spokesperson, learn to identify your key light. It is usually the brightest light on you. As you look at the camera, it will be approximately forty-five degrees to your right or left. Often you will be asked to angle your body or face slightly to the side of the key light.

- **Continuity.** You often will not shoot the script in chronological order; you will shoot "out of sequence." They will get all the shots from a certain camera angle or location, and then they will move to the next angle. You may get all the "master" or wide shots first and then go back and get the close-ups. It is easier and quicker to have the actors shoot out of sequence than it is to make the camera crew constantly move all of the equipment back and forth. The more you shoot things "out of sequence," the more attention you will have to pay to continuity.

  Props, body positions, set pieces, etc., all must be in the same position as in the previous shot, even if the previous shot was done hours or days earlier. Your movements, hands, and props need to be consistent so that the shots can be edited or "cut together" properly. For example, at the end of the last shot, were you holding the mug in your right hand or left hand? Were you wearing your glasses in the wide shot? On what line did you remove them? You will need to remember these things so that you can repeat them exactly when you shoot the same scene from a different angle. I sometimes make a note in my script so that I have an accurate recollection when we return to the scene later.

  Further, never play with props or set pieces unless you have a specific reason to do so. You never want to be the one that messed up the continuity!

- **Wrap.** "That's a wrap" means it is quitting time; the shoot's done. You will also hear, "Let's wrap for the day," or "You are wrapped."

Location shoots.

Location shoots can be interesting, to say the least. I have shot in hospitals, emergency rooms, waiting rooms, "clean rooms," corporate offices, model homes, private homes, restaurants, stores, storage facilities, countless manufacturing plants, the county morgue, Minneapolis parks in the summer, St. Paul streets in the winter, a North Dakota wheat field, Ohio railroad tracks at night in the rain, and even in the Boundary Waters in the lightning and thunder!

At a location shoot you will rarely have a dressing room or a trailer. You will often be on your own to change and do makeup in whatever public facility is available—the van, grip truck, storage closet, a tent, or your car. The

> A wild location shoot: "I was a spokesperson for a group of personal injury law firms while standing on the highest suspension bridge in the world in Royal Gorge, Colorado."
> —Clem Birch

lower the budget, the less consideration is given to an actor's comfort. Be ready for whatever may come. Usually you will have at least a decent public restroom at your disposal, but not always. (In the North Dakota wheat field, my restroom was a squat behind the grip truck. Glamorous!)

Studio shoots.

Studio shoots are more predictable and often more comfortable—less audio trouble, fewer passers-by looking into the camera, controlled lighting, etc. You will also typically have a dressing room of some kind.

Just plain crazy shoots.

Most shoots will happen in a studio, at a retail location, in a corporate setting, or at a private home with other actors and a small crew. However, once in a great while you may be called for something completely different!

Foam suit acting: "I had to ice skate while wearing an enormous dot-shaped foam rubber suit (with a very small hole for me to see through). The production company forgot to ask the talent one minor question during the auditions: 'Do you know how to ice skate?' Luckily I am a decent skater; the poor guy I shot with was panic-stricken. He drew blood where he held on to my arm!" (Ann Whiting).

"I have played a lung, a banana, and a Santa Bear" (Jim Cunningham).

"I sang as a chicken for a casino spot. I am not proud, but I did" (Teri Parker-Brown).

"I was hired to put on a giant eyeball mascot outfit. My head went inside this massive fiberglass eyeball, and my legs went into a yellow fabric tube that made up the 'stalk.' The client's intent was that I would hop about as we went through their corporate office to greet the employees. Disappointingly, my huge, bulbous eyeball head could not fit through the double doors at the front of the building. We tried and tried, but my giant head would not squeeze through. Their last-minute solution was for me to lurk outside in the parking lot so that employees could see me out the window, while I hopped about, all by myself, for about fifteen minutes. Hop hop hop. They said I did much better than the last person they hired to be the eyeball. I've always treasured that compliment" (Heidi Fellner).

Birthday suit acting: "I had all of my body hair (and I do mean all, except eyebrows) shaved off on camera for a product video for surgical shears. Nurses, camera crew, directors, clients—all got pretty "up close and personal" (David Coral).

Acting with animals: "I shot a commercial in Des Moines for a high-speed internet company. The commercial featured a few mad scientists and their monkey assistant ("Spencer") all in matching lab coats. They were conducting an experiment that involved asking me questions, and whenever I responded with the correct answer, the monkey would jump off the stool, land on my shoulder or on top of my head, and pop a treat in my mouth.

"The treat that I was given was actually a black glass bead—supposedly a raisin. The gag at the end of the commercial was that the monkey was giving me what the scientists thought were raisins and the monkey was actually giving me 'poo.' There's a cute exchange at the end when the monkey puts both hands up to his mouth as if to say, 'Oops!'

"All day we worked scenes, and he dutifully put the glass bead in my mouth. However, at one point, his curiosity got the best of him—it was the tempting smell of my saliva on the bead—and in the middle of a take he shoved the bead in his own mouth. We happened to be shooting the close up. The trainer yelled "Spencer!" at which point he quickly spit the bead into his little fingers, extended his arm and dropped it in my mouth, a string of saliva still connected to his lip. The crew said the lights illuminated the saliva arc perfectly. I kept my composure until the director yelled 'cut,' and the entire room broke down in hysterical laughter. Weeping, wet-your-pants laughter. I said, 'If I get monkey pox, I'm taking you all down with me'" (Solveig Anderson).

What do I bring to a shoot?

I tend to forget things when I race out to a gig, so I have a printed checklist that I consult every time I leave for a shoot. You will want to customize this list for yourself.

Wardrobe: (They will tell you specifics.)
Blouses/shirts
Dresses/skirts
Suits
Slacks
Scarves/ties
Belts
Shoes
Nylons/socks

Accessories/props (if needed):
Jewelry
Hair accessories
Purse
Briefcase
Contact lenses
Glasses
Lint roller (if you have pets)

Makeup: (Bring your own unless you are certain of a makeup artist.)
Base, eye shadow, blush, mascara, liner
Powder and brush or puff
Hairbrush or comb, hairspray
(Men: at least powder and comb)

Job-specific items:
Script (if they sent one)
Client names, production company names
Phone numbers, directions
Ear prompter and batteries (if you use one)

Personal or comfort items:
Reading material (for down time)
Cell phone/pager (turned off on the set)
Purse or wallet (with minimal valuables)
Water, thermos of coffee or tea, snack

Whatever you are told for wardrobe, always bring at least three choices. I usually bring four or five. Bring a variety of color choices as well. You never know what the background color of the set will be. You do not want to clash with it, and you definitely do not want to wear the same color as the background or you will fade into it.

For further details about wardrobe, see Chapter 3.

If you have an ear prompter, always bring it (unless you know it is a non-speaking role).

I tell my ear prompter students to bring their prompters to every audition and every shoot. You often will not need it, but sometimes it comes in handy. If the client changes the script or adds to it and you do not have time to memorize, you will have the option to pull out your prompter. It saves lots of stress.

I was on a shoot in Phoenix a few years ago. Mid-way through the afternoon, the teleprompter broke. They called to rent another, but we would have to wait three hours to get it. I had packed my ear prompter, so we were wrapped long before the replacement teleprompter would have arrived. Happy client, happy crew, and happy me at the hotel pool in 114 degree heat.

Bring a snack? Why?

If you are a person who can easily go more than four or five hours without eating, skip this section. If, like me, you get grumpy if you do not eat every few hours, this might be very important.

At bigger shoots, most production companies will provide snacks at what is commonly known as the "craft service" table; thus, no need for you to bring anything. Most clients will also provide lunch at a shoot; however, this is not always the case. Free lunch is great, especially if it is a good caterer! More often than not it is the corporate cafeteria, sandwiches, or pizza. If you have special dietary concerns, you may want to bring something along. Do not expect personalized service!

> Cover up your wardrobe or change before you eat. Stains on your wardrobe could really slow down a shoot!

Smaller shoots may not have craft services. Some locations will have nary a pop machine, much less a Starbuck's nearby. Once in a while you work for someone who apparently does not need to eat, and meal breaks are few and far between. Thus, my "shoot packing list" always contains a snack, water, and thermos of coffee or tea. This is my insurance against crabbiness, low blood sugar, and poor concentration. Bring a little something. Often you will not need it; but when you do, you will be so happy you have it!

Lunch time etiquette.

One lunch rule that you should know: Crew eats lunch before actors. Let them get into the lunch line before you. This is not always true, but be sure you are aware of the rule. (You will need a minute to change out of your wardrobe anyway.) The bigger the shoot, the more likely this unwritten rule is to be applied. Often, the crew has to get back to the set to prep for the next shot before work can continue. Actors should let everyone else get lunch before they dive in, unless it is obviously okay for you to go ahead.

A note about safety.

Crews and directors are very good about taking care of your safety. While I have rarely been put in a situation where I feel unsafe, crews and directors are under pressure to "get the shot." Sometimes we have to do whatever it takes in order to get it. However, if it crosses the line and becomes a safety issue for you, do not be shy. Do whatever you can to get the shot, but if it feels unsafe, speak up. It is not worth risking your safety to get the shot a little more quickly.

Shooting on film vs. shooting on tape or digital.

Most productions are shot on digital or tape formats. Occasionally for a big commercial or certainly for a feature film, you will shoot on film. You do not need to know all of the technical details, but digital and tape are cheap, film is expensive. It takes more time to set up the shot for film. Focus and lighting are far more sensitive. You have to be very good about hitting your marks and getting the shot efficiently. It is easy to "roll" multiple takes on digital. Not so for film.

> I played a short order cook in a hot, greasy restaurant kitchen for a commercial. (It was a spot for a temp service—"Do you hate your job?" kind of a thing.) The grill was dark, so there was no light hitting my face. The remedy was a big glass light bulb two feet above the grill over intense heat. The camera operator said it would be fine, "It is a quick shot." Both the lighting technician and I could only imagine the glass exploding into my face from the heat. I insisted, and they put a metal screen over the light just in case. It wasn't perfectly safe, but at least I wasn't going to have glass shards flying at my eyes.

Always be ready for multiple "takes."

Rarely will you get the shot in one take. More often than not, you will do several takes of each shot. Some industrial shoots will move on to the next shot as soon as you have completed the previous shot, but this is rare. Most directors will get the "keeper" (the best version of the shot, the one they want to keep) and then they will get a "safety" (another good version of the shot just in case they need it).

The more complicated the shot, the more "takes" you will have to do in order to get it. For example, if you have a shot requiring actors to speak and move, extras moving in the background, the camera moving on a "dolly" (a camera mounted on a specialized cart that rolls on train-like "dolly tracks") and a camera operator zooming in and changing focus, you have many variables that can go wrong in a shot. This type of shot will likely require several rehearsals and several takes to get it right. The more consistently you can perform your piece of the puzzle in each and every take, the more they will appreciate you. The director can then concentrate on the rest of the shot, not you.

"Reaction shots," "room tone," "alts," etc.

There may be a variety of shots they will need to get in order to edit the program or commercial. Sometimes in a scene with two or more actors, they will get "reaction shots." These will be close-ups of you smiling, nodding, listening intently, etc. When they shoot this, you may feel silly at first, but you will get used to it. If the editor has a problem making two shots "cut together," sometimes a few seconds of a reaction shot will make the cut work. (You do not have to know why or how, just know that you will sometimes have to give them a minute or two of reactions.)

The editor will also need room tone. All you have to do is stand there in silence for a minute while they record the natural sound in the room. They will record this through your microphone if you are wearing one. Again, you do not necessarily need to know exactly why they need this, just know that they may need it during the editing process.

Sometimes they will need alternate versions of the same shot. Either they need this for two different versions of the program or commercial, or the client has not decided which way is best, so they shoot it both ways and decide later. It is much easier to get the alternate version at the time of the shoot, rather than to come back and try to duplicate the shot weeks later. The director will often shorten this terminology to "alt." You will hear: "Let's get the alt before we move on." Or, "Okay, now give me the alt."

What's "green screen"?

Occasionally, you will do a shoot on green screen. This is a special effects technique. Basically, they will record you on camera in front of a solid green background. When they edit, they can then "chroma-key" out all green in the shot, and insert another background—often an animated background of some kind.

For green screen, you cannot wear any green at all. If you were to wear a green scarf on a green screen shoot, for example, it would appear as if your head is floating above your body with no neck. The green scarf will completely disappear. The director or your agent will tell you if you are shooting on green screen. Simply leave any green wardrobe at home.

Some shoots are long and difficult, others are easy.

Some days you will work hard, other days you will sit around a lot.

- **Spokesperson gigs**. On the days that you are the spokesperson, you may be on your feet talking to the camera all day. Once in a while, the spokesperson only has a couple of paragraphs to do on camera, and then it is an easy, quick day. If the script is twenty to thirty pages or more, you will really earn your pay!

- **Day player.** A day player role means you have some lines, or even a lot of lines, but you are not the principal role. These can be easy days with lots of down time or they can be very busy, involved days.

- **Non-speaking roles.** You might expect non-speaking roles to be the easiest, but this is not always the case. Sometimes these are very busy, hands-on gigs. Sometimes you will be demonstrating a product or a process for a video in which a voice-over narrator will describe what you are doing. In these cases, there can be many shots that require very specific physical action from you.

One of my most memorable non-speaking shoots involved a training video for hotel housekeepers, many of whom did not speak English. Rather than try to make several versions of the video in different languages, they produced one visual version with voice-over narration in the various languages. The shoot lasted three full days, with oodles of shots of me cleaning every conceivable nook and cranny of a hotel room. The toilet shot was my personal favorite, including several takes from different angles, not to mention the time it took to light the toilet and me. (I am in it for the glamour.) The shoot was long and physical.

Another interesting non-speaking shoot was a video used for market research for a new product that was not yet on the market. I had to sign a confidentiality agreement, so I cannot tell you what the product was, or I'd have to shoot you. However, it involved tearing open a specially-designed package and pouring out its contents. Easy enough, except that they had only two prototypes of the package on the set. I had two chances to get the shot right. Further, there were about eight other steps I had to do in this shot before I even got to the actual tearing part. Pressure was on. I did several rehearsals (without tearing) before we actually shot, just to be sure not to screw up the entire thing.

- **Extras.** An extra is also a non-speaking role, but you are strictly in the background. Nothing you do is featured in the shot. Often if you are an extra at the shoot, there is a lot of down time. You simply sit around just in case they need you. You will do things like walk through the shot or sit at a table in the background.

If memorization is required, make sure you do it!

When you memorize for an industrial, you do not necessarily have to memorize as perfectly and flawlessly as for a stage gig. However, do not show up unprepared. Time is money. Never make a director and crew wait around while you need multiple takes because you did not do your homework. When you book a shoot, always ask your agent if there is a script to memorize. Memorization is simply a discipline that is integral to the job.

Of course, you will occasionally make mistakes or forget a line at a shoot (we all do), but if you do your homework, you will minimize mistakes. If you did not get the script ahead of time, it is their fault. If you have had it for a day or more, you have no excuses. (If the script is long, they should get it to you several days ahead of time.)

An ear prompter might reduce your memorization load for some jobs. (See Chapter 3 for details.)

Do not expect the director to direct you!

That may sound ridiculous, but most commercial and industrial directors come from a technical or communications background, not an acting background. They will tell you where to be and when to talk. They will give you a general idea of what the client wants. The delivery is then up to you. Use your acting instincts and give them your best, truthful take. They may "tweak" your interpretation from there; however, do not expect them to help you with the acting part of it. Once in a while you will work with a director who gives great direction, but most will not.

What do I do if I am sick for a gig?

In most cases, the show must go on. If you absolutely cannot do it, you will have to be replaced. When you know it is a possibility, call your agent *immediately* so they can have a pinch-hitter ready. A gig rarely can be rescheduled around you.

If you can do the shoot and do it well, take your aspirin, vitamin C, decongestants, or whatever it takes to get you through. If you have laryngitis or the flu, and you know you will not be able to do the shoot well, call your agent right away!

"Call-time" means earlier than that.

First and foremost, never show up to a gig late. The client is paying for many crew members, studio time, and equipment rental. If you are late, you may be holding up a lot of people and costing the client a lot of money.

Establish the habit of arriving to gigs ten to fifteen minutes early. For print shoots, you should arrive even earlier than that. Arrive prior to your call-time and allow extra time for parking problems, traffic, and getting lost. Often at a shoot they will not be ready for you when you arrive, and you may sit around for a while. I would rather wait around occasionally than face the tension of being late and holding things up.

If you know you are going to be late, do not panic and think your career is over. Just call your agent so that they can alert the client—but this should be a very rare occurrence.

Conflict on the set.

You will occasionally see disagreements between directors, producers, and/or clients on the set. Stay out of it. Nothing good can come of an actor's involvement in such things. Let them settle their disagreements and just wait until it is time to do your job. Often the conflict has nothing to do with you. Sometimes it is about your delivery or your appearance. Sometimes they will huddle up and whisper before they fill you in on their discussion about you. You just have to wait and do as you are told. Do not become flustered or take it personally; it just comes with the job. (You are a commodity, remember?)

> "On set, remember you are just there for the day. You are a hired gun. You aren't the director, and you don't have to be right. Let all the other folks do their job, and you do yours. If you do have an opinion about how something should go, step lightly. You will very quickly know whether or not it is appropriate to say something—if you are listening."
> —Greta Grosch

When conflict happens, just do your job. If it involves you, simply tell them what options they can expect from you, and let them settle the battle. If you think your agent can be of assistance, by all means call and ask for help. If it involves finances, definitely refer them to your agent. In any event, keep your cool and be professional.

I once had a producer begin a shoot day by literally yelling and swearing at a director—about my hair of all things. Though they auditioned me on camera and had seen me many times, there was a communication problem and the producer expected me to show up as a blonde. Without giving all the silly details, I calmly offered to call my agent so she could send a perfectly wonderful blonde actress, or I could attempt to do a cheap, temporary spray-in color, or I could do the shoot as a brunette. I ended up having an entire can of drug store, Halloween, spray-on hair color applied to my head to satisfy this producer. I'm quite certain it looked horrible, but he won, so that is all that mattered. I had to just stay calm, not take it personally, and do my job.

Melinda Kordich tells the story of a huddled conference on a commercial set. They were whispering and occasionally looking over at her. Eventually they called the makeup artist over, whispered some more, and then sent her to talk with the actress. Apparently, they liked her and they liked the wardrobe, but they were concerned that, well, she appeared to be too "flat-chested." Her response? "Well for God's sake, tell me something I don't know! Let's stuff my bra and get on with it!" Melinda adds, "The clients (all men, by the by) could not look me in the eye."

Actor etiquette on the set.

There are some sure fire ways to become unpopular at the shoot. If you want to increase the chances that you will be hired again, keep these things in mind. Some of them seem obvious, but I have seen it all happen, and I have been the culprit a few times.

- **Always be ready for the next shot.** Sometimes directors will tell you when you have a short break. Often they will not say anything. You will finish a shot, they will start re-lighting for the next shot, and they forget to "break the actors." That is typical. The important thing is never leave the set unless you first check with the P.A. or the director. Once you have been around for a while, you can usually tell when you will have a few minutes free, but be sure to confirm this before you leave. Always be ready for the next shot at a second's notice. You never want to be the one holding up a shoot!

- **Taking breaks.** Union actors are supposed to have scheduled breaks. Non-union actors have nothing defined. Usually there is plenty of down time for actors on a set. However, when it is a long day with precious few opportunities for breaks, be ready to work hard, but do not be too shy to say what you need. If a director seems to forget that I am human and not a lighting instrument, I sometimes will say, "Let me know when there's a good time for me to step out for a minute or two." That lets them know that you are attentive to the need to get the shots done efficiently, but also reminds them that occasionally you must tend to personal needs.

- **Never make them wait for you on your cell phone.** If you have to return a call, do so when you are sure you have a break and be ready to hang up and turn it off quickly when they need you again.

- **Turn cell phones off.** Never leave your cell phone on. Always turn it off on the set. Turn it on only when you have a break away from the set.

- **Never direct your fellow actor.** That is the director's job. It is very bad form for you to direct another actor. If a friend asks your opinion, go ahead and answer—but that is the only exception to the rule. (Even then be careful what you say if you do not want to lose a friend!) If you direct another actor, you are not only stepping on the actor's toes, you may be offending the director as well. Even if you think you are just being helpful, bite your tongue.

- **Never make lighting suggestions, writing suggestions, directing suggestions, etc**. On an industrial or commercial set, your job is to deliver a script, move when you are told, and sometimes act. Anything else is not your job. You risk offending if you try to jump in where you do not belong.

  Occasionally on an industrial shoot, the director or client may stop the shoot to say, "It sounds awkward." You may then chime in and say, "It doesn't feel quite right to me, either." They may ask, "How would you say it?" That is an invitation to give suggestions, so go ahead. Other times, a group re-write will happen with several people offering suggestions. Perhaps you can safely chime in then. However, most of the time you will want to pause until the impulse passes, rather than risk offending.

- **Be positive.** We all have our good and bad days, but try to leave negativity at home. Most of the actors I work with are great fun. A couple of times I have worked with actors who ooze negativity; they complain to their fellow actors constantly about this agent or that director or this or that shoot. Just remember that when you are working, there are dozens of other actors out there who would love to have your gig that day. Do not take it for granted, and be careful to whom you complain. You may be having a bad day, but it is usually a very important day for the client.

- **Professionalism on the set.** This may seem obvious, but I have seen actors rub clients or directors the wrong way by committing a faux pas here and there. Carry a professional attitude on the set and in the studio. Of course, this does not mean you have to be stuffy; however, be careful not to be too casual. Read the mood on the set and get a feel for the corporate culture before you relax too much. I have worked with actors who have told jokes or performed their best impressions on the set, and the client seemed to be irritated by it. Remember that the actors' down time is often work time for director and crew; we break while they plan and set up the next shot. If they are chatting, then join in. If they are trying to concentrate, get out of the way and allow them to focus.

  When we actors are all backstage and in the dressing room, the culture can be a lot more casual and loose, to say the least! When we enter the corporate world, the rules change. Be a chameleon and adjust easily to the corporate culture. If you are the type of actor who is very gregarious and entertaining, know when it is okay, but sense when to keep quiet. And watch your language; you never know if someone will be offended by it. (Clients have complained to agents about this!)

  The bottom line: Never give a client reason not to hire you again. When in doubt, talk less and listen more.

- **Expect overtime.** Avoid planning anything right after a shoot. More often than not you will be done on time, but you never know. If you have not arranged for an early release in advance, you will need to stay until the job is done. Sometimes shoots can last into the wee hours of the morning. (Feature film shoots often go long.) A friend once did a twenty-three-hour industrial shoot. Great overtime pay, but a scheduling nightmare! This is an extreme example, but overtime happens. Be prepared to stay late if needed.

  > If you have a definite rehearsal or work conflict, you must request an early release at the audition or time of booking.

- **Questioning the director's direction.** Most directors will trust your interpretation and will offer simple suggestions. Once in a while you will get what feels like bad direction. I then give them my best, truthful interpretation close to what they want. If they want me to take it even further into something that feels like just plain bad acting, so be it. Just give it to them anyway. Their job is to direct; your job is to act—even if it feels like bad acting.

- **Me, me, me.** This is a common new actor symptom. This may sound harsh, but it must be said: Occasionally your friends and other actors will be interested in all of your latest auditions and jobs, but the crew will be totally uninterested. Refrain from discussing every aspect of your acting career; the business of acting may be new and exciting to you, but it often is not as interesting to others. Enjoy those conversations with your actor friends in classes and over coffee, but suppress them on the set.

- **Do not waste time making excuses.** Everyone "blows a take" now and again. You are not expected to be perfect on every take; actors will forget lines, miss marks, and trip over words from time to time. That is expected. Relax. Avoid becoming flustered and wasting time with lengthy apologies. A quick "Oops, sorry" or "My bad" will suffice; then simply re-group, take a deep breath, and immediately get ready for take two.

- **Take interest in the client's business.** Sometimes a client wants to tell us all about their business or product, thinking they are being helpful to us. They often do not realize that the script gives us most everything we need to know to do the job of acting. However, taking a sincere, active interest in a client's business is simply good networking, and often their business is more interesting than you might expect at first glance. Understanding their product, business, or corporate culture may not actually change the way you play the role at the shoot, but it will help to establish a potentially valuable relationship.

Script changes and other curve balls.

Clients sometimes change their minds. Re-writes often happen in the middle of the shoot. Expect it. Your job is to stay calm and deliver whatever you are given. A few changes here and there are doable; however, if they give you a bunch of new copy to memorize on the spot, do the best you can. Instant memorization of long copy is next to impossible for most of us. If they do this to you, it is not your fault. Just stay calm and focused, breathe deeply, do the best you can, and know that you are not the first actor to be in this uncomfortable position! Relaxation will aid memorization. (Actors have been known to place cheat sheets all over the set, as long as they are not in the shot!)

Hurry up and wait.

I mentioned earlier that there is a lot of down time at a shoot. Waiting is just part of the job. It is difficult to know exactly how long it will take to get the shot. If yours is just one of many shots, the schedule can be very difficult to predict. You are usually being paid a day rate, thus you will get the same pay if you are there for an hour or for the full shift. Bring something to read and simply relax. If you get done early, that is a bonus.

Delays can happen for a myriad of reasons, and shoots can frequently run behind schedule. "Hurry up and wait" is just a reality of the job.

Final word about your job on the set.

Our job as actors in commercials and especially industrials is more about functioning efficiently than it is about acting. Yes, we usually have to be able to act in order to book the work. However, once you are on the set, your job is to function as efficiently as any other piece of the puzzle.

Keep in mind the client's needs and the director's needs. In addition to getting good shots in order to communicate the message, they need the shoot to be on schedule and under budget. The more relaxed and focused you are, the more efficiently you will function. I like to think that getting my shots done on or ahead of schedule is part of my job. Sometimes that goal is out of my control. However, as often as I can, I do my part to keep it moving.

Show up to a shoot ready to work efficiently. Even if you have a million-dollar contract to shoot a feature film, remember that a shoot is never about you—it is about getting the shots. Your job is to help make that happen.

CHAPTER 9

Training and Classes

Just do it, but don't spend a fortune.

Athletes train year round and constantly work on the fundamentals of their particular sport. Musicians practice daily or they "lose their chops." Dancers train and rehearse for hours in order to be fit, flexible, and fluid. Hmmm. Are you seeing a pattern here?

There are vastly different opinions about where you should go to get actor training and what "method" you should study; however, most knowledgeable people agree about one thing: Talent alone is not enough. You need to learn how to develop and use that talent.

Learning to act.

You cannot learn to act by reading about it, though there are many great books about acting. Nor can you learn to act in a vacuum; you need interaction with other actors and eventually an audience. The study of acting requires that you get on your feet and do it. Get yourself up on stage: community theater, church or synagogue, school theater, scene work with friends, monologue groups—wherever you can, act. Classes will make more sense to you if you have some experience to draw upon as a context for your training. Start auditioning wherever you can, and start searching for good, affordable classes. This chapter will help you start your search for actor training.

> "To be an actor requires talent. But beyond talent, it takes a sound mind and body . . . a trained voice and fine standard speech . . . an insatiable curiosity about the human condition . . . an unshakable desire to be an actor . . . and tenacity and discipline to make something of the talent."
>
> —Uta Hagen, legendary actress, teacher and author. From an ad in **Backstage**, May 2002

What kind of training do you need?

It depends on what you want from the biz. Do you see yourself on stage? Do you dream of a film and TV career? Or, do you want to try to make money in commercials and industrials or voice-overs?

Good actor training will help you in your pursuit of all of the above. Many of the most successful actors on-camera and in voice-overs are experienced, trained stage actors. Regardless of your career focus, I recommend at least basic acting and improvisation classes for any actor.

In Appendix F you will find an extensive list of training options in the Twin Cities.

Do I have to take classes?

No. I know some successful people in the biz who are not trained actors. People with a natural gift for communication may indeed have success without ever taking an acting class. If acting classes do not interest you, try your hand at the biz without them. You might be a natural.

That said, I think everyone can benefit from classes. I would not be making a living in the biz if not for several classes I have taken. Sometimes you don't know what you don't know! Coming out of college with a theater degree, I thought I had it all figured out. In hindsight, I had no idea how much more I had to learn. (I still have a lot more to learn!)

I have seen actors grow by leaps and bounds during classes. When a light bulb goes on in an actor's head, it can be blindingly bright!

Why take classes?

There are a myriad of benefits to taking acting classes. I find the study of acting fascinating, and I have thoroughly enjoyed almost all of the acting classes I have taken. Classes allow you to simply act without the pressure of an audition or an audience. In class, you can experiment and play, make bigger, riskier choices and learn what works for you and what does not. Some reasons for taking classes:

- To add tools to your actor toolbox.
- To learn new acting methods.
- To learn more about yourself.
- To practice relaxation and concentration in preparation for auditioning and performing.
- To gain feedback from a new and objective teacher.
- To learn camera technique.
- To exercise your vocal instrument.

- To exercise your physical instrument.
- To build confidence.
- To combat self-consciousness.
- To learn to "be in the moment."
- To meet other actors and network.
- To actually get to act during the times that no one is casting you.

Respect for the art of acting.

I simply love great acting. I have immense respect for the art and craft of it. Watching inspired, gifted actors in a well–crafted show is magical. However, such inspired performances do not happen by accident.

I have come across many actors who feel they do not need training:

"I've been cast a few times, so why do I need classes?"

"I have experience—I've already taken an acting class."

"I did a bunch of shows in high school and college, so I already know what I'm doing."

Trust me, I have been there. I am embarrassed to admit how frustrated I was during my first year of auditioning for Twin Cities' stages, being cast as "only" the maid or the "second cigarette girl from the left." However, I appreciated the roles I got, and it did not take long for me to realize how much I still needed to learn. My arrogance soon turned to humility, and I got myself into the best classes I could find. I also quickly realized that playing those "smaller roles" was excellent experience and networking for me.

> Jenni Lilledahl (co-owner of the Brave New Workshop, founded by Dudley Riggs) trained in Chicago at Second City for a couple of years. She told me, "The question in Chicago is not: 'Are you training?' It's '**Where** are you training?'" In the bigger markets, it is just expected that an actor is studying.

When you listen to great actors talk, you will hear many of them refer to their "acting coach" or their most recent teacher. Watch *The Actor's Studio* on Bravo and you will hear Academy Award and Tony Award winning actors talk this way. Many accomplished actors are constantly training.

You can dabble in the world of commercial acting and amateur theater without taking any classes. If you are not driven to work professionally, feel free to treat acting as a hobby. If you have natural talent, you will land some gigs once in a while. Train or not; it is up to you. Just know that this is a competitive business. What is going to help you get an edge?

College and university programs vs. other classes: Do I need a degree in theater?

There are lots of folks auditioning around town with degrees in acting. There are many others who have no college acting experience whatsoever. If you are young and determined to be a professional actor in New York or L.A., you may want to look into getting a degree in acting. If your plan is to be an actor in this city, the credentials are helpful but not essential. A theater degree may help get you in the door with a local agent or director, but it is ultimately your talent and your audition that will get you the role. Many succeed without a theater degree.

For those who wish to pursue a degree, contact the University of Minnesota's theater department for information about their programs, as well as joint programs with the Guthrie Theater. In addition, many nearby small colleges have vibrant theater departments. For information about nationally-known theater schools, refer to Appendix N for books about the biz. Specifically, consult *How to Sell Yourself As an Actor*, sixth edition, by K. Callan, pages 103-108 (Sweden Press, 2008). She lists her recommended theater schools and their contact information.

Which "method" is best?

When I was first learning to act, I searched for a way to put it all together, to figure out "the right way to act." I often became confused and overwhelmed by all of the different methods, theories, and exercises. If you become similarly confused or overwhelmed, simply remember that the essence of acting is truthful human behavior. Some exercises will work for you; some will not.

It will be up to you to decide what works best for you as you study with different teachers. Try on all of the different methods that your teachers offer to see what fits. Many of us use pieces from many different methods. As you study with different teachers and work with different actors, you will begin to realize your strengths as well as areas that need work. Your own personal method will evolve as your work and experience grow.

Spend your time and money on teachers with whom you connect. Switch classes if you feel you are stagnating. If you cannot master "their way," it may simply be a method that does not fit your needs right now. Give it a serious and earnest effort, but do not immediately assume there is something wrong with you if you don't get it. Five or ten years from now you may want to revisit a method that did not work for you the first time around; maybe you will get it the second time around. See Appendix N for a brief bibliography of references to jump-start your learning.

Learning to play your instrument: Your voice and your body.

Most actors would agree, regardless of an actor's method, you have to learn to how to play your instrument—your voice and your body. If the audience cannot hear or understand you, the truth of your emotions and the creativity of your choices simply will not matter. If your body is not working in harmony with your voice and your emotions, you cannot fully express the truth of the moment. Perhaps you can get away without vocal and movement training if you only want to dabble in commercials, but if you want to work on the stage you need to learn to play your entire instrument.

Your voice is a main component of your physical instrument. If you have never learned to use your voice properly—breath support, easy and open vowels, clear diction, etc.—I would recommend some good vocal training. (See Appendix F.)

You may also wish to seek out some movement training. Some people are naturally physical; others seem to lack a connection between mind and body. If you are a trained dancer or a skilled athlete, movement training may not be a priority for you. If you have never trained your body, you may want to look into adding some kind of regular movement work to your life: dance, yoga, mime, pilates, etc.

Objectively examine your own instrument to discover what may need more work. When you start doing scene work or performances, the comments and notes you hear from teachers and directors will begin to reveal a pattern. Listen carefully to any feedback you receive, and you will discover what kind of work you may need.

Classes and training: Options in the Twin Cities.

When I am in New York, I always pick up *Backstage*, the trade publication for the business of acting there. There is also *Backstage West* for L.A. actors. Chicago's version is *PerformInk*. When I thumb through these papers, I am sometimes envious of all the opportunities there—not only audition opportunities, but also the myriad of training opportunities. Options for training here in the Twin Cities are not as plentiful, but our options are constantly increasing.

There are quite a few teachers and classes in town from which to choose. It can be tough to know where to begin. In college or university training, the school will lay out courses and prerequisites for you. That is not the case if you are searching for classes on your own. Here are some suggestions to shape your search.

As with teachers of any subject, you will click with some and not with others. Teaching is a talent and skill unto itself. (Just because someone is a great actor does not necessarily mean he or she is a great teacher.) Rely on your instincts as you search for training. Once you get started, networking and advice from other actors will help you in your search.

Where do I find the most up-to-date information about classes?

See Appendix C for the main communication networks for local actors. Most acting teachers will advertise on one of the actor websites, minnesotaplaylist.com or callboard.org.

Some teachers will keep an e-mail list and notify prospective students when there is an upcoming class. When a teacher is recommended to you, contact him or her directly to be included on the list.

Further, most agency and casting directors' offices will post information about local classes. Take a look at their bulletin boards when you are there.

How do I know if a teacher is giving me what I need?

Since actors rely on their own truthful emotions and reactions, some actor training can feel very personal and even make you feel a bit vulnerable. With a good teacher, this will feel quite safe. A good teacher will not press you to expose and elaborate upon personal experiences. That is for therapy, not acting class. In your pursuit of acting, it is good to challenge and explore your own behavior and reactions. However, if acting class begins to feel uncomfortable, manipulative, insulting, or inappropriate, trust your gut feeling and do not continue training with that teacher.

Sometimes scenes in class will flop and will not feel good. You will not always leave an acting class feeling wonderful and exhilarated. A teacher's job is not to always pat you on the back and tell you that you are a wonderful actor. A good teacher will challenge you. On the other hand, what if a teacher makes you feel uncomfortable as a human being, tears you down, or attempts to make you dependent upon him or her for your acting career? It is a good bet this is a teacher with whom you do not want to work. Good teachers do not want to create a dependent relationship. On the contrary, good teachers foster independence and teach you the tools you need to create your own art.

If you ever feel pressured to continue classes with a particular teacher or school, know that good teachers want what is best for you and will allow you to follow your instincts without pressure. If it seems their motives are driven by money or ego, then walk away.

How do I choose good classes? Practical considerations.

Overall suggestions:

- Shop around. The going rate for classes should be no more than $10 to $25 per hour of class time. If it is more than that, it should be a great class with very few students.

- Class sizes should be limited. If it is a seminar with no on-camera or scene work, then bigger classes are fine. If it is an on-camera, voice, or scene class, even ten to twelve students in class can be too many. Know the prices and class size limits before you pay.

- Get details about the teachers. Ask about the teacher's acting experience and training, as well as teaching experience. Whenever possible, find out what other actors say about a particular teacher.

- Never be pressured into signing up for anything. If you feel pressured to take a class, tell them you need to think about it for a while. If it is a legitimate class, the opportunity will still be available after you have had the opportunity to sleep on it. If you interview with an agency for representation and they press the hard sell on classes they themselves offer, there is a chance that financial profit is taking precedence over your professional development.

Be cautious about package deals and promises.

The number of modeling and unaccredited acting schools is growing. They used to advertise only in the newspapers. Now some of them are paying to advertise on radio and TV. They are found in shopping malls, trying to convince people to be models or actors. I elaborate on this subject in Chapter 13. In many cases, they target teens and parents to convince them of their child's potential as an actor/model.

I have said it before, and I will say it again: You do not need to spend a lot of money in order to work in the Twin Cities. If you choose to sign up for an entire package of classes and pay for them all up front, treat this as an investment in your business.

- **Know with whom you are dealing.** Investigate any organization carefully before you pay. The Better Business Bureau is a good place to start. Do a search on the internet to see what comes up when you type in the organization's name. Some organizations promise audition opportunities along with their classes. Apparently they have connections to casting people at well-known production companies. I have been told that these connections and opportunities are, at least in some circumstances, real. If you do not want to move to L.A., but you still want the opportunity to audition for these big opportunities, then I guess you can pay thousands for their package of classes in order to gamble on such audition opportunities. However, know that your odds of being cast in any big, national audition are slim.

- **Get the refund policy in writing.** Seriously, is there anything in the world you pay big money for up front without having some kind of warranty? Paying up front with no refund policy may be a bad business decision for you, but a good business outcome for the organization.

- **Know what you are getting.** Ask the organization for as much *specific* information as possible. Who teaches the classes? What are their credentials? What is the teaching philosophy? Ask for a detailed breakdown of the goals for the class.

- **Ask for a copy of the written contract** before you sign anything. If they refuse this request, walk away. If there is much fine print in the contract, it is always wise to have an attorney look it over.

- **Get references.** Are there other students to whom you can talk before you make a decision?

- **Ask about individual classes**. Can you take a class or two before you make a decision about a full package?

It is possible to sign up for a package of classes for $2000 to $3000 or more. I would try a class or two at a time and invest the extra money elsewhere.

Classes for kids.

Parents and teens, see Chapter 13 and Appendix F for more information.

Do I have to learn to sing and dance?

No. I hear this question from newer actors from time to time. Personally, I do not sing very well and I am not a trained dancer—so I do not do musicals, and I do not take voice lessons or dance classes. There is no pressing need. (Though I do consider both from time to time, just for fun.)

If you want to do musical theater, then you may wish to get some training. Again, see Appendix F for some options.

Forming your own support group, monologue group, or artist's circle.

Some actors band together to form their own theater group or "artist's circle." (This term comes from the book by Julia Cameron entitled *The Artist's Way: A Course in Discovering and Recovering Your Creative Self*.) Other actors gather either formally or informally to rehearse and work monologues or scenes. I highly recommend something like this; it holds you accountable to other actors and it gives you an audience. Again, acting does not happen in a vacuum; you need interaction with other actors and an audience. If you have such a group, you may also want to hire an acting coach to work with the group regularly. Many acting teachers would be happy to avoid expensive, time-consuming marketing efforts and have a class come to them!

I'm a beginner; are there specific classes you would recommend?

If you are a beginner, allow me to suggest a course of action for you. However, know that there is no right or wrong way to learn. Just get out there and get started! (See Appendix F for contact information for each class listed below, along with many more.)

- First, start auditioning. Get yourself on stage wherever and whenever possible in school or community theater. (See Appendix C for audition sources.)

- Network with other actors. Get together and read scripts, work on scenes and monologues. Start an artist's circle. This will get you up on your feet and will give you a context for your training. If you have not met many other actors yet, take a class or two and you will quickly find them.

- Get some improvisation training as soon as possible. Improv will help you dive in, work with other actors, listen, connect, and respond spontaneously. Beginning improv classes are fun, low-stress ways to get up on your feet and "play" in the world of the actor. Classes are filled with actors and non-actors alike. It is an excellent first step. Check out the classes at the Brave New Workshop or with Stevie Ray.

- Check out Cheryl Moore Brinkley's "Acting Fundamentals" and "Voice Fundamentals" classes. For more detail about Cheryl's classes, go to bvocal.net.

- Beginners may also wish to check out Don Cosgrove's "Basic Acting Skills" class. This would be a great place to give acting a try. Don teaches several different classes. Check out the list at thetalentcenter.com.

- Beginners who would like to give commercial acting a try may also contact Bill Cooper. He has been in the biz for years and can give you some personalized camera training.

- Michelle Hutchison teaches camera acting at Lynn Blumenthal Casting. Once you have a few basics, Michelle's class is a great option.

- Do not forget to look into your local community education offerings. Acting classes are occasionally advertised, and close to home might be perfect for you.

- Once you have a foundation, seek out some scene study classes. Try classes at the Guthrie—that is where many of us started. If you are a novice actor, do not be intimidated by the name. The Guthrie's beginning and intermediate classes are filled with novice actors. You will not be alone.

Then start to focus on any areas you wish to pursue: stage, camera or voice-over work. Consult Appendix F for a more extensive list. Contact information for all of the classes identified above (and many more) can be found there.

I'm an experienced actor. How do I find training for professionals?

There are several local instructors who teach experienced actors all the time. Cheryl Moore Brinkley, Steve Hendrickson, Michelle Hutchison, and Cynthia Uhrich immediately come to mind. Contact them to discuss your needs. (See Appendix F for details about these instructors and several more.)

Jane Brody (from Chicago) and Anthony Vincent Bova (from New York) travel to the Twin Cities from time to time to teach workshops. Their classes are specifically for more experienced actors.

Many teachers and directors would be happy to coach individuals or small groups even if they do not specifically advertise classes. If you have a good rapport with a certain director, this may be a great option for you. Find a director you like and ask if he/she is willing to teach. If you get a small group of dedicated and reliable actors together, many directors and teachers will work with you. You will have to negotiate schedule and pricing.

> "Practice your craft so when the good stuff comes along, you will shine!"
> —Jean Rohn, casting director

See Appendix F for many more options, and keep checking callboard. org and minnesotaplaylist.com.

Watch actors work!

Some of my best training has come from watching great actors. You can learn a lot by watching terrific, professional actors here in the Twin Cities! If you want to be an actor, start seeing more theater right here in town.

Final words about training: Just do it.

Acting is like any other skill or craft: Raw talent will only get you so far. Keep stretching, flexing, and working out!

CHAPTER 10

Theater in the Twin Cities

The best part of the biz

That bold statement (on the right) ought to give you a pretty good idea of the vibrant theater scene we have here in the Twin Cities! Theater opportunities abound. New theater companies appear constantly. Some make it; some disappear and are quickly replaced by others. There are so many theaters that it is difficult to keep track of who's who! This chapter will offer some resources to help you find the opportunities that are right for you.

> "No city in the country outside of New York has more theaters per capita or spends more on performing arts than the Twin Cities."
> —From **Business Week,** as found on the Minnesota Association of Community Theaters' website, 2004

I am far from the most experienced and connected stage actor in town, though I have worked several times on the stages of Park Square Theater and Theatre in the Round, among others. I have also seen hundreds of shows from here to Chicago to New York to London. Our theater scene is as vibrant and exciting as any other city, with performances every bit as terrific as you will see in the bigger markets. There are stages here with talented, experienced, veteran performers, as well as dozens of stages with opportunities for novice actors. This chapter is intended for beginning actors as well as more experienced artists.

How many theaters are in the Twin Cities?

The number is constantly changing. Almost every month I see an ad for a performance by some brand new theater company. In Appendix G you will find a list of theaters, theater companies, and theater spaces—including web addresses and the basics about each theater. You will be surprised when you see how many theaters there are!

Take a virtual tour of Twin Cities' theaters.

These sites will link you to just about every theater in town.

- Minnesota Playlist is a terrific resource for the theater community. The site contains audition notices, a theater calendar, reviews, articles, a talent listing—just about everything you can imagine about performing arts in Minnesota (minnesotaplaylist.com).

- The Minnesota Association of Community Theaters' website has everything you would ever want to know about community theater in the state. You will find links to community theaters, events, auditions and job notices (mact.net).

- The Ivey Awards are the local version of the Tony Awards. The website contains lots of information about the local professional theater scene, with links to every professional theater in town (ivey-awards.com).

- The new Play by Play Bookstore is a great resource for all things theater in the Twin Cities. Just as the Drama Book Shop is important to New York actors, Play by Play Bookstore will become a hub for our theater community. Visit and support this great new resource for local actors: Play by Play Theatre Bookstore and Opening Night Gifts, 1771 Selby Avenue, St. Paul (playbyplaybooks.com).

- TC Theatre Connections website will give you amazing insight into the local theater scene: Podcasts of interviews with Twin Cities performers, directors, designers and administrators; links to many web resources; news about show openings and closings; and links to many theater websites (tctheater-connection.com).

Go to shows!

The best way to learn about the theater scene is to start seeing theater. See everything that intrigues you. Attend shows at theaters where you want to work. Read the programs; if you like an actor's work, check their bio to see where else they work. If you like the director's work, watch for his or her name in audition notices.

> "There also might be something to be said for going to some of the smaller productions and talking to the actors after the show or even the ushers or ticket takers. Usually these people are also kin to the artists' world, so if someone is new, this might be a good place to start. Go to a show, and start asking around about the business of the community. Someone is bound to have two pretty valuable cents to come away with."
>
> —Eric "Pogi" Sumangil, Mixed Blood, Theater, Chanhassen Dinner Theatre, Frank Theatre, Ordway, Guthrie Theater

Theater tickets can be expensive. If you cannot afford to see as many shows as you would like, watch for "industry nights" or "pay what you can" nights. Several local theaters offer these performances, typically on Monday nights. Reserve your tickets early; these shows often sell out, as you can imagine.

Where do I find out about stage auditions?

Appendix C will give you a listing of audition hotlines, websites, and other sources. Most actors routinely check these. If you are new in town, they will be your lifelines to the Twin Cities' theater scene. Consult them regularly.

Getting a foot in the door . . .

Audition, audition, audition. It is the only way to get into the game. Auditioning is networking. You need to get out there to meet people and establish contacts. Each audition is a potential "foot in the door." An audition can be extremely successful, even if you do not land the role. Often you will not be cast the first time you audition for a director. He or she may already have someone in mind or may be hesitant to take a risk on an unknown actor, so it may take you a while to "break in." Each audition helps to build your reputation and your network.

Here are some comments from local actors about getting a foot in the door:

> Audition, audition, audition! No one will know who you are if they don't see you. The community here is by far one of the most friendly, and inevitably someone will be nice enough to help you. But you have to get out there (Adena Brumer, AEA, Guthrie Lab, Chanhassen, Ordway, Ten Thousand Things, History Theatre, Latte Da, Children's Theatre).

> Audition, audition, audition, audition, audition. And volunteer to help on productions as a tech or production person. Meet the people. Introduce yourself to them. Get in their faces. Work on their shows (Zach Curtis, Guthrie, Illusion, Children's Theatre, Mixed Blood, Old Log, Actors' Theater of Minnesota, Ten Thousand Things, Park Square).

> Go to auditions. Talk to people. This is a relatively small town. Once you start to get to know a few people, the circle widens pretty quickly. Even a small project can lead to bigger things eventually (Greta Grosch, AEA, Hey City, Comedysportz, Plymouth Playhouse).

Go to shows and see what kind of work is being done at specific venues, so when you do audition you have a good idea as to what material to perform to suit their venue. This is a small community and it won't take long to get the word out! (Michelle Hutchison, AEA/AFTRA/SAG, Guthrie, Guthrie Lab, Mixed Blood, Park Square).

For more experienced actors.

If you have a great deal of experience and training, you may wish to take a more proactive approach. If you would like to work with a particular theater or director, send a headshot and resume, and request a meeting. If a director is intrigued by your resume, he or she may want to meet you. (I do not recommend this for beginning actors. You will need to get some good experience on your resume before a director will be interested. Save time and postage until you have a resume that may catch someone's attention.)

More advice from actors:

Send headshot and resumes to theaters you would like to work at, network, and try to get referrals from actors you know (Kirby Bennett, Park Square, Theatre in the Round, Buzzworks, Mystery Café).

Contact the theaters (either at the Equity level or mid-tier) and ask when they hold general auditions. I'd also attend theater around town and get the contacts via the programs (Maggie Bearmon-Pistner, Theatre in the Round, Starting Gate, Gremlin, Theatre L'Homme Dieu, Pioneer Place).

I have found that most casting and artistic directors *will* meet with an actor if they ask. It gets you an introduction, and you tend to get a sense if they are going to have any interest in you whatsoever (Carolyn Pool, AEA, Park Square, Jungle, Ten Thousand Things, Actors' Theater of Minnesota, History Theatre).

Word of mouth—establishing your reputation.

Often, opportunities are available only via word of mouth. It is not uncommon that directors cast a show without any kind of audition at all; they simply cast actors they know. This can be frustrating for newer actors, but if you are talented and reliable, you will eventually break into the word-of-mouth loop.

There are plenty of auditions that are advertised and open to all. The first time you audition for a director, you introduce yourself and make a first impression. With each subsequent audition you establish your reputation and credibility. Once they know you, directors may invite you to an audition or callback or, better yet, offer you a role without an audition. Further, directors do occasionally call each other for casting recommendations or references. When you are new, the word-of-mouth loop certainly will not be working for you; but if you stick around long enough, you will become connected.

When asked, "Where do you find out about theater opportunities?" many actors replied, "Word of mouth."

> Word of mouth mostly . . . unfortunately that springs from working with other actors, directors. . . . "Work begets work" in my dictionary . . . so, it creates a "Catch 22" so to speak; you have to be working to get work. It is hard to get a roll going when you start from a complete stop. So, I think it is wise to keep communication open with people you have worked with in the past, dropping a line to a former director to remind them of you, calling other actors who are working and finding out what is going on in the community. A lot of my opportunities have been borne from this (Michelle Hutchison).

> After spending a number of years here, I have found word of mouth really valuable. People hire people, and it's about whom you know. It becomes about the connections you make over time. Once you are able to step out of your own way (and swallow your pride) you can start asking other people for help. I used to call up theaters to ask if I could audition for them; now they are starting to call me—time and connections. I know that might be frustrating for newcomers, but it's really true. Say yes to opportunities that arise, get out there, get seen, and meet people (Greta Grosch).

Be reliable and persistent, and keep auditioning. Eventually someone will take a chance on you, and word of mouth will begin to work in your favor.

Do a little research and know what shows are coming.

Theaters often announce their upcoming seasons well in advance on the website and sometimes in the newspaper. Do some research, learn about the shows, or read the scripts. If there is a role for you, prepare for the audition in advance.

Preparing in advance can be occasionally frustrating if the role (or the entire show) is cast without an audition. This has happened to me more than a few times. It can be disappointing, but reading scripts and preparing is never a waste of time. It is a good workout for you; further, when you attend the production, you can watch with a more educated eye.

How much are stage actors paid?

In general, actors in the Twin Cities do not do stage for the money. Yes, there are some actors who rely on their stage earnings as all or part of their living; however, the majority of Twin Cities' actors must have other sources of income.

> "Check theater websites to see the upcoming seasons. . . . Usually by the time auditions go into the paper, those of us who know they are coming have already been preparing for weeks. I think that gives us an advantage. Plus, things audition very far in advance and can catch you by surprise if you aren't paying attention."
>
> —Teri Parker-Brown AEA, Chanhassen Dinner Theatre, Ordway, Children's Theatre, Troupe America

Stage actors here are paid anywhere from nothing to several hundred dollars per week. Pay varies greatly based on many factors: actor's union status, theater status (community, not-for-profit, or professional), and theater size (based on number of seats in the house and box office receipts). The following pages will give you some idea of what you can expect to be paid if you perform on a Twin Cities' stage. Please note: This is local only, not actors performing in Broadway touring shows.

Actor's Equity Association—minimum salaries for Equity (union) actors.

Union members are generally the highest paid stage actors in town. Actor's Equity Association (AEA or "Equity") is the union for stage actors and stage managers, and is a sister union to AFTRA and SAG. (See Chapter 5 for more about AFTRA and SAG.)

Many different types of contracts cover Equity actors working on Twin Cities' stages, thus the pay varies. The types of Equity contracts include: League of Regional Theatres (LORT), Dinner Theatre, Small Professional Theatre, Guest Artist, and Special Appearance. For example, Guthrie actors work under a LORT agreement. Each agreement spells out expectations for actors and producers, salary minimums, benefits, etc. Actors and theaters can negotiate for higher salaries, but the contracts clearly define the minimums.

Further, each contract has its own variations based upon the size of the theater, the number of performances per week, box office receipts, etc. Because of the many variations, it is impossible to say what the average actor earns. In general, actors who work on stage under Equity contracts in the Twin Cities can make from around $160 per week (smaller theater, fewer performances) to between $600 and $800 per week (larger theater, eight performances per week). Established performers playing principal roles at the largest theaters may make closer to $1,000 per week or more. That is a very general description. Consult the AEA website for greater detail. You can read many of these agreements online at actorsequity.org. On the home page, go to "contracts," then "national agreements," then search the documents. You have the option to open PDF files to read various contracts.

Actor's Equity audition information (www.actorsequity.org).

The regional office for Actors' Equity is in Chicago. The Minneapolis/St. Paul area hotline is 612-924-4044. The hotline has a recorded message about auditions and union news. (If you are not a member or a candidate, this hotline will be of very little use to you.) You may also find local and national audition information on the website under "casting call."

Local stages that hire Equity actors.

Very few local stages use *exclusively* Equity actors; the Guthrie, Old Log, and the Ordway main stage cast primarily Equity actors.

Actors report that Equity Small Professional Theater contracts are common around town.

Many mid-size theaters have some kind of contract with Equity for a limited number of performers, thus they hire both Equity and non-Equity actors. Appendix G contains a list of nearly every theater in town with basic details including whether or not they cast Equity actors.

Should I join AEA?

Joining this union generally involves registering for candidacy to join and working a certain number of weeks in an accredited theater before gaining membership. (Check out the website for

> "I have had my Actor's Equity card for almost ten years now. I waited until I was thirty years old and knew that I could effectively compete at the new level. I have never looked back. I have been doing theater for twenty years and quite frankly feel I deserve to get paid for a job well done."
> —Seri Johnson, AEA, Chanhassen Dinner Theatre, Old Log

the details.) Of course, you will have to be cast in a show at an accredited theater before you can consider joining.

Initiation fees are approximately $1,000, and yearly dues vary based on your pay under Equity contracts. If you are experienced enough to be cast in an Equity house, then you probably already know the basics.

If you are new to acting, you probably do not need to worry about this union for quite a while. You will want to gain experience and training before even considering membership in Actor's Equity. If you want to know more, go to the website and consult the detailed FAQ section.

Average pay for non-union stage actors.

While Equity actors are paid minimum salaries, non-union actors have no such guidelines. Stage actors can be paid anywhere from nothing to a stipend for the entire run of the show to weekly salaries similar to the lower Equity rates.

Community theater actors (at Theatre in the Round or Lakeshore Players, for example) work on a strictly volunteer basis. There is no pay.

Actors at small theaters often make a stipend of between $50 and $300 for the entire run of the show, including the rehearsal process. The amount will vary from theater to theater and from show to show. Actors report that $100 to $125 is typical at many theaters such as: Gremlin, Minneapolis Musical Theatre, Pig's Eye, Starting Gate, Theatre Pro Rata, and Theatre Unbound.

Other theaters may pay on a per-show basis. Several years ago at Park Square I was paid a stipend of $200 for the six-week rehearsal period, a per show fee of $40 for student matinees, and $25 for evening performances (eight shows per week). This type of arrangement is common.

Still other theaters may follow the Equity model of a weekly salary, though the salaries are usually not as high as Equity minimums. Some of these theaters include Actors' Theater of Minnesota, The Brave New Workshop, Frank Theatre, Great American History Theatre, Illusion Theater, Jungle Theater, Minnesota Jewish Theatre, Mixed Blood, Ordway McKnight Stage, Park Square Theatre, Ten Thousand Things, Theater Latte Da, and Troupe America. (Please note that at least some of these stages hire both Equity and non-equity performers.)

Again, all of the information above is subject to change. Equity contracts specify minimums, but without an Equity agreement pay can vary greatly depending upon each theater's budget. This information is provided only to give you a general idea about what stage actors are paid here in the Twin Cities.

With so many theaters in town, how do I know where to audition?

If you are a *novice actor*, audition everywhere you can. Start with school, church, synagogue—anywhere that you can get up on your feet and act. Try any community theaters in your area and build from there. (See a list of community theaters in Appendix G.) Volunteer at any nearby theaters; usher, build sets, hang lights—anything to get a foot in the door.

For *experienced actors* who are new to town, search appendix G and note the theaters that cast at least some equity actors. These theaters are likely to attract more experienced actors. Here's some advice from the locals: I asked the question, "At which theaters do you prefer to work?" Their responses might give you a few ideas about where to start.

> When in doubt, start at Theatre in the Round; most of us have. I love Theatre in the Round with all my heart . . . arena acting and a tremendous staff . . . nearly guaranteed reviews and season ticket holders who are smart theater goers (Linda Sue Anderson, Theatre in the Round, Starting Gate, Torch, Workhouse).

> Ten Thousand Things—best theater in the Cities (Zach Curtis).

> Park Square—nice theater, sells well, pays! (Kirby Bennett).

> Guthrie, Ordway because it's so delightfully professional—everyone knows their jobs and does them well. An actor gets a bit pampered at those houses. I also like the History Theater because they do interesting work, and stage management is consistently good there (Patty Nieman).

> Chanhassen is kind of like a family. It is a hard nut to crack, but once you are in they take pretty good care of you. Ordway was great, too—really professional. I also really liked the Children's Theater (Teri Parker Brown).

> Ten Thousand Things for the audience and its mission, and the Guthrie for how you're treated as an actor (Adena Brumer).

> Of course I love the Guthrie. I mean, who wouldn't? The pay is exceptional, and every need you may have is addressed. Mixed Blood Theatre is exceptional as well. The theater is intimate, and the artistic staff is accessible. Loved Dudley Rigg's [Brave New Workshop] as it was

creative and my input was invaluable. Would love to work at the Jungle (Michelle Hutchison).

Exciting theater happens just about every night around town. We have loads of talent here, and great folks with whom to work. I have not worked at all of the theaters listed above, but I have been an audience member at all of them. I agree with the comments above, and must add my vote for the two most exciting theaters in town: Ten Thousand Things and Theatre Latte Da. Go see their shows. You will see what I mean.

Which theaters produce musicals?

We have a wealth of gifted musical theater artists in town. There are only a few theaters that specialize in musicals: Chanhassen Dinner Theatres, Minneapolis Musical Theater, Theatre Latte Da, Nautilus Music-Theater works, the Ordway, and of course, Minnesota Opera and SkyLark Opera.

Several other theaters may produce musicals, though infrequently, including: Park Square Theater, Ten Thousand Things, the Guthrie, Actor's Theater of Minnesota, Bloomington Civic Theatre, Children's Theatre, Great American History Theatre, the Phipps, and several community theaters.

If you are a musical theater artist, watch the audition notices carefully. If you have musical theater experience, by all means submit your headshot and resume to the theaters listed above.

So many theaters, so little time!

"I love small theater, but it is herding cats to keep up with these groups, and so many slip through the cracks" (Graydon Royce, theater reviewer for the *Star Tribune*, January 6, 2007). This is in reference to his wish list for the theater community in 2008. One wish is for "some kind of a micro-theater alliance, an organization that makes a greater sum of these parts."

Even a professional who is paid to keep up with the local theater scene has a difficult time keeping track of it all! Until some kind of small-theater alliance happens, my listing in Appendix G will have to suffice in giving you the big picture. The best way to learn about the local theater scene is to go out and experience it for yourself!

Who are the best directors around town?

Ask ten actors and you will get ten different answers. Some directors are well known and have directed here for years; other new directors enter the scene all the time. It would be impossible to list them all.

However, local actor/teacher Shirley Venard has a great recommendation for her students at the University of Minnesota: If you want to learn about a particular director, simply search for his or her name on the internet. If a director's shows have been reviewed in the papers or online, you will certainly find some of those reviews and articles via the internet. From there, you can learn about the theaters at which they have directed, as well as some of the actors with whom they have worked. This kind of search will not tell you everything you may wish to know, but it will give you some basic information prior to auditioning for a particular director.

Twin Cities Unified Theater Auditions.

Several years ago, the first annual Twin Cities Unified Theater Auditions were held at the Brave New Workshop. (More recently, they have been held at the Jungle Theatre.) This is a fabulous opportunity for actors. Representatives from several theaters and agencies spend the day in one theater watching a parade of actors perform. For a $15 fee, you get to strut ninety seconds of your best stuff to several theaters and agencies all at once. The unified auditions are usually held in March or April. Watch the *Star Tribune* Sunday classifieds, and check minnesotaplaylist.com and callboard.org. When you see the ads, sign up right away. The 140 audition slots go quickly. Check the prerequisites, however; these auditions require that you have experience on your resume before you sign up.

The Minnesota Association of Community Theatres.

There are great opportunities for novice actors at community theaters. While there are some professional actors who choose to do community theater for no pay, there are mostly amateur actors on the stages of Minnesota's community theaters. Some of these amateurs have a tremendous amount of experience; some have very little. The Minnesota Association of Community Theatres (MACT) is a fabulous organization. Whether you are a novice actor or a veteran, MACT has something to offer.

While the actors on the community theater stages are not paid for their work, the directors and some of the designers often are. I have had wonderful experiences at a couple of the local community theaters, working with very talented, experienced directors and designers. Check out the MACT website: mact.net.

The Minnesota Fringe Festival.

The Fringe is another great opportunity for all kinds of actors and artists. This huge ten-day festival happens in August every year. According to the 2008 annual report (as posted on fringefestival.org) there were 1080 participating artists and 40,926 tickets issued. (The Minnesota Fringe Festival is touted to be the largest Fringe in the country.)

Anyone can perform in the Fringe. Check out the website for details about applications and the lottery process (usually in February). Four hundred dollars is the approximate fee which covers rent for five performances, technical and box office staff, a listing in the Fringe programs, a listing on the website, plus sixty-five percent of the box office proceeds for your show. It is up to you to choose, rehearse, and promote the show.

Some performances are elaborate; some simple. Some feature established, well-known works; some are brand new scripts. Some showcase veteran actors; some showcase novices. If you have not been to any Fringe shows, I highly recommend that you attend! Visit the website to find more information and to register. In July of each year, the website posts the schedule of performances for the August festival.

An added bonus to attending fringe shows: With your fringe button you can get discounts at many local theaters throughout the year. Visit the website to register for regular e-mail updates.

The Playwrights' Center.

We are lucky to have an organization in the Twin Cities dedicated to live theater. I think the Playwrights' Center is the very heart of creativity for theater here, particularly for new works. The Playwrights' Center's website states:

> As both a community for new work and a hub for playwrights around the country, The Playwrights' Center offers opportunities for both playwrights and non-playwrights. Each year, The Playwrights' Center supports programs and services that meet the developmental needs of over 300 member writers across the country. As a service organization, the Center seeks to create links between writers and the tools they need to support their work. In addition to providing writers with access to in-house playwright services staff, the Center also contracts over 200 veteran actors, directors, dramaturgs and artists each year to guide and serve playwrights as they develop their scripts.

Watch for the public readings of new plays. If you are an aspiring writer, you should check out their classes. If you are an experienced actor, watch for the auditions they hold each year. They hire actors to read plays for both public readings and workshop readings. The pay is minimal, but the experience is terrific. Check out the website (pwcenter.org). The address is:

The Playwrights' Center
2301 Franklin Avenue E.
Minneapolis, Minnesota 55406-1099

Working as an extra at the Guthrie.

The Guthrie Theater often holds auditions for actors to be extras (or "essentials") in *A Christmas Carol* and other productions. I have never done this, but actors I know have enjoyed the experience and have learned by watching the work of Guthrie actors, directors, and designers.

Before you audition, just know that it is a big commitment for little pay. Rehearsals may occur on weekdays, and you are expected to faithfully attend.

Should I list my headshot and resume on one of the local websites? Will it help me find work on stage?

There are a few sites that contain listings for local theater professionals and actors. To find acting work, you really need to audition. A listing alone will not bring you work; however, it is an inexpensive way to find some exposure and possible networking opportunities in the local community. Visit the sites to discern for yourself the value of registering with each.

An on-line database of Minnesota artists and organizations, www.mnartists.org "offers to Minnesota-based artists a central gathering place on the web," and "offers the public a new way to explore art and get to know artists."

The website, www.minnesotaplaylist.com, contains a searchable database of Twin Cities' actors and other industry professionals. There is a small fee—approximately $20 every six months, $35 for the year.

Minnesota Playlist is a terrific resource. Check it regularly for all kinds of articles, audition notices, and classes. When you buy a listing in the talent directory, you are supporting the only performing arts magazine in the Twin Cities area. The talent listing promotes actors, designers, directors, and production people. You can upload photos of recent productions, post video and audio links, etc. Check it out and consider supporting this great resource for the local theater scene.

Other paid opportunities for performers.

Be sure to consult Appendix O to learn about other paid performance opportunities at theme parks and with educational tours.

See live theater!

Audition for everything you can, and when you are not auditioning, go to a show! We have a talented theater community in the Twin Cities. If you want to work in the theater, learn by watching and supporting the business.

CHAPTER 11

Film and TV

You want to be a star? You are in the wrong town.

During the 1990s, excitement ran high about the state of the film industry in the Twin Cities. *Fargo, The Mighty Ducks, Iron Will, Jingle All the Way, Grumpy Old Men, Drop Dead Fred, and Drop Dead Gorgeous* (among many others) were produced here. The Twin Cities seemed to be developing into a new hot spot for motion picture production. The scene is not as exciting these days, but since 2005, business has picked up slightly. *North Country* was partially shot in northern Minnesota, *Sweetland* in western Minnesota, *A Prairie Home Companion* in St. Paul, and, most recently, the Coen Brothers' *A Serious Man* was shot in the Twin Cities. Several other less publicized movies were produced here during that time. We all hope for more to come our way soon.

Despite the decline, there are still opportunities for actors in film and TV. Though there have not been an abundance of major motion pictures produced here in the last several years, there are many filmmakers producing independent films. Further, according to the Film and TV Board's Minnesota Production Guide, there are several TV series in production, including shows for HGTV, ESPN, The Discovery Channel, Outdoor Channel, PBS, National Geographic, Food Network, The Travel Channel, and USA Network, among others. Though film and TV opportunities are not numerous, they do exist if you know where to look for them!

The Minnesota Film and TV Board.

The main source of information about the film and TV business in town is the Minnesota Film and TV Board. From the website: "The Minnesota Film and TV Board's mission is to build and promote the art and commerce of the moving image industry." While most actors will not have much direct contact with the Film Board, it is a good idea to keep tabs on what they are doing and how we can help the cause. If any great film or TV opportunities come this way, you can bet that the Minnesota Film and TV Board has a hand in it somewhere. Consult their website hotline frequently if you want to keep up with the film industry here.

Two things to remember about the board: First, they do not exist to promote opportunities for actors; their mission is to promote the entire industry. Actors are just a small piece of the puzzle. Second, the board is a non-profit organization. All actors in Minnesota might want to ponder this idea: "Ask not what the Film Board can do for you, but what you can do for the Film Board." Former Film and TV Board executive director, Craig Rice, said something to that effect in the annual Film Board gathering a few years ago. Current executive director, Lucinda Winter, and her tiny staff run the Film Board on a tight budget.

Something you should know about the Minnesota Film and TV Board.

From the website:

> We are a non-profit public/private partnership, which means we receive funds from the State of Minnesota that must be privately matched. For every dollar we raise privately, the state releases $3 of our funds, which makes every contribution, no matter how small, that much more powerful.

Here is an idea: What if every actor in town were to give $10 to the Film and TV Board? That donation would then add $30 from the State of Minnesota. I cannot think of a better way to maximize your tax-deductible contribution and take control of a few of your tax dollars! Spread the word; there is an easy donation page on the website! Or mail a check to:

Minnesota Film and TV Board
Designer's Guild Building
401 N. 3rd Street, Suite 440
Minneapolis, Minnesota 55401

The Minnesota Film and TV Board's website (mnfilmtv.org).

Occasionally, acting opportunities are posted on the website's "hotline" section. You will also find interesting articles, a filmography, and TV-ography of productions here in our home state.

Check out the Minnesota Production Guide.

On the Film Board's website you will find the Production Guide. Its primary function is to provide the film and TV industry—including those from out of state—with all the necessary information they need to shoot here. While the guide is not necessarily of specific use to actors, it is an interesting book to peruse. Find it at mnfilmtv.org.

When major motion pictures come to town, how do I get into them?

First, know that you are highly unlikely to become a film star in a movie shot here. While major motion pictures are occasionally produced here, the big name roles are rarely, if ever, cast here. The major roles are almost always cast on the coasts, though smaller roles are sometimes available for local actors. Auditions for such roles are usually offered through the casting directors and/or agents, and most often these are available to union (SAG) actors. (See Chapter 5 for union information.)

While it is next to impossible for brand new actors to land any speaking roles, it is often relatively easy to be an extra. These opportunities may be advertised in the Sunday *Star Tribune,* on the actor websites, or through an agency. (See Appendix C for a more complete list of audition sources.)

Roles for major motion pictures that are advertised locally.

You will occasionally see an ad in the paper or on the actor websites for a feature film audition to be held at one of the casting director's offices. This will usually be a search for a child's role of a specific age and type. If the audition is at one of the casting director's offices, you can be assured it is for real. Also know that it could very well be a national search. They will audition perhaps a hundred children here and hundreds of children in several other cities. If you show up for one of these, be prepared to wait in line knowing that your odds are long, but the opportunity is real.

You will rarely see an ad for adult roles in major films. They will fill these few roles through the talent agencies.

Modeling and acting schools offering TV and film opportunities for your children.

Some schools promise big audition opportunities for your kids. For these opportunities, you may have to pay thousands of dollars to take classes. For various reasons, I choose not to associate with these organizations. You will have to be the judge of how to spend your money on educational opportunities for your children. Please see Chapter 13 for much more information about kids and the acting biz.

I want to be an extra!

The easiest way to be in a movie is to be an extra. Know that this job does not pay well, it is not glamorous, and it means little on a resume; however, it is a way to get a glimpse of a movie set.

For a very full day (sometimes ten to fifteen hours or more), an extra will make from nothing to $150. There are so many folks who are willing to be extras that the going rate is very low and the hours can be very long. The typical rate is $35 a day. Even then, your agent's commission can be taken out of that $35. Thus, do not do extra work for the money.

When I was just starting out, the fabulous classic *Drop Dead Fred* was shooting in town. I did a couple of days on that film. A typical extra day involves sitting for long hours in a holding room until they are ready for you on the set. Sometimes this holding room will not even have enough chairs, so you may pass the time sitting on the floor. You are then herded in and positioned. They rehearse and shoot the scene several times, and then you are herded back to your holding room to sit for hours longer.

While it is not necessarily exciting and glamorous, it is something that new actors may wish to consider doing once or twice. It is interesting to see a movie set and the huge crew involved, and you will learn first hand what "hurry up and wait" means. If you are lucky, you will spend your time in the holding room networking with other new actors. If you are smart, you will also bring a good book or deck of cards to pass the time!

My brush with fame on this movie? Listening to Phoebe Cates whine about how long it was taking to get the shot. Imagine a whiny, loud, twenty- year-old voice: "Acting time. I want to act now!" (Hmm, does she get *any* acting time anymore?)

What is a stand-in?

A stand-in is a small step up from an extra. You may be paid a few bucks more, and you may get to spend a little more time on the set. Your role is to stand or sit in the place of one of the characters so that the crew can light the shot with a real person in place. Once the set is ready, they move you out and the featured actors in. My only experience as a stand-in was in another classic of the American cinema, *The Mighty Ducks*. Being a stand-in is not much more exciting than being an extra, but if you have never seen it before, it is interesting to watch all that is involved in lighting a shot.

My brush with fame on this one? As I was herded off of the set and the featured actors came in, I learned that I am taller than Emilio Estevez. Exciting. The scene I worked on as a stand-in? Cut from the film. Even the chair I sat in ended up on the proverbial cutting room floor.

Independent films and student films.

There are many independent filmmakers in town. Occasionally they will search for actors via the want ads or the various websites. Rarely will these be paying jobs for actors. It is expensive to make a movie or video, so the filmmaker's budget will be spent on shooting and editing. Filmmakers often invest their own money in order to hone their filmmaking skills. Doing an independent film is a great way to hone your own camera acting skills. Many actors do student films and low-budget independent films for the experience, and to get a copy of their scenes for a demo reel. (See Chapter 3 for more information about demos and reels.)

I have done just a few independent films with two local filmmakers, Joel Itman and Jon Springer. All gave me valuable experience. I landed the first role via an ad in the paper and the other two via word of mouth. (The films are not well known, though Jon Springer is a respected local filmmaker. His film, *The Hagstone Demon*, has gotten great reviews.)

If you answer an ad in the paper, you have no way of knowing the talent or experience of the filmmaker, nor will you know the quality of the script. If the filmmaker is sincere about his or her work, you will probably have a great experience.

Again, anyone can post an audition notice. Be sure to trust your instincts when you show up for the audition. If it does not feel right, walk away. You may be wise to attend any unknown auditions with another actor. While I have not heard of negative experiences from actors in the Twin Cities, always use good judgment. Walking away from an audition that does not feel right will not ruin your career. If it does not feel professional, you probably do not want to work with them anyway.

Where do I find out about independent film opportunities?

Check the usual sources listed in Appendix C. Matthew Feeney's *Walden Entertainment* may be a great place to learn about opportunities to work as an extra.

Friend and fabulous actor Charles Hubbell suggests that you check www.ifpnorth.org—the source for independent filmmakers. This is a hub for local independent filmmakers, so if you network with this organization, you may find some opportunities.

Charles also suggests that you contact the Minneapolis Community and Technical College Film Department. Supplying them with your name and e-mail address can help them find you when students are looking for actors to help with their various projects. (Beginning actors may want to gain a little experience on your resume and comfort in front of the camera before you pursue independent film work.)

Signing contracts for independent films.

If you do an independent film that the filmmaker hopes to sell, you will likely be asked to sign a contract. For an actor, this type of contract gives the filmmaker the right to use footage of you in the film, and it may specify financial compensation, if any. (For more details about this type of contract and others, see Chapter 16.)

How do I find out about TV opportunities?

There are not many TV opportunities in town, but if any come your way they will likely happen via an agent or personal contacts. Local companies produce the various TV series that are shot here, and many find talent through local agencies. Most of the shows shot locally are not sitcoms or dramatic series. They are more often informative entertainment in which actors serve as hosts.

There are also creative folks in town who produce and pitch their own TV series ideas. *Comedy Hotel* (on local channel 45) and *Let's Bowl* (on Comedy Central) are two that immediately come to mind. (Though sadly, they are no longer on the air.) Unless a producer chooses to advertise an audition, word of mouth and professional contacts are the only ways that I know to get in on this type of project.

If you do land a television acting or hosting gig, you may wish to have an agent involved in the contract negotiations. If it is a low budget, local-cable-access deal, this may not be necessary. However, if there is talk of a show going regional or national, you may want to seek out good advice and representation.

How does a TV show find its way to Minnesota?

Often, shows that are shot or produced here have been developed here. A production company will develop ideas for shows and will pitch their ideas to the networks.

In 2003, I attended a great event hosted by the Minnesota Film and TV Board that dealt with how to pitch and sell shows to cable TV channels. Representatives from the Discovery Channel and the Food Network (among others) were there to discuss how they find new shows and what they are seeking. Many local production companies were in attendance, and some had the opportunity to pitch their concepts to these representatives.

When pitching a show, producers seemed much like an actor at an audition. They had a very limited amount of time to "show their stuff." There are thousands of production companies across the country trying to pitch their ideas, just as there are hundreds of thousands of actors auditioning. It can be just as difficult for producers to be noticed as it is for actors.

Before an idea becomes an actual show, the production company may need to produce a pilot to show the network. Occasionally, they will need talent for these shows, and that is where we actors come in. Some production companies will use talent that they already know, and some will hold auditions. Again, these auditions will usually happen via your agent.

Reality TV

Sadly, it seems that reality TV is here to stay. Yes, they audition here for some of these things. If you want to be an actor, do not bother. If you just want your fifteen minutes of fame, go ahead.

The advent of reality TV coincided with threats of actor, writer, and director strikes. Production companies and networks feared financial hardship when confronted with a lack of acting, writing, and directing talent. Reality shows are a way to "talent-proof" TV so that advertisers will still pay the bills when strikes happen.

The greater the number of reality TV shows, the fewer the jobs available for legitimate actors. To be quite honest, I think most reality TV is mind-numbing, trashy sensationalism. (Okay, I sometimes watch *American Idol* and *The Biggest Loser*, but. . . .) Occasionally there are reality show auditions here in the Twin Cities. The producers advertise in the media or they call local talent agencies and casting directors. Audition for these things if you would enjoy it, but do not do it to become an actor. Know any reality TV "stars" who are now successful actors? (Other than Jennifer Hudson, of course.)

Home shopping network opportunities

The shopping networks book talent through talent agencies and sometimes via ads in the paper. Shop NBC shoots here in town. Shopping is not my thing (and shopping from my TV really is not my thing) so I have never pursued this. However, if it sounds interesting to you, watch for audition notices in the paper or cultivate a relationship with the agencies that book this work. (See Appendix A for a listing of agencies.)

The pay can vary. Recently a friend looked into a shopping gig that would pay $25 per hour to be an on-air host and around $250 to do promotional spots for the show. This is well below the going non-union and union rates for hosting any kind of show. However, it is great money compared to most temp-agency office work, so if you would enjoy it, go for it.

Another friend hosted a shopping show for a while, but negotiated his contract to be on a commission basis. He reports that he made pretty good money. If you pursue this, you may wish to investigate working for commission.

Additional film and TV resources for those who are curious.

While the following organizations are not in the business of offering opportunities for actors, you may want to check them out to learn much more about the filmmaking community in town. (Do not call them with acting issues; they likely will not have anything for you.) These organizations will link you to many more. (Check Appendix L for a little more detail about each.)

- Screenwriter's Workshop (screenwritersworkshop.org)
  528 Hennepin Avenue, Suite 507, Minneapolis, Minnesota 55403
- IFP Minnesota Center for Media Arts (ifpnorth.org)
  2446 University Avenue W., Suite 100, St. Paul, Minnesota 55114
  (Independent Feature Project is national organization, ifp.org.)
- Intermedia Arts Minnesota (intermediaarts.org)
  2822 Lyndale Avenue S., Minneapolis, Minnesota 55408
- Minnesota Film Arts (mnfilmarts.org)
  309 Oak Street S.E., Minneapolis, Minnesota 55414
- Minnesota Women in Film and Television (mnwift.org)
- Walker Art Center (walkerart.org)
  1750 Hennepin Avenue, Minneapolis, Minnesota 55403
- Shoot in Minnesota (shootinminnesota.org)
- Twin Cities International Film Festival, October, 2010 (tcfilmfest. com)

The 48 hour film project.

If you have no experience in film, this annual event is a great place to start. Attend as an audience member and you will see dozens of local fillmmakers at work. Or, dive in head first and audition or volunteer! (48hourfilm.com/Minneapolis).

Final word on film and TV opportunities.

I wish I could offer more information and encouragement to aspiring film and TV actors. If your goal is to be a movie or television star, you are simply in the wrong town. While there are opportunities here, they certainly are not star-making vehicles. If you are determined to work in film and TV in this area, stay in touch with the organizations listed above and the Minnesota Film and TV Board. If something big is happening, you will be sure to hear about it through one of these organizations.

CHAPTER 12

Voice-overs

Nice work if you can get it.

Voice work is some of the most coveted work in this business. When you listen to a voice-over, it sounds easy to do; but do not underestimate the skill it takes to be a good voice talent. It is great work if you can get it. This chapter will help you give it a shot.

They say that voice-overs are almost impossible to break into.

Yes, and no. Voice work is a very competitive part of the business here in the Twin Cities. However, new people do break in all the time. In the early 1990s I produced my first voice-demo and shopped it around to the agents. It took a few years to break in, but eventually I did.

> If I had listened to the people who said it was impossible, I would not be doing voice-overs today.

I have listened to hundreds of voice-demos while screening new talent for my agency. Of the hundred or more demos submitted for each two-year cycle, there are always a handful of new folks who catch our attention. Five or six new people make it onto the agency roster each time the agency produces a new demo, and often these new people have success.

Though it is difficult to break in, it is not impossible. Brace yourself for the inevitable rejections and gather your patience. If you really want to do voice work, go for it! Here is lots of practical advice to help you get started.

Changing technology is changing the voice-over world.

The past ten years have brought about *major* changes in the voice-over business. First, high-speed internet technologies have allowed clients to easily hire voice talent from other markets. In essence, local actors are competing with voice talent from all over the country.

Second, many are taking advantage of new technology to do voice-over work from home. A moderate investment may enable actors to produce voice auditions and even voice-over jobs from a home studio. It may sound simple, but audio quality is always a challenge. Finding clients and marketing your work is another challenge. First, I will focus on the local voice-over business from a traditional approach. Later in the chapter, I will tackle the internet voice-over market and the home studio pros and cons.

Are there really a lot of opportunities to do voice-overs in the Twin Cities?

Yes, there are lots of opportunities for both union and non-union actors. It may not seem that way to everyone because a good percentage of the voice work goes to the same, limited pool of talent. There are folks in town who make their living doing primarily voice work. There are many others who book only occasional voice-overs. Several of the successful agencies in town have voice-demos that contain dozens of different voices—most of whom work at least once in a while.

> "There's a misconception out there that anyone can do voice-over work if they have a good/interesting/strong set of pipes. Not so. Yes, you need to have a voice that people want to listen to, and a deep voice or an interesting sound may work to your advantage. However, you also need to be able to nail a cold read, deliver nuance, and have serious interpretation skills."
>
> —Laura McDonnell, actor/agent, NUTS, ltd.

What does it take to be a voice talent?

In many ways, voice work requires the greatest amount of skill from an actor. You have only your voice to convey everything. Your eyes, face, and gestures are not there to support you. Many gigs require tremendous subtlety, impeccable timing, and the ability to cold read well. The longer the copy, the smoother you must be. Studio time is expensive for the client, so there is no time to wait around for you to get it right. Further, if you cannot get it right, then the audio engineer has to spend extra time, sometimes hours, piecing together your work. Either the client is billed for that time, or the studio must eat the cost. (And in that case, they may not call you again!)

To be a successful voice talent, you need at least some, if not all of these qualities:

- A great voice—smooth, clear, rich, easy on the ears.
- An interesting voice—raspy, cute and perky, deep and gravelly, etc.
- Excellent cold reading ability.

- Excellent diction and enunciation. (If you have a speech impediment, even if it is subtle, your success may be limited.)

- Acting talent and skill.

- Ability to take direction and *immediately* translate it into performance ("speed it up," "slow it down," "warmer," "brighter," "more energy," "more conversational," "more intimate," etc.).

- Consistency, flexibility, and spontaneity—all at the same time.

And, of course, you need a great voice-demo (discussed in detail later).

"My friends tell me I have a great voice. They say I should do voice-overs."

Who are "they"? Do your friends know anything about the biz? I cannot tell you how often agents hear this. You may indeed have a great voice, but to an agent, this line does not mean a thing. Do not approach an agent this way.

If you want to get into voice work, it will take a lot more than a great voice. If you have a great sounding voice, that is a good start, but it is only a start. You will be competing with some of the finest, most experienced actors in town. Do not be intimidated; just know what you are up against, and know that you need to prepare yourself to face the competition. If you have a great voice, you will need to demonstrate it with a great voice-demo.

A lot of commercials just sound like announcers. What is so difficult about doing an announcer style read?

Nothing. Many actors can easily read like an announcer. Announcer-type voice gigs require a great voice and smooth reading. Voice talent who do primarily announcer-style reads can sometimes get away without being great actors, but they typically have great pipes and great cold-reading skills. Most voice work requires precise timing, acting ability, and direct-ability. If you cannot take direction and execute that direction quickly and adeptly, even an announcer with a great voice will not have a lot of success in the voice-over business.

Voice-over work is mostly for actors who do cartoon voices, right?

No. You commonly hear about famous actors doing the voices for Disney animated movies and such, but that is just the tip of the iceberg. The voice-work for actors here in the Twin Cities is quite different from the work available in Hollywood. There may be a little work here for cartoon-style voices, but the vast majority of local voice work is much more straightforward. The following pages will give you a sampling of the great variety of voice-overs that are recorded here.

What's a typical voice gig like?

Most actors love to do voice work. The jobs are often short and sweet, and they pay well. You do not have to pack wardrobe, dress up, or do makeup. Once you are an established voice talent, you do not have to audition for many of your gigs. Voice work is the gravy of the biz.

Voice work does not have quite the same varied circumstances as on-camera work, but you will still find a variety. Most voice-overs are done in a recording studio, but there are exceptions.

Radio and TV commercial voice-overs are almost always done in a studio. There are dozens of audio studios in town. Many production companies have their own in-house studios as well. Some of the biggest and best known studios in town for high-quality audio production are: Audio Ruckus (a 2007 merger of Cookhouse and Voiceworks), Sound 80, Babble-On, and Aaron Stokes Music. The folks at all these places are great to work with.

For commercial voice-overs with short copy, you need to be adept at reading copy accurately so that they can direct the subtleties—over and over and over again. Often, you have to nail precise timing on nearly every take. Thirty seconds of commercial copy has to be done in less than thirty seconds, or the take is no good. (The studio can sometimes "compress" a second or so, but they count on you to be able to get it done.) A ten second "donut" has to be done in less than ten seconds. (A donut is a section of copy that falls between lyrics in the music, other sound effects, or audio clips.) With experience, voice talent can develop this sense of timing.

Demo-spots. Occasionally voice talent are called to do demo-spots. These are sample commercials produced for test marketing. They do not actually shoot the spot, they use the voice-over with animated drawings. Here is how it works: The ad agency will propose several spots to the client. The client will choose a few, and then they will make those into demo-spots. The demo-spots are then shown to consumers for feedback. (For example, how is this spot received by soccer moms in Des Moines?) Actors are paid less for demo-spots than for commercials—around $150 for union work, $100 for non-union.

Tags. Ah, tags! That's a beautiful word in the voice-over business. A tag or tag line is the extra bit of information at the end of a commercial. For example: If there are several locations for stores in a region—the Twin Cities, Rochester, Duluth, and Fargo—they will use the same spot, but add a different tag for broadcast in each location. The beauty of this? You get paid an additional fee for each tag. Often the fee is $50 to $75 or more per tag. Do the math! (When you do tags, be sure to call your agent after the job to confirm the number of tags so that it gets billed properly.)

Industrial voice-overs are done at a huge variety of locations—from big audio studios to home studios to corporate conference rooms to storage closets. (Sometimes the storage closet is the quietest place in the building.) The majority of industrial voice-overs are done in studios, but it depends on the budget of the job and the sound quality needed.

Industrial voice-overs done in the studio are much like commercial voice gigs, except the copy is usually longer and time limits are not as strict. I have done industrial voice gigs ranging from a sentence or a paragraph to hundreds of pages that require multiple days in a studio.

Subjects and uses for industrial voice-overs are broadly varied:

- Phone response systems or on-hold messages.
- Interactive computer training or e-learning.
- Audio training; for example, CDs or mp3s to which sales people listen as they are driving.
- Educational materials for schools.
- Medical training.
  - Educating patients prior to a medical procedure.
  - Training doctors how to do the procedure itself. (The video shows the medical procedure while the voice-over describes it.)
- Sales training.
- Safety training.
- Training for any material production process you can imagine.
- Kiosks in stores: Push a button and your voice announces the piece of music the customer is about to hear.
- Point-of-purchase videos: TVs showing a product demonstration next to the retail product display.
- DVDs included within product packaging—video instructions about how to assemble or use the product.
- Kiosks at trade shows: Touch the screen and hear a description of a manufacturing process.
- Pre-recorded announcements at conventions/awards banquets, etc.
- Marketing pieces on company websites.

That list just skims the surface, but it gives you an idea of what an industrial voice-over might be.

Audio books.

There are not a lot of audio books recorded here. Big publishing companies in bigger markets (New York) hire actors there. I am told that publishers use the same voices over and over, making it tough for new folks to break in. However, there are occasional opportunities here. I have been fortunate enough to land a couple through connections with my agent and local audio engineers. If you discover how to get into this field, do let me know!

What do typical voice-over gigs pay?

Rates vary for different types of voice-overs. If you are represented by a good agency, a voice job will typically pay at least $150 to $200 per hour, often more. This amount can vary widely based on how the client plans to use the recording.

- Non-broadcast industrials typically pay $200 per one-hour session for non-union actors, slightly more for union actors. (Each additional hour will usually be $50 to $100 per hour or more, depending upon the agency and union status.)

- For broadcast use, the rate will vary by local, regional, or national use. A TV commercial voice-over airing locally will pay between $200 and $300 (again, depending upon the agency and union status). If a spot airs nationally, it can pay closer to $1000 or more. (See Chapter 5 for specific rate comparisons for union and non-union work.)

These are basic examples of the variations in pay, but you can easily see why I say that voice-over work can be the most coveted work in the biz. Please note that the jobs that pay in the thousands are much less common. Even for successful, experienced voice talent, these are too few and far between!

What's an "audio-demo" or "voice-demo"?

A voice-demo is to the voice talent what a portfolio is to the print model. Your demo shows the agent or client what you can do in front of a microphone. It is normally a one- to two-minute sampling of short clips of commercial and industrial voice-overs. (For the Los Angeles market, I am told that demos are expected to be only forty-five seconds.) For more experienced voice talent, the demo contains actual work that they have done for clients. Beginners will need to go to a studio with copy (scripts) in hand, and hire the audio engineer to record and produce your work, complete with sound effects and music. (Details about how to produce a voice-demo follow later in this chapter.)

Do I have to have a voice-demo?

Yes. An actor who is right for a specific role may occasionally be called to audition for or do a voice-over gig without having a voice-demo. Usually these actors are already well known by the agency or client. However, if you want to seriously pursue voice-over work, you must have a professional-sounding demo. Good agencies have talented pools of voice-over artists. If you are new, they will have no idea what you can do unless you show them. The voice-demo is the only way to show your stuff.

What is the difference between my voice-demo and an agency's demo?

An agency demo—currently offered to clients on the web and on CD—contains their entire team of voice talent. Generally, you submit your own ninety-second demo to an agency. If you are chosen to be on the agency demo, you will have to edit your demo according to the agency's specifications. Each actor's demo is then compiled onto the agency demo; the CDs are then sent to clients and recording studios, and all actor demos are posted on the agency website. Most local agents have twenty to forty men and twenty to forty women on the roster. Numbers will vary.

Currently, actors submit demos via CD or mp3 file. Clients often use agency websites to screen talent, rather than pulling out the CD. Digital formats may soon make CDs obsolete.

How can I hear a sample of professional voice-demos?

Go to agency websites to listen to their voice-demos. (Appendix A lists web addresses for local talent agencies.)

My agent does not send me out for voice work. Why?

You will rarely be considered for voice work unless you have a professional demo. I know actors who complain that they are not considered for voice work, but they have never bothered to make a demo. Do your homework or you cannot expect an agent to consider you.

Even if you do produce a voice-demo, your agent may still not accept you onto the agency demo. It is a very competitive, subjective business. Either work with a coach to keep trying to improve yourself and your demo, or shop your demo around to other agents.

Should I answer an ad in the paper? "Complete demo for under $200!"

New voice-over instructors appear from time to time. If you see an ad for a flat rate for a complete voice-over demo, be sure to ask questions and listen to samples of their work. Ask if they will supply original copy, or if they use the same scripts for more than one actor. You want your demo to be polished, professional, and unique.

I have listened to some of the bargain basement demos, and they often sound the same—dull. You should shop around and trust recommendations from fellow actors and your agent.

If you have a brother-in-law who owns a recording studio and you can record there for free, that is great. However, you had better know what a good demo sounds like, because he likely will not. (See Appendix H for voice-over coaches, engineers, and studios.)

How easy is it to get onto an agency's demo?

Most people who are on an agent's demo stay on it for years. In any given demo cycle—two to three years is typical—only a handful of people leave. The agent may cut some, some move out of town, and some join or leave the union. Thus, there are rarely more than a handful of places available on an agent's voice-over roster.

Usually, 100 or more people are competing for those few spots. I have helped to screen hundreds of demos submitted to my agent over the past several years. About three-fourths of them do not make the first cut. If we hear potential, we put it into the maybe pile. The rest go straight to the trash. If that seems harsh, think about it this way: Would a corporation meet with a job applicant if he or she does not submit a professional resume? Would a good band consider bringing on a lead guitarist if he or she is still taking intermediate guitar lessons?

If someone submits a demo that shows little talent or training, or shows a total lack of understanding of the voice-over business, the demo gets tossed in the trash. You would not believe what people send in! We have received CDs from people with a few minutes of a radio call-in show they once hosted; we have listened to demos from people who do many animal impressions and various bizarre sound effects with their mouths; we have listened to CDs of people reading Shakespeare (and not well); we have listened to demos of people shouting out pro-wrestling and monster-truck commercials, etc. I have no clue what these people think they are going to do in this business. The problem is, they have no clue either.

On the other hand, we receive many good demos as well. After the first cut, the agency team listens to the remaining demos. Many of these folks are quite talented. The final cut often takes into consideration the current roster of agency voice talent and the agency's need at that particular time. Sometimes even actors with great demos do not make this cut simply because the agency already has plenty of actors with the same sound and style. Of hundreds of demos, probably ten to fifteen make it to the actual interview. The final candidates are interviewed and auditioned, and only a handful of these folks are invited onto the agency roster.

My guess is that most agents' numbers are similar. Most actors would love to do voice work. It is extremely competitive. You really have to have a great demo to get agencies to consider you.

Can I get voice work if I am not on an agent's demo?

Yes, but it can be challenging. First, you may try to market yourself locally the old-fashioned way—sending your demo (CD via snail mail or digital demo via e-mail) all over town to ad agencies, recording studios, and production companies. I know of a couple of actors who could not get an agent to represent them for voice work, so they did their own leg work and marketing. I am sure most of their CDs ended up in the circular file; however, the small amount of work they got was enough to get the agent's attention. They proved themselves marketable, and both ended up on agency demos.

Or, second, you may wish to purchase home audio equipment and try your luck in the internet voice-over pool. Details about this follow later in this chapter.

Where do I go to get training or coaching for voice-overs?

There are a few voice-over classes in town; I have listed these in Appendix H. You are looking for a coach who directs you like you are an actor, not as if you are a poet at a literary reading or a radio DJ. Voice work is not about sounding a certain way; it is about communicating. Voice-over coaching should be focused on good communication and good acting.

Further, there is no need to train for years to try your hand at voice-over work. Work with a good coach. Then, when you feel confident and ready, produce your demo and get it out to agents. Experienced actors may need only a few sessions to learn the specifics of interpretation and the microphone. Many talented actors have achieved voice-over success through on-the-job training only. Newer actors may need several sessions to gain experience and confidence.

Also know that if you have a vocal problem or a diction problem, you may be wise to first focus on breath support and diction before you attempt voice-over coaching. There are good vocal coaches in town, too. (See Appendix F for suggested classes.)

Voice-overs are not the same as jingle singing.

Jingle singing is another subject entirely. I am not aware of any agencies that specifically represent singers, though occasionally clients may audition singers via talent agencies. Talent agencies usually know which talent are professional singers or musical theater artists. The composers and audio engineers who produce jingles often use well-known local singers. If you are not a known singer, you may be at a disadvantage. You will need to produce a separate demo for your pursuit of this type of work, and you will need to send it to studios and ad agencies on your own. My guess is that producing such a demo is expensive. I would not commit to this expense until you first get a foot in the door of the theater, music, or commercial/industrial industry in town. Once you are in, your connections may lead you to commercial singing opportunities.

Do I have to pay to be on an agency's demo?

Yes. It is expensive to produce quality CDs and websites. It is also expensive to duplicate and then distribute CDs to clients. Maintaining audio files on an agency website only adds to the expense. Agencies will share these costs with the actors. Typically voice talent will pay from $200 to $400 to be on the agency demo. Most agencies use their demos for a two- to three-year cycle. Thus, you will need to pay that amount every two or three years to be included on subsequent demos. (This is in addition to the cost of producing your own ninety-second demo.)

It is an expensive proposition, but keep in mind that if you book only two or three voice gigs, you will cover your expenses. As always, remember that you do not want to give this kind of money to anyone unless you know they have a solid reputation in the biz.

Which studios can help actors produce voice-over demos?

Almost any recording studio can help you produce a voice-demo, but you would be wise to use a studio that actually produces real commercials for clients. Again, Appendix H lists many reputable studios.

Before you book studio time, know that an audio engineer will not hold your hand through the process. Audio engineers are not voice and acting coaches. They may have some good feedback for you, but they generally will not direct you to the subtleties of the script. Consider bringing a voice-over coach with you to the studio.

Further, you will need to bring your own commercial copy—selections that are right for your type and your voice. Expect to pay for three to five hours of total studio time to produce a demo. This will include your time to read the copy and the audio engineer's time to edit and add music and sound effects. At $75 to $300 per hour, studio time is expensive. Be sure to be organized before you go in.

Voice-over work from your own home studio.

There is an ever-increasing buzz about actors who are pursuing voice-over work via the internet from their own home audio studio. Real clients are holding auditions and hiring voice talent via the internet. No one really knows how this new twist in voice-overs will alter the business in the coming years. Change is coming.

There will always be a need for the superior audio quality that the best recording studios provide. I would say that the majority of voice-work in town is recorded with talent live in the studio rather than remotely from home. Further, an actor at home could rarely match the experience and knowledge of a top-notch audio engineer.

That being said, there is an established, on-line voice-over business. For an introduction to this new world, visit some of the websites that market voice-over talent: voicebank.net, Voice123.com, and Voices.com. Voicebank.net hosts many talent agency demos. Several local agencies now use voicebank to host their on-line demos. These sites have thousands of individual voice demos—some better than others, of course. Clients can search these voices, post an audition to the masses, or invite individuals to audition for their projects. Sounds blissfully easy? There are some challenges to working the voice-over market this way.

What equipment do I need?

I am not a technical expert nor am I an expert in this new voice-over world. I have my own equipment at home, but have not yet mastered its use. I may eventually enter the on-line voice-over game; for now, I simply hope to use it to audition from home. My investment was about $600. You can spend far more.

Don Cosgrove (thetalentcenter.com) teaches a class, "Make $$ on the internet with your voice!" Don has been in the biz for a long time, and his classes are reasonably priced. If you are curious about the internet voice-over world, by all means work with Don. He will walk you through the basics, including the equipment you need.

Another great resource for setting up a home studio is *The Voice Actor's Guide to Home Recording* by Harlan Hogan and Jeffrey Fisher

(Thomson Course Technology, 2005). The subtitle is: "A money- and time-saving non-technical guide to making your own voiceover demos and auditioning from home or on location." The book discusses all aspects of the business—from computer and technical needs, to navigating the web, to auditioning and reaching clients. The technical discussions in this book still make my head spin, but if you have just a little bit of technical savvy, this book will help you get started.

What is the upside of this new voice-over world?

- This is a way to get into the game without wading into the world of talent agencies. If the agencies are not interested in you, you can still try your hand at voice-overs.

- Even if you are with an agent, you will often be waiting for the phone to ring. Marketing your voice-over talent on the internet may allow you to seize some control over your own career, rather than waiting for your agent to drive your career.

- When/if you get work, you can work from home.

- The hourly pay can be quite good.

- For established voice talent, this can be a beautiful addition to what you already do. I know several experienced actors who have their own studios. They do not need to begin marketing from scratch; they simply offer the home recording option to their clients as an added feature. Further, they can audition from home without running to the agency studio for every audition.

Local voice-over artist Veronica March adds: "Another 'upside' to the new internet voice-over world is that it is a great way to practice your auditioning skills. I have always felt that even if I never booked a job through Voice123.com or Voices.com, I'd gotten my money's worth in the subscription fees by having access to the widest array of copy you could imagine—everything from traditional TV and radio spots to audio books, documentaries, voice messaging, web-based training, promos, animation, etc."

- If a client hires you, you may become a favorite of that client; thus, they will hire you without subsequent auditions. Any successful voice talent builds their volume of work through this kind of repeat business.

The challenges?

- **Cost:** The initial investment will be from a few hundred dollars to thousands. Microphone and basic software are at the low end of that scale, more elaborate technology and a quality-recording booth at the high end.

- **Technology:** For those of us somewhat intimidated by or impatient with technology, this seems a daunting challenge. Don Cosgrove says you can do this without technical expertise. However, to really swim with the big fish, you may need to deal with a little more technology. Some online voice talent offer their services via an ISDN line. This additional technology comes with significant expense. Further, to be your own full-service talent studio, a basic knowledge of editing may be necessary.

- **Expanding competition:** Your competition is nationwide. Online, you will compete with thousands of voices, and this number will only grow. On Voice123.com, I did a quick search for my competition: non-union, middle-age female voices who do commercials and promotions. The search yielded 1136 people. To be heard above the growing throng will require significant marketing efforts.

- **Audio quality:** Differences in audio quality are evident, even to the untrained ear. You may be able to get in the game with minimal expense, but the best talent invest in quality.

- **Availability and time:** It takes time to audition. It takes time to weed through the audition postings on the websites. It takes time to field requests for auditions in your e-mail inbox. If you are not at home near your computer and audio-studio, you will not be able to reply to all of the auditions quickly enough. If your lifestyle does not allow quiet time at the computer to get it all done, this may not be the right path for you.

- **Pricing and billing:** You will need to act as your own agent. Marketing, pricing, billing, and financial records will all rest on your shoulders. In the traditional voice-over world, prices vary widely with the client's use of your work. Broadcast, non-broadcast, internet use, point of sale—I do not know the going rates for everything, and I have been doing this for years. If you are content to work for a simple hourly rate, this may not matter to you.

- **Marketing:** To have great success, you likely will need to do some kind of marketing and advertising, or you will be buried amidst the thousands of other voices.

Success stories.

Despite my trepidation about this new voice-over market, I know of several success stories. I have met a few people who make quite a bit of their income from home. These tend to be established voice-over actors who now work for their clients from home studios. These folks have high-quality equipment.

My friend Veronica was new to the talent world about two years ago. She is a diligent and hard-working marketer; she has talent; and she works to make the most of it. She attacked the voice-over world from all fronts: She trained with great coaches; she produced a killer voice-demo; she established a great website for her new business; she pursued the talent agencies, distributed professional marketing materials to studios and ad agencies, invested in great equipment and technology, and established herself on

> **If you are serious about pursuing voice work, get some training and learn what you are doing before you spend a lot of money on studio time.**

the internet voice sites. She is not yet reaping incredible wealth, but her business continues to grow.

If you want to dabble in the voice-over market, you certainly do not need to invest that kind of time and expense. You may be able to make a little money on the side with a small investment of money and energy. However, if you want to make a significant income doing voice-overs via the internet, know that it may not be as simple as getting a microphone and setting up shop on a website.

A great resource for experienced, professional talent.

Celia Siegel was a top voice-over agent both here and in L.A., becoming an expert in the field of voice-over talent marketing. She now manages a handful of top voice-over talent and markets them to national clients. She also offers consulting services (coaching, branding, and marketing) to those who are determined to grow their voice-over business.

She has a wealth of information and expertise. If you are serious about voice-over work as a business and not just a hobby, and if you have the time, energy, and resources to fully commit, then you would be wise to work with Celia (and her right-hand woman and copywriter, Marnie). Visit celiasiegel.com to learn more.

Producing a voice-demo: A crash course.

Again, see Appendix F for actor training options and Appendix H for specific voice-over resources. If you are determined to try it on your own or if you are an experienced actor who may not need extra training, I hope the following guidelines will be helpful.

Prepping for your studio session.

Listen to professional demos. Go to agency websites to listen on-line. You need to know what a good demo sounds like before you can make one of your own. Be sure to listen for demos of your "type." For example, do not try to emulate a demo with a lot of comedy and character voices if you are a straightforward corporate type.

Choose copy. To find ideas, magazine ads often contain well-written copy. Read them for inspiration and a guide to style as you write your own copy. You only need to write a sentence or two for each cut of your demo. Choose magazines that market to your type. Guys may want to look at sports magazines, *Popular Mechanics* or *Family Handyman*. Young moms and dads should look to parenting magazines. If you have a young sound, look at teen magazines. If you have a more mature sound, try upscale magazines: *Food and Wine* or *Minnesota Monthly*.

Do not over-rehearse! Rehearse and practice on other copy, but do not over-do the spots you might include on your demo. You might want to rehearse using a recorder at home. Play it back to be sure you like what you hear, but be sure not to read and listen so much that you have the sound of your read imprinted into your mind. You will want to be spontaneous and fresh in the booth, not stuck in a rhythm or pattern that you have rehearsed.

Do not fill the demo with radio-style announcer spots. You hear lots of "announcers" on radio and television. If you have a great set of pipes (a deep, rich voice), you might want to include one or two announcer style spots, but avoid using too much of this. Agents get lots of demos from folks doing radio-style spots. These are not going to catch an agent's attention. If you are reading for an announcer or narrator role, read it with some real communication happening, not just a canned announcer sound. If you do not know the difference, get some coaching.

Do not do a lot of crazy characters. If you do character voices *really* well, then include what you do well. However, unless you are a master at character voices, keep it to a minimum. There are exceptions to every rule; there are a few people in town who specialize in character voices. If you are really good, you may be able to compete with them. If you do funny characters, be sure your copy is funny, too.

Do not do a variety of all the dialects you can do. We stage actors like to think we can do great dialects: cowboy, cockney British, leprechaun Irish, Russian, Jamaican, etc. I have done some decent dialect work on stage, but I doubt I would pass for a native in any of them. If your dialect is not flawless, do not put it on the demo. There is a rare need for dialect voice work in this market. If they need dialects, they will call in the native speakers whenever possible. Then the agent will call their stage actors to audition for it. They will rarely cast it from your demo. If you are not native to a particular region, think twice before putting it on your demo.

Include variety. Again, variety means neither goofy characters nor every dialect you have ever done on stage. Variety in attitude is what you are going for: tongue-in-cheek, laid back and flip, seductive, intimate, teasing, compassionate, high-energy, giddy, sarcastic, etc. Look for copy that coaxes an attitude from you.

Get coaching. You would be wise to get a bit of coaching before you hit the studio. (If you are a non-actor, definitely get coaching or take a class.) A coach can help you narrow down your copy choices. The more prepared you are before you get to the studio, the less you will pay in hourly studio rates.

Choose a studio and make an appointment. You will need to schedule about one or two hours to record your voice, and two or three hours for the engineer to produce the spots. A good engineer will help you edit your spots and add appropriate music and sound effects to compliment your work. If you are organized, three or four hours should be enough. If you are really new to voice work and your ducks are not in a row before you go in, you will need more time. (More time = more expense.)

Again, studio time can cost from $75 to $300 per hour or more. That is why you need to be organized and prepared!

In the studio.

Relax. You are not performing for anyone. You can change or revise anything you record. Unless you are up against a tight deadline, you can always go back to the studio a week later and make revisions. It will cost you, but it is often worth it. Just as in the writing process, you might want to do a rough draft and polish it later.

Bring water. I often bring tea as well. Coffee and caffeine will dry you out.

 Studio etiquette. Be on time or early. Your clock is running at the start of your appointment time, not the time you arrive. Also, never touch the microphone or microphone stand. Your engineer will handle it. (You may adjust your copy stand.) Never blow into a microphone.

The microphone. Generally you will want your mouth to be five to eight inches from the microphone, closer if the copy is soft and intimate, a bit farther away if you will be loud. Be aware of "p-pops." If you read directly into the microphone, your plosives (p, b, t) might pop in the microphone. You will usually hear it when it happens. Simply turn your head slightly so that the airflow from your mouth is not flowing directly into the microphone. Your engineer will help you with this.

Be in the moment. If you are an actor, you know what this means. On stage, you do not want to be self-consciously listening and critiquing yourself as you work. You want to be free to communicate in the moment. The same concept applies when you are in front of the microphone. Bring your acting skills to the booth. Do not plan the read. Do not rehearse how you want it to sound. Do not mimic a certain style or sound. Communicate. Who are you talking to? How are you trying to affect them? What action are you playing?

Be physical. A good voice talent is in motion as he/she works. Let your physical energy out while you are reading the copy. It does not matter how you move and gesture as long as the microphone does not hear you moving. If you are stiff and tight physically, it will be apparent in your voice.

Do not edit before you record. You do not need to know exactly what excerpt of each spot will go on your demo. Record them all and decide what to use in which order after you record. Bring in a carefully selected variety of copy—perhaps ten to twelve choices. Record them, then listen and make editing decisions with the studio engineer and your coach.

Editing the demo.

Some audio engineers will take what you have recorded and edit it on their own. If they have done lots of demos, you can trust them. However, be sure to speak up if you do not like something in the finished product. With digital recording these days, changes are easy to make. Other engineers will have you listen in while they edit the demo.

Trust your gut feeling. Your best stuff will strike you when you hear it. If something is not good, it will bother you. Re-record it or throw it out.

Trust your audio engineer. A good engineer knows what he or she hears. They have recorded and edited hundreds of TV and radio spots and hundreds of demos. Trust their opinions when choosing which cuts to use. They can be objective about you. We actors are simply awful at being objective about ourselves.

Be assertive. If you really do not like something, do not let the engineer hurry you through it. Re-record or insist on different music. If something in the edited version really bothers you, then change it. You are paying for the studio time, so be sure that you are a satisfied customer. Yes, trust your engineer, but do not be afraid to voice your opinions. (However, if budget is a concern, be mindful of the clock!)

Choosing music. A music bed helps some spots, and some are better without music. Your engineer will have a music library from which to choose. You can sit back and relax while they search for music for certain spots. Usually their feel for the style of the spot and music is great. Remember that it is your read that matters most. The music is simply the icing on the cake.

Length. Your demo should be a maximum of two minutes. Many agents require a shorter version, often sixty to ninety seconds. Other agencies will request two demos: a sixty-second commercial demo and a sixty-second narration demo. If you do not have agency representation yet, produce a ninety-second demo with a variety of commercial and industrial reads.

Number of cuts. There is no pre-defined number of spots. Commercial cuts should be no longer than ten to fifteen seconds. Some cuts will be only a few seconds. Narration cuts may be longer—perhaps fifteen to thirty seconds. Good demos have a fun variety of rhythm. Your first demo might be pretty simple: five to nine cuts of ten to fifteen seconds each. That is fine. Each time you do a new demo (typically every couple of years), it will be better than the previous.

Previously recorded spots. Be sure to bring a CD or digital version of any real work you have done. Some of it might fit nicely on your demo. Hopefully someday you will have enough work that you only will need to edit your real spots together to make your demos.

Lead with your best. Your first two or three cuts should be your most real, most marketable stuff. If you do not know what your most marketable voice is, be sure to get feedback. A studio engineer or coach will have a pretty good idea once he or she hears you read several pieces of copy. You need to lead with your best because most clients will listen to the first ten seconds of a demo, and, if they do not hear what they are looking for, turn you off and move on to the next actor.

Once your demo is done.

Have several copies made and send them to any agent with whom you would like to work. Do not expect prompt replies from agents. If they are not interested, you likely will not hear anything at all from them. Some agencies produce new demo CDs every couple of years; others simply add new voices to the agency website periodically. Between those times, they may simply toss new demos into a box to review at a later date. Do not be surprised if months or a year go by before you hear anything. A follow-up phone call often will not do you much good. If you are not sure they have received it, feel free to send another one.

If you do not have any success for a year or more, consider making a new and improved demo. Sending the same demo year after year probably will not help. It could be that the agent did not hear enough on your first demo to convince them to give you a shot. Keep working and keep improving.

Getting feedback.

Some voice-over teachers will advise you to send your demo to an agent and request feedback. Some agents may take the time to do this; most will not. As I have said, agents receive hundreds of demos. They rarely will take the time to call an unknown actor to give feedback. They are simply too busy doing business with clients. Do not be disappointed by this; it is just a reality of the biz.

Agents are really nice folks who do not want to disappoint you or dash your hopes. It is difficult to give constructive feedback to a total stranger. When I am asked to critique someone's demo, I'm well aware that this person has spent good money to produce it. I am sometimes hesitant to give blunt, honest feedback, even when I know that is what would be most helpful. Agents are similarly hesitant.

Ask your coach or other actors for feedback. If you know an experienced voice talent, that person may be willing to share some insight. If you have little success with your first demo, seek a different voice-over coach for an objective opinion.

> "Stick-to-it-tiveness and sheer determination are key to this business. If you have these qualities plus a lot of patience you may make it—but it will more than likely take a long time and cost some dollars to get started. If you are determined to be in this business, then do it. It took me about five years of practicing and taking classes and doing scratch demos and agent nagging before I got in with what I consider a good agent. Then it was another few years before I started to get some decent work of any quantity. It is a hard biz to break into, and competition is stiff. Most people do not make it because they get frustrated and give up."
>
> —Anne Burnett, local voice-over artist

Perseverance.

This is perhaps more important in pursuing voice work than in any other part of the acting biz.

Perseverance and patience, great pipes and skill—you will need them all. If and when you break in, it will be worth the effort.

CHAPTER 13

Kids and the Business

With the emphasis on the word business!

I taught junior high English and senior high speech in the public school system for four years before I decided to act full time. I am a teacher at heart, and I have some very strong opinions about kids and acting.

In addition to teaching junior and senior high, I have interviewed dozens of kids and their parents for my agent; I have worked with kids in commercials; I have acted with and directed kids on stage—so I have been around this block a few times. I have also done some research in hopes that this chapter will help you find the right avenues for your child's acting pursuit. The chapter contains only suggestions and ideas; it is up to you to decide what is best for your child.

Parents, please keep in mind the subtitle of this chapter. This is big business. Too many parents approach the professional acting and modeling world as if they were signing up the kids for a school activity or recreational program: They expect to be treated fairly, and they expect their child to be given a fair chance. Business is not about fair play; it is about making money. Folks in the business are not paid to look out for the best interests of your children. That is your job.

Personally, I would suggest little league, soccer, dance classes, piano lessons, summer camp, swimming lessons, school plays, and art classes—anything your child might enjoy—instead of professional acting and modeling work. On the other hand, if your child really wants to try acting and modeling, then support your child's dreams and goals. You as the parent just need to be smart about it. Educate yourself; do not fall for the first sales pitch that claims your child will be a star.

Commercial acting and modeling vs. school plays and educational theater.

Please note that in this chapter I deal primarily with the pursuit of professional acting and modeling work, rather than educational and amateur theater opportunities. Let me be clear: I am all for children doing theater—in schools, churches, communities, etc. Children learn poise, confidence, teamwork, and responsibility from experience in the theater. It is a great place for a child to exercise his or her creativity and imagination. If your child wants to be an actor, encourage all of the theater experience he or she can find!

The world of commercial acting and modeling is a different story. If you sense any lack of encouragement in the tone of this chapter, it is simply because the world of professional acting and modeling can be tough even for adults. I believe that children should be playing and learning, not necessarily trying to make money. Childhood goes by much too quickly; children have the rest of their lives to make money. However, if your child is excited about acting and modeling, and he or she seems to be playing and learning while pursuing it, great. The work can be educationally and (less frequently) financially rewarding. Proceed with enthusiasm, but also proceed with caution.

> "They learn something else that will be a source of enrichment and enjoyment for the rest of their lives—a love and appreciation of live theater. They will learn to look at a play with a truly discerning eye and know something about the process that made it all happen."
> —Jan Hilton, founder of NUTS, ltd. and long-time Theatre in the Round board member

Educate yourself!

Once you determine that your son or daughter wants to be an actor or model, it is time to educate yourself. Suddenly your child expresses the desire to act, and you have no idea where to go. Too many parents answer the first ad they see in the paper and then trust whatever they are told. Would you run your own business that way? Would you select a contractor or repair person from the first ad you see? Shop around and learn before you pay. This is a big business in which lots of money changes hands. There are many marketing and salespeople placing ads and giving presentations designed to separate you from your money.

There is no direct route to finding success in this business. However, there are signs along the road. Read on and learn to recognize them.

I have good news and bad news. First, the bad news . . .

The first half of this chapter contains the bad news: avoiding rip-offs and unnecessary expenses, coping with the drawbacks of the job, etc. You need to know the realities before pursuing this business. The fun part comes later!

Parents, ask yourselves: "Why are we doing this?"

Lots of kids want to be actors. Often, once they get a taste of some of the realities of the job, they change their minds. Parents do, too. My overall rule is this: A child's acting career should be child-driven, not adult-driven. Moreover, it should certainly not be money-driven or stardom-driven. Before you help your child pursue acting, ask yourself, "Why?" Be sure the answer is only because your child really wants to do it.

Two examples: Years ago, I did a few video shoots with a terrific kid named CJ. (Little CJ is now nearly six feet tall!) CJ's mom once told me that he enjoyed the work so much, he would rather do a shoot than go to the cabin on vacation! This was a kid who loved the work, loved the auditions, and had the patience of a saint on the job. On the other hand, I once worked with another terrific freckle-faced kid who booked quite a bit of work. After a year or two, he decided he simply did not like the work very much; thus his mom told the agency that he would not be available anymore. I applaud both of these parents for letting the child drive the career decisions.

If children want to act, they should want to act as much or more than they want to swim on the swim team, sing in the choir, or play with the chess club. If your child enjoys those other things, then do them. Kids should be kids, not little plastic actors ruled by over-zealous stage moms.

That being said, there are lots of kids who just love this acting stuff. If your child is drawn to the world of acting, then absolutely help him or her fill that yearning.

Do not do it for the money.

Few kids make much money in this business. Yes, there is money to be made. If your child books a professional job, he or she will receive professional pay; but do not hold your breath waiting for lots of big paychecks. A little bit of work now and again is quite possible; however, few stars are born here in the Twin Cities. Folks will try to tell you that they can help you "be discovered." Know that stardom and riches are highly unlikely.

Your child's job will also be your job.

If your child has some success in this business, you will need to play the role of chauffeur and chaperone. Auditions and shoots most often happen during the workday. Theater rehearsals often happen during evenings and weekends. Your job will have to allow a bit of flexibility, or you will need to enlist the help of a willing relative or friend.

Kids are often treated as adults by the business.

Much of the information in other chapters of this book will also apply to children. As far as the business is concerned, a professional actor is a professional actor—at age five or ninety-five. Finances, taxes, unions, agents, etc.—you will encounter all of these if you choose to seek professional work for your child. Be sure to consult other chapters of this book when you have specific questions.

Helping your child cope with rejection.

Chapter 2 deals with the subject of survival in a very subjective business. Even experienced, successful actors must deal with rejection. It will be your responsibility to help your child understand the ups and downs that come with being an actor.

> In order to prevent your child from being disappointed about not getting the job, make the audition the goal. If the child feels good about the audition, he or she has gained something important and should be made to feel that way. If they should book the job, great, but the goal should be to enjoy and learn from the audition. If they come out of the audition feeling that they didn't do well, see if you can find out why, and find positives in that, too. Learning what to do better next time is a positive, if the parent can help the child to frame it that way (Jan Hilton).

Be a parent first. This business can be fun and educational for children. Parents can go a long way toward making it so.

Do I need to spend a lot of money to get my child into acting and/or modeling?

Nothing makes me angrier in this business than entities that prey on starry-eyed children and their unwitting parents. You have a legitimate chance to get into the game in the Twin Cities market with only a good photo, a resume, and some postage.

The pursuit of acting work can be quickly soured by an encounter with rip-off artists. I have heard from many frustrated parents who have paid big money and received little value in return. Learn from their experience! As in the adult acting world, there are unethical people who prey on the desires of children who are dying to be actors. Know what you are going to get before you pay for anything in your child's pursuit of acting.

The hard truth: Kids who can really act or who have a truly "great look" may very likely have opportunities in this business without spending much money up front. Kids who do not possess natural acting talent and a really "great look" may not get many opportunities, no matter how much you spend. Acting talent can be honed, polished, and improved; but true talent cannot be taught. Likewise, a really good modeling look can be polished, but cannot be taught. All the money in the world cannot buy talent.

Your child is about to be judged primarily on appearance. Personality will play a role, but look is essential. Look, personality, skill—in that order. It is true for adults, and it is true for kids. To get work, your child must first have a good look for commercial work, then the personality and temperament for it, and finally skill. Skill that one may learn in classes is the last, and perhaps least-important factor. Even the most talented, adorable children will likely be rejected more often than cast. Spending a lot of money on photos and classes may not make a great deal of difference in finding professional opportunities.

> If you are brand new to this business, drop everything right now and go to the Federal Trade Commission's website (www.ftc.gov). Read their brochure titled: "If You've Got The Look . . . Look Out: Avoiding Modeling Scams." While the title says modeling, the advice applies to actors as well. Call to request a copy: 1-877-FTC-HELP. Or, go to the website and search "modeling schools." If you read this short brochure, you will have a much better idea about how to avoid trouble and unnecessary expense!

While there are some good acting classes available for children, it is my opinion that what your child will learn from time spent on stage in school and community theater may be as valuable as anything he or she will learn from an expensive class. Before you spend a lot of money, think like a parent and like a businessperson. Will you get a return on your investment? (That return should be in educational value, not just dollars!) And do not believe everything you are told. Read on to learn about the red flags.

Should we attend a model and talent search advertised on the radio or in the newspaper?

Sure, if it sounds interesting, but keep a very tight grip on your wallet and checkbook. Better yet, leave your checkbook and credit card at home. Some so-called "model and talent searches" may quickly turn into a search for your money.

Caution: Children and teens see images of actors and models in magazines and on television. They hear stories of glamour in ads on the radio for modeling and talent searches. They plead with their parents to take them. Or worse yet, parents hear the ads and imagine nothing but dollar signs, and then parade into such searches with their children in tow, all dolled up in ribbons and bows or glamorous makeup. A few glittering success stories are shared, along with convincing speeches about discipline, responsibility, staying away from drugs, etc. Of course they mean what they say, but such speeches also help to win a parent's trust. At some of these gatherings, parents who think they are attending a talent search may actually find themselves at a carefully prepared sales pitch for classes and photo packages.

Parents have told me about more specific sales strategies. Parents and children attend a talent search advertised in the paper or on the radio. They call the child into the audition room; the child performs and is praised lavishly by the director of the audition. The director then meets with parents and child. The same praise relayed to the parents. Just when the parents are puffed up with pride and the child is bubbling over with dreams of stardom, the sales pitch strikes: "We can help your child achieve this potential, complete with opportunities to be seen by casting directors from Hollywood—if you train with us. Our complete package of classes is available to you, today only, for the discounted price of $3000." The child is tugging at daddy's sleeve, "Oh, please, daddy?" Thus, the sales pressure comes from not only the sales pitch, but from the child as well. Under that type of pressure, what is a poor parent to do? You thought you were attending an audition for opportunities; now you are at risk of disappointing your child and being to blame for ruining his or her big chance! This sales strategy works frightfully well. Thus, many starry-eyed children, teens, and parents sign on the dotted line and shell out big bucks, never stopping to consider the reality and long odds which have been obscured by the glittering dream.

> "A child breaking into the modeling or acting profession needs a good headshot, a parent to get them where they need to go and a quality agent who teaches them the business. Modeling school is not a requirement."
> —Meredith Model and Talent Agency

I imagine that wonderful young actors are occasionally discovered at these searches. I am sure there are some legitimate audition opportunities. The classes they offer may be educational, and the classroom facilities may sparkle. But do not check your business sense at the door. If the classes or photo packages sound like fun and you can afford them, go ahead and sign up. However, glittering opportunities sometimes lose their luster after a good night's sleep. The offer of a "special discount if you pay today" is simply an effective sales technique designed to close the sale.

If you are caught in a pressure sales situation, perhaps it is time to teach your child an important lesson on the value of a dollar and how much you can really afford. What is the child willing to do to help pay for these opportunities? Is this a teachable moment?

See Chapter 7 for more about model and talent searches and auditions.

Some model and talent "agencies" may be a front for modeling schools. Watch out for the old "bait and switch"!

Some modeling schools may be either tightly or loosely affiliated with modeling and talent agencies. While there are legitimate modeling and acting schools, some use a marketing ploy that makes me cringe a little. "Agency seeks new faces! No experience required!" "Hundreds of modeling and acting jobs—you could be a star!" You show up at what you think is an audition, and you are actually offered a package of classes for a price. "If you take our classes, you will be a real, professional model!" You may learn how to be, but that does not matter if you do not have a look or the talent that clients want to hire.

> "When we see [modeling school] on someone's resume, and if that's all they have on their resume, we usually send them a 'no thank you' note."
> —Geanette Poole of Talent Poole

Some agencies do indeed have connections to TV shows and casting folks on the coasts—real opportunities—but they are a select few. They parade and flash their success stories in front of star-struck potential customers, and then they pull out the brochures of classes that "got their stars where they are today." More likely the stars got there largely on their own look and talent.

This is my opinion; however, some of the best agencies in town echo this evaluation. Many books written about the business of acting say exactly what I am saying here.

If an agent tries to convince you to take expensive courses, then use your business sense and follow the money. Who's profiting? Are they making their profits by booking actors for work, or are they making their money on commission by selling classes? Sometimes it is tough to tell. Often, based on what they see in your audition, agents will have recommendations of classes that might help you. Sometimes it is great advice. A recommendation of a class or training can be a benefit to you; on the other hand, a pushy sales pitch may suggest financial benefit to the agent. If you feel pressured to pay, tell them you need some time to think about it before you make that kind of investment. The classes might be very good, but do your research to find out if the classes and the agent are reputable before you pay.

Trips to the coasts to "be discovered."

Sooner or later you will hear about trips or conventions in New York or L.A. to be seen and discovered by agents and casting people. A few agents and schools in town help coordinate these trips to "talent conventions" run by national or international associations.

At these conventions, there are agents and casting people who attend and watch the performances your child will do there. Actors who attend compete in many categories and age groups: sitcom, TV commercial, real people, dramatic monologue, fashion print, commercial print, theatrical headshot, team singing, pre-teen talent of the year, etc. The agents and casting folks watch these performances, judge them, and apply rankings—winners, runners-up, etc. Are actors ever "discovered" through these things? One website of a local agency reports of people who were "discovered" or "signed" by someone as a result of these conventions.

I also know that some actors have really enjoyed the experience. A twelve-year-old friend and her mom shared with me that they "had the time of their lives. It was a great experience." I am quite certain that many who attend have a great time.

The downside? These trips may be very expensive. You pay to enter, pay for photos and comp cards, pay for hotel rooms, pay for travel for the contestants and parents, etc. The cost to you can be thousands of dollars. I will go out on a limb and guess that someone is making some pretty good profits from the contestants' fees. If I had the extra cash, I would take the family to Disney World or put it into my child's college fund. If you have the money and these trips sound like fun, go for it. Others have gone before you and have had a great time. However, as I have said before, think like a businessperson. What is the likelihood that you will get a return on this investment? If spending $3000 or more on a trip like this is going to be a financial hardship for your family, do not do it. If you are counting on "being discovered," odds are you will be disappointed. Even if your child does receive some interest from Hollywood agents or casting directors, it is still a tough business that may involve relocating. You probably cannot audition regularly for real jobs in Hollywood if you live in Minnesota.

The most common totally unnecessary expense?

Expensive "photo packages" for kids are not necessary. Some agencies may expect you to buy a photo package; however, most of the local agencies will require only a good photo or headshot.

My friend recently took her six-year-old son to a local agency/ school. They told her she would need a portfolio done in order to pursue work with them. Depending on the particular package, it would cost between $375 and $590. He is six years old. A $400 to $500 portfolio for a six-year-old beginning model/actor who will look very different a year from now—is it necessary? None of the agencies with which I have ever been associated would require this. Now, you may indeed need such a photo package to pursue work with that particular agency, but know that there are other great agencies in town that require no such photo package.

While professional *models* will eventually need a portfolio or "comp card," neither adult *actors* nor child *actors* have any need for these. Actors need one good headshot. As your child ages, you will need an updated headshot every year or two anyway. Get a good, reasonably-priced headshot every year or two, not an expensive package. For many local agencies, a good school photo will be enough to get you started. (See Chapter 3 for more information about headshots.)

Know that modeling is a different issue, discussed at length in Chapter 14. If your child begins to have some success in modeling, you may want to put together a portfolio of work that he or she has done. You may even want to pay to have a few extra photos taken; but do this with the guidance of a reputable agency.

If you are just starting out in the business of acting, save your money and send a resume and headshot (or just a school photo) to the agencies.

Outright scams.

Please see Chapter 7 for a list of red flags that may indicate which so-called "opportunities" may really be scams. There are many folks who will try to take your money; know what to watch out for!

What is the fun side of acting for kids? What kind of acting work is available for my child?

Kids do almost every type of work that adult actors do.

- Stage (for both professional and amateur actors).
- Commercials (for local and sometimes regional or national spots).

- Industrial and educational videos. An industrial is anything that is not for broadcast. This term covers a huge variety of projects, usually for training or marketing purposes.

- Voice-overs. This term covers radio and TV commercials and industrial voice-overs. (Voice work is much more rare for kids. See Chapter 12 for details about voice-overs. Know that most agencies do not put kids on their agency voice demo. When voice-over opportunities arise, auditions are held.)

- Print work and modeling. (See Chapter 14 for details about modeling.)

- Student films, lower-budget independent films, and the rare major motion picture or made-for-TV movie. (The leading roles in major movies are almost always cast in the bigger markets. Smaller roles are sometimes available for local actors. See Chapter 11 if you are curious about the film and TV business in town.)

All of the above opportunities are available to young actors here in the Twin Cities.

Where do I find out about auditions and opportunities?

Audition opportunities for kids and adults are listed in the same places. See Appendix C for audition sources. Further, see Chapter 7 for much more information about auditioning.

How do I know if my child "has what it takes"?

It is almost impossible to know. The great thing about parents is that you think your child is the prettiest, handsomest, most-talented child ever. You are biased, and that is as it should be! The important thing is to find out what your child loves to do. First see if your child loves to act. Try school plays, performing at your church, synagogue, or community center, dance classes, and acting classes. Does your child love to perform? Does he or she just light up with delight when in front of others? That is a good start.

Also discern whether or not your child has the temperament for this work. It sometimes requires immense patience. They will be looked at, scrutinized, dressed, primped, directed, ordered, etc. Then they will have to wait around, and then wait some more, then hurry up and wait again. Waiting is the most common activity in the business, and your child will need to be patient. (So will you!)

Test the waters before you invest. Audition for plays and send a photo and resume to the talent agencies in town. (See Chapter 4 and Appendix

A for information about agents.) If your child loves it and you get some good feedback, swim in a little deeper. If you get a few nibbles in terms of legitimate jobs and audition opportunities—being called back or cast for a commercial or industrial, or being cast in a theatrical role—these might be good indicators that your child has some potential in the biz. If the only nibbles you get are those that want your money up front, this is not a good indicator of whether your child has it or not; it simply indicates that these folks want your money.

What's the best "age range" to pursue acting and modeling?

Kids of all ages—infants to teens—may get acting and modeling work.

I once did a commercial for a hospital in which I played a nurse in the maternity ward. They employed six different infants. For the actual shot, they used whichever baby was not crying at the time! All of the kids (with moms) were paid equally.

I have done commercial and industrial shoots with kids of all ages: a family on vacation for an insurance commercial, young soccer players piling into a mini-van for a car dealership spot, mom and child with a medical condition for a medical training video, a teacher with teenagers planning their prom for a prom supply company, etc. Clients need kids of all ages for their projects.

For professional commercial and industrial work, I have heard it said that age seven to eleven is prime time. At seven, kids are old enough to read, take direction, and understand what they need to do on a set; at eleven kids have not reached the occasional awkwardness of puberty. Watch commercials; these are the kids you see most often.

Of course, the world of advertising and fashion modeling obviously seeks out teens. This work depends almost entirely on your look, regardless of age and training. (See Chapter 14 for more information about modeling.)

When your child expresses a desire to be an actor or model, that is the time to try it.

Should I enroll my child in classes?

If your child wants to take classes and you can afford it, absolutely. I believe in all kinds of educational opportunities for kids.

There are several not-for-profit organizations and theaters that offer great classes for kids. Among the best are the Children's Theatre, Stages Theatre Company in Hopkins, Youth Performance Company in Minneapolis, and Steppingstone Theatre in St. Paul. The Guthrie Theatre, the

Chanhassen Dinner Theatre and the Brave New Workshop will occasionally offer great programs for kids, too. (See the resources listed in Appendix F for a more complete listing.)

Also check out local sources. A local community education department, community theater, or a nearby college or university may offer theater opportunities or summer theater camps for kids.

There are a handful of acting and modeling schools in town. I have spoken with many parents about their children's experiences there, and the feedback often varies with the quality of each instructor. Some parents have regretted spending the money on classes. Others have raved about their children's experiences. One mother in particular said that the classes her daughter took did not necessarily result in real acting and modeling work, but what she gained in poise and professionalism was worth every penny. If you can easily afford it, try a class or two at the modeling schools. They may be a good educational opportunity. If your child enjoys classes and you feel they are a good educational experience for the money, then go ahead and try a couple more.

Just know that children can and do find success in the Twin Cities talent market without ever taking a single class outside of their regular school day. Weigh what is best for your child.

How do I find good classes for my child?

Look for affordable educational opportunities and activities. Any activity that allows your child to perform—to do improvisation, to do scenes and plays—is great acting training. What your child really needs to learn is to be poised in front of a group, while at the same time to be relaxed and free to play when they perform—not stiff, controlled, and polished.

If you want to pursue more formal acting classes and experiences for your child, see Appendix F for a more extensive list of organizations Some are expensive; others are very affordable. (Just because something is more expensive does not mean it is better!)

The same rule for adult classes is true for kids' classes: Shop around. Do your shopping based on some of the following criteria: (These are not solid rules, just suggested guidelines.)

- Price: The going rate for classes is around $10 to $20 per hour of class time. If it is more than that, it had better be a fabulous class with very few students.

- Class size: Class size should be limited. An acting class should be filled with activity and performing, not hours of watching others perform. Even ten to fifteen students per instructor can be too many students.

- Teacher's credentials: Ask questions. Get details about the credentials of teachers. Has the teacher worked in the field they teach? Do they have a degree in the field? Have they taught children before?

- Observe: Ask if you (the parent) can observe a class session before you sign up. Observe how the teacher interacts with the kids. Observe the "creative buzz" and enthusiasm of the students.

- Observe the children's responses to the teacher. Observe what they are learning: Are they becoming more stiff and controlled and polished, or are they learning to be free to interact in the moment of the scene? Are the teachers trying to free the child's instincts, or form the child into a plastic, cookie-cutter mold? These may be tough distinctions if you do not know acting, but it may help you look for the subtleties.

- Do they have a curriculum for the class? What are the objectives or learning outcomes of the class? What will your child leave the class knowing that he/she did not know before? Can they state these learning outcomes clearly, or do they have objectives available in writing? The instructor may not have a formal, written curriculum; however, he or she should be able to state the activities and outcomes clearly.

Schools or classes may not always be able to satisfy all of the suggestions listed above, but keep these things in mind as you shop for classes. As always, trust your gut feeling. If something does not feel right, do not do it and do not give in to pressure. A good class opportunity will always be there at a later date after you have had time to think about it and investigate.

Multi-year programs at acting or modeling schools.

Schools may offer deep discounts for paying in advance for extended course work: two-, -three-, or four-year plans or memberships. Remember that kids' interests sometimes change with the wind. What they are crazy about this month may be old news next month. One mom told me that her daughter loved the classes as an eighth-grader, but by ninth grade she was so busy with school theater, choir, and dance line that she did not have time for the classes anymore. There was no refund policy, so the discount was not as cost-effective as they had initially hoped.

Read the contract carefully before you pay. Your child may love the classes every year. On the other hand, if your child loses interest, you may be a frustrated parent fighting with your child about not attending classes for which you have already paid.

How many local agents represent children?

Most of the agencies have kids on their rosters. Some focus more on children, while others have only occasional opportunities for kids. Some have weekly or monthly open calls to interview new talent; others will schedule interviews two to four times per year. (See Appendix A and Chapter 4 for further information about local talent agencies.)

What do I send to an agent? My child does not have a resume yet!

Time to type up a resume! See Chapter 3 for further information about resumes. Many of the principles for an adult actor's resume also apply to a child's resume.

The resume does not need to be lengthy. If your child has theater experience, obviously include that and print it up like an adult acting resume. Even small roles in school plays are important on a resume. Good stage experience will help get an agent's attention. Most children will not have a lot of formal theater experience, so keep the resume simple.

Include any performance experience: school or community plays, speeches, dance recitals, music recitals, performance classes, etc. Include any experience that says your child is comfortable being up in front of people. Also include any special interests and skills. I do not mean "cute" details such as "she loves to play with her

> "Past accomplishments are important, but a young performer's motivation, look, manner, energy, talent, and future moneymaking potential are all necessary ingredients in the entertainment business."
> —www.sag.com

pink ducky in the tub." This may be cute to you, but it is not useful information for the agent. Special interests and skills include: musical abilities, dance, sports skills, hobbies such as skateboarding and roller-blading, juggling, special artistic talent, etc.

Resumes for kids should also include parents' names, all phone numbers, and the child's date of birth. For your first submissions to agencies, also include your home address. Once you begin to audition for clients, you will remove your personal phone numbers and addresses, and replace them with your agent's phone number. (Again, see Chapter 3 for further information about resumes.)

Do not worry if your child does not have much to put on a resume. If your child has great potential, the camera will see it despite the sparse resume.

Do I need to get expensive headshots and photos for my child?

Professional headshots are great, but your child does not absolutely need one. You do need to have a good photo of your child, but school photos may suffice for beginners. As it is, you will spend plenty on inexpensive headshots every year simply to keep up with your child's changing look. Yes, some parents get professional headshots taken for their children every year or two. Yes, this projects a professional image. If you become serious about this and your child really enjoys it, then you will eventually want to invest in professional headshots. (See Chapter 3 for details about headshots.)

Get a professional headshot if you can easily afford it. Call the photographers listed in Appendix D to compare prices. If you are just testing the waters—if your child has expressed an interest in acting or modeling but you are not sure about it—simply send a good school photo with resume to the agents. (If you are pursuing modeling work, the photo should be a "three-quarter shot" or full-body shot rather than just the headshot, and be sure to include measurements.)

Each agent will have preferences about photos, and some may insist on professional headshots. Once an agent wants to represent you, ask for their opinion. However, if an agent pushes you to spend a lot of money with their favorite photographer, be careful.

Further, you only need one headshot. You will need multiple copies, but you do not need a different photo for every agency. If you do arrange with an agency to have photos taken, often they will want the agency logo and contact information printed on it. Be sure to ask for a copy (or proof) without the agency logo; you want to be able to use the headshot to submit to other agencies and theaters. I would take issue if they tell you that the photo can only be used exclusively for their agency. It is your money. If you are spending hundreds, get what you need. The other agencies do not want to send you out on auditions using a headshot that advertises their competition! You need one good headshot to submit for everything.

Do not spend money to do a composite or comp card. This may be useful for models, but unnecessary for actors. If your child wants to act, there is no need for such a thing. (If your child wants to be a model, you may eventually want to do a comp card, but do not do this right away. See Chapter 14 for modeling information.)

Finally, be sure your name and phone numbers are on the resume, and be sure staples at each corner securely attach the resume to the headshot. If your child is very young and has no resume, at least be sure that all contact information is on the back of the photo.

Again, you do not need to make a big investment in order to take a test drive in the business. Send out a nice photo and professional resume, and see where the road leads you. If your child has a "good look" and a bit of performance experience, agents will likely be interested in seeing you.

What can we expect at the agent interview?

Kids who interview with an agent should show up in their everyday school clothes, not their "Sunday best." Agents just want to see who you are and what you look like. Often, the most important quality is how well your child can relate to different people. I do not mean that your child needs to be able to have intellectual conversations with the agent. Simply, can your child be him/herself in new situations?

Older children and teenagers will read a script or two to gauge acting talent. Younger children will simply be interviewed. Agents are looking for real kids who can show their personality.

Remember that this is a business, not an educational institution. A large number of actors, including children, will be rejected by an agency rather than signed by an agency. Agents will be very nice at the interview, of course, but when it comes to making the business decisions, they will only represent the kids they think clients will cast.

Be sure that you are the one who gives your child some positive feedback for a job well done at the interview. The agents might not gush like you think they should.

Parents need to know when to support, and when to get out of the way!

I have interviewed kids for my agent, and I have seen just about everything. Most parents are great. They are proud of their kids, helping them to pursue their interests and to learn a little bit about professionalism along the way. Once in a while you run into a "stage mom" or "stage dad." Telltale signs: misbehaved children whose parents think they are just wonderful; parents who talk through the entire interview so I never even hear from the child; or plastic, overly-coached kids who do not seem free to be themselves anymore.

Believe it or not, your behavior can be as important as your child's behavior! Pushy stage parents drag their kids from interview to audition, doing most of the talking about how great their child is. If your kid is truly great, we will see that without a word from you. Further, pushy and doting stage parents may end up with a carefully rehearsed, plastic kid. If you want your child to do pageants, go ahead. However, all that focus on looks, hair, and just the right frozen smile might just snuff out any little light of natural acting talent your child may have. It is your child's natural look and personality that are important, not how he or she is made to look. You want your child to feel free to be spontaneous and natural, not rehearsed.

There are some terrific kids who are seldom called by agents because the parents are such a pain. On the other hand, there are parents that are so nice to work with that their kids actually get more calls from the agents. First and foremost, the parent must be reliable and easy to work with. The same behaviors that can help or hinder an adult's acting opportunities can also affect your child's opportunities. (See Chapter 4 for further details. Many of the suggestions for adult actors also apply to parents of child actors!)

Of course, you need to accompany your child on auditions and jobs. Be there to support when needed, but then stay out of the way as much as possible. At the audition and the job, allow your child to interact naturally. Unless you are needed, it is best to fade into the background. Be attentive and aware for discipline or safety reasons, of course, but let your child do his/her thing with as little interference from you as possible.

Most parents I meet are supportive and attentive. They know when to supervise and ask questions, and when to step back and allow their kids to shine. It is truly a pleasure to work with these parents. Believe me, it does make a difference!

Do I need to update my child's photos every year?

Yes, or at least every two years. If an agent is representing you, they will need new photos as your child grows. Obviously, kids change rapidly! Be sure to keep your agent supplied with updated photos. A half-dozen copies are plenty for most kids to send to agents. If your child begins to work more often, you may need to provide more than that.

What if they want my child to be on the website?

Most agencies showcase talent headshots on the agency website. Some agencies feature children and adults on the web, other agencies choose to keep kids' photos off of the web. They provide photos to clients upon request. There is often a fee to put your child's photo on the website. Weigh this decision as you would any other business decision, and see Chapter 4 for a detailed discussion of agency websites.

Commercial work vs. school obligations.

Any agent in town will understand that school comes first. Some jobs will require that your child miss school. Clients will often forget to consider school scheduling when they plan their shoots. It is up to you to decide how much school can be missed and when.

Similarly, school concerts, games, church events, and other extracurricular commitments are important. If your child will be really upset about missing a concert or a game, turn down the commercial audition and honor the child's previous commitment. Perhaps ask your child to make the choice; it might be a good way to teach them to prioritize and make difficult choices. Just remember (speaking as a former teacher and coach), your child has to deal with those teachers and coaches every day; honor commitments to school, teachers, coaches, teams, choirs, etc. No agent will fault you for wanting your kid to be a kid first and an actor second!

However, if you do need to refuse a job, be sure to turn it down prior to the audition or at least at the time of the audition. Once you have auditioned and said that you are available for the shoot date, you need to honor the commitment to the client. Changing your mind mid-stream may cause great difficulty and expense for the client as well as frustration for the agent!

Commercial work as educational experience.

Teachers are often frustrated with parents who pull their kids out of school. However, supportive parents who communicate with teachers are terrific. Be sure to communicate with your child's teachers if your child has to miss school.

I spoke with one parent who works with the child's teacher to build educational opportunities around the shoot. The child writes a report to present to the class about the experience, or they look at the script as a class and discuss the writing, etc. In one instance, the child did a mini-interview with several of the personnel on the shoot, and reported about what kinds of jobs are available in the business. If your child needs to miss school for a job, there are good ways to create additional learning opportunities in place of the lost day of class.

Kids and the unions.

Professional child actors can be members of the actors' unions. Again, in the business of acting, children are often treated the same as adults. All of the union rules that apply to adults also apply to children. See Chapter 5 for a detailed discussion of union and non-union work.

Further, the Screen Actor's Guild website (SAG.com) has quite a bit of information for young performers and parents. You may wish to take a look.

My child really wants to try commercial acting and/or modeling. Where do I start?

Here is an idea that comes right out of my former school-teacher brain: If your child is older than ten or eleven, assign a

Make your child do the homework first, rather than running around in a stressed-out frenzy!

reading of this chapter, plus Chapters 1 through 4. (If your child wants to model, add Chapter 14 to the assignment.) Have your child report back to you a well-thought-out approach to the pursuit of commercial acting or modeling—or at least the first few steps. Have your child address and stamp the envelopes for the initial mailing to agents. (Addresses are listed in Appendix A.) This will teach your child that this is a business, and there is work to be done before one ever "makes it." If your child actually follows through with this, then he or she must really want it.

Final words.

There is much more that can be said about your child's potential acting career. You now know the basics and several resources that may help you, as well as the red flags. Appendix F contains many more useful resources.

Chapter 14 contains more information about modeling. Keep reading if your interests lead you in that direction.

Finally, and I cannot stress this enough: Be sure that your pursuit of this business stems from your child's desire to act and perform, not because you are chasing financial reward and stardom—and certainly not because you are chasing some lost childhood dream of your own. (If you want to act, start over at Chapter 1 of this book and read it with yourself in mind. Go ahead and act; you can start at any age!) If this is truly your child's dream, then absolutely chase it, but do so armed with knowledge and good business sense.

Modeling and Print Work

Look is everything.

I have done about a dozen print shoots in all the years I have been in this business. A mere twelve print gigs do not an expert make, though I can offer you some basic advice and resources that will help you start your pursuit of a modeling career.

Modeling is a tough business (emphasis on the word "business"), but if you really want to try it, go for it! It can be very rewarding, and there are lots of opportunities in the Twin Cities. Just be sure to prepare yourself so you can make the most of any opportunities that may come your way.

Many thanks to Robyn Johnson (professional model) for providing some of the detailed information about the local modeling business.

> "Big corporations make millions of dollars annually selling unattainable dreams to aspiring models. They sell conventions, modeling courses, comp cards, websites . . . profiteering on what should not be a volume-driven thing. They have blurred the truth--all in the name of profit."
> —modeltruth.com

The bad news, then the good news!

Again, the bad news first. In Chapters 2, 7, and 13, I discuss at length the existence of those who are waiting to profit from your desire to be an actor. This is equally true for modeling; it actually may be worse.

There are far more people who want your money than those who can offer employment. Frequently, what you believe is an audition for work or representation may turn out to be a sales pitch for photos, classes, or expensive on-line national talent listings. Many people spend thousands trying to break in, yet never make a penny.

The advice and resources in this chapter will help you evaluate your options.

Warnings from the Federal Trade Commission.

As I mentioned in Chapter 13, the very best place to begin your search for modeling opportunities is at the Federal Trade Commission's website, ftc.gov. Ploys to take your money are so prevalent, the government has provided free consumer education in a document titled, "If You've Got The Look . . . Look Out: Avoiding Modeling Scams." Read it! Call to request a copy (1-877 FTC-HELP), or search the website using the key word, modeling.

> What could be more flattering? Someone approaches you at the mall and says, "You could be a model. You've got the look we're after. Here's my card. Give me a call to set up an appointment." People have always said you are good looking. Now, visions of glamour, travel, and money flash before your eyes.
>
> It is true that some successful models have been discovered in everyday places like malls, boutiques, clubs, and airports. But the vast majority of would-be models knock on door after agency door before work comes their way.
>
> If and when you make that follow-up appointment, you will probably find yourself in an office filled with lots of other model and actor hopefuls. Then the spiel starts. What you thought was a job interview with a talent agency turns into a high-pressure sales pitch for modeling or acting classes, or for "screen tests" or "photo shoots" that can range in price from several hundred to several thousand dollars (from "If You've Got the Look . . . Look Out").

These classes and photo shoots may be educational and enjoyable, but some local talent and modeling agencies will tell you that you do not need them at all. (Advice from several agencies to follow.) Before you pay, research to determine the best path for you. The Federal Trade Commission's website offers much more information.

How should I spend my money to get into modeling?

Only you can decide how to spend your money. There are successful models who have launched careers with only a letter, a single photo, and a few postage stamps. I suggest two basic guidelines as you consider your options:

1. When the person giving you advice is also asking for money, get a second opinion.

2. Before you spend money, use good business sense and ask yourself, "What kind of return will I get for this investment?"

As you pursue modeling, you will likely encounter the following:

- Model searches and conventions.
- Kiosks and personnel at shopping malls who claim they can "discover" you.
- Photos and photo packages.
- Modeling schools and classes.

I will discuss each of these in a little more detail; but overall, when you consider spending money in the modeling business, remember to apply the two basic guidelines on the previous page.

Should I attend a "model search" or a national "convention" to be discovered?

Occasionally you will see ads for "model and talent searches." If attendance is free, then go ahead, but leave your checkbook and credit card at home. If they ask for money once you arrive, be sure to apply the two guidelines.

You will also hear about trips to New York or Los Angeles to compete and audition in front of agents and casting people. If it sounds like a fun trip and you can easily afford it, go ahead. If you want to do it as a financial investment in your career, you would be wise to consider the likelihood of getting a return on that investment.

Before you commit, ask for a list of all of the agents and casting directors who will be in attendance. What types of projects have they worked on in the past? Who are their current clients? How many models will be seen? Dozens? Hundreds? Thousands? If you are spending thousands of dollars for such a convention, you should know what you are actually getting for that investment.

Further, as I said in Chapter 13, to work in a major market you probably have to live there. Even if you were to catch the eye of anyone with casting influence, are you ready for the travel demands of a job on the coasts? You can meet local agents and casting directors right here in town. If you want to meet agencies from other markets, be sure you are ready to travel if and when they need you.

When you answer ads for something like this, just check your ego at the door and use your best business sense. Again, please see Chapters 7 and 13 for more information about talent searches and conventions.

Know that some of these things may not be searching for you; they may be searching for your wallet.

Should I sign up for classes and auditions when they "discover" me at the mall?

Please ask yourself the following questions: "Why are these companies paying to have a kiosk at the mall?" "Is there really a great demand for new models and actors?" "How many other prospects have they approached?"

Any working model or actor will tell you that there is not enough employment for all the pretty and talented people in town as it is. Sure, once in a great while, these searches at the mall may find some great new face who will actually become a working model. However, they may also find many teenagers and parents who will pay for photos and classes. My guess is they are at the malls because they are making money—and they will happily take yours.

Sure, the classes or photo packages they are selling may be educational and enjoyable. As you decide what is right for you, simply apply the two guidelines given previously.

Do I need a comp card? If I have a comp card, do I appear to be more professional?

Perhaps, if you really have the experience that goes with a good comp card. If you do not have experience, buying an expensive photo package may not help you.

A composite, or comp card is an approximately 5 x 8 card with several photos of you. Typically, a great three-quarter shot with your name will be on one side, and three to five different shots will be on the back, along with all your stats and your agent's name and number. These other shots will vary, but will often show a full-body shot, a few shots that will demonstrate your personality, style, or attitude, and a shot or two of any specialty modeling that you do (hand model, body parts, etc.).

There are lots of aspiring models sending out comp cards. Some agencies and schools tell prospective models that they need comp cards and portfolios in order to pursue work. Some may charge hundreds or thousands of dollars to produce such cards. I imagine these expensive comp cards are intended to suggest that an aspiring model has actual experience in front of the camera. However, because agents are well aware of modeling schools in town that promote or sell photo shoots and comp cards, agents also know that many comp cards come from people who have no experience whatsoever. (Experienced agents can tell the difference.)

Most agents in the Twin Cities will look at all the headshots, three-quarter shots, comp cards, and photos they receive. Having a comp card may not give you an advantage over the people who send single photos. I would try sending a simple photo to the agencies before spending the extra money on a comp card. Consider this investment as carefully as you do any other investment of your hard-earned money.

Should I take modeling classes?

That is up to you. Some will say, "No way." Others will tell you that such classes are beneficial. You will need to evaluate this for yourself.

From a purely business standpoint, modeling classes are not necessary. You may gain enjoyment and education, but it is debatable whether or not such classes will increase your professional modeling opportunities. Many models have been successful without ever taking classes. Your look will dictate ninety-five percent or more of your success. Classes and training will not give you "that look." Be sure to read the quotes on the coming pages from local agencies and consult the other resources listed in this chapter.

On the other hand, if you want to experience and learn about the world of modeling, take classes. If you sign up for modeling classes, please do it primarily for the learning experience. No one can guarantee that you will ever get work; spending all the money in the world for classes and training may not significantly improve your chances of booking professional modeling jobs. If some actual professional opportunities come your way as a result of such classes, consider that to be the icing on the cake.

I have met many aspiring models who have regretted spending the money for modeling classes; I have met others who have been satisfied with their class experience. A parent once told me that her daughter had gained tremendous poise and confidence at modeling school. Through classes, you can experience the world of modeling without facing real-world rejection.

If the price tag is too high for your budget, consider whether or not your money would be more wisely invested in a college fund. Send a good, inexpensive photo to the agencies instead. Only you can make that decision.

Modeling school or modeling agency: What is the difference?

There are legitimate modeling schools, and there are legitimate talent and modeling agencies, but the two are very different businesses. Some entities seem to intentionally blur the lines. With a school, *you pay* for classes and training; with an agency, *you are paid* for any professional modeling work that you may book through that agency. Big difference.

When you answer advertisements for modeling opportunities, remember the fundamental difference between schools and agencies. Before you do business with an organization, simply ask them to be clear about what they do.

How do the local agents answer the question of classes and training?

- Agency Models and Talent: "I tell them to call a working model to get one-on-one training. We will train them for free if they sign exclusive. Get a little acting training. Models are actors, as they need to convey emotion without words. Do not go to a 'modeling school.' If we want you, we will help you without charging you for advice."

- Meredith Model and Talent Agency: "It is an agent's responsibility to teach its talent what their responsibilities are in the business. No modeling classes are necessary if you are intelligent. If an agency wants to send you to a $2000 contest, you'd be better off spending the money in front of a camera building up your portfolio."

- Moore Creative Talent Inc.: "If you are not a certain height, weight, look, etc., spending a lot of money on classes and pictures is not necessary."

Further, Susan Wehmann of Wehmann Models/Talent Inc. is quoted in the *Star Tribune*: "Not one top model I've worked with in twenty years went to modeling school." The article goes on to say, "Wehmann agrees that schools can generate confidence, but so can sports and theater or other activities" (John Ewoldt, "Model Teens" in Minneapolis *Star Tribune*, July 10, 2003).

A word about safety.

Trust your instincts. If you are called to interview or audition, and something feels wrong or dangerous, just leave. If you were sent by an agency, call your agent immediately. If you are a young person, do not attend an interview or an audition alone—unless an agent or other knowledgeable person can vouch for the entity that is holding the audition. I have not heard of any such problems here in the Twin Cities, but let a little bit of wisdom be your guide.

"I'm serious about this! I really think I have what it takes to be a professional model."

Okay, you have read my cautions above and you really want to go for it. Read this chapter to get started, and then be sure to refer to more complete resources. You will find many books and websites about modeling, Here are two that I recommend:

- Model Truth (www.modeltruth.com). This is an advocacy organization for models. They offer an affordable DVD ($19.95) filled with information from professionals in the business. I watched it, and I can assure you that it contains sound advice for aspiring models. Check out the website to decide if it might be useful to you.

- *The Complete Idiot's Guide to Being a Model* (2nd edition) by supermodel Roshumba Williams with Anne Marie O'Connor (Alpha Books, 2007, Radiant Jewel, Inc.).

I know the titles of *Idiot's Guides* and *Books for Dummies* are a bit insulting, but this one is a good reference. It is packed with information, including descriptions of the types of modeling, what it takes to become a model, the particular physical requirements for successful models, how to conduct yourself at interviews, financial information, a great glossary of terms, and much more. It is comprehensive and clearly organized. And the $18.95 price tag is a bargain for the wealth of information it gives.

Will I be evaluated only on my looks?

Whereas your "look" is important in acting, it is everything in modeling. If you want to be a model, you had better brace yourself for acceptance, criticism, or rejection based totally on your looks. Before you even consider this pursuit, answer this question: Do I have a "look" that's marketable compared to what I see in print ads? If you do not have the natural body type and look, you will not be able to create it, or you will seriously compromise your health trying.

You need to be tough in this business. If you want to model, you need beautiful—and sometimes, thick—skin!

A word about your health and well-being.

Your body is your business! Dance, pilates, yoga, free weights, running and nutrition all are important. Even more than in acting – clients do not hire talent who appear to be unhealthy. Your health is critical.

In the world of professional modeling, you will face all kinds of demands: "You have to change your hair." " You have to fix your teeth." "You have to lose ten pounds." This is a tough business. If you get a foot in the door, constructive criticism may feel very personal. Separate your business from your self-esteem. You are selling a product (your appearance and personality); you are not selling your soul. Keep the two very separate in your mind and the blunt comments about your product will not feel quite so personal. Remember, the business is about money, not about boosting your self-esteem or protecting your health. You must care for your own emotional and physical well-being.

Finally, eating disorders run rampant in the modeling world. Robyn Johnson tells the story of a professional model advising a younger model to adopt her diet of carrots and ice cubes. Terrible advice! Even if you have some success, you will not be able to model forever. Your health is much more important than a few modeling jobs. Do not damage your health for the sake of this business. (Parents especially: Watch for signs of eating disorders. The Melrose Institute in Minneapolis has some great resources if you have questions and concerns.)

What do I need to do to get started as a professional model?

If you think you have potential to be a professional model, your next step is to simply send your "stuff" to local agencies and see if you get a response.

By "stuff" I mean:

- A good photo.
- A brief, professional cover letter.
- Your stats: date of birth, height, weight, measurements, and clothing sizes.

Do not send a family photo or a group shot of you and your friends, even if you look great in the shot. The photo should be a clear, good quality photo of you at your everyday best.

If you want to spend a little more to make a professional impression, pay to get a good three-quarter shot taken by a photographer who knows the business. A good shot that has been professionally reproduced will cost you from $150 to $500, depending on the photographer you use. (See Appendix D for photographer information.)

If you do get replies from agents, some may be willing to train you for free. This is the very best way to start—interest from an agent who will help guide you at no cost. If this happens, consider this a fairly reliable confirmation that you have potential.

If you get no response to this mailing, remember what a competitive business this is. You will be one among thousands of aspiring models who have tasted rejection. Welcome to a big club! If you are determined, keep at it and do not let the rejection get to you.

If you have a "marketable look," the agents will want to see you. If you do not have that particular look, they may never want to see you. It is as simple as that. If you get no response, do not give up entirely. Send your stuff to the agencies again every six months. Try a different photo or invest in a professional photo. Their needs may change and your look may change, thus increasing their interest.

Sexy vs. promiscuous photos.

This may seem obvious, but I am amazed at some of the promiscu-ous-style photos that occasionally arrive at the agency office. There is a big difference between the professional modeling world and businesses that produce "pin-up calendars." There is a difference between attractive, sexy photos and promiscuous-looking photos. I will not delve into great detail, but suffice it to say, you will need to draw your own line when it comes to the professional and artistic interpretation of your photographs. Visit local agency websites to study your competition. Notice the style of the photos to get an idea about what local agencies want. Then view photographers' websites to be sure their style will suit your image. Be sure you and your photographer are on the same page about the image you want to project.

Do I need special wardrobe and makeup items?

For print jobs, often the client will provide wardrobe and a makeup artist, but not always. If your agent does not specify wardrobe, hair, and makeup details when you are booked for the job, always ask. If the client will be pro-viding wardrobe and a makeup artist, simply show up with a clean face and simply-styled hair. Your makeup artist will take care of the rest.

For auditions and some shoots, you will need to provide your own wardrobe and makeup. You should always have the basics ready to go for any call that comes in. Just as for acting jobs, you should have a simple makeup kit and a few outfits that are clean and pressed. Depending on your type, your basic wardrobe should consist of at least a couple busi-ness outfits (for adults) and a couple stylish, casual options—along with scarves, shoes, belts, and hair accessories. (See Chapter 3 for more infor-mation about makeup and wardrobe needs.)

What's a "go-see"?

A "go and see" or "go-see" is to a model what the audition is to the actor. You go to the client's office so they can see what you look like in person. Sometimes they will interview you if it is for a big, important shoot; but more often they will just snap a quick photo and send you on your way. To an actor, a go-see often feels like a cattle-call. They sometimes see hundreds of people for a few little shots. However, if you book the job, the pay is often really good.

What is a portfolio?

A portfolio is a book of selected photos of your work. Professional models carry this with them to all interviews and go-sees. When you are new, you will not have a portfolio yet; your goal is to build one through professional opportunities. The longer you have been in business, the better and more complete your portfolio will be.

What is a tear sheet?

Tear sheets are the photos from magazines and catalogs of work you have actually done. When you start to work, be sure to collect the tear sheets and keep them in your portfolio.

Do I need a composite or a portfolio?

If you are primarily an actor, do not bother with either. Period. A professional model will need these eventually, but not right away. I asked a few local agencies about the need for photos:

- Agency Models and Talent: Would love a book full of good pictures and a killer comp, but would settle for one good three-quarter shot. If you are a commercial model, you can start with a three-quarter shot and build. Do not go to a "modeling school." Send good snapshots to agencies that do not have a school affiliation. If we want you, we will help you without charging you for advice.

- Meredith Model and Talent Agency: They need to submit a photograph (doesn't need to be professionally taken, but it doesn't hurt). Minimum of 4 x 6, composite card or 8 x 10 (either a headshot or three-quarter shot) and resume. If you have what it takes, a good agent and a 4 x 6 photograph will get you in the door.

- Moore Creative Talent Inc.: Just send a snapshot, not necessarily a portfolio. If you get a professional shot, get a three-quarter shot.

- Wehmann Models/Talent Inc.: Send a headshot and comp, if available. Would like to see comps, great photos or tear sheets, current stats. If you are putting together a comp, let the agents pick photos; we know what clients look for!

  One big mistake that many aspiring models make is spending tons of money on photos, portfolios, and composites before they get an agent. This is a total waste of money and time, and people who tell you otherwise either do not know what they are talking about or are scamming you. . . . All photos taken without an agent's guidance are essentially useless because the photos may not capture the image the agent plans to build for you and promote to the fashion industry. When agents are looking for new models, they want to develop the model's own natural beauty into a marketable style, so spending a lot of money on professional photos that probably will not project the image they are after is not necessary" (*The Complete Idiot's Guide to Being a Model*).

Now that is a strong statement; and again, "agent" is not synonymous with "modeling school." Modeling schools may encourage you to get a composite or portfolio done, but schools will not be marketing you; an agent will be doing the marketing. You would be wise to follow the advice above and wait for an agent's guidance. If you begin to achieve some success in modeling, you will certainly want to invest in professional photos. However, I think it is abundantly clear that if you have a great look and the right measurements, a simple photo or professional three-quarter shot can get you noticed by a good agency.

What type of modeling might be right for me?

Fashion modeling is very different than commercial print work. Some models can cross over and do different types of work. An agent can help you discern what may be the right fit: runway, high fashion, commercial print, bridal, etc. For example, runway models are typically 5'8" or taller. Fashion models generally wear sizes 0-4. Bridal samples are usually sizes 6 or 8. Genetics and bone structure will largely dictate what you can and cannot do in the business. According to Robyn Johnson, one of the first hurdles in modeling is to accept the type of modeling you can do.

What measurements do I send to agencies?

When you send your photos, be sure to send accurate measurements, too. Women need to provide weight, height, bust, waist, hips, hair color, and eye color. Men need to send height, weight, chest, waist, inseam, hair color, and eye color.

- Height: measure flat-footed without shoes.
- Bust: measure at the fullest part of your bust line. (It is not your bra size.)
- Waist: measure at the smallest part of your waist.
- Hips: measure at the fullest part across your bottom.

Don't lie! Stylists and costumers buy wardrobe based upon the information you give on audition forms. Be sure you always provide accurate sizes and measurements!

What about runway modeling?

I have no experience here whatsoever. (At 5'4" and 140 pounds, go figure!) While several agents suggested that they recommend no classes for aspiring models, the Wehmann agency responded: "Maybe runway class if a model has runway potential." I am sure runway work has some very specific requirements and skills that one would need to know before actually walking down a fashion show runway.

Before your pursue runway classes, be sure you are the "runway type." Send out your photos and stats, and let a reputable agent discern this for you. Please consult the other, more complete resources listed in this chapter if you wish to pursue this type of work.

What about "fit modeling"?

You may occasionally be called to be a fit model. Even if you do not want to be a model, you may be able to get into this kind of work if you are the right size for the industry.

Basically, the clothing industry needs to try their products on real humans, not just mannequins. Models of certain sizes and measurements are hired to try on clothes for fittings. It requires patience, as you may need to try on several different garments and have them pinned, adjusted, etc. It is not glamorous, but it will pay a good hourly rate.

Should I model for a hair show?

Occasionally, you will see ads looking for models for hair shows. If you work as a model for a hair show, quite often you will have to consent to anything they want to do with your hairstyle—including cut and color. It is a great way to get a new, trendy style; but keep in mind, for the acting and modeling profession, you must look like your headshot. If you dramatically change your style, you may have some casting challenges while you wait for the purple highlights to grow out. (Most hair shows would not go that extreme, but you get my point!)

Can an actor get print work?

I do not qualify as a model by any stretch of the imagination; however, I get a smattering of print jobs, and I am happy to have the work when it comes my way. We all know about fashion models because we see them in magazines. We may not notice other types of print work, because the "models" in these shots look like everyday people. That's the kind of print work they hire actors to do. Actor/models are often hired to be the talent for corporate brochures, medical product brochures, product packaging, photo illustrations in textbooks, print ads for household products, etc. The list is endless, but not necessarily glamorous!

My illustrious print resume includes such sophisticated and exciting gigs as the mom playing a board game on a game box, a rep selling windows on advertising flyers, a shopper in a furniture store ad, a bank teller on a billboard, and a physical therapy patient on medical product packaging. I have also done a bit of "body parts" modeling. The inside of my mouth was photographed for a dental procedure brochure. My hand was made up to look like a third-degree burn for a medical textbook. My feet had their own close-ups for a foot care program. I even did a shoot in the buff for a medical product. (Although this was a long, uncomfortable story, it was a very professional shoot—very clinical—and it paid well; it was just well outside of my comfort zone!)

The best story I have heard recently is a call to my agent, looking for a senior citizen's buttocks for a brochure for a prescription skin care product. It is a glamorous business! (But the model chosen was paid well for lying down all day.)

Why not hire everyday people if that is the look they want in the shot?

Sometimes they do; but often "everyday people" do not know the industry and do not have patience for the tedious nature of shooting. Actors know that it often requires dozens of takes to get the shot. Actors know that it takes a long time to light the shot. We understand camera angles and what the camera "sees" in a shot. We know how to take direction without taking it personally. If the shot requires any emotion or truthful response, actors know how to give that for the camera, too.

And can you imagine an average person receiving a call requesting them to lie face down on a table all day while their rear-end is photographed? Only actors and models are crazy enough to take that call seriously.

If I am an actor, what do I need to do to pursue print work on the side?

Nothing more than you are already doing for your acting work. You still need to have a particular look for a print job, so do not expect your phone to ring off the hook with bookings. Agents usually call actors they know when everyday people print jobs come up. Send your headshot or three-quarter shot and resume to the agents, and if you are right for a print job, they will call you.

If you are sending your headshot and resume to an agency that has a print department, be sure to address one submission to the on-camera department and another to the print department. Do not expect them to communicate and share your stuff between departments. Each area likely has its own files. You want them all to have you on file.

What are the modeling agencies in the Twin Cities?

If you search the internet or check the yellow pages, several modeling agencies appear. I wish I could give you a review of each, but I simply do not know them all. I know that each of the following agencies have represented friends and colleagues for professional modeling jobs.

- Agency Models and Talent
- Allensworth Entertainment
- Caryn Model and Talent Agency
- Meredith Model and Talent Agency
- Moore Creative Talent, Inc.
- Wehmann Models/Talent, Inc.

See Chapter 4 and Appendix A for more detailed information about these agencies.

How much are models paid?

There is no union governing print work, thus no standard pay scale. Agents seem to establish their own rates. Hourly rates or day rates can vary widely. Just as in acting work, the level of exposure for any job affects the pay. If the shot will only be shown to a limited audience for a one-time event, the pay will be lower. If the shot will be seen via national distribution (for example, in a major magazine or on product packaging sold nationwide), the pay will be significantly higher.

For the print work I have done (in corporate brochures and such), I have received $50 to $100 per hour. My appearance on a billboard in a small market paid several hundred dollars for a very quick shoot (under an hour). I recently attended a go-see for a photo to be used on product packaging. The quoted rate was a $2500 buyout. (The buyout would cover the day rate and national exposure, plus the rights for the client to use the shot in other ways as specified by the contract.) I did not book that one, but it sure would have been nice. I cannot even fathom what supermodels must get for cover shots on magazines!

Be sure to consult other resources if you want more detailed information about pay rates for models.

Which photographers do agencies recommend for models?

If you choose to have professional shots taken before you have guidance from an agency, use photographers who have actual clients. Be sure the photographer is experienced in the world of professional modeling. I asked several local agencies to recommend photographers for models. The following names appeared on their lists: Lee Stanford, Erika Ludwig, Tom Kanthak, Kevin White, Joan Buccina, John Wagner, Jason Tieg and Steve Winters. See Appendix D for contact information for these photographers.

One local agency added: "Go to New York City if you want real fashion photography." I imagine if you want to play in the big leagues of fashion modeling, you need to go to the center of that universe. However, I would advise you to test the waters here first. If you want to swim with the big fish in New York, you should do quite a bit of research before you dive in.

Good luck!

This chapter contains the basics to help you get started. If a reputable agency is interested in you, they will help you figure out your next steps.

Much of the information throughout this book applies to models as well as actors. Consult other chapters for further information (particularly Chapters 2, 4, and 16).

There are many opportunities for models here in the Twin Cities. If you have the right look and a positive, professional attitude, you hopefully will experience some success in the business.

CHAPTER 15

Standup Comedy*

The Twin Cities—a good place to start.

My friend and colleague Joe Lovitt wrote this chapter. Joe is a successful commercial and industrial actor, writer and standup comic. If your acting pursuits also include an interest in standup comedy, I hope his advice will be helpful to you!

The Twin Cities has a thriving standup comedy community. Ask any national headlining comedian where he or she most likes to appear, and Minneapolis will usually be on the list. That is because the Twin Cities has a reputation for having sharp standup comedians who do not settle for "lowest common denominator" humor, and smart, enthusiastic audiences who appreciate them.

The area hit its "standup stride" in the 1970s and 1980s when it provided the training ground for a number of comic talents. The list includes comics such as Louie Anderson, Jeff Cesario, Alex Cole, Scott Hanson, Dave Mordal, and Joel Hodgson *(Mystery Science Theater 3000)*. Standups who went on to successful careers in comedy writing include Joel Madison and Sid Youngers *(Roseanne),* Greg Fidler *(The Tonight Show, Prairie Home Companion),* Lizz Winstead (co-creator of *The Daily Show* on Comedy Central), Peter Tolan (executive producer, *Rescue Me*; co-producer, *Home Improvement;* writer, *Analyze This;* creator, *Murphy Brown, The Larry Sanders Show)* and Don Foster (writer and story editor, *Roseanne, Dharma and Greg,* and *Two and a Half Men*). (Thanks to Stevie Ray, local comic and improv instructor for adding to this list of writers.)

Getting started.

A number of classes in standup comedy have been offered through community education programs and through the Learning Annex. Check the Learning Annex website (www.learningannex.com) or your local community education department to see if any classes are currently offered.

---

* By contributing author, Joe Lovitt.

Also, check out the Sunday workshops offered at The Joke Joint in Bloomington (details at the end of this chapter).

The best education you can get is by attending a few comedy shows. Each typically consists of an MC who opens the show by doing ten to fifteen minutes of material, then introduces the other two acts. The *feature* act performs twenty-five to thirty minutes of material. The *headliner* may perform for forty-five to sixty minutes, or even more.

Open mic nights.

An open mic (pronounced "mike") night can be found nearly every night of the week in the Twin Cities. Each open mic night has its own procedures, so call ahead to find out when you should arrive, how to sign up, etc. Most follow these guidelines:

- Arrive at the comedy club an hour and a half before show time. At that time, the manager posts a sign-up sheet for anyone looking for stage time that night. Do not be late; the sign-up sheet is usually only available for a half-hour. If you are performing for the first time, be sure to put a notation next to your name to that effect. Managers usually try to give priority to first timers.

- A half-hour before show time, the manager posts the show order for the evening. The show order contains the comics' names and the amount of stage time each one has been allotted.

- First-time and beginning comics usually receive three minutes of stage time, although some clubs will offer five minutes, so be prepared to fill the time you are given. Beginning comics appear early in the show. Comics who have shown promise and progress in writing new material are next in the lineup; each of them may receive five minutes. They are followed by established comics, who are given anywhere from seven to ten minutes. The final comic is usually given ten to fifteen minutes with which to close the show.

- Some open mic nights have an MC, usually the person who will be the MC that week at the club's regular shows. The MC opens the show with seven to ten minutes of material, then introduces each comic. Comics are brought up from the audience, not from backstage.

- Prior to performing, find out what system the club has for letting you know your time is up. Most clubs have a light that is visible from the stage. The light will be turned on to indicate you have thirty seconds left. When your time is up, the light will begin flashing. Do not go over your allotted time! If you do, the club may not give you stage time for several more weeks.

What's next?

Even after you have survived your first open mic set, you may not be put on the list at that club for another few weeks. Do not let that discourage you from coming back to that club's open mic again. There are only so many new comics the manager can put up every week. Besides, there are plenty of other clubs to keep you busy. Keep signing up, keep writing, and keep performing. If you are funny, persistent, and prove you are capable of coming up with new material, you will go from three-minute sets to five-minute sets. Then seven. Then ten. By that time, the booker should already have introduced himself or herself to you. It does not hurt for you to take the initiative and introduce yourself to a booker. Just don't be pushy. That will only hurt your chances in the long run.

After you have demonstrated your talent on open mic night, a booker may then ask you to do a *guest set*. This is a seven-minute set during a regular show. You will appear between the MC and the feature act. This unpaid performance gives the booker a chance to see how well a paying audience responds to you. If all goes well, after a successful guest set or two the booker will hire you as an MC. Talent and persistence will determine whether or not you will move on to feature and headliner status.

Working as a comic

Most Twin Cities comics act as their own agent. They call clubs and send them demo tapes and promotional materials. They schedule their own club dates. Those comics fortunate enough to have an agent usually have one who books them nationally. (Note, agents who represent comics are not the same as local talent agents!)

One of the best ways to get work as a standup comic—at least when starting out—is to network with other standup comics. You will learn which bars and restaurants in the region are booking comics for weekend shows. Other comics may hire you to open, co-feature, or co-headline with them.

Some club managers and bookers also book comics for other venues in the region. Once you are established as a working comic, let them know if you are available to travel and take on out-of-town or out-of-state gigs. Even if they do not book you themselves, they may recommend you to bars and smaller clubs who often call the larger clubs looking for talent recommendations.

When and where are the open mic nights?

It all starts with hitting the stage at an open mic night. Here are a few of the local open mic nights. (All of this information is subject to change, so be sure to contact the venue to confirm.)

Acme Comedy Company (Mondays)
708 N. First Street, Minneapolis, Minnesota
612-338-6393
Sign up between 6 and 7 p.m., show at 8 p.m.

The Beat Coffeehouse
(check the website calendar for scheduled events)
1414 W. 28th Street
Minneapolis, Minnesota
612-910-0360
thebeatcoffee.com

Rick Bronson's House of Comedy (Tuesdays)
4th Floor, Mall of America
408 E. Broadway
Bloomington, Minnesota
952 858-8558
houseofcomedy.net

Minnesota Comedy Club (Wednesdays)
Welsch's Big Ten Tavern
4703 Highway 10
Arden Hills, Minnesota
651-777-7255
minnesotacomedyclub.com

Grumpy's Bar, Death Comedy Jam (call for open mic details)
1111 Washington Avenue S.
Minneapolis, Minnesota
612-340-9738
Rookie comics are welcome, but the majority of the show consists of experienced local veterans.

Other Grumpy's locations:

2801 Snelling Avenue N., Roseville, Minnesota
651-379-1180

2200 Fourth St. N.E., Minneapolis, Minnesota
612-789-7429

Comedy Corner Underground (Fridays—call for details.)
Corner Bar
1501 Washington Avenue S.
Minneapolis, Minnesota
612-339-4333

The Joke Joint (Sundays)
2300 East American Boulevard
Bloomington, Minnesota
612-327-0185
jokejointcomedyclub.com

Details about the open mic night can be found on the website.

Final words from Beth.

Three other resources you may wish to check out:

- The website, www.comedy.openmikes.org, lists several other open mic nights in the area. I cannot vouch for the reliability of the information here, so you would be wise to call each venue to verify the information.

- Sunday comedy workshops at the Joke Joint in Bloomington. For details, visit jokejointcomedyclub.com.

- *The Comedy Bible: From Stand-up to Sitcom: The Comedy Writer's Ultimate "How To" Guide* by Judy Carter (Simon and Schuster, 2001).

Even if you do not have an interest in standup comedy, go to an open mic night—it is a blast! Thanks to Joe for this information, and watch for his name at local comedy clubs.

If you want to do standup, you are a braver soul than I—not to mention funnier. Good luck!

CHAPTER 16

Legal and Accounting Issues

My least favorite subject!

As I have said throughout this book, this is a business. As in any business you have to confront the issues of record keeping, finances, contracts, legal formalities, and taxes.

I am neither an attorney nor an accountant nor a tax expert. I am by nature somewhat inept at these things. While I may be a bit more organized than the average actor, like most "artists" my passions and skills lie in the realm of the artistic rather than things logical and numerical. Any advice I have here has come from experience forced upon me rather than anything I have studied by choice. For every issue I discuss here, you would be wise to consult a legal expert, an accountant, or a tax expert. Use the information that follows as an introductory guide to help you get organized and possibly avoid trouble; but if you find yourself in trouble, find yourself an expert!

This chapter is divided into three sections: Contracts and releases, record keeping, and taxes.

CONTRACTS AND RELEASES: SIGNING ON THE DOTTED LINE.

Occasionally, agents ask actors to sign various agreements, managers ask actors to sign contracts, clients and production companies ask actors to sign releases, etc. Some of these documents are a normal part of the business, but not all of them. *Never sign anything if you do not know what you are signing!*

Contracts in general.

If anyone pressures you to sign a contract of any kind, walk away. Anyone who is legit will allow you time to review the contract, consult others, and even consult an attorney before you sign. If they pressure you to sign right away, they are probably someone with whom you do not want to do business.

Exclusivity contracts and agreements.

If you "go exclusive" with an agency, you will probably sign an agreement or contract of some kind. (Being exclusive means you agree not to work with any other talent agency.) Such a document is standard operating procedure and is for the protection of the business relationship. Before signing, be sure the agent is reputable and be sure exclusivity is for you. Be sure the terms and conditions to dissolve the contract are clearly spelled out for both sides. You may want to get out of the agreement someday, so be sure you have that option before you sign. An exclusive agreement with an agency should be a good arrangement for both parties. (See Chapter 4 for details about agents and exclusivity.)

Contracts for Film and TV.

If you do an independent film, one that the filmmaker hopes to sell, you will likely be asked to sign a contract. For an actor, this type of contract gives the filmmaker the right to use footage of you in the film and may specify financial compensation, if any. If the film is likely to be widely released and make some money, you may want an agent or attorney to be involved. However, most independent films never make much money and are never widely aired. Filmmakers here are often honing their talent and investing their own money to get the film made. Many actors do student films and low-budget independent films for the experience, not for the money. A typical contract will guarantee the actor a copy of the film and a tiny percentage of any profits.

Should I sign with a manager?

A Twin Cities actor with a manager is a very rare thing indeed. Successful, busy actors on the coasts hire managers for their schedules, finances, and business relationships. Here in the Twin Cities the vast majority of actors have no need for a manager.

I have heard of managers in L.A. who have roots and/or connections here in the Twin Cities. I also know a local manager who represents top voice-over talent to national clients. It may be wise to build connections before you tackle bigger markets. However, until you have quite a bit of experience and you are in demand, a manager is a waste of money. Do not allow yourself to be pressured, do not pay money up front, and be sure to check references before you sign. Read the fine print to be sure you can dissolve an unsatisfactory relationship without penalty. Further, consulting an attorney is often a good idea before signing any important business agreement.

Signing a talent release at the end of a gig.

Releases are routine, but some can be troublesome. It is standard operating procedure to give talent a release to sign at the end of a shoot. Production companies and clients must have permission to use your likeness in their productions. This is a necessary legal formality for their protection. However, attorneys write up documents that protect their clients from any and every foreseeable problem, sometimes leaving the other party high and dry. They write such documents because their client is paying them, and the other party is not. Too often, we actors blindly sign without reading, because we want to please the client and not make waves. They say, "Oh, it is just the standard release for legal purposes. Everyone just signs it. It is a formality."

That statement is often true. It is just a formality, and it will rarely hurt you. However, depending upon the language, these documents occasionally haunt actors. Read them carefully! If you have any doubts, your agent should always read and approve the release before you sign. Telling the client you cannot sign until your agent approves it can be difficult, especially if all the other actors are blissfully signing away. Your agent has negotiated rates with the client for the particular usage of the gig. If you blindly sign a release, you may unknowingly be giving the client the rights to use the footage much more extensively than what was negotiated by your agent.

Following are some sample statements, similar to releases that I have actually (ignorantly) signed. It does not take a rocket scientist to see the danger in signing such things:

> Actor agrees to use of his or her performance in any
> and all media including television, radio, Internet, etc.,
> throughout the world without limitation.

The problem with this one is that they can use you on any other media, anywhere in the world at any time in the future, and you cannot get a penny for it. Let your agent negotiate and collect the appropriate fees for additional use of your likeness.

Here's another scary one:

> Actor agrees that he or she will not at any time in the
> future authorize the use of his or her likeness or voice in
> any commercial advertising for any competitive product
> or services.

OR

> I understand that photographs of me will be used in
> advertising of [client's product] and their value would be

diminished if I appear in competitive advertising. As long as [client] continues to use photographs in its advertising, I will not allow similar photographs to be taken of me.

The above two paragraphs would limit your ability to work for the client's competitors. Competitors may not want to use you anyway; however, if a client wants a guarantee that you will not work for the competition, they will have to pay for that guarantee. Signing something like this may limit your ability to work and may open you up to litigation in the future. A good agent will back you up on this and will charge the client an additional fee for such a demand. If a client wants you exclusively for their product, limiting your relationships with other clients, they should pay accordingly.

And another:

I hereby authorize [client], its successors, licensees, assignees to use and reproduce audiovisuals of me, and to circulate them for any and all purposes and in any manner, including publications and advertisements of all kinds in all media.

This one not only gives them the right to put your little face anywhere in the world, it also gives them the right to give your little face to lots of other folks to use anywhere in the world. You will likely never see a penny for it.

If you blindly sign these things, you are giving the client the right to use your likeness anywhere and everywhere without further compensation. One story will illustrate the danger here: I once did a commercial for a furniture store. It was a "buyout," so I was getting around $1200 for the spot. This buyout gave the client the rights to show this one commercial in multiple markets for multiple years if they chose to do so. (Union actors reading this are now choking—this is the down-side of being non-union. Though $1200 is a great day rate, the potential for abuse by the client is unreal.) Anyway, in blissful ignorance at the end of the shoot, I signed their release. Lo and behold, my face (along with the three other actors in the spot) began showing up in four different commercials edited from the same footage. Further, our faces appeared in a full-page ad in the Sunday *Star Tribune* and *Pioneer Press*. Finally, though I played a customer in the spot, my face appeared in an ad in the Yellow Pages (in every home and business in the Twin Cities metro area) as if I was a representative of the store. This was either abuse of the agreement between the client and my agent, or a miscommunication of the terms of the buyout.

However, remember the release I blindly signed? Though the buyout rate gave the client permission to use the footage in *one* spot to play in multiple markets for multiple years, the client assumed that the buyout fee along with this release covered them for every use and abuse of my likeness anywhere and forever. Fortunately, my agent fought and won additional compensation. However, had it gone to court, the fact that I signed the release may have given us a shaky legal leg.

Discuss this issue with your agent, and do not sign a questionable release unless your agent has approved it. I realize that it may be awkward at the shoot, but apologize to the client, explain that while you trust that particular client, unscrupulous clients do exist, and you are simply trying to protect yourself. Fax machines are everywhere. Call for your agent's fax number and ask the client or production company to fax it. If the shoot is after hours, they will have to give you a copy to share with your agent during the next business day.

Most clients are honest and will not abuse your services even if you do sign one of these things. Blame the legal departments for the language, not necessarily the client. When you sign releases, most of the time it will not come back to haunt you. Again, read carefully; the risk is up to you.

What if it is after hours and the client insists?

If a contract contains a passage that makes you uncomfortable, you have the option of crossing out the passage, initialing in the margin next to the passage, and asking the client to add his/her initials. I have done this a few times. Often the production assistant is not authorized to initial, and the client is not available on the set. If you cannot obtain the client's initials, the legal ramifications are unclear (according to my attorney), though it does put the client on notice that there may be a problem. If the client insists that you sign, cross off objectionable passages, initial the changes and ask for a copy. If you are wise, you will ask for a copy of any release you sign and share it with your agent.

What kind of a release can I sign?

The releases need to be clear and fair. You can sign releases that your agent has reviewed and approved, or releases that you know to be fair. When you have been around for a while, you may be able to recognize a release that is safe for you to sign. When in doubt, run it by your agent.

An example of a release that is acceptable from an actor's point of view follows. This one clearly grants the client and production company the right to use the footage, but only for this particular video. It is not an unlimited-use agreement like the preceding examples.

I grant [production company and client] the right to photograph scenes in which I appear on (shoot date) and consent that such pictures may be used in the production, duplication, and distribution of [client and specific title of video produced that day] for use within [client's company name].

This gives the client the right to use the footage that was shot that day for the specified project only. Fair and clear. Again, most clients have no intention to cheat you. Read releases carefully, and consult your agent if you have concerns.

Non-disclosure agreements.

If you are hired to participate in any kind of marketing study for a new product, you may be asked to sign a "non-disclosure" or confidentiality agreement. This type of document generally states that you agree not to talk about or reveal the product information to anyone. I have signed a handful of these. Read carefully, and then be sure not to talk. The information that I agree to keep confidential generally seems unimportant to me (who would want to know anyway?), but it is important to the client. Sign and honor the agreement.

The bottom line.

Do not sign anything if you have not read it. Do not sign anything that you do not understand. Do not sign anything with unclear language about usage and money until your agent approves it.

RECORD KEEPING.

Why do I have to keep detailed records? Doesn't my agent keep track of my paychecks?

Remember that you are a small business selling a product; you are the president, C.E.O., V.P. of sales, marketing, accounting, and human resources. You do have an agent, who is essentially a marketing manager for several key accounts—she books the gig, bills the gig, forwards the money to you, and issues a 1099 at tax time—but that is it. All other tasks and roles in your company go to you!

Again, I am not a tax expert. However, I have learned from my mistakes, and here are several suggestions to keep you from making similar (potentially costly and embarrassing) mistakes!

Perhaps you are like I was twenty years ago, accustomed to a regular paycheck at regular intervals. I was a public school teacher; I got a check for the same amount every fifteenth and thirtieth of the month, and taxes were taken out. Tax time was simple, and budgeting was very clear. (My budget still did not balance, but the math was easier then.) Now I never know when I will receive paychecks, and I am often unsure of the exact amount. Budgeting is a nightmare, and tax time has often been worse. Keeping accurate records will help.

What kinds of records should I keep?

When you are starting out, it is easy to keep track of a few jobs a year. When you start doing more auditions and booking a few more gigs, it will be essential to keep track of everything.

Normally, you do the job, it goes as expected, and you receive your check in a timely manner. Then record keeping is easy. Record the job and the pay, and file it away. If anything about the job or payment goes awry, you will be glad you have kept good records.

Your records for each and every gig should include the following information:

- Audition date, time, and location.
- Shoot or session date, call time, and location.
- Agent who sent you (very important if you are listed with more than one agent; you will occasionally forget).
- Wardrobe you wore to the audition.
- Name of the client and/or production company.
- Approximate amount of money due to you.
- Amount actually paid to you.
- Commission paid to your agent.
- Check numbers.
- Invoice number or job numbers (if your agent uses these).
- Potential tax deductions: mileage, parking fees, and any other costs associated with the audition or job. (See IRS information below.)

Record-keeping formats.

It is likely you will be able to devise an effective system for yourself; however, I have included (in Appendix I) a sample job sheet that I have used for years. Feel free to copy it or modify it as you please. It is not brilliant, but it has been functional for me. There are also actors' accounting notebooks and software available for purchase. Again, see Appendix I.

If you are computer literate, you may be able to design a simpler, more efficient system. Accounting programs such as Quicken or Microsoft Money can be customized to add different fields in order to keep track of job details.

Why do I need to keep such detailed records?

You may never need to go back and refer to many of these details; however, if you ever encounter problems, you will be glad you have them in ink.

It seems like a no-brainer, but you need to keep track of which jobs have been paid and which have not. Do not bug your agent with questions if you simply cashed the check and forgot. Record keeping is part of your job. The agent can look it up for you, but they sure do not want to spend a lot of time digging through files for you. Do this often, and you will have an annoyed agent.

If you keep good records, you can glance through your paperwork and recognize past due accounts. If it has been more than seven or eight weeks and you still

> "It is the talent's responsibility to keep detailed records of auditions, shoots, voice-overs, and job payments. I cannot tell you how frustrating it is when a talent calls to ask, 'Has that one thing that I auditioned for last week been cast?' or, 'I did that job where I played a single mom a while back; has it paid yet?'"
>
> —Laura McDonnell, actor, agent, NUTS, ltd.

have not been paid for a job, it is time to call your agent. (Do not call if it has been only two or three weeks. Union actors are supposed to be paid within a couple of weeks; non-union actors are rarely paid that quickly.) If you have the date and client's name right there in your records, it will be much easier for your agent to find the paperwork. Searching the files when you provide no dates and names can be very frustrating.

Accurate records may help you avoid being underpaid. If clients like a spot you have done, they may decide to run it again a year or two later. If you are in the union, you will receive residuals for this. If you are non-union, you may have to work for any additional pay. If you see the spot running again, you can search your records for the exact shoot date and the pay you received. If you did not receive a buyout up front, they may owe you more money. If your records accurately confirm date, financial figures, client, production company, etc., you may be able to help your agent get you more money. (Union contracts may give you more clout and accurate records for this type of situation. If you are non-union, you and your agent are on your own.)

You will also want accurate records just in case the IRS comes to call. Which brings me to my least favorite subject.

TAXES AND THE DREADED IRS.

Again, I am not qualified to give tax advice. If you start making any money in this business, get a good tax advisor. A few suggestions may help you with planning, record keeping, and avoiding some of the costly mistakes I have made.

If they do not withhold taxes, I probably do not owe any; or at least I can get away without paying any, right?

Oh so wrong. You may be able to get away with it, but I sure would not risk it.

If you are hired as an independent contractor, you are responsible for paying the taxes on all of this income. The IRS requires that you make quarterly estimated tax payments, due April, June, September, and January of each year. A good accountant can help you figure the approximate amount of these payments.

Do not do what I did. My first relatively successful year in the business was great—until tax time. Did I save for taxes that year? Of course not. I figured I just did not make that much, so how bad could it be? I left my accountant's office, fighting tears, holding a bill to the IRS for a sum greater than I had imagined. I had to swallow my pride and, for the first time in my adult life, call my parents to ask for money. (My dad did not want me to quit my "real job" in the first place; I swore I would be able to make it without his help. Ouch. Admitting you are wrong is almost as painful as owing the cash to the IRS.) I am glad I have a generous, forgiving dad; he made things easier. But planning ahead and paying my quarterlies would have been much better.

Also know that you may owe penalties for late payment if you do not pay your quarterlies. The IRS wants their money on time, not a year later.

How do I know if I have been hired as an independent contractor or an employee?

Your agent can help you with this; however, it is not complicated.

If you are hired as an *employee*, you will need to fill out tax forms for that employer, forms W4 and I9 at the very least. (You will also need to show ID—a driver's license and social security card or a passport. This is standard procedure for any employment.) As an employee, even just for a one-day shoot, taxes will be deducted from your check. When you receive your check, the check stub will clearly show the withholding for state and federal taxes; you will also receive a bill from your agent for the ten to fifteen percent agency fee. (Your employer pays you, and then you pay your agent.)

If you are hired as an *independent contractor*, no forms will be needed. Your agent will bill the client; the client will pay your agent; your agent takes her ten to fifteen percent and sends you a check for the rest. You simply receive a check from the agency with no tax information whatsoever.

If there is no check stub with tax details, know that you were hired as an independent contractor and you probably owe taxes.

What happens at tax time?

You will receive a W2 from any company who hired you as an employee. (Sometimes this comes from a payroll service.)

You will receive a 1099 for your other income. If you receive more than $600 as an independent contractor from any one source, that source must issue you a Form 1099 each January for the previous fiscal year. The form will most likely come from your agent. If you are employed on stage, the 1099 will come from the theater.

I cannot tell you what to do with your W2s and 1099; that is what I pay my accountant to do. (I can only suggest that you gaze at the 1099 or W2 proudly, with the realization that you are a working actor!)

Tax deductions.

Tax deductions are perfectly legal. We pay a lot in taxes, and there is no reason to pay more than you owe!

However, deductions from your taxes can be very confusing. The laws frequently change, so here is where you may really need a good tax advisor. The following list contains items and costs that *may* be tax deductible for performing artists. However, there are restrictions and technicalities. Entire dull books are written on the subject. I am simply suggesting that you track all of these expenses very carefully. Save and file all receipts. Write the details of each expense on the receipt before you file it. Note check numbers and dates, along with the specific job, audition, or networking connection for which the expense was paid. Organize all the receipts and totals by category, and then take it all to your accountant to figure out. If you are ever audited, you had better have a good paper trail to verify all of your deductions: car mileage log, receipts, dates, details of subject matter for business meals, etc.

Also, be aware of another very confusing technicality: Items for employee work are often not deductible (or less deductible) than items for your independent contractor work. Blame the tax code! Keep track of it all, and be sure to note what was used/purchased for employee gigs as opposed to all other gigs and auditions. An able accountant is invaluable.

Items that *may* be tax deductible for actors.

- Actor coaching, training, classes, seminars, etc.
- Vocal coaching and lessons.
- Agent fees.
- CDs and DVDs used for research and training. (Be careful here: If you rent a movie for fun, it is not deductible. On the other hand, if you have an audition coming up for the Coen brothers, for example, the cost to rent a few of their movies to research the style may be deductible.)
- Concert/film/theater tickets—if for research purposes.
- Books, plays, scripts and sheet music that are specific to your preparation for work and auditions.
- Cell phone. (If it is used primarily for business.)
- Long distance business calls.
- Some auto expenses. (See details below.)
- Parking fees for jobs and auditions.
- Bus fare, cab fare for seeking employment.
- Business equipment: ear prompters, microphones, editing software, etc.
- Gifts for business associates. (Gifts for opening night, cast members, directors, agents, etc. The limit is $25 per person.)
- Business meals/entertainment expenses (partially deductible; be sure to note on all receipts the subject matter of the business meal and the names and titles of those present at the meeting).
- Headshots and photo duplication.
- Computer software and supplies if used for business purposes.
- Resumes and duplication.
- Copying, fax, postage for business purposes.
- Office supplies.
- Costumes and costume maintenance.
- Hair care, makeup, manicures, etc. (Your own routine hair care and makeup are likely not deductible. If a client specifically requests a hair color, trim, or manicure for the shoot, it may be deductible.)
- Piano tuning/repair (if you are a singer who needs to rehearse).
- Trade publications (*Back Stage News*, *American Theater Magazine*, etc.)

- Professional organization dues, union initiation fees and dues.
- Rehearsal space rental.
- Advertising: demos, websites, mailings to agents, casting directors and clients, mailings to advertise your latest show, etc.
- Travel expenses for employment.
- A portion of your health club expenses if your appearance is very significant to your employment.

Note: If you use any the above items for other day-to-day purposes, they are probably not deductible. To be deductible, an item must be solely for employment/acting/audition purposes. For example, if you purchase a suit for an audition or gig that you also wear to your day job, it is not deductible. If it is a costume that you wear *only* for auditions and gigs, it may be legally deductible.

Once again, confirm all of this with a qualified, professional tax advisor. My advice here is simply to jump start your planning and record-keeping process.

Keeping track of mileage.

Your mileage to and from gigs, auditions, rehearsals, etc., may be tax deductible. A few miles here and there may not seem like much, but it can really add up. However, in order to claim this as a deduction, you first must keep accurate records. I record mileage information in my calendar next to the job entry. You may want to keep a mileage log in your car. Though it is tedious to total it all at the end of the year, it is worth it. If you claim mileage as a deduction, the IRS will require written evidence.

Not all of your mileage is deductible. As with anyone who has a job, your trip to work and back home may not be deductible. If your job requires you to make several trips in between, those miles may be deductible. For example, I drive to an audition, and then to a voice gig, then to my agent's office to drop off the extra headshots she requested, then I go to another audition, then to my evening theater rehearsal, and then home. My first trip out in the morning is not deductible. My final trip home is not deductible. The miles in between may be deductible.

Finally . . .

Be a good business manager. No one will take care of your records for you. Record keeping is key, and so is a good tax accountant to help you sort it all out. Take a little time to establish your own system; once you get started, it is not difficult to stay on top of it. See Appendix I for specific resources that will help make it all easier.

CHAPTER 17

Other Markets: Resources

Know before you go . . .

The closest I have come to being a working actor in another market is a 1984 summer internship at Wisdom Bridge Theatre in Chicago. That was a long time ago, and the theater no longer exists. So much for having out-of-town connections!

Explore resources and prepare carefully before you make the big move to New York, Chicago or L.A. Minneapolis/St. Paul is a great place to learn and gain experience. It is a great place to stay if your desire is to be a working actor with a livable lifestyle. If your goal is to work in film and TV, you will eventually have to move.

There is nothing like networking and connections. If you are going to move, keep your eyes and ears open for actors who have been there or those who are planning to go. Ask questions. Occasionally you will see an ad for a class about the L.A. market taught by someone who has worked there. If you are serious about making the jump, I recommend that you get all the information you can.

Get your SAG card.

I have frequently heard that you should be a SAG (Screen Actors' Guild) member before you head to L.A. It is difficult enough to get a foot in the door with agents and casting directors. Being non-union might be an additional impediment for you. If your goal is to move, look into all of your union options here long before you leave town. (See Chapter 5 for more information.)

Two great resources for all markets:

- *How to Sell Yourself as an Actor*, sixth edition (by K. Callan, Sweden Press, 2008) is my favorite resource about being a professional actor on the coasts. It gives a very practical approach for those determined to make it as an actor in any market. It is well written and easy to read, with great advice about the business side of being an actor.

- *How to be a Working Actor*, fifth edition (by Mari Lyn Henry and Lynne Rogers, Back Stage Books, 2008) is another great resource about the world of acting, written by professionals who know the business from all angles.

Smaller markets.

The two books listed above both touch on pursuing acting work wherever you are. More specifically, K. Callan's book discusses how to research acting opportunities in any hometown in her Chapter 5: "There's no place like home." Other books and directories about smaller markets may exist, though you may not find them in major bookstores or national booksellers' websites. I have seen some small market references on the shelves at the Drama Book Shop in New York. If you need to relocate, search the website (dramabookshop.com) or call to ask what they may have.

Of course, the internet may help in your search; but do not trust everything you read. I have seen many "directories" that claim to have information about the business in Minnesota, but the information is usually incorrect or incomplete. Use good business sense when you approach unknown agencies.

Chicago.

My old hometown has a thriving acting community. My life is here in the Twin Cities, but a piece of my heart remains in Chicago.

- *Performink: Chicago's Entertainment Trade Paper. The Art, the Business, the Industry* (performink.com). If you are planning a move to Chicago, check out performink.com. It is the website for Chicago's trade paper. The website will link you to just about every theater organization in the city. Twin Cities' actors may want to check the site to find great articles, too.

- *The Book: An Actor's Guide to Chicago*, seventh edition (by Carrie L. Kaufman, Performink Books, 2007). If you are going to pursue work in Chicago, this is a must. It is incredibly complete. Reading it made me want to move back.

- Act One Studios (www.actone.com, 312-787-9384, 640 N. LaSalle, Chicago). Oh how I wish we had an Act One in the Twin Cities! Act One offers a wealth of classes and workshops, and the website contains a links section that will hook you up with dozens of Chicago resources—from theaters, to agents, to headshot photographers. They also offer an inexpensive workshop for actors who are new to the Chicago area. If you want to work in Chicago, you want to know about Act One Studios.

- Chicago Artists Resource website. Visit Chicagoartists.org and click on theater to find a myriad of Chicago and national resources.

New York.

There are dozens, perhaps hundreds of books written about the business on the coasts. The following are just a few of the key resources that are well organized and detailed. I have been fortunate to spend a bit of time in New York, so I have had the opportunity to do a little research there.

- *Backstage: The Performing Arts Weekly* (www.backstage.com) This is the weekly trade paper of the acting world in New York. (There is a New York version and a west coast version.) This is a must if you are going to move to one of the coasts to pursue acting. It contains audition listings, ads for classes and schools, great articles, reviews, etc. Visit the website for further information or to order a subscription. You may subscribe via print or online. If you want to get a copy locally, some Barnes and Nobles bookstores carry it.

- The Drama Bookshop (www.dramabookshop.com, 250 W. 40th Street, New York, NY 10018, 1-800 322-0595, 212 944-0595). This should be one of your first stops when you go to New York. It is at the southern edge of the Broadway theater district, a couple blocks south of Times Square. It has everything from scripts, to books about the business, to rehearsal space, to mailing labels for all kinds of industry contacts. They frequently offer free workshops, book signings, and play readings. Go to the website to register for their e-mail newsletter. They will have just about any book or resource you would ever want.

- *ACT New York 2005: The Actor's Pocket Guide to New York City*, by Larry Silverberg, Smith and Kraus, 2004. A very comprehensive listing of who's who and what's what relating to acting in New York. The first chapter is a great listing and review of some of the best acting coaches in the city.

- *An Actor's Guide: Making it in New York City* (by Glenn Alterman, Allworth Press, 2002). Practical information about living and working in New York. The book opens with a discussion of the question, "New York or Los Angeles: Which is best for you?"

- *The New York Agent Book: How to Get the Agent You Need for the Career You Want*, sixth edition (by K. Callan. Sweden Press, 2008). If you think the agent game in Minneapolis can be confusing and frustrating, read about New York! The book discusses each New York agent and what they do, as well as sharing a ton of great advice about working in New York.

- *An Actor Prepares . . . To Live in New York City: How to Live Like a Star Before You Become One* (by Craig Wroe, Limelight Editions,

2004). This book is less about acting and the business, and more about surviving and thriving in New York.

Los Angeles.

La-la land (L.A.) is a mystery to me. I have visited there and I know folks who have moved there (many never to be heard from again), but I have no desire to ever live there. I am just not a Los Angeles type. The short list below is a tiny fraction of the resources you will find about show business in Los Angeles. You will note that two of the three are by Kristi Callan. I have read a few of her books; I love her writing style, and if you read reviews online, she seems to be *the* expert at creating and composing useful, professional guidebooks for actors.

If you decide to make the jump to L.A., I wish you much luck, you brave soul. I hope the following resources may be of help to you.

- *Backstage West: The Performing Arts Weekly* (www.backstage.com). This is the West Coast version of *Backstage*. If you go to backstage.com, you will need to click on "subscribe" to get to the specifics of the west coast version. You may choose to subscribe to the print version or online. Again, it is a must if you are going to move to L.A. to pursue acting. It contains audition listings, ads for classes and schools, great articles, reviews, etc.

- *The Working Actor's Guide to Los Angeles* (edited by Kristi Callan. Aaron Blake Publishers, 2006, www.workingactors.com). This is a complete source book for actors in L.A. It is periodically updated with contact information for theaters, production companies, acting schools, casting directors, etc. Visit the website; many of the listings in the book are also online.

- *The Los Angeles Agent Book: How to Get the Agent You Need for the Career You Want* (by K. Callan. Sweden Press, 2008). Again, the agent game in L.A. is enormously complicated compared to the Twin Cities. The book discusses each L.A. agent and what they do, as well as providing a ton of great advice about working in L.A.

Check out the "Ice Pack."

Minnesotans who relocate to the coasts occasionally gather as the "Ice Pack" to meet, greet, and network. The official gatherings may be listed on the Minnesota Film and TV Board website (mnfilmtv.org). Be sure to look into this if you head to New York or Los Angeles. Search the site for the words, Ice Pack, or contact the Film and TV Board to ask about the Ice Pack list.

When you jump, do not just close your eyes and hope for the best.

Thousands of actors and wannabes head to the coasts each year with stars in their eyes. If you make the move, be sure you have done your homework and as much networking as possible. Research and networking will help you knock on the right doors, and, with a lot of luck, your talent and training will get you through some of them.

I have heard that in L.A., the Twin Cities has a reputation for developing good actors, thus the agents on the coasts may take an extra glance. I have no idea if this is true, but when you go, be sure to represent us well. It would be nice if that positive Twin Cities reputation could grow.

Whether you stay here in the Twin Cities or you head for the bright lights of Broadway or sunny L.A., enjoy the journey. And break a leg!

Afterword

I often say, "I pretend for a living." This is a fun business, and I cannot imagine myself in any other career. However, do not confuse the word *fun* with the word *easy*. Everyone I know who stays in the biz works incredibly hard. Successful actors do not sit at home waiting for the phone to ring! They are constantly working it, working at their acting craft, and working the biz.

Entering this career is neither practical nor sensible. It only makes sense if you are dying to be an actor and nothing else will satisfy you. It was a little bit crazy of me to leave a full-time, tenured teaching position in order to give acting a whirl, but I felt compelled. It was not practical, but it was what I needed to do.

If you feel the same way, join me. If you cannot be satisfied in life until you try it, then follow the advice I give in this book so you can chase this dream in a sensible, practical way. Balance the crazy dream with a sane approach.

Above all, acting is play. Do not get so bogged down in the business and the money that you forget what attracted you to the biz in the first place. Just play, pretend, communicate, create—and enjoy the ride.

If you notice that any information in this listing is incomplete or out of date, please let me know! Send an e-mail to beth@actingbiztc.com. Changes and updates will be posted on my website, actingbiztc.com.

Acknowledgments

Great thanks to everyone who helped create this book!

The editors of my early drafts—for offering extensive, fantastic feedback: Jan Hilton, Gigi Jensen, Celia Forrest, Bob and Carol Thomas, Sarah Teich, Doug Leland, Jillian Dunham, and David and Carole Chaplin. And subject matter experts who clarified many facts: Stevie Ray, and Robyn Johnson.

Colleen Aho, executive director of the local AFTRA office, and Cathy Fuller, former AFTRA president. Their input for Chapter 5 was invaluable. I am grateful for their time and expertise in clarifying much of the information.

My dear friends at NUTS, ltd. for their loyalty and friendship—including all of you who have been NUTS over the years; You know who you are!

Jan Hilton, who taught me much about the business side of this crazy biz.

My research assistants, contributors, and friends: Susan Spongberg, Colleen Barrett, Joe Lovitt, and Megan Kelly.

Linda Klemmer and Debbie Klemmer-Rush of Voice Plus/Actors Plus for their loyalty during the past two decades.

Jane Brody who taught me much of what I know about acting and for offering words of encouragement.

Casting directors who have offered expert input: Jean Rohn, Kelly Gallagher, Lynn Blumenthal, Michelle Hutchison, Lynn Steele, and Barbara Shelton.

Cheryl Moore Brinkley, outstanding teacher, colleague, and friend. Your input, advice, and friendship have been invaluable, both personally and professionally.

The dozens of actors who have filled out questionnaires and responded to e-mails with information, opinions, and stories. Many asked to remain anonymous. You know who you are, my friends, and I truly appreciate your contributions.

Various talent agents who gave their time to answer questions and offer input.

Students in my past acting classes. Your questions and wisdom helped create this book.

Attorney Deb Orenstein and Springboard for the Arts.

Leonard and Karen at Kirk House Publishers for their support, and the confidence and enthusiasm to make this book happen!

Last, but certainly not least, my family: Your encouragement, love, support, and patience are overwhelming and endless. Words simply cannot suffice.

Agents

The information about each agency below has been provided by the agency or comes directly from the agency's website. I know experienced actors who are represented by each, and I know that each agency below has booked actors for legitimate work for which the actor has been paid. I cannot vouch for the business practices of any agency: rates, fees, sales of classes/photo packages, etc. See each agency website for more detailed info.

I have not listed every agent in town, as I cannot personally vouch for all of them. I have listed only the agents that I feel I can recommend to you with some measure of confidence. An omission here means that an agency is fairly new to town, or that I simply do not recommend them. There may be some new agents who have opened up shop since the publication of this book. However, if you stick with the list below, you will have found most of the good agents in town.

Agency Models and Talent
700 Washington Avenue N., # 210
Minneapolis, Minnesota 55401
agencymodelsandtalent.com
612 664-1174

Established: 1996
Non-union
Represent Fi-core actors? Yes
Commission: 15 percent
Modeling and print department: Yes
Represent children: Yes
Affiliated with any acting/modeling
schools? No
Fee to be on the agency's website:
Changes as our cost goes down

Interested talent should submit photo and resume and/or voice-over demo (no more than two photos, keep attachments under 2MB)

Mail:
Agency Models and Talent
Attn: New Talent Division
700 Washington Avenue N., #210
Minneapolis, Minnesota 55401

E-mail: newtalent@agencymodelsandtalent.com

Allensworth Entertainment, Inc. Minnesota
8120 Penn Avenue S. #151D
Bloomington, Minnesota 55431
allensworthentertainment.com
952-567-1141

Established: 2008
Union and non-union (SAG franchised)
Represent Fi-core actors? Yes
Commission: 10 percent union, 15 percent non-union
Modeling and print department: Yes
Represent children: Yes
Fee to be on the agency's website: $25, additional $25 to include actor's reel

Affiliated with any acting/modeling schools? No

Interested talent should submit photo and resume and/or voice-over demo

Mail:
Allensworth Entertainment, Inc.
Minnesota
8120 Penn Avenue S., Suite 151D
Bloomington, Minnesota 55431

E-mail:
Stephanie@allensworthentertainment.com

West coast office:
Allensworth Entertainment, Inc.
291 S. La Cienega Boulevard, Suite 107
Beverly Hills, CA 90211

Caryn Model and Talent Management
4229 Excelsior Boulevard
St. Louis Park, Minnesota 55416
carynmodels.com
952-945-6600

Established: 1990
Union and non-union
Represent Fi-core actors? Yes
Commission: Union 10 percent, non-union 20 percent
Modeling and print department: Yes
Represent children: Yes
Fee to be included on the agency's website: $80 set-up fee + $9.99 per month
Affiliated with any acting/modeling schools? "Caryn and Chuck Rosenberg own Caryn International: however, Caryn Model and Talent Management is completely independent."

Interested talent should submit photo and resume to:

Mail:
Caryn Model and Talent Management
4229 Excelsior Boulevard
St. Louis Park, Minnesota 55416

NUTS, ltd. (Non-union talent service)
820 N. Lilac Drive, Suite 101
Golden Valley, Minnesota 55422
nutsltd.com
763-529-0330

Established: 1985
Non-union
Represent Fi-core actors? No
Commission: 15% (10% from exclusive talent.)
Modeling and Print department: no (occasional print opportunities come our way.)
Represent Children: yes (over age 5, theater/performing experience preferred.)
Fee to be included on the agency's website: No fee. Adult actors are included on our website for free. We do not place children's photos on our website.
Are you affiliated with any acting/modeling schools? No

Interested talent should submit photo and resume (and/or voice-over demo) to:

Mail:
NUTS, ltd.
820 N. Lilac Drive, Suite 101
Golden Valley, Minnesota 55422

E-mail: No e-mail submissions. They only accept submissions via the postal service.

Lipservice Talent Guild
2010 E. Hennepin Avenue, Box 16
Minneapolis, Minnesota 55413
lipservicetalent.com
612-338-5477

Established: 1973
Strictly union: SAG/AFTRA/AEA
Represent Fi-core actors? No
Commission: 10 percent (used to fund the guild)
Modeling and print department: No (though occasionally print finds its way to them)
Represent children: No
Fee to be included on website: No
Affiliated with any acting/modeling schools? No

Interested talent should submit photo and resume and/or voice-over demo:

Mail:
Lipservice Talent Guild
ATTN: Membership Committee
2010 E. Hennepin Avenue, Box 16
Minneapolis, Minnesota 55413

Do not stop by in person, fax or e-mail submissions! Please read the information on the Lipservice website before submitting materials.

Meredith Model and Talent Agency
800 Washington Avenue N., Suite 511
Minneapolis, Minnesota 55401
meridithagency.com
612-340-9555

Established: New Jersey 1977, Twin Cities 1991
Union: SAG/AFTRA franchised
Do you also represent actors for non-union jobs? Unknown
Represent Fi-core actors? Unknown
Commission: 10 percent
Modeling and print department: Yes
Represent children: Yes
Fee to be included on the agency's website: Unknown
Are you affiliated with any acting/modeling schools? No

Interested talent should submit photo and resume and/or voice-over demo to:

Mail:
Meredith Model and Talent Agency
800 Washington Avenue N., # 511
Minneapolis, Minnesota 55401

E-mail: Photos via e-mail will not be reviewed. Photos need to be a minimum of 4x6", not to exceed 8"x10", and do not have to be professionally taken.

East Coast office:
Meredith Model Management
767 Frederick Court
Wyckoff, NJ 07481
201-560-9981

Moore Creative Talent, Inc.
3130 Excelsior Boulevard
Minneapolis, Minnesota 55416
mooretalent.com
612-827-3823

New talent info line: 612 827-3200
Established: 1958
Union and non-union, SAG/AFTRA franchised
Represent Fi-core actors? Yes
Commission: 10 percent
Modeling and print department: Yes
Represent children: Yes
Fee to be included on the agency's website: $50 for actors, $250 for make-up artists
Affiliated with any acting/modeling schools? No

Interested talent should submit photo and resume(and/or voice-over demo) to:

Mail:
Moore Creative Talent, Inc.
3130 Excelsior Boulevard
Minneapolis, Minnesota 55416

E-mail: Does not accept e-mailed pictures or resumes.

Voice demos via e-mail to: voiceover@ mooretalent.com

No walk-ins.

Talent Poole
1595 Selby Avenue
Suite 200, The Park Building
St. Paul, Minnesota 55104
talentpoole.com
651 645-2516

Established: 1997
Non-union
Represent Fi-core actors? No
Commission: 10 percent
Modeling and print department: No, only occasional print work.
Represent children: Yes, age 5 and up.
Fee to be included on the agency's website: One time fee of $20 to post the photo and resume. Photo updates: $10. $25 annual fee for voice talent.

Are you affiliated with any acting/modeling schools? No

Interested talent should submit photo and resume (and/or voice-over demo) to:

Mail:
Talent Poole
Attn: Tom Poole
1595 Selby Avenue
Suite 200, The Park Building
St. Paul, Minnesota 55104

E-mail: Tom@talentpoole.com

Interested voice talent should submit mp3s or CDs

Mail:
Talent Poole
Attn: Geanette
1595 Selby Avenue
Suite 200, The Park Building
St. Paul, Minnesota 55104

E-mail: geanette@talentpoole.com

Wehmann Models/Talent, Inc.
1128 Harmon Place, Suite 202
Minneapolis, Minnesota 55403
wehmann.com
612 333-6393

Established: 1984
Union: AFTRA/SAG/AEA franchised
Represent Fi-core actors? No
Commission: 10 percent
Modeling and print department: Yes
Represent children: Yes
Fee to be included on the agency's website: $100
Are you affiliated with any acting/modeling schools? No

Interested talent should submit photo and resume (and/or voice-over demo) to:

Mail:
Wehmann Models/Talent, Inc.
1128 Harmon Place, Suite 202
Minneapolis, Minnesota 55403

E-mai: Julia@wehmann.com

Other agencies

I know little about the following agencies. I do not personally know any actors who have booked work through them, possibly because they may specialize in areas other than acting (modeling, music, etc.). Pursue representation if you wish.

Vision Management Group, Inc
111 Washington Avenue N., Suite 200
Minneapolis, Minnesota 55401
visionmodels.com
612-359-0828

Arquette and Associates
801 Washington Avenue N., Suite 118
Minneapolis, Minnesota 55401
Arquetteagency.com
612 339-8500

*A Model Management (new agency, 2009)
720 West Lake Street, Suite 101
Minneapolis, MN 55408
Awithastar.com
612 259-7388

Perfectly Petite
2500 W. County Road 42, Suite 108
Burnsville, Minnesota 55337
perfectlypetite.com
952 882 9626

JMG
219 N. Second Street, Suite 401
Minneapolis, Minnesota 55401
612 338-2077

Casting Directors

Though I have listed phone numbers here, actors should not call. If you know a casting director well, then feel free to use the phone number; however, if you are a new actor, just submit your headshot and resume through the mail. They will call you if they want to see you!

A&E Casting (est. 2007)
Toni Trussoni and Eric Mahutga
681 17th Avenue N.E., Suite 202
Minneapolis, Minnesota 55413
612-310-5333
aandecasting.com

Bab's Casting (est. 1989)
Barbara Shelton
420 North 5th Street #312
Minneapolis, Minnesota 55401
612-332-6858

Note: They do not keep a file of actors' headshots at Bab's Casting, so there is no need to send yours. They will call you through an agency if they want to see you.

JR Casting (est. 1994)
Jean Rohn and Kelly Gallagher
www.jrcasting.net

Talent submissions:
P.O. Box 46638
Eden Prairie, Minnesota 55344

Studio address:
400 First Avenue N., Suite 515
Minneapolis, Minnesota 55401
612-396-9043

Lynn Blumenthal Casting, Inc. (est. 1989)
Lynn Blumenthal
401 N. Third Street, Suite 660
Minneapolis, Minnesota 55401
612-338-0369
lbcasting.com

Lynn Steele Casting (est. 1988)
4905 Abbott Avenue S.
Minneapolis, Minnesota 55410
612-924-9269
612-889-5487
steelecasting.com

Walden Entertainment
Matthew Feeney
8120 Penn Avenue S. Suite 157
Bloomington, Minnesota 55431
walden-entertainment.com
651-983-0505

Specializing in casting extras and Minnesota-based indie films. Check the website to sign up for their mailing lists.

Auditions and Opportunities

If there is an audition in town, you can bet you will find it through one of the sources below. Remember that advertising on a website or in the paper does not guarantee that the advertiser is credible and legitimate. Most of the listings are for real, but be sure to trust your instincts and do some research when you are dealing with an unknown organization.

For stage, film and TV auditions.

Callboard:

Play by Play Theater Bookstore and Opening Night Gifts
1771 Selby Avenue
Saint Paul, MN 55104
playbyplaybooks.com

A brand new resource for the Twin Cities theater community, Play by Play will have a callboard in the store with auditions, classes and jobs, and will allow theatres to leave "sides" for auditions. Play by Play will offer a large selection of new and used books related to the performing arts - theatre, film, dance and opera. Free coffee, loads of theatre related events, along with artsy greeting cards and unique gift items await actors, dancers, students, educators, and audience members.

Theater hotlines:

Minnesota Association of Community Theatres hotline (auditions, jobs, news): 612-706-1456, 1-800-290-2428

Actors' Equity Association hotline (for professional, Actors Equity Association members only): 612-924-4044

Websites:

minnesotaplaylist.com—Minnesota Playlist contains an abundance of information about performing arts in Minnesota: job postings, auditions, classes, articles, etc. Minnesota Playlist (formerly Twin Cities Theater and Film Alliance) is fast becoming the virtual hub of theater in the Twin Cities. Check it regularly!

mnfilmtv.org—The Minnesota Film and TV Board has a detailed website with job postings and audition notices. If any major films come to town, opportunities will be listed on the Film and TV board's site. Click on Hotline.

callboard.org—The Callboard is an online community for the local small theater scene. If there's something going on in local small theater, someone will talk about it here. Many local theater companies post their auditions here.

mact.net—The Minnesota Association of Community Theaters has a very complete website that offers theater listings and theater news, as well as auditions and job postings.

matthewfeeney.com—Matthew Feeney is an entrepreneur, performer, networker extraordinaire, and an all around good guy. On his website you will find a link to his company, Walden Enterprises. Click on the link to sign up for e-mail notices for theater auditions, classes, low budget independent film auditions, extras casting, etc. This is a great resource, especially for novice actors.

mntalent.com—Discussions and audition information about the local acting biz. Audition opportunities are occasionally posted here. This site is not as active as others above, but you may want to check it out.

ifpmn.org—The Independent Film Project is an organization for filmmakers. In the site's classifieds, you will need to weed through the many N.Y. and L.A. listings to find the few that may be for Minnesota. There are very few specific audition listings for actors, but if you keep in touch with this organization, you will learn much more about the local independent film scene, and you may learn about auditions that are not posted on the usual sources.

Sunday *Star Tribune* **classified ads:**

The *Star Tribune* jobs section used to be the place to advertise auditions and classes. Use of the internet has caused a decline in newspaper ads. Theaters, acting teachers, independent film producers, headshot photographers, and casting directors still occasionally use the classifieds to get the word out to the masses. Just check the Sunday *Star Tribune* jobs section; you will find "performing arts" listed at the very end of the section. (It used to be the "550 section"—we all called it "the 550s." At the beginning of 2009, they removed the numbers.) Each week you will find a variety of auditions.

Commercial, industrial, print and modeling auditions:

These types of auditions almost always come through an agent or a casting director. When corporate or commercial projects are advertised through other sources, they are often lower budget projects that the agencies will not take.

Voice-over auditions:

Most voice-over work in town comes through local talent agencies. There are exceptions to this, of course. The production of your voice demo and the relatively new world of voice-over work over the internet are complicated issues. See Chapter 12.

Headshot Photographers and Printers

Pricing information for headshot duplication varies. Phone each individual business for their most current pricing.

Headshot printers.

Local:

Digigraphics
2639 Minnehaha Avenue
Minneapolis, Minnesota 55406
digidigi.com
612 721-2434

Digigraphics is where most local actors go to have headshots professionally printed. Once you have chosen your headshot from your photographer, you will then take the digital or paper version to Digigraphics. You will need to specify how you want your name to appear on it. There's a small set-up fee for this. Then you will need to tell them how many copies you want. They will then keep your master on file for easy re-ordering when you need more.

Their prices vary based on the cost of their supplies at any given time. The more copies you order, the less each copy will cost. For example, if you order 50 copies, the cost may be around $1.50. If you order 250 copies, your cost may be less than $1.00 per print. It is more cost effective to order in bulk.

Digigraphics is where I have always had my headshots printed, and I have been very pleased with the quality of their work. (Plus, I prefer to keep my money in the local economy whenever possible.)

Out of town duplication sources:

Such sources may be less expensive than local sources. You may wish to call to check out the current pricing and procedures. I have never used them, thus I cannot personally vouch for the quality of the work; however, other actors have recommended them. Check the website for current pricing.

ABC Pictures, Inc.
2838 N. Ingram Drive
Springfield, Missouri 65803
1-888-526-5336
ABCPictures.com

Spotlight Printing
Garden Grove, CA
1-888-954-8467
spotlightprinting.com

Headshot photographers.

The following photographers have been recommended by various local talent agencies. If you are with an agency, ask about the agency's favorite photographers. Take a look at the websites listed below for examples of each photographer's work. Note that websites often show more of the photographers' commercial and editorial work; only a few show actor headshots. Some post pricing on the website, many do not. Call to find out current prices for headshot sessions.

During your session, your photographer will shoot a specified number of shots or a specified number of rolls of film (though I doubt many still shoot on film). After your session, the photographer will give or send you a disk or a contact/proof sheet with all of the shots. You will then choose the shot you like best. Most will shoot both headshots and three-quarter shots upon request. See Chapter 3 for detailed information about headshots.

Jennifer Bong
612-706-9000
jenniferbongfoto.com

Joan Buccina
612-379-2911
buccina.com

Scott Dahlseid Photography
dahlseidphotography.com

Richard Fleischman
612-991-5879
www.fleischmanphoto.com

Tom Kanthak
612-337-0242
reactionstudios.com

Erika Ludwig
612-338-5776
elphoto.net

*Ann Marsden
612-834-2662
annmarsden.com

Sarah Morreim
651-592-8314
smorreimphotography.com

Kathy Quirk-Syvertsen
612-823-5136
kathysyvertsen.com

David Sherman
612-672-9216
davidshermanphoto.com

Lee Stanford
612-338-7901
leestanfordphoto.com

Craig VanderSchaegen
612-245-8389
craigvanders.com

John Wagner
612-296-0010
johnwagnerphotography.com

*Dani Werner
612-706-8392
daniphoto.com

Steve Winters
612-309-6504
stevewintersphotography.com

*These are my personal favorites. But keep in mind they are the only two I really know from this list, so I am biased! I have seen lots of photos by Ann and Dani over the years, and they are consistently excellent. Actors love how comfortable they feel during sessions.

Unions

See Chapter 5 for more information about Actors' Unions.

Actor's Equity Association—the union
for theatre actors and stage managers
www.actorsequity.org

Casting Hotlines:
    Minneapolis Hotline: 612-924-4044
    Central Region: 312-641-0418

Regional Equity office:
    125 S. Clark Street, Suite 1500
    Chicago, IL 60603

AFTRA—American Federation of Television and Radio Artists
www.aftra.com

AFTRA Twin Cities local:
    Shawn Hamilton, president
    Colleen Aho, executive director
    2610 University Avenue W., Suite 350
    St. Paul, Minnesota 55114
    651-789-8990

SAG—Screen Actors' Guild
www.sag.com

Chicago/Midwest SAG office:
    1 East Erie, Suite #650
    Chicago, IL 60611
    800-724-0767

Classes and Training

There may be many more options than those listed here. Be sure to check the local websites regularly (Minnesotaplaylist.com and callboard. org) and ask other actors for their ideas. I will update my website (acting-biztc.com) with any new options I come across. If you know about good opportunities not listed here, please send the information to me at beth@ actingbiztc.com.

A listing below does not necessarily imply a personal endorsement. If I have first-hand knowledge of a teacher or organization, I have added my comments.

Please contact the teacher or organization for current offerings and prices. As you research, remember to ask about class size. (The greater the number of students in a class, the less actual performance time you may get.) Average class costs seem to be between $10 and $25 per class hour. If it costs much more than that, it should be a very small class! Individual instruction and private coaching will run higher—$25 to75 per hour or more. Keep in mind that good training is available in the Twin Cities at a reasonable cost.

Beginners, do not forget about your local community education department. Many communities offer basic acting and performing classes. This would be a very affordable way to begin your search. (Experienced actors, if your local community education department does not offer classes, why not look into teaching one?)

Private or small group instruction and coaching.

Many teachers and directors would be happy to coach individuals or small groups. If you get a small group of dedicated and reliable actors together, many directors and teachers would love to work with you. You will have to negotiate schedule and pricing.

Various stage acting classes (including improvisation)

Bloomington Arts Center
1800 W. Old Shakopee Road
Bloomington, Minnesota 55431
bloomingtonartcenter.com

Offers a wide variety of art classes with occasional theater classes.

Anthony Vincent Bova
Bovaactorsworkshop.com

Anthony travels from New York to the Twin Cities occasionally to teach weekend workshops. I observed a sample class. He is terrific (for experienced actors).

The Brave New Institute at The Brave New Workshop founded by Dudley Riggs
2605 Hennepin Avenue S.
Minneapolis, Minnesota 55408
www.bravenewworkshop.com

The Brave New Workshop is one of my favorite places in town. Their classes stress improvisation for truthful communication, not specifically for comedy. They also offer various other acting classes with guest instructors. Be sure to check the website for the latest offerings. (Improv is great for actors of all experience levels.)

Cheryl Moore Brinkley
bvocal.net

Classes are located at various venues, including The Brave New Workshop and Theatre in the Round.

Cheryl is not only an expert in her subject matter; she is a gifted teacher. I highly recommend all of Cheryl's classes: Acting Fundamentals, Voice Fundamentals, TV Acting Technique, Scene Study, Audition Techniques and private coaching. (I've done them all.) She offers options for novice actors as well as trained, experienced artists. Her website gives all the details.

Jane Brody
Excellent actor training, though not for beginners. She was a casting director in Chicago for years and a professional actor before that. She comes to Minneapolis occasionally to teach a variety of classes, including cold reading, auditioning for TV and film, monologues, and new techniques in acting. I highly recommend her classes. When she comes to town, she will advertise on Minnesotaplaylist.com and callboard.org as well as through the agencies.

Chanhassen Dinner Theaters
chanhassendt.com

Performance training in musical theater for teens and adults—singing, acting, dancing—taught by Chanhassen Dinner Theatre professionals.

The Guthrie Theater
612-347-1197
guthrietheater.org (click on "learn")

Check the website to view their "Classes and camps" list. I took several of their classes during my first few years in the biz—from improv to monologues to scene study. Often there are many beginners in Guthrie classes, allowing for a great low stress atmosphere. On the other hand, intermediate to advanced actors looking for more intense training may find the presence of so many beginning actors to be occasionally frustrating. If this is you, be sure to look for their more advanced classes. Teachers at the Guthrie are, as you would expect, highly qualified and reputable.

Steve Hendrickson
beau-geste.org
Power_auditions@mac.com

Outstanding actor Steve Hendrickson is also an outstanding teacher. Actor Zach Curtis says, "Any time Steve Hendrickson offers his 'how to audition classes,' take them. He knows better than anyone." Visit the website for details about classes and private coaching.

Sandra Horner
sandrakhorner.com
SKHperformance@aol.com

Sandra teaches Meisner technique and scene study. Meisner work is tough, but rewarding. I benefited greatly from Sandra's class, as well as private coaching with her. Sandra moved to L.A. in 2000, but continues to teach in Minneapolis. Watch Minnesotaplaylist.com and callboard.org for her free sample classes. For beginners and experienced actors.

In the Moment Actor's Studio
itmacting.com

Cynthia Uhrich
308 Prince Street, Fourth Floor
Lowertown
St. Paul, Minnesota 55101
612-870-4310

Beginning acting, advanced acting. See Cynthia's website for details. I hear nothing but positive reviews about her classes.

David Lind—Michael Chekhov technique
actorsbreath.com

David Lind hasn't offered classes recently, but may offer them again. Contact him via his website to find out. His classes feature the Michael Chekhov technique.

From the website: "The Michael Chekhov Acting Technique consists primarily of work with the 'imaginary body' and the Psychological Gesture (PG). By working with the 'imaginary body,' the actor is able to effect both physical and psychological changes. This is neither a physical approach to acting, nor a psychological one. Chekhov referred to his work as 'psychophysical.' Elements of the technique: imaginary body, centers, qualities of movement, character archetypes, atmosphere, psychological gestures, radiating, ensemble work, etc."

Lundstrum Center for the Performing Arts
1617 N. Second Street
Minneapolis, Minnesota
612-521-2600
lundstrumcenter.com

I do not have any personal experience with the Lundstrum Center. The instructors listed on the website have great credentials. From the website: "The Lundstrum Center for the Performing Arts is a Minnesota non-profit corporation offering training in dance, voice, and drama for the experienced performer as well as the absolute beginner. All classes are taught by professionals in the business." "Work study and grants are available." Classes include offerings for adults as well as children in modeling, acting, musical theatre, and dance.

Lyric Arts Main Street Stage (community theater)
lyricarts.org
Anoka, Minnesota

Workshops for children and adults are listed on the website.

MacPhail Center for Music
501 S. Second Street
Minneapolis, Minnesota 55401
612-321-0100
macphail.org

A great variety of music classes. Actors may be interested in their musical theater and voice classes.

Lev Mailer
levmailer.com

I have no personal experience with Lev Mailer's classes, but actors have spoken highly of him. Visit the website to see his classes, or call for more information.

Minneapolis Community Education
Minneapoliscommunityed.com

Beginning improvisation, beginning theater and acting classes.

Phipps Center for the Arts
109 Locust Street
Hudson, Wisconsin 54016
715-386-2305
thephipps.org

The Phipps offers a variety of classes: dance, music, acting, etc. Check out the website for details.

Phoenix Theater Works, Reggie Phoenix
651-503-1613
phoenixtheaterworks.org

Reggie Phoenix teaches classes at the Children's Theater, including group and individual classes, audition technique, monologue, and scene work.

Stevie Ray's improv
Minneapolis, Minnesota
612-825-1832
stevierays.org

I have not taken classes here, but they have a good reputation. Check them out as another reputable option for improv training. Check the website for the latest class offerings, or register for their e-mailing list.

Studio 206 in the Ivy Building
Ivy Building for the Arts
2637 27th Avenue S.
Minneapolis, Minnesota
ivystudio206.com

From the website: "206 is a workspace committed to supporting artists of all disciplines in exploring new ground in performance and art. Not a theatre or a school but a platform . . . a place to ask questions and take risks. 206 provides an environment where artists at all points in their creative lives can research, create, rehearse, and show work. With the intention of inspiring the highest rigor and craft, it also offers training in the form of ongoing workshops and residencies in physical and hybrid (interdisciplinary) approaches to performance." See the website for details, and watch Minnesota-Playlist.com for specific offerings.

Rebecca Surmont
rsurmont@comcast.net
612-597-4496

Voice and movement coach, Physical acting/Corporeal Mime teacher. Rebecca is an experienced local actress, and former company member with Margolis Brown.

The Talent Center
Don Cosgrove
71 Imperial Drive E.
West St. Paul, Minnesota 55118
651-306-9670
thetalentcenter.com

Check the website for information about a variety of classes. Don has done all aspects of the biz for many years. His classes include: basic acting skills, acting for non-actors, on camera and voice acting, private ear prompter and teleprompter training, audio and video demo tapes, and more. This is a good place for beginners to get a start.

TC Connections
Eric "Pogi" Sumangil
pogmyster@hotmail.com

Pogi offers his consulting services to new and experienced actors—a one-stop resource for actors either new to town or just starting out in the biz. He plans to offer classes in auditioning, networking, or to do meet & greets with directors or casting directors. He offers "marketing and brand management for actors, doing headshot and resume reviews, listing casting and talent agencies for mailings, etc." (Pogi works in commercials and industrials, and has worked with these theaters: Mixed Blood, Theater Mu, Chanhassen Dinner Theatres, Ordway, Guthrie, Frank Theater, as well as stages in San Diego.)

Theatre in the Round
245 Cedar Avenue
Minneapolis, 55454
Theatreintheround.org

TRP offers a variety of classes with experienced theater professionals. This is a great place for both beginners and experienced actors. Visit the website and click on: "opportunities," then "classes and workshops."

Tumblemonster Stunt School
tumblemonster.com
2015 Silver Bell Rd., Suite 180
Eagan, MN 55112
651-269-2708

Yes, stunt training here in Minnesota!

Wesley Balk Opera/Music-Theater Institute
wesleybalk.org

Intensive three-week summer session for the professional artist. They have also offered "a six-week introductory class in the basic principles of Performing Power, the approach to integrated singing-acting first developed by famed director Wesley Balk." Affiliated with Nautilus Music-Theater. See the website for details.

Workhouse Theatre
4400 Osseo Road
Minneapolis, Minneapolis
Workhousetheatre.org

Acting, improv, scenic design, and mask-making are recent offerings, for children and adults.

On-camera/commercial acting classes.

Even if you are only interested in commercial acting, do not ignore the list above! As teacher Cheryl Moore Brinkley said to me recently: "I think of camera training as a technical *specialization* of acting, not the gateway to the craft." Having some basic experience in stage acting will give you a better foundation for your on-camera work. Many of the following teachers will accept beginners. Others will require that you have some actor training and experience as a prerequisite.

Cheryl Moore Brinkley
bvocal.net

Excellent camera technique training; Cheryl's teaching helped me immensely. She asks that her camera students have some acting experience prior to taking her camera class; call her to discuss your situation. See listing above.

Jane Brody
See listing above.

Bill Cooper
Actor/On-camera acting coach
612-616-3159
billcooper.info

Bill offers one-on-one training primarily with novice actors trying to develop their acting craft and get involved with the biz. Audition techniques, commercials, ear prompting, etc. He helps with resumes, cover letters, reels, websites, taxes, and topics related to the talent business. He offers six to eight week workshops on "Television & Film Scene Study" and "Write, Act, Direct."

Matthew Feeney
MatthewFeeney.com

Matthew teaches "VIP Extras Class," "Business of Show Business," and on-camera audition classes. See the website for details, and to register for his mailing lists. He is a great resource for beginners.

The Guthrie Theater
612-347-1197
guthrietheater.org (click on "learn")
Minneapolis, Minnesota

Check the website for occasional on-camera classes offered by Guthrie professionals.

Lundstrum Center for the Arts
See listing above.

Lev Mailer
See listing above.

The Talent Center
See listing above.

Casting directors.

Local casting directors occasionally offer classes. Not only will they have great feedback for you, it will also be a valuable opportunity to get to know them (and vice versa). You will get honest feedback from a client's perspective about where you fit in this market.

For all of these classes, watch callboard.org, Minnesotaplaylist.com, and your talent agency's bulletin board. You will love all of these folks. They are truly a pleasure to work with. (See Chapter 6 for much more information about casting directors.)

Lynn Blumenthal of Lynn Blumenthal Casting has taught an on-camera class in the past. (It is a great class.) Currently, Michelle Hutchison teaches the classes at Lynn's office. (See her listing in this section.)

Jean Rohn and Kelly Gallagher of JR Casting teach classes about the biz with on-camera coaching sessions. Highly recommended, especially for actors who are new to the commercial side of things.

Barbara Shelton of Bab's casting offers more advanced classes from time to time. You will love her, too—fun, honest, and down to earth.

Michelle Hutchison
funnyhutch@aol.com

Classes are held at Lynn Blumenthal Casting, 401 N. Third Street, Suite 660, Minneapolis, Minnesota 55401
Michelle is an experienced pro with an extensive acting resume; I hear great feedback about her classes. She is currently the casting associate at Lynn Blumenthal Casting. She teaches actors how to audition for film and TV projects in six weekly, three-hour sessions. When Michelle offers a new class, you will see it on callboard.org and minnesotaplaylist.com.

Classes and training for children and teens.

In addition to the resources listed here, be sure to contact your local community education department, community theater, and colleges to inquire about opportunities for children and teens. There may be fabulous, affordable classes and summer camps right in your own backyard!

Organizations are listed in alphabetical order. A listing here does not imply an endorsement. If I have experience with a teacher or organization, I note that accordingly. (And be sure to consult Chapter 13 for much more information about children and the biz.)

Arts in Minnesota Summer Programs Guide
mcae.k12.mn.us/aim

The Perpich Center for Arts Education publishes an annual summer program guide. It becomes available in late spring. It is a compilation of summer programs in arts education all over the state.

Bloomington Arts Center
Bloomingtonartcenter.com
Bloomington, Minnesota

Offers a wide variety of art classes with occasional theater classes.

The Brave New Institute at The Brave New Workshop founded by Dudley Riggs
2605 Hennepin Avenue S.
Minneapolis, Minnesota 55408
612-332-6620, ext. 205
bravenewworkshop.com

Check the website for the latest offerings. Specific opportunities for youth have included: "Youth Pizza Jams," spring break events, a summer youth improvisation program, and a youth performance team. (See a more complete listing above in this section.)

CB Productions
cbproductions.org

Theater group for home-schooled youth, offering classes and productions. Part of the Minnesota Homeschooler's Alliance, a statewide non-profit. For ages twelve to seventeen. See the website for detail.

Chanhassen Dinner Theatres, summer programs
501 W. 78th Street
Chanhassen, Minnesota 55317
952-934-1525
chanhassentheatres.com

Performance classes for ages thirteen to adult, taught by Chanhassen Dinner Theatre professionals. All experience levels are welcome. Also, "First Act Summer Theatre Camp"—acting, dance, voice, movement, and production for ages eight to eighteen.

Children's Theatre Company
2400 Third Avenue S.
Minneapolis, Minnesota 55404-3597
612-874-0400
childrenstheatre.org
ctc4teens.org

Extensive class offerings for children ages three to eighteen. See the website for complete schedules, registration forms and information. Some offerings require an audition while others are open to all. Young actors age eighteen or older may audition for their performing apprentice program.

Commonweal Theatre Company
206 Parkway Avenue N.
Lanesboro, Minnesota 55949
commonwealtheatre.org

See the website for details about a variety of educational opportunities, including student matinees, theatre skills classes for high school juniors and seniors, and college/post-grad apprenticeships. (approximately 125 miles southeast of the Twin Cities)

FAIR School
Wmep.k12.mn.us/fair
Crystal, Minnesota

The Fine Arts Interdisciplinary Resource (FAIR) School is a magnet school for students in grades four to eight.

Guthrie Theater—Classes at the Guthrie
www.guthrietheater.org

A great variety of offerings for kids of all ages. Opportunities include affordable sampler classes and full-day or week-long summer camps. Check the website for details.

Great River Shakespeare Festival
Winona, Minnesota
grsf.org/education

Summer classes, workshops and programs for learners of all ages, in conjunction with the Summer Festival.

Harmony Theatre Company and School
centerharmony.org

Performance space:
Center for Independent Artists
4137 Bloomington Avenue S.,
Minneapolis, Minnesota

School:
6121 Excelsior Boulevard
St. Louis Park, Minnesota

From the website: "Harmony welcomes children and adults of all backgrounds to participate in and create theatre." See the website for further details.

Michelle Hutchison

Classes are held at
Lynn Blumenthal Casting
401 N. Third Street, Suite 660
Minneapolis, Minnesota, 55401
Funnyhutch@aol.com

Michelle Hutchison occasionally offers on-camera classes for kids and teens. She's a talented professional. In the past, she has offered summer "On-Camera Acting Camps for Kids and Teens." Contact her for more information and current class schedules, and watch callboard.org and MinnesotaPlaylist.com.

In the Heart of the Beast--post-show puppet workshop

1500 E. Lake Street
Minneapolis, Minnesota
Hobt.org

Check the website for their Saturday morning puppet shows for kids and post-show puppet workshops for families.

Lundstrum Center for the Performing Arts

1617 N. Second Street
Minneapolis, Minnesota
612-521-2600
lundstrumcenter.com

Dance, voice, and drama classes for kids, teens, and adults. See the website for details.

Lyric Arts: Mainstreet Stage

420 E. Main Street
Anoka, Minnesota 55303
763-433-2510, ext 101 (for questions about workshops)
lyricarts.org

A non-profit community theatre offering a variety of classes for students in kindergarten through grade twelve. Classes for both beginning and experienced actors.

MacPhail Center for Music

501 S. Second Street
Minneapolis, Minnesota 55401
612-321-0100
macphail.org

A great variety of music classes. Actors may be interested in their musical theater and voice classes.

Main Street School of Performing Arts

1320 Main Street
Hopkins, Minnesota 55343
952-224-1340
Performing-arts-school.org

MSSPA is a tuition-free public high school in the Hopkins School District. Four-year charter school with an arts-centered curriculum.

Masquer's Theatre Company

292 Lake Street
Forest Lake, Minnesota 55025
651-464-5823
masquerstheatre.org

Summer theater camps for ages four through seventeen. See the website for details.

Minneapolis community education

Minneapoliscommunityed.com

Recent offerings included Broadway Kids (kindergarten through grade three) and all kinds of dance classes.

Minnesota Association of Community Theatres (MACT)

mact.net
612-706-1456, 800-290-2428

MACT is a great organization of community theaters all over the state. The MACT website may not advertise specific classes; however, use it to search for community theaters in your area. Contact local community theaters about possible offerings for children.

Minnesota Institute for Talented Youth

Mity.org

Check the website for a variety of opportunities, including a week-long summer theater program.

Minnetonka Arts
Minnetonkaarts.org
952-473-7361, ext. 16

Summer arts camp for children ages five
through twelve and teens.

Old Gem Theater
oldgemtheater.com
New Richmond, WI

The website lists a variety of offerings for
kids.

Park Square Theatre
20 W. Seventh Place
St. Paul, Minnesota 55102
parksquaretheatre.org

Park Square does not currently offer specific classes for kids; however, they offer
immersion days for school groups. If you
are a teacher or your child is in drama or
literature classes, check the website or
call for more information.

Penumbra Theatre
270 N. Kent Street
St. Paul, Minnesota
penumbratheatre.org

See the website for details about student
matinees and the "Summer Institute for
Activist Artists," ages thirteen through eighteen. The Summer Institute is a four-week
summer program that is "highly intensive
and for committed students only."

**Perpich Center for Arts Education—Arts
High School** (grades eleven through twelve)
6125 Olson Highway
Golden Valley, Minnesota
Mcae.k12.mn.us

Tuition free public high school. Academics plus instruction in six arts areas:
dance, theater, music, literary arts, media
arts, and visual arts.

Phipps Center for the Arts
109 Locust Street
Hudson, Wisconsin 54016
715-386-2305
thephipps.org

The Phipps offers all kinds of classes and
opportunities for kids and adults: visual
arts, performing arts, dance, acting,
etc. Summer theater camp for kids, too.
Check out the website for details.

**Pillsbury House Theatre: Chicago
Avenue Project**
Pillsburyhousetheatre.org
3501 Chicago Avenue S.
Minneapolis, Minnesota

Neighboorhood kids get the chance to
work with professionals to create and
perform in their own plays.

Sabes Jewish Community Center
4330 S. Cedar Lake Road
St. Louis Park, Minnesota
sabesjcc.org

A great variety of classes including dance
and acting, plus summer theater programs
for kids.

St. Olaf College Summer Theater Camp
Northfield, Minnesota
stolaf.edu/camps

Residential theater camp, ages thirteen
through seventeen. New in 2009 is a "master
class" option for advanced theater students.

**St. Paul Conservatory for Performing
Artists**
Landmark Center, 75 W. Fifth Street
St. Paul, Minnesota 55102
651-290-2225
Spcpa.org

Tuition-free public high school, grades nine
through twelve. Academics, plus instrumen-
tal and vocal music, theater and dance.

Stacia Rice
torchtheater.com

Once or twice a year, well-known local actress Stacia Rice teaches acting classes for
girls, ages 8-11, 12-15, and 16-18. Visit
the Torch Theater website, scroll to the
bottom, and e-mail your request to be on
the mailing list for classes. Stacia focuses
on confidence, finding creativity, what it
means to create a character, etc.

StageCoach Theatre Arts School
stage-school.com

From the website: "StageCoach Theatre Arts Schools provide part-time, weekend training in dance, drama, and singing for students aged four through eighteen." Classes are held in various metro locations. See the website for details.

Stages Theatre Company
1111 Main Street
Hopkins, Minnesota 55343
stagestheatre.org

I highly recommend this organization. Stages offers a variety of opportunities for ages five through eighteen, including summer workshops. A "Conservatory Program" is available for the serious student of acting, ages twelve through eighteen. There is a '"Junior Conservatory" for ages nine through eleven. See the website for more information.

Steppingstone Theatre for Youth Development
314 Landmark Center
75 W. Fifth Street
St. Paul, Minnesota 55102
651-225-9265
steppingstonetheatre.org

Steppingstone is all about creativity and theater for kids. Great opportunities for kids ages three-and-a-half through seventeen. Theater classes are offered throughout the school year, with camp opportunities in the summer. Actors ages nine through eighteen may audition for their shows. Classes include creative dramatics, tech theater, acting, musical theater, advanced acting, and many more. See the website for much more detail.

Yellow Tree Theatre
320 Fifth Avenue S.E.
Osseo, Minnesota 55369
yellowtreetheatre.com

Recent offerings: "Fun with Theatre" classes for ages six through nine and ages ten through twelve. Summer Musical Theatre Camp for ages seven through thirteen. See the website for details.

Youth Performance Company
3338 University Avenue S.E.
Minneapolis, Minnesota 55414
612-623-9080
youthperformanceco.com

Performances are held in the
Howard Conn Fine Arts Center
1900 Nicollet Avenue
Minneapolis, Minnesota 55403

I taught a couple of classes here a few years ago and I think it is a terrific organization. There is a creative buzz around the place, and kids truly love to be there. Classes seem to have the right mix of fun and education. Classes are offered year-round for ages five to eighteen, with a great variety of summer camps. See the website for more information.

Theaters

This list is divided into several sections:

- Professional theaters
- Amateur/community/volunteer theaters
- Theater spaces
- Theaters for children and youth
- Improvisation / sketch comedy theaters
- Theater festivals

For the purposes of this list, the primary distinction between "professional" and "amateur" is whether or not the theater pays its performers. This distinction may have very little to do with the quality of any given performance. Please note that the designation of "professional" can mean many things!

My apologies if any theaters have been omitted from this list. With so many theaters in town, it is likely that I have missed one. Please let me know of any omissions so that I may correct this on my website and in subsequent editions.

Note that the numerous high school, college, and university theaters are not included in this listing. Dance theaters are listed. Companies that are strictly dance are not covered in this book.

For spelling fanatics: Theater/theatre is correctly spelled both ways. I have attempted to maintain the spelling given by a theater's own communications. Some organizations even spell the theater's name one way and the website the other.

This list is designed to be an overview of the theater scene. The best way to learn about a theater is to attend its shows. The next best way is to visit the theater's website. As beauty is in the eye of the beholder, I have chosen not to add comments about many of my favorite theater companies. It is up to you to discover your own favorites and to discern where to audition.

Details about pay: A listing in this section indicates whether the theater: (a) pays its performers and/or (b) considers itself to be "professional" by virtue of its membership in the Ivey Awards. Many theaters listed here are established theaters that absolutely do pay their artists, though a listing here in no way guarantees you will be paid. A few guidelines to clarify:

- Local theaters that hire only non-Equity performers typically pay a stipend ranging from $25 to a few hundred dollars. This will vary greatly. This stipend is usually a one-time payment covering the entire rehearsal and performance period.

- If a theater casts Equity actors, pay is dictated by contract with the union.

- If a theater casts both Equity and non-Equity actors, this theater may be more likely to pay their non-Equity artists a more substantial stipend, per show fee, or weekly salary. The specifics are noted where the information was available.

A few of the organizations listed do not pay their performers, but are included here for various reasons, particularly if they are service organizations that may be of interest to professional actors.

All of this information is subject to change! Please note that the theater scene is constantly changing. The information here has been provided by the theater, from the theater's website, or in some cases from my personal experience with the theater as an actor or audience member. I cannot guarantee the certainty of any information listed here. You must verify that all information is current before you rely on audition, pay, or location information. Use this listing as a starting point for your own research.

The phone numbers listed are generally not for audition information. Rely on the theater's website or listed audition sources. Some of the theaters invite submissions of headshots and resumes. This is noted where applicable.

I have included the theater's mission statement if it helps to define a specific niche or community served by the theater. These statements may not be the mission as defined by the theater; rather, they include any distinguishing information such as theatrical styles, locations outside the metro area, unique mission statements, etc.

Ivey participant means they pledge to meet the requirements to participate in the Ivey awards. This includes the requirement to "compensate their artists and staff on a regular basis." A few theaters report that their actors are "volunteers," yet they are also Ivey participants. I have no explanation for this inconsistency; ask the theater when you audition. See www.iveyawards.com for details about membership requirements.

Last, but not least, a huge thank-you to talented local actress Megan Kelly for her wonderful assistance in researching and compiling this list. If this list proves helpful to you, Megan deserves much of the credit!

Professional theaters.

20% Theatre Company
tctwentypercent.org
Administration: 612-227-1188

Performance space: varies—Theatre Garage, The Bedlam, etc.

Non-Equity, stipend

Auditions: Posted on minnesotaplaylist.com, callboard.org, 20% website, e-mail announcements, occasional notification to organizations or colleges.

Send headshot and resume to:
Claire H Avitabile, Artistic Director
20% Theatre
5152 Aldrich Avenue N.
Minneapolis Minnesota, 55430
or claire@tctwentypercent.org

Mission: To produce new and progressive work by female, transgender, and gender-queer theatre artists, while also supporting the same gender minorities artistically behind the scenes.

3AM Productions
3amprod.org
Admnistration: 612-781-3019
E-mail: info@3amprod.org

Performance space (varies):
Grain Belt Bottling House
78 13th Avenue N.E.
Minneapolis, Minnesota 55413

Non-Equity

Mission: To create a total artistic experience by incorporating different mediums into the realm of theatre, i.e. visual art, music and multimedia. By using unconventional spaces and new approaches to produce work, 3AM seeks to tell the story by inspiring discussion and fostering change.

3 Sticks Theatre Company
threestickstheatre.org

Performance space: varies—Southern Theatre, Theatre Garage

Auditions: Posted on minnesotaplaylist.com, callboard.org.

Send headshot and resume to:
Jason Bohon
Sticks
P.O. Box 300044
Minneapolis, Minnesota 55403

8Ball Theatre
eightballtheatre.com

Performance space: varies

Auditions: See website for mailing list information

Ivey participant

Actors' Theater of Minnesota
actorsMN.org
Administration: 651-290-2290
Box office: 651-227-2464

Performance space:
Lowry Theater
16 W. Fifth Street
St. Paul, Minnesota

Non-Equity/ $50-$75 per performance, sometimes offer Equity contracts

Auditions: Actors are cast from their files and auditions posted on minnesotaplaylist.com.

Send headshot and resume to:
allen@actorsmn.org or
Actors Theater of Minnesota
350 St. Peter Street, Suite 254
St. Paul, Minnesota 55102

Ivey participant

Ballet of the Dolls (dance–theater)
343 13th Avenue N.E.
Minneapolis, Minnesota 55413
balletofthedolls.org
Administration: 612-623-7660
Box office: 612-436-1129

Performance space:
The Ritz Theatre
345 13th Avenue N.E.,
Minneapolis, Minnesota 55413

Company members paid salary or independent contracts. No auditions held.

Mission: To create a variety of professional, full-scale dance-theater productions that include deconstructions of famous ballets, original works for dance-theater, and works created for families and children; extending unique dance-theater vision through education programs with on-site and outreach program activities that include in-school residencies, the Dolls Performance Workshop for Youth, and free performances by the company in support of community events.

Ivey participant: Company members and production staff have been recipients.

BALLS Cabaret (cabaret performances)
members.toast.net/prthomas/ballswbs/balls.htm
southerntheater.org/balls.htm
Administration: 612-340-0155, ext. 25
Box Office: 612-340-1725

Performance space:
Southern Theater
1420 Washington Avenue S.
Minneapolis, Minnesota 55454

Non-Equity, no pay

Auditions: no auditions; call 612-340-0155, ext. 25, to get a spot in the line up

Leslie Ball, creator

Bedlam Theatre Company
bedlamtheatre.org
Administration: 612-341-1038

Performance space:
Bedlam Theatre
1501 S. Sixth Street
Minneapolis, Minnesota 55458

Send headshot and resume to: Artistic directors Maren Ward and John Bueche

Mission: To produce radical works of theater with a focus on collaboration and a unique blend of professional and community art. . . . As a venue, Bedlam supports a year-round calendar of local, national and international artists, in theater, dance, music, puppetry, performance art, and more.

Ivey participant

Bloomington Civic Theatre
Bloomingtoncivictheater.com
Box office: 952-563-8575

Performance space:
Bloomington Center for the Arts,
1800 W. Old Shakopee Road,
Bloomington, Minnesota 55431

Non-Equity, $200 stipend

Auditions: Posted on minnesotaplaylist.com.

The Bottling Company
http://thebottlingcompany.wordpress.com
Administration: 612-559-3251
Box office: 612-559-3251

Performance space:
Grain Belt Studios
79 13th Avenue N.E.
Minneapolis, Minnesota

Non-Equity—stipend

Auditions: Not posted and by invitation only. Contact thebottlingcompany@gmail.com if interested. (Company is primarily former U of M theater students.)

Mission: Minneapolis-based ensemble dedicated to politics, classics, and films.

Brave New Workshop
(improv and sketch comedy)
bravenewworkshop.org
Administration: 612-332-6620

Performance space:
Brave New Workshop
2605 Hennepin Avenue S.
Minneapolis, Minnesota 55408

Non-Equity—pay weekly salary based on experience and time with the company.

Auditions: Hire from classes or submit headshot and resume

Send headshot and resume to:
Brave New Workshop
Attn: Katy McEwan
2605 Hennepin Avenue S.
Minneapolis, Minnesota 55408

Ivey participant

Buffalo Gal Productions
buffalogalproductions.com
Administration: 612-203-5521

Performance space: Loring Playhouse,
History Theater, Fringe Festival

Mission: Non-profit organization which
produces and creates original and rarely
seen Broadway and off-Broadway works
by, for, and about women, creating opportunities for artists and audience members
to participate in new theater experiences.

Ivey participant

The Burning House Group
burninghousegroup.org
Administration: 612-623-9396

Performance space: Theater Garage

Equity guest contracts/non-Equity

Auditions posted: Minnesotaplaylist.com,
callboard.org, website

Ivey participant

Chanhassen Dinner Theatres
(musical theater)
chanhassentheatres.com
Administration: 952.934.1500
Box office: 952.934.1525

Performance space:
Chanhassen Theatres
501 W. 78th Street
Chanhassen, Minnesota 55317

Equity and non-Equity—weekly salary
$400-$600

Auditions: Posted in Sunday Star Tribune.
Auditions held at Chanhassen Theatres.

Ivey participant

Cheap Theatre (storytelling)
Administration: 612-870-6583

Performance Space:
Black Forest Inn,
1 E. 26th Street,
Minneapolis, Minnesota 55404

Non-Equity

Children's Theatre Company (professional theater for adult and child actors)
childrenstheatre.org
Administration: 612-874-0500
Box office: 612-874-0400

Performance space:
Children's Theatre Company
2400 Third Avenue S.
Minneapolis, Minnesota 55404

Equity and non-Equity—all adult positions paid

Auditions: Advertised in Pioneer Press,
Star Tribune, and www.childrenstheatre.
org/news/auditions.html.

Mission: To create extraordinary theatre
experiences, and to advance theatre as
a means of educating, challenging, and
inspiring young people.

Ivey participant

Comedy Sportz (improvisational theater)
comedysportztc.com
Administration: 612-870-1230

Performance space:
Calhoun Square
3001 Hennepin Avenue S.,
Minneapolis, Minnesota 55408

Also, remote shows for church groups,
businesses, schools.

Non-Equity—pay per show

Auditions: Often hire out of classes,
sometimes audition, posted in Sunday
Star Tribune, on website.

Send headshot and resume to:
Doug Ocar
3001 Hennepin Avenue S.
Minneapolis, Minnesota 55408

Commonweal Theatre Company
Commonwealtheatre.org
Administration: 507-467-2905
Box office: 507-467-2525

Performance space:
Commonweal Theatre
208 Parkway Avenue N.,
Lanesboro, Minnesota 55949

Non-Equity: $200-$250 per week plus six to eight hours of additional duties (box office, etc.)

Auditions: Auditions held for each season. Commonweal Theatre attends UPTAs and Twin Cities Unifieds. Apprenticeships available.

Send headshot and resume to:
Commonweal Casting
P O Box 15
Lanesboro, Minnesota 55949

Commedia Beauregard

cbtheatre.org
Administration: 651-797-4967
Box office (Brown Paper Tickets):
1-800-838-3006

Performance space: varies

Non-Equity—stipend

Auditions: Posted on minnesotaplaylist.com, callboard.org, and theater website.

Mission: To translate the universal human experience to the stage: to expand horizons and share knowledge of all cultures, translating between languages and between arts to create theater that is beautiful in expression.

Ivey participant

The Cromulent Shakespeare Co.

cromulentshakespeare.org
Administration: 612-326-3289

Performance Space (varies): Black Forest Inn, Theatre Garage

Non-Equity—stipend

Auditions: Posted at www.cromulent-shakespeare.org, minnesotaplaylist.com, callboard.org.

Ivey participant

Duck Soup Players

(volunteer service organization)
ducksoupplayers.com
Administration: 651-433-4039

Performance space: on-site at senior citizens' centers, hospitals, etc.

Non-Equity, volunteer only

Auditions: No auditions. If interested contact 651-433-4039 or ducksoupplayers@aol.com.

Mission: To provide, at no cost, persons of limited mobility with a live professional-quality theater experience. These persons include the elderly in high-rises, the hospitalized, and the institutionalized, primarily in the Twin Cities metro area.

Ensemble Productions

ensembleproductions.org
Administration: 612-559-8444

Performance Space:
Spill the Wine
1101 Washington Avenue S.
Minneapolis, Minnesota 55415

Non-Equity

Flaneur Productions

flaneurproductions.com
Administration: 612-203-9560

Auditions: Do not normally hold auditions.

Non-Equity—split box office or stipend

Ivey participant

The Flower Shop Project

theflowershopproject.com
Administration: 612.870.9740

Performance space
Bryant Lake Bowl,
810 W. Lake Street
Minneapolis, Minnesota 55408

Non-Equity—pay by stipend $100

Auditions: minnesotaplaylist.com, theater website

Mission: To create and produce new works of theatre that are smart, ballsy, and fundamentally entertaining. Goal is to produce original scripts from within the company, as well as to solicit and produce scripts from other local playwrights.

Ivey participant

Four Humors Theater
fourhumorstheater.com

Performance space (varies): Bedlam Theater, Old Arizona Theater, North American Fringe Festival Tour

Non-Equity

Ivey participant

Frank Theatre
franktheatre.org
Administration: 612-724-3760

Performance space: Ritz Theater, Guthrie's Dowling Studio

Equity/Non-Equity—small stipend

Auditions: Posted on minnesotaplaylist. com or join audition e-mail list on franktheatre.org.

Ivey participant

Girl Friday Productions
girlfridayproductions.org

Performance space (varies): Theatre Garage

Non-Equity—stipend

Auditions: Posted in Sunday *Star Tribune*, minnesotaplaylist.com, and e-mail notice to those who request it via info@girlfridayproductions.org.

Mission: To inspire audiences and provide career development for artists via outstanding, actor-driven theatrical productions that illuminate the human condition.

Ivey participant

Great American History Theatre
historytheatre.com
Administration: 651-292-4323
Box Office: 651-292-4323

Performance space:
History Theatre
30 E. Tenth Street
St. Paul, Minnesota 55101

Equity and non-Equity—weekly salary

Auditions: Posted on AEA hotline and Minnesotaplaylist.com.

Send headshots and resumes to:
Ron Peluso
History Theater
30 E. Tenth Street
St. Paul, Minnesota 55101

Ivey participant

Great River Shakespeare Festival
Grsf.org
Box office: 507-474-7900, ext. 110

Performance space: Winona State University

Equity/non-Equity

Auditions: See website for details. Apprentice acting company, technical and administrationistrative internships.

Mission: To be "the" place in America to attend plays by Shakespeare.

Gremlin Theatre
gremlin-theatre.org
Administration: 651-228-7008

Performance space
The Gremlin Theatre
2400 University Avenue W.
St. Paul, Minnesota

Equity/non-Equity—stipend

Auditions: Posted on minnesotaplaylist. com, callboard.org, theater's website.

Ivey participant

Guthrie Theater
Guthrietheater.org
Administration: 612-225-6000
Box office: 612-377-2224

Performance spaces:
McGuire Proscenium Stage
Wurtele Thrust Stage
Dowling Studio
818 S. Second Street
Minneapolis, Minnesota 55415

Equity and non-Equity—weekly salary and stipend

Auditions: Posted in Pioneer Press, Star Tribune, and guthrietheater.org/opportunities/auditions.

Submit headshot and resume to:
John Miller-Stephany
Associate Artistic Director
Guthrie Theater
818 S. Second Street
Minneapolis, Minnesota 55415

Mission: An American center for theater performance, production, education, and professional training. By presenting both classical literature and new work from diverse cultures, the Guthrie illuminates the common humanity connecting Minnesota to the peoples of the world.

Ivey participant

Hardcover Theater

Hardcovertheatre.org
Administration: 612-581-2229

Performance space (varies): Bryant Lake Bowl, Playwright's Center

Non-Equity—stipend ranges $50-$250 for actors, $50-$400 for designers

Auditions: Posted: on minnesotaplaylist.com, callboard.org, hardcovertheatre.org; sign up for audition notifications on the website.

Mission: To create entertaining, thought-provoking, and stylistically original adaptations of literature for the stage. As part of this mission, they seek to celebrate the power and beauty of language, promote literacy, reading, and historical understanding, expand the vocabulary of the theater by experimenting with staging devices, especially —"direct address," in which actors speak directly to the audience.

Hometown Theatre

hometowntheatre.org

Performance space (varies): Mounds Theater, Fringe Festival, Pioneer Place

Non-Equity, limited Equity—$50 per show

Auditions: Posted on minnesotaplaylist.com, callboard.org.

Submit headshot and resume to
Greg Eiden, Artistic Director
Hometown Theatre
928 123rd Lane N.W.
Coon Rapids, Minnesota 55448
or to gregeiden@hotmail.com

Ivey participant

Illusion Theater

illusiontheater.org
Administrationistration and box office:
612-339-4944

Performance space:
Illusion Theater
528 Hennepin Avenue
Minneapolis, Minnesota 55403

Equity/non-Equity—pay per weekly salary

Auditions: Invite only or posted on Sunday Star Tribune and minnesotaplaylist.com.

Submit headshot and resume to:
Illusion Theater
528 Hennepin Avenue, Suite 704
Minneapolis, Minnesota 55403

Ivey participant

In the Heart of the Beast Puppet and Mask Theatre (puppet theater)

hobt.org
Administrationistration and box office:
612-721-2535

Performance space:
Avalon Theater
1500 E. Lake Street
Minneapolis, Minnesota 55407

Non-Equity—puppeteers paid an hourly wage for rehearsal, then per show.

Auditions: Rarely held, contact directly if interested. "We employ more of an 'apprentice' type of model. Most people enter as unpaid interns or volunteers and then work up to being paid. We are always interested in meeting new puppeteers and encourage those interested in the field to contact us."

Ivey participant

Interact Theatre
interactcenter.com
Administration: 612-339-5145

Performance space (varies): Mixed Blood, Old Arizona, Dowling Studio

Non-Equity—monthly stipend

Auditions: Open auditions are not held. Guest artists are sometimes used.

Mission: To provide artists with disabilities skills and opportunities for creative expression, artistic growth, professional performance and exhibition opportunities, and opportunities to earn income from their work; to challenge existing stereotypes that assume people with disabilities are not capable; to challenge the arts community to recognize and include the unique talents and vision of people who have long been marginalized.

Ivey participant

Jon Hassler Theatre
jonhasslertheater.org
Administration: 507-534-2900 or 866-548-7469

Performance space:
Jon Hassler Theater
412 W. Broadway
Plainview, Minnesota 55964

Non-Equity—weekly salary covering rehearsal and performance. Housing provided.

Auditions: Posted per show on minnesotaplaylist.com.

Joseph Scrimshaw Productions
josephscrimshaw.com
Administrationistration and box office: 612-280-9210

Performance space: Theatre Garage, Bryant Lake Bowl, Fringe Festival

Limited Equity contracts/non-Equity—pay by stipend, per show, or stipend based on percentage of profits.

Auditions: Posted on minnesotaplaylist. com, callboard.org.

Submit headshot and resume to:
Joseph Scrimshaw Productions
4336 Oakland Avenue
Minneapolis, Minnesota 55407

Jungle Theater
Jungletheater.com
Administration: 612-822-4002
Box office: 612-822-7063

Performance space
Jungle Theater
2951 Lyndale Avenue S.
Minneapolis, Minnesota 55408

Auditions: Posted in the Sunday *Star Tribune*, minnesotaplaylist.com.

Equity/limited non-Equity—weekly salary

Send headshots and resumes to:
Jungle Theater
Attn: Joel Sass
2951 Lyndale Avenue S.
Minneapolis, Minnesota 55408

Ivey participant

Live Action Set
liveactionset.org

Performance space (varies): Soap Factory, Dowling Studio

Ivey participant

Margolis Brown Theater Company
(moved to East Coast, sometimes returns for performances and workshops)
margolisbrown.org
Administration: 612-791-7287

Performance space (varies): Illusion Theater

Join mailing list on website for information updates.

The Mechanical Division
mechanicaldivision.com
Administration: 612-810-5111

Performance space:
Lakeville Area Arts Center
20965 Holyoke Avenue
Lakeville, Minnesota 55044

Non-Equity

Auditions: Posted in the Sunday *Star Tribune*, minnesotaplaylist.com, fringefamous.com.

Send headshot and resume to:
The Mechanical Division
602 Seventh Street N.E.
New Prague, Minnesota 56071

Ivey participant

Ministry of Cultural Warfare
(comedy theater)
mocw.org

Performance space (varies): Bryant Lake Bowl, Fringe Festivals, Intermedia Arts

Non-Equity—"If we make a profit, we split it."

Auditions: see website

Minneapolis Musical Theatre
aboutmmt.org
Administration: 952.544.1372

Performance space:
Illusion Theater
Hennepin Center for the Arts
528 Hennepin Avenue
Minneapolis, Minnesota 55403

Non-Equity—$200 stipend

Auditions: Posted for season on website, minneasotaplaylist.com, callboard.org.

Submit headshots and resumes to:
Minneapolis Musical Theatre
8520 W. 29th Street
Minneapolis, Minnesota 55426

Mission: Dedicated to providing community access to high quality yet affordable works of musical theatre never before—or very rarely—seen by Twin Cities audiences.

Ivey participant

Minnesota Centennial Showboat
showboat.umn.edu
Administration: 612-625-4001
Box office: 651-227-110

Performance space:
Showboat on Harriet Island
St Paul, Minnesota

Non-Equity—U of M theater students only

Minnesota Jewish Theatre
mnjewishtheatre.org
Administration: 651-647-4315

Performance space:
Hillcrest Center
1978 Ford Parkway
St. Paul, Minnesota

Equity/non-Equity

Auditions: Posted in Sunday *Star Tribune*, minnesotaplaylist.com, callboard.org.

Ivey participant

Minnesota Opera
mnopera.org
Administration: 612-333-2700
Box office: 612-333-6669

Performance space:
Ordway Center
345 Washington Street
St Paul, Minnesota

Non-Equity—Dancers: weekly salary; chorus/supers: hourly plus performance fee; principals: per performance.

Auditions: Held every spring by appointment only. Call 612-342-9572 for information.

See website for more details.

Minnesota Shakespeare Project
mnshakespeare.org
Administration: 612-871-5168

To be considered for an audition or interview, submit headshot and resume to:
Minnesota Shakespeare Project
4253 Newton Avenue N.
Minneapolis, Minnesota 55412

Ivey participant

Minnetonka Community Theatre
minnetonkatheatre.com
Administration: 952.401.5748
Box Office: 952.401.5898

Performance space:
Arts Center on 7
18285 Highway 7
Minnetonka, Minnesota

Few Equity guest contracts, primarily non-Equity volunteer

Auditions: Sunday *Star Tribune*, minnesotaplaylist.com, theater's website.

Mixed Blood Theatre
mixedblood.com
Administration: 612-338-0937
Box Office: 612-338-6131

Performance space:
Mixed Blood Theatre
1501 S. Fourth Street
Minneapolis, Minnesota 55454

Equity/non-Equity

Auditions: Posted on minnesotaplaylist.com, callboard.org. Attends the Twin Cities Unified Auditions and holds periodic auditions

Submit headshots and resumes to:
Mixed Blood Theatre
Attn: Jack Reuler
1501 S. Fourth Street
Minneapolis Minnesota 55454.

Artists of color, multilingual actors, and actors with disabilities are especially encouraged to audition.

Mission: A professional, multi-racial theatre promoting cultural pluralism and individual equality through artistic excellence. Using theater as a vehicle for artistry, entertainment, education and social change, Mixed Blood Theatre addresses artificial barriers that keep people from succeeding in American society. Mixed Blood's purpose is to produce plays using culture-conscious casting, provide the finest forum in the nation for theatre artists of color to practice their craft, take artistic risks in the selection and production of plays, reach a non-traditional theatre audience, produce educational programs on racial and cultural themes.

Ivey participant

Mu Performing Arts and Theater Mu
muperformingarts.org
Administration: 612-824-4804

Performance space (varies): Mixed Blood, The Ritz

Non-Equity, occasional Equity guests

Mission: Mu Performing Arts is the Midwest's foremost pan-Asian performing arts organization, and is home to Theater Mu, an Asian-American theater company, and Mu Daiko, a Japanese taiko-drumming group. Founded as Theater Mu in 1992, Mu has come to be known for its unique blending of Asian and Western Artistic forms in the expression of Asian and Asian-American stories and music.

Ivey participant

Mystery Cafe
(murder mystery dinner theatre)
themysterycafe.com
Administration: 763-566-2583

Performance space:
The Mystery Café Comedy dinner theater
Crowne Plaza Minneapolis North
2200 Freeway Boulevard
Brooklyn Center, Minnesota 55430-1737

Submit headshots and resumes to:
Mystery Cafe
5701 Shingle Creek Parkway, Suite 612
Brooklyn Center, Minnesota 55430

Mystery Café also provides corporate and team building shows.

Nautilus Music–Theater
nautilusmusictheater.org
Administration: 651-298-9913

Performance space:
Nautilus Musical Theatre Studio
Northern Warehouse
308 Prince Street, Suite 250
St. Paul, Minnesota 55101

Auditions: Submission information on website.

Mission: Since 1986, Nautilus (formerly The New Music-Theater Ensemble) has been dedicated to the development of new operas and other forms of music-theater, along with innovative productions of existing work. Goals include the formation of partnerships between creators, performers, and audiences, and the creation of professional training programs for artists. They use music-theater as a tool to create enriching experiences for artists and audiences, supporting the individual and collective growth of the human spirit.

Ivey participant

Nimbus Theatre
nimbustheatre.com
Administration: 651-229-3122

Performance space:
Minneapolis Theatre Garage
711 W. Franklin Avenue
Minneapolis, Minnesota

Non-Equity/volunteer

Auditions: Posted in Sunday *Star Tribune*, minnesotaplaylist.com, callboard.org, audition e-mail list (join on theater's website).

Ivey participant

No Refunds Theatre Company

norefundstheatre.com

Performance space (varies): Red Eye, Fringe Festival, Bryant Lake Bowl

Limited Equity guest contracts/non-Equity—small stipend

Auditions: Posted on minnesotaplaylist.com.

Off Leash Area (award-winning, contemporary performance works)
offleasharea.org
Administration: 612-724-7372

Performance space:
Our Garage
3540 34th Avenue S.
Minneapolis, Minnesota 55406

Non-Equity—pay per show

Auditions: Sometimes post on minnesotaplaylist.com, invitation, and e-mail list.

Ivey participant

Old Gem Theater
(forty miles from Twin Cities)
oldgemtheater.com
Box office: 715-246-3285

Performance space:
Old Gem Theater
116 S. Knowles Avenue
New Richmond, Wisconsin, 54017

Non-Equity/some guest Equity contracts—pay per rehearsal stipend and per show

Send headshot and resume to:
Kathy Welch, Artistic Director
116 S. Knowles Avenue
New Richmond, Wisconsin 54017
or e-mail boxoffice@oldgemtheater.com

Auditions: Posted on website and e-mail list.

Old Log Theater
oldlog.com
Administration: 952-474-5951

Performance space:
Old Log Theater
5185 Meadville Street
Excelsior, Minnesota 55331

Equity/non-Equity—weekly salary, approximately $400-$500

Auditions: Contact Tom Stolz for audition information via administration phone

Submit headshots and resumes to:
Old Log Theater
Box 250
Excelsior, Minnesota 55331-0250

Ivey participant

Olson Brothers Entertainment
donthugme.com
Administration: 877-877-8135

Non-Equity—approx $75 per show

Auditions: Posted on minnesotaplaylist.com.

Submit headshots and resumes to:
phil@philolson.net

Ivey participant

Open Eye Figure Theatre
(mixing screen projections, figures, music,
human actors, and shadow puppetry)
openeyetheatre.org
Administration and box office:
612-874-6338
Studio: 612-823-5162

Performance space:
Open Eye Theatre
506 E. 24th Street
Minneapolis, Minnesota

Creators: Michael Sommers and Sue Haas

Ivey participant

Ordway Center for the Performing Arts
(home to locally-produced and touring
shows)
ordway.org
Administration: 651-282-3000
Box office: 651-224-.4222

Performance space:
Ordway Theater
345 Washington Street
St. Paul, Minnesota 55102

Equity/non-Equity—$400-$600 weekly
salary

Auditions: Posted on website, min-
nesotaplaylist.com, audition hotline
651-215-2100.

Ivey participant

Outward Spiral
outwardspiral.org
Administration: 612-703-1258

Non-Equity

Auditions: If interested in joining Outward Spiral as a volunteer, sponsor, board
member, or in any other capacity, contact
info@outwardspiral.org.

Mission: Dedicated to producing theatre
from a queer point-of-view. They strive to
entertain, educate, and act as a catalyst
for social change through inclusive, multi-
cultural, provocative artistic expression.

Pangea World Theater
pangeaworldtheater.org
Administration: 612-822-0015
Box Office: 612-203-1088

Performance space: Intermedia Arts,
Avalon Theater, and others

Non-Equity

Auditions: posted on minnesotaplaylist.com

Mission: Illuminates the human condition, celebrates cultural differences, and
promotes human rights by creating and
presenting international, multi-disciplin-
ary theater.

Ivey participant

Park Square Theatre
parksquaretheatre.org
Administration: 651-291-7005
Box office: 651-291-7005

Performance space:
Park Square Theatre
Historic Hamm Building
20 W. Seventh Place
St. Paul, Minnesota 55102

Equity/Non-Equity—pay per show

Auditions: Posted per show on website,
minnesotaplaylist.com, or call auditions
hotline at 651-767-8491.

Mission: Seeks to enrich our community
by producing and presenting exceptional
live theatre that touches the heart, en-
gages the mind, and delights the spirit.

Ivey participant

Patrick's Cabaret
(cabaret performances, space rental)
patrickscabaret.org
Administration: 612-724-6273
Box office: 612-721-3595

Performance space:
Patrick's Cabaret
3010 Minnehaha Avenue S.
Minneapolis, Minnesota 55406

Auditions:Visit website for information.

Mission: Supports artists in their growth and development by encouraging artists of all experience levels to try new things, take risks, or present works in progress. We serve a diverse range of artists, from emerging to experienced, from teenagers to seniors. The Cabaret's first commitment is to serve the needs of local performing artists, specifically reaching out to artists of color and GLBT/ queer-identified artists and those with disabilities.

Paul Bunyan Playhouse
(professional summer theatre 225 miles north of the Twin Cities)
paulbunyanplayhouse.com
Box office: 218-751-7270

Performance space:
The Historic Chief Theatre
314 Beltrami Avenue
Bemidji, Minnesota 56601

Non-Equity/limited Equity contracts— weekly salary

Auditions: Posted on theater website, held in Bemidji; sometimes post Twin Cities auditions on minnesotaplaylist.com and callboard.org.

Send headshot and resume to: artistic director via address on website

Pendulum Theatre Company
Pendulumtheatrecompany.org
karla@pendulumtheatrecompany.org;

Karla Reck, artistic director

Non-Equity

Auditions: posted on website

Mission: To allow Christ to be a blessing to all people by producing living art that explores the complexities of human nature and relationships, cultivating lifelong theatre enthusiasts, and providing a nurturing and stable environment where professional theatre artists can explore their craft and thrive in their art.

Penumbra Theatre
penumbratheatre.org
Administration and box office:
651-224-3180

Performance space:
Martin Luther King Center
270 N. Kent Street
St. Paul, Minnesota

Equity and non-Equity

Mission: Creates professional productions that are artistically excellent, thought provoking, relevant, and illuminate the human condition through the prism of the African-American experience.

Ivey participant

Perpetual Motion Theatre
perpetualmotiontheatre.org

Non-equity

Auditions: private company, collaborates for performances for the Fringe Festival

Mission: An experimental theatre ensemble based in Minneapolis. They focus on creating theatrical works that combine physical and movement-based techniques with narrative and character-driven scripts.

Phipps Center for the Arts
(twenty-five miles from the Twin Cities)
thephipps.org
Administration: 715-386-2305

Performance space:
The Phipps
109 Locust Street
Hudson, Wisconsin 54016

Non-equity

Auditions: Posted on website.

Pillsbury House Theatre
Pillsburyhousetheatre.org
Administration and box office:
612-825-0459

Performance space: Pillsbury House
Theatre, 3501 Chicago Avenue S., Minneapolis, Minnesota 55407

Equity with an SPT contract

Auditions: Interested actors call
612-825-0459.

Submit headshots and resumes to:
Faye Price
3501 Chicago Avenue S.
Minneapolis, Minnesota 55407

Ivey participant

Pioneer Place on Fifth
(seventy miles from the Twin Cities)
ppfive.com
Box office: 320-203-0331

Performance space:
Pioneer Place Theater
22 Fifth Avenue S.
St Cloud, Minnesota

Limited Equity contracts/non-Equity—per show salary

Auditions: Most shows are tours or remounts so auditions and submissions are not actively pursued.

Playwright's Center
(does not produce full shows, but often work culminates in a public staged reading)
www.pwcenter.org
Administration: 612-332-7481

Equity/non-Equity—pay per hour

Auditions: once per year, posted on website

Send headshot and resume to:
Sarah Gioia, Casting Associate
The Playwrights' Center
2301 Franklin Avenue E.
Minneapolis, Minnesota 55406-1099

Mission: Champions playwrights and plays to build upon a living theater that demands new and innovative works.

Prufrock Theatre
prufrocktheatre.org

Red Eye Theater
redeyetheater.org
Administration: 612-870-7531
Box Office: 612-870-0309

Performance space:
Red Eye Theater
15 W. 14th Street
Minneapolis, Minnesota

Limited Equity/non-Equity

Auditions: Posted on minnesotaplaylist.com, callboard.org.

Mission: A multidisciplinary creative laboratory that supports the development and production of pioneering performance work.

Ivey participant

River's Edge Playback Theatre
riversedgeplayback.org
Administration: 651-917-1976

Performance space:
Collaborative Village Initiative
2020 Elliot Avenue S.
Minneapolis, Minnesota 55404

Non-Equity

Mission:Improvisational theatre in which audience or group members tell stories from their lives, and watch them enacted on the spot by an ensemble of actors. Community improv workshop held once per month.

Ronin Theatre
ronintheater.org

Non-Equity

Auditions: posted on website

Mission: Devoted to crafting quality theater, training actors, and providing them with the chance to develop themselves through a variety of genres and performance styles. They hope to provide actors with a real chance to challenge themselves artistically, in order to grow into a better performer.

St. Croix Festival Theatre
(fifty miles from the Twin Cities)
www.festivaltheatre.org
Administration and box office:
715-483-3387

Performance space:
The Festival Theatre
210 N. Washington Street
St. Croix Falls, Wisconsin 54024

Few guest artist contracts/non-Equity—approximately $200-$350 per week, some stipend and volunteer positions also available

Auditions: Posted on minnesotaplaylist.com. E-mail boxoffice@festivaltheatre.org to join the audition e-notice list.

Submit headshot and resume: to address above

St. Croix Off Broadway Dinner Theatre
(twenty-five miles from the Twin Cities)
www.stcroixoffbroadway.com
Administration and box office:
715-386-2394

Performance space:
Best Western Hudson House Inn
1616 Crestview Drive
Hudson, Wisconsin 54016

Non-Equity—pay per show

Auditions: Posted on minnesotaplaylist.com, callboard.org. STOBDT attends Twin Cities Unifieds.

Send headshot and resume to:
St. Croix Off Broadway Dinner Theatre
Personnel
412 River Hills Road S.
River Falls, Wisconsin 54022
(include dates available and position interested in)

Sandbox Theatre
aboutthisplay.com
Administration: 612-554-1302

Performance space:
Red Eye Collaboration Theater,
5 W. 14th Street
Minneapolis, Minnesota

Non-Equity—pay by stipend

Auditions: Primarily a collaborative ensemble, if interested in joining please contact porkchop@aboutthisplay.com or Sandbox Theatre, 3301 Emerson Avenue S., Minneapolis, Minnesota 55408.

Auditions posted on minnesotaplaylist.com, by personal invitation, and e-mail list

Ivey participant

Seasons Dinner Theatre
theseasonsatbunkerhills.
com/dinner-theater
Administration and Box Office:
763-755-4444

Performance space:
Bunker Hills Golf Course
12800 Bunker Drive
Coon Rapids, Minnesota 55448

Non-Equity

Shakespeare and Company
Shakespeareandcompany.org
Administration: 651,779,5818

Non-Equity

Performance space:
Outdoor Classical Repertory Theatre
Century College
White Bear Lake, Minnesota

Auditions: Held in the spring for the summer season, check the website in March/April.

Shakespeare on the Cape
http://shakespeareonthecape.wordpress.com/

Performance space:
Grainbelt Brewery Bottling House Theatre
79 13th Avenue N.E.
Minneapolis, Minnesota

Non-Equity

Skewed Visions
skewedvisions.org
Administration: 612-201-5727

Equity if necessary, mostly non-Equity—pay by stipend

Auditions: Rarely held, if interested in collaborating please contact the company directly.

Submissions may be sent to:
Skewed Vision
681 17th Avenue N.E., Suite 209
Minneapolis, Minnesota 55413

Mission: Create original, multidisciplinary, site-specific performances for or tailored to particular locations.

Ivey participant

Skylark Opera (formerly NorthStar Opera)
NorthStarOpera.org
Administration: 651-292-4309

Performance space:
E. M. Pearson Theatre
Concordia University
St. Paul, Minnesota

Equity guest contracts/non-Equity—flat fee for large roles, hourly wage for smaller roles

Auditions: Sunday *Star Tribune*, on website, e-mail invitation.

Submit headshots and resumes to:
Artistic Director Steve Stucki
Landmark Center, Suite 414
75 W. Fifth Street
St. Paul, Minnesota 55102

Spark Theater + Dance
sparktheater.com
Administration: 612-870-2585

Ivey participant

Stages Theatre Company (children and youth)
stagestheatre.org
Administration: 952-979-1111

Performance space:
Stages Theatre Company
1111 Mainstreet
Hopkins, Minnesota 55343

Auditions: For ages ten to twenty-one only, unless otherwise listed; audition dates posted at www.stagestheatre.org/auditions.htm.

Ivey participant

Starting Gate Productions
startinggate.org
Administration: 651-645-3503

Performance space:
Mounds Theatre
1029 Hudson Road
St Paul, Minnesota 55106

Few Equity contracts/mon-Equity—pay by stipend

Auditions: Posted on www.minnesotaplaylist.com, www.startinggate.org/auditions.asp.

Send headshot and resume to:
Starting Gate Productions
Attn: Richard Jackson
PO Box 16392
St Paul, Minnesota 55116

Ivey participant

SteppingStone Theatre for Youth
(children and youth)
steppingstonetheatre.org
Administration and box office:
651-225-9265

Performance space:

SteppingStone Theatre
55 Victoria Avenue N.
St. Paul, Minnesota

Non-Equity youth theatre and education

Ivey participant

Stevie Ray's Improv Company
(improvisation)
www.stevierays.org
Administration: 612-825-1832

Performance space:
Sheraton Bloomington Hotel
7800 Normandale Boulevard
Bloomington, Minnesota 55439

Non-Equity

Auditions: Notices sent via e-mail to other local improv companies.

Swandive Theatre
swandivetheatre.org

Teatro del Pueblo
teatrodelpueblo.org
Administration: 651-224-8806
Box office: 651-225-8106

Performance space:
Baker Center
209 Page Street W.
St Paul, Minnesota

Few Equity contracts/non-Equity—pay per show, some stipends for contract work

Auditions: Posted on minnesotaplaylist. com, callboard.org, on website, and e-mail lists.

Submit headshot and resume to: Christina@teatrodelpueblo.org

Mission: Based in the West Side's Latino community, Teatro del Pueblo promotes Latino culture through the creation and presentation of performing arts. Teatro develops and supports Latino artists, provides educational opportunities for all to experience Latino culture and promotes cross-cultural dialogue.

Ivey participant

Ten Thousand Things Theater Company
tenthousandthings.org
Administration: 612-203-9502

Performance space (varies): shelters, prisons, low-income centers

Equity (SPT4)/non-Equity—pay weekly salary

Auditions: Posted on minnesotaplaylist. com, theater's website. Open auditions once a year.

Mission: Ten Thousand Things brings lively, intelligent theater to people with little access to the wealth of the arts—who in turn help us to reimagine theater. Performing at homeless shelters, prisons, and other low-income centers, using the region's finest actors, this bare-bones, high-quality theater company invigorates ancient tales, classic stories, and contemporary plays through its search for raw, open interactions between actors and audiences.

Ivey participant

Theater for the Thirsty
theaterforthethirsty.com
Administration: 612-529-3821

Performance space: Northwestern College, various churches

Non-Equity

Auditions: Two-person theater company, with a few external members.

Mission: Entertaining and imaginative theater that explores redemptive themes and leaves your mouth feeling minty-fresh.

Ivey participant

Theater Latte Da
(the art of musical theater)
Latteda.org
Administration: 612-339-3003

Performance space: McKnight Theater, Southern Theater, Pantages Theater

Equity Contracts/non-Equity

Auditions: Posted on minnesotaplaylist. com, callboard.org.

Ivey participant

Theatre L'Homme Dieu
(professional summer theater, 135 miles from the Twin Cities.)
tlhd.org
Box office: 320-846-3150

Performance space:
Theatre L'Homme Dieu
Alexandria, Minnesota

Primarily non-Equity

Auditions: Not currently holding auditions; imports shows from various Minnesota professional theaters.

Theatre Limina
theatrelimina.org
Administration and tickets: 612-825-8949

Performance space:
Bryant Lake Bowl
810 W. Lake Street
Minneapolis, Minnesota

Non-Equity

Ivey participant

Theater Mu (see Mu Performing Arts)

Theatre of Fools
theatreoffools.com
Administration: 612-823-1118

Auditions: None; husband and wife organization, produces two-person shows.

Ivey participant

Theatre Pro Rata
theatreprorata.org
Administration: 612-874-9321

Performance space:
Gremlin Theater
2400 University Avenue
St. Paul, Minnesota 55114

Limited Equity contracts/non-Equity—pay by stipend

Auditions: Posted on minnesotaplaylist.com, callboard.org, on website, e-mail list (sign up on website), occasionally invite-only auditions.

Submit headshot and resume to:
Carin Bratlie at info@theatreprorata.org
or inquire at this e-mail for mailing address

Ivey participant

Theatre Unbound
theatreunbound.com
Administration: 612-207-3659

Performance space (varies): Bryant Lake Bowl, Paul & Sheila Wellstone Community Center, Playwright's Center

Non-Equity—pay by stipend

Auditions: Posted on minnesotaplaylist.com, callboard.org.

Mission: Committed to affecting the theatre community on a grass roots level. By opening up opportunities for women actors, directors, playwrights, and designers, they give them the power to affect the theatre community on a larger scale.

Ivey participant

Torch Theater
torchtheater.com
Administration: 952-929-9097

Performance space (varies): Theatre Garage, History Theater

Some Equity contracts/non-Equity

Auditions: Hotline 952-929-9097.

Ivey participant

Triple Espresso
tripleespresso.com/minneapolis
Administration: 612-871-1414
Box office: 612-871-1414

Performance space:
Music Box Theater
1407 Nicollet Avenue
Minneapolis, Minnesota

Equity/non-Equity—pay per show

Ivey participant

Troupe America
troupeamerica.com
Administration: 612-333-3302

Performance space: Plymouth Playhouse, touring shows

Equity/non-Equity—pay by weekly salary or per show, additional per diem for housing and transportation for touring

Auditions: Posted in the Sunday *Star Tribune* and on minnesotaplaylist.com; attends SETCs, UPTAs.

Submit headshot and resume to:
Curt Wollan
528 Hennepin Avenue, Suite 206
Minneapolis, Minnesota 55403

Upright Egg Theatre Company
Uprightegg.com

Urban Samurai Productions
urbansamurai.org
Administration: 651-983-6626

Performance space:
Jewish Community Center
4330 Cedar Lake Road S.
St. Louis Park, Minnesota

Non-Equity—pay by stipend

Auditions: Posted on callboard.org, minnesotaplaylist.com.

Submit headshot and resume to:
urbansamuraipro@gmail.com

Ivey participant

Urban Spectrum Theatre
urbanspectrumtheatre.com
Administration: 612-869-5080

Non-Equity—Pay by stipend

Auditions: Posted on minnesotplaylist.com.

Send headshot and resume to:
urbanspectrum@yahoo.com

Walking Shadow Theatre Company
walkingshadowcompany.org
Administration: 612-375-0300

Performance space (varies): Pillsbury House Theatre, Red Eye Theatre, People's Center Theatre, etc.

Primarily non-Equity/limited Equity—all positions paid, amount varies

Auditions: Not currently holding open auditions, e-mail info@walkingshadow-company.org, with headshot and resume for consideration.

Ivey participant

Wild Yam Cabaret (cabaret performance)
wildyamcabaret.org

Performance space:
Mad Hatter's Teahouse
943 W. Seventh Street
St. Paul, Minnesota

Non-Equity

Auditions: Contact swfr@minn.net if interested in performing.

Workhaus Collective
workhauscollective.org
Administration: 612-332-7481, ext. 20

Performance space:
The Playwright's Center
2301 Franklin Avenue E.
Minneapolis, Minnesota

Some Equity, non-Equity

Mission: Fueled by the desire, as playwrights, to communicate directly with audiences with shows that are adventurous and event-driven: a full-bodied experience that can only happen in live theatre. Workhaus is a diverse group of nationally recognized playwrights based in the Twin Cities.

Ivey participant

Workhouse Theatre Company
Workhousetheatre.org
Administration: 612-386-5763

Performance space:
The Warren
4400 Osseo Road
Minneapolis., Minnesota 55412

Non-equity

Mission: The Workhouse Theatre's mission is to provide the residents of the Camden neighborhoods with an opportunity to attend and to participate in quality presentations of theatrical works.

Ivey participant

Yellow Tree Theatre
yellowtreetheatre.com
Administration and box office:
763-493-8733

Performance space:
Yellow Tree Theatre
320 Fifth Avenue S.E.
Osseo, Minnesota 55369

Non-Equity—Pay by stipend

Auditions: Posted on minnesotaplaylist. com, callboard.org.

Submit headshot and resume to above address or jason@yellowtreetheatre.com.

Community/amateur/volunteer theaters.

A listing here simply means that actors are not paid. Directors and designers may be paid; in fact, some community theaters (like Theatre in the Round) may pay their directors or designers more than some of the "professional theaters" previously listed! This will vary.

Further, this categorization is in no way a commentary on the quality of the artists' work. I have worked with a few of these theaters, and I have attended performances at several more. I have been entertained and impressed, and, in fact, the entertainment value has sometimes been vastly superior to some of the professional theaters I have attended. When artists come together for the sheer love of theater, magical things often happen.

Also know that professional actors, directors, and designers frequently work at some of these theaters. The more established among them often have great audience attendance; as a result, these theaters will often draw talented and experienced artists. Personally, I would rather work for free in front of full houses than be paid a small stipend to play to empty seats! Do not rule out a community or amateur theater just because you will not be paid.

Many of these theaters welcome volunteers, and it is a great way to get your foot in the door of the local theater scene. Volunteer to usher, paint sets, work backstage, work the box office, etc.

The list that follows is a sampling of community and amateur theaters in the metro area. There are many more all over the state. You may wish to visit the Minnesota Association of Community Theatres' (MACT) website for links to more (mact.net, click on "Member Theatres"). Many of these theaters list auditions on their websites and on minnesotaplaylist.com. The MACT hotline may advertise auditions as well: 612-706-1456, 800-290-2428. In addition, there are community theatres that may not be members of MACT. Keep an eye out for advertising in your area.

ANOKA
Lyric Arts
lyricarts.org

BLOOMINGTON
Bloomington Art Center Gallery Players
bloomingtonartcenter.com

BROOKLYN PARK
Prime Time Players
thetalentcenter.com/radio.htm
(theater by and for seniors)

BURNSVILLE
Applause Community Theatre
applausecommunitytheatre.com

CHASKA
Chaska Valley Family Theatre
cvft.org

EDEN PRAIRIE
Eden Prairie Players
edenprairieplayers.org

ELK RIVER
Elk River Community Theatre
erct.org

FOREST LAKE
Masquers Theatre Company
masquerstheatre.org

LAKEVILLE
Chameleon Theatre Circle
chameleontheatre.org

LITTLE CANADA
Heritage Theatre Company
www.heritagetc.com

MAPLE GROVE/OSSEO
Cross Community Players (Christians Reaching Out in Social Services)
crossplayers.org

MINNEAPOLIS
Corcoran Park Players

Morris Park Players Community Theatre
morrisparkplayers.org

Theatre in the Round
theatreintheround.org

Gilbert and Sullivan Very Light Opera
www.gsvloc.org
(non-Equity—no pay for actors; orchestra paid $17 stipend per performance)

MINNETONKA
Minnetonka Community Theatre
minnetonkatheatre.com

MOUNDS VIEW / NEW BRIGHTON
Mounds View Community Theatre
mvct.org

NEW HOPE
Off Broadway Musical Theater
(outdoor summer theater)
obmt.org
(actors are volunteers, some staff positions paid; submit to obmt@yahoo.com or mail to
OBMT Board
12920 46th Avenue
Plymouth, Minnesota 55442)

PRIOR LAKE
Prior Lake Players
priorlakeplayers.org

ROSEVILLE
Rosetown Playhouse
rosetownplayhouse.org

SHAKOPEE
River Valley Theatre Company
rivervalleytheatrecompany.org

ST. ANTHONY
St. Anthony Community Theater
sactheater.org

ST. PAUL
Lex-Ham Community Theater
lexhamarts.org

5th Season Entertainment
5thseasonentertainment.com

WHITE BEAR LAKE
Lakeshore Players
lakeshoreplayers.com

WOODBURY
Woodbury Community Theater
woodburycommunitytheatre.org

Theater spaces.

The following theaters are not companies, they are spaces that local theater organizations sometimes use or rent. Some of these spaces are primarily used for theatrical productions; many others are café cabaret spaces that are used for live music and various performances. (Often these spaces are part of the annual Fringe Festival.) Again, I have not included the many high school, college, and university theater spaces in the area.

Acadia Café
Acadiacafe.com
1931 Nicollet Avenue S.
Minneapolis, Minnesota

Bryant Lake Bowl
bryantlakebowl.com
Box office 612.825.8949
810 W. Lake Street
Minneapolis, Minnesota

Capri Theatre
thecapritheater.org
2027 W. Broadway
Minneapolis, Minnesota

Cedar Riverside People's Center
Peoples-center.org
425 20th Avenue S.
Minneapolis, Minnesota

Cedar Cultural Center
Thecedar.org
416 Cedar Avenue S.
Minneapolis, Minnesota

Center for Independent Artists
www.c4ia.org
4137 Bloomington Avenue S.
Minneapolis, Minnesota

Center for Independent Artists exists as a producing, convening and service organization for artists from diverse physical, cultural, and aesthetic perspectives, offering a place for visibility, intersection, conversation, and career support. It celebrates the role of the independent artist as visionary in society. The Center nurtures independent artistic vision, fosters diverse cultural perspectives and seeks to build an educated, enlightened citizenry.

The Directors' Studios – rehearsal space
tdstudios.us
1170 15th Avenue SE
Minneapolis, MN 55414
612-746-1372

Fitzgerald Theater
fitzgeraldtheater.publicradio.org
10 E. Exchange Street
St. Paul, Minnesota

Grainbelt Brewery Bottling House Theatre
79 Thirteenth Avenue N.E.
Minneapolis, Minnesota

Hennepin Center for the Arts
Little Theater
528 Hennepin Avenue S.
Minneapolis, Minnesota

Hennepin Stages
Hennepintheatredistrict.org
Upper level and lower level theaters
824 Hennepin Avenue S.
Minneapolis, Minnesota

Hillcrest Center Theater
(home of Minnesota Jewish Theater)
1978 Ford Parkway
St. Paul, Minnesota

Historic Theatre Group
(Orpheum, State, Pantages)
Hennepintheatredistrict.org

Orpheum
910 Hennepin Avenue S.
Minneapolis, Minnesota

State
805 Hennepin Avenue S.
Minneapolis, Minnesota

Pantages
710 Hennepin Avenue S.
Minneapolis, Minnesota

Howard Conn Fine Arts Center
612-623-9180
1900 Nicollet Avenue
Minneapolis, Minnesota

Hopkins Center for the Arts
Hopkinsmn.com/hca
1111 Main Street
Hopkins, Minnesota

Intermedia Arts
intermediaarts.org
2822 Lyndale Avenue S.
Minneapolis, Minnesota 55408

The Lab Theater
thelabtheater.org
700 N. First Street
Minneapolis, Minnesota

Loring Playhouse
1633 Hennepin Avenue
Minneapolis, Minnesota

Lowry Lab Theater
Lowrylabtheater.org
carol@theaterspaceproject.org
350 St. Peter Street
St. Paul, Minnesota

Lowry Theater
16 W. Fifth Street
St. Paul, Minnesota

Mounds Theater
Moundstheater.org
1029 Hudson Road
St. Paul, Minnesota

The Music Box Theater
1407 Nicollet Avenue S.
Minneapolis, Minnesota

Patrick's Cabaret
patrickscabaret.org
3010 Minnehaha Avenue S.
Minneapolis, Minnesota

Paul and Sheila Wellstone Community Center
neighb.org (click on "performance space")
179 Robie Street
St. Paul, Minnesota

The Phipps
ThePhipps.org
109 Locust Street
Hudson, Wisconsin

Playwright's Center
pwcenter.org
2301 Franklin Avenue
Minneapolis, Minnesota

Plymouth Playhouse
plymouthplayhouse.com
Best Western Kelly Inn
2705 Annapolis Lane N.
Plymouth, Minnesota
currently operated by Troupe America

Old Arizona Theatre
Oldarizona.com
2821 Nicollet Avenue
Minneapolis, Minnesota

The Red Eye Theater
redeyetheater.org
15 W. 14th Street
Minneapolis, Minnesota

Ritz Theater
Ritztheaterfoundation.org
345 13th Avenue N.E.
Minneapolis, Minnesota

Sabes Jewish Community Center
sabesjcc.org
4330 S. Cedar Lake Road
St. Louis Park, Minnesota

Southern Theater
southerntheater.org
Box office: 612-340-1725
1420 Washington Avenue S.
Minneapolis, Minnesota

Theatre Garage
Box office: 612-870-0723
711 W. Franklin Avenue
Minneapolis, Minnesota

Varsity Theater
Varsitytheater.org
1308 Fourth Street S.E.
Minneapolis, Minnesota

Walker Art Center, McGuire Theater
walkerart.org
1750 Hennepin Avenue
Minneapolis, Minnesota

Theater for youth and children.

The following provide performance opportunities specifically for kids (some professional, some amateur/educational). See the websites for more details. Contact community theaters in your area to discover more possibilities.

Please note that organizations on this list provide performing opportunities. If you are looking for classes and workshops, many of these offer such opportunities, but see Appendix F for many more.

Blue Water Theatre Company
www.bluewatertheatre.com

Performance space:
Eisenhower Community Center
Plymouth, Minnesota

Chaska Valley Family Theatre
cvft.org
1661 Park Ridge Drive
Chaska, Minnesota 55318
Community theater for families

Chicago Avenue Project
puc-mn.org (click on "Pillsbury House Theater," then "Chicago Avenue Project")
3501 Chicago Avenue S.
Minneapolis, Minnesota

Children's Theatre Company
childrenstheatre.org
2400 Third Avenue S.
Minneapolis, Minnesota
see listing in professional theater section

Circus Juventas
Circusjuventas.org
1270 Montreal Avenue
St. Paul, Minnesota

Outward Spiral Theatre/Empowered Expressions
Outwardspiral.org
District 202
1601 Nicollet Avenue
Minneapolis, Minnesota
Outreach for students, dedicated to giving voice to queer youth and cultivating community.

Stages Theatre Company
stagestheatre.org
1111 Mainstreet
Hopkins, Minnesota
see listing in professional theater section

SteppingStone Theatre for Youth
steppingstonetheatre.org
55 Victoria Avenue N.
St. Paul, Minnesota

Upstage Musical Theatre Workshop
upstagemtw.org
Performances:
Old Arizona Studios
2821 Nicollet Avenue
Minneapolis, Minnesota

Young Artists Initiative
youngartistsmn.org
463 Maria Avenue
St. Paul, Minnesota

Youth Performance Company
youthperformanceco.com
3338 University Avenue S.E.
Minneapolis, Minnesota
Improvisation and sketch comedy

Brave New Workshop
Bravenewworkshop.com

Comedy Sportz
Comedysportztc.com

Stevie Ray's Comedy Cabaret
Stevierays.org

Twin Cities Improv Festival
Twincitiesimprovfestival.com

Theater festivals

There are several other, smaller theater festivals every year, including ten-minute play festivals at various theaters. Watch the Star Tribune, City Pages, and minnesotaplaylist.com for listings.

Great River Shakespeare Festival
grsf.org
Summers at Winona State University, Winona, Minnesota; see the professional theater listings for details.

Minnesota Fringe Theater and Performance Festival
fringefestival.org
August every year, application process and lottery happen in January/February.

Minnesota Association of Community Theaters (MACT) One-Act Festival
mact.net
Every two years.

Voice-over Demos, Video Demos, and Voice-over Demo Production

I strongly recommend that you work with a voice-over coach before you spend any money on studio time. Audio engineers may be able to help you with a little bit of basic direction, but this is not why you are paying them and it is not their area of expertise. Take a class or get some coaching from someone who knows the voice-over business before you pay big bucks for studio time. Your coach will likely recommend a studio for you. Know that most studios will charge $100 to $200 per hour, so be sure you are organized before you go in! The average demo takes two to four hours of studio time to complete—one to two hours if you already have real commercial spots to edit together, three to four hours if you are starting from scratch.

If you are thinking about cutting corners, you probably do not want to use your sister's boyfriend's cousin's recording studio, unless they have actually done professional commercial work before. If you want a professional sounding demo, you want to work with professionals who actually produce commercials. See chapter 12 for more information about voice-over demos.

Voice-over classes and coaching.

Look for other coaches and classes on minnesotaplaylist.com and callboard.org.

Cheryl Moore Brinkley
bvocal.net
Cheryl offers voice-over coaching for both new and experienced actors. Contact her to discuss details.

Guthrie Theater: Jim Cada
612-225-6172
guthrietheater.org

Celia Siegel
Celiasiegel.com
Celia Siegel was a top voice-over agent both here and in L.A., becoming an expert in the field of voice-over talent marketing. She now manages a handful of top voice-over talent and markets them to national clients. She also offers consulting services (coaching, branding, and marketing) to those who are determined to grow their voice-over business (not for beginners).

The Talent Center: Don Cosgrove
651-306-9670
thetalentcenter.com
71 Imperial Drive E.
West St. Paul, Minnesota 55118

Theatre in the Round: Larry Russo
theatreintheround.org

John Wehrman
wehrmanvoice.com

Professional recording studios.

I have worked with the folks at most of the following audio production studios; other actors have recommended a few. They have all assisted actors in producing voice-over demos from time to time. Whether or not they will be interested in helping you with your demo depends upon how busy they are at any given time. If they are busy with clients, your demo project may be less attractive to them. Do not be insulted if they will not take your project; it simply means that business is good. (There are many, many more recording studios in town, and I am sure some of them have produced actors' demos.)

A few of these are large audio production studios with several engineers on staff. If they have time and you have the budget, they will be able to help you produce a professional sounding demo.

DO NOT CALL for advice about producing a demo. DO NOT CALL to ask if they have work for you. These folks are professional recording engineers, not teachers and advisors. None of them will be interested in cold calls from beginning voice-over artists. Take your questions to your voice-over coach. Call the studios for pricing and availability when you are organized and ready to record.

Aaron Stokes Music
612-373-2220
aaronstokes.com
708 N. First Street, Suite 135
Minneapolis, Minnesota 55401

The Audio Guy
612-729-3772
theaudioguy.net
Minneapolis, Minnesota

Audio Ruckus
612-333-2067
audioruckusrecording.com
10 S. Fifth Street, Suite 440
Minneapolis, Minnesota 55402

Babble-On
612-375-0533
babble-on-recording.com
12 S. Sixth Street, Suite 1221
Minneapolis, Minnesota 55402

Buzz Cutz Audio, Inc.
612-333-2899
buzzcutzaudio.com
210 N. Second Street, Suite 50
Minneapolis, Minnesota 55401

HDMG
Ben O'Brien, audio designer
952-943-1711
hdmg.com

Intuitive
612-872-0444
totallyintuitive.com
2544 Pillsbury Avenue
Minneapolis, Minnesota 55404

Morantz Music Audio Production Services
612-313-2611
morantzmusic.com
105 Fifth Avenue S., Suite 150
Minneapolis, Minnesota 55401

Splice Here
612-767-1111
splicehere.tv
119 N. Second Street
Minneapolis, Minnesota 55401

Undertone Music
612-339-8911
undertonemusic.com
600 N. Washington Avenue, Suite 305,
Minneapolis, Minnesota 55401

Tri-Audio Productions
763-425-6092
Brooklyn Park, Minnesota

Video demo editing.

Chapter 3 notes that a video demo is unnecessary in this market. It may be a handy tool if you start to get lots of work, but do not bother to produce one from scratch. If you eventually have a lot of clips to edit together into a demo, here are a couple of suggestions.

Once you have done some work, you will probably know some folks at production companies or independent filmmakers who may be willing to edit your demo during a slow day or week. It will probably cost you a minimum of $100 per hour to hire a studio and engineer (likely more) unless you have a great connection that will give you a great deal. I once bartered voice-over services in exchange for editing my demo; that may be possible for you if you get to know clients well.

If you do not have a great connection, you may wish to consult the *Minnesota Film and TV Board Guide* to find some studios. Your local community TV or cable channel may also be a possibility for lower-cost editing. (For more detailed information about video demos, consult Chapter 3.)

Paul Ryan is a local on-camera talent who offers assistance editing a video demo. He is the owner of PFR Productions and the founder of talenthelpers.com, a resource for talent. He charges a very reasonable price. Visit the website and click on video demo reel.

Paul Ryan at PFR Productions
952-892-1938
talenthelpers.com

Record Keeping, Tax Accountants

Record keeping and tax organization resources.

The Organized Actor: Workbook and Planner (organizedactor.com)

The website contains descriptions of the organizers along with much more advice, including an opportunity to sign up for an e-mail newsletter.

Performer Track (performertrack.com)

Performer Track is a new on-line system to help you keep track of all aspects of your business—logging all auditions and jobs, tracking union status, pay, contacts, directions, etc. It works great. It began as the *Hold-on Log* for actors, a workbook-style organizer then morphed into ActorTrack software. Performer Track is their brand-new on-line system that takes the place of their other products. If you use their product, you will be included in their e-mail newsletter. Most of the newsletter information pertains to an actor's life on the coasts, but some of the articles are quite interesting.

Paper records.

I have been living in the last century when it comes to my financial records. On the next page is my sample "job page." If you are technologically challenged, feel free to copy or modify my antiquated paper system as you choose. I use the upper third for audition information. If I book the job, I then use the middle space for all of the job details. The lower third deals with all of the pay issues. If I do not get the audition, I simply put a big X through the pay box. (Sadly, forms with the big X sometimes pile up!) If I do book the gig, I put the amount due to me on the last line of the page. That way, I can quickly thumb through my job pages to figure my current accounts receivable. If the box above the amount due is empty, it means the check has not arrived. Once I fill in that box, I file the job page.

I keep my job pages in a three-ring binder, along with large envelopes in which to store check stubs, agency invoices, etc. Keeping all of this together during the year will make tax time a little easier.

AUDITION

Date:

Time:

Location:

Client:

Shoot Date:

Wardrobe:

YEAR: 20_____

AGENT: _____

SHOOT   **VOICE-OVER**   **LIVE** (Circle one)

Date: Call time:

Wardrobe:

Location:

Client and/or production company:

Names:

Program title:

IRS SPECIFICS: (circle one)   **PAID** Date: _____

Independent Contractor   Check number: _____

Employer: _____   Gross pay: _____

Expenses/possible tax deductions: Taxes withheld: _____

(parking, etc.)   Agent fee: _____

                                  Actual check amount: _____

AMOUNT DUE:

Accountants who do actors' taxes.

A listing here does not imply an endorsement. There are thousands of tax accountants out there. Actors have recommended the following accountants; thus, they are at least aware of the unique tax implications for artists. It is up to you to determine the best tax professional for you. If a website is listed, you may wish to visit the website to discern the personalities and specialties of each business. Accounting services are not cheap; having your taxes done will likely cost at least $100 and up to $500 or more.

Fox Tax, LLC
612-824-2829
foxtaxservice.com
503 First Avenue N.E.
Minneapolis, Minnesota 55413
IRS-certified enrolled agents.

Karen Hefner at HR Block
952- 837-1155
7650 Edinborough Way, Suite 250
Edina, Minnesota 55435
IRS-certified enrolled agent.

Steve Hendrickson
beaugestemn@msn.com
Steve is a professional union actor who also does actors' taxes. His preferred contact method during tax season is his e-mail address (above). He is not an accountant, but he has been preparing tax returns for professionals in the performing arts (including actors, directors, writers, dancers, singers, and designers) for over twelve years. His clients include "sea-soned veterans and fledgling neophytes." When preparing a return, he generally goes to the client's house or apartment. For more information, e-mail to arrange a phone consult.

Ingersoll Financial Service
612-722-4291
4116 Cedar Avenue S.
Minneapolis, Minnesota 55407

E. Marty Malone, CPA
651-631-9490
New Brighton, Minnesota
Marty is a professional non-union talent and CPA. Marty has been doing actors' taxes for nearly twenty years.

ROR Financial Services, Dick Miller
612-822-7177
Rortax.com
4500 Park Glen Road, Suite 425
St. Louis Park, Minnesota 55416

Tax advice for actors

The Actor's Tax Guide: What Professional Actors and Other Performers Need to Know About Income Taxes (ActorsTaxGuide.com). Written by an actor, for actors. Download a pdf of this tax guide.

Costumes and Make-up Supplies

Costume sources.

Theater companies

Local theaters will often rent costumes and props. I have rented costumes and wigs from several local theater companies, including The Guthrie, Theatre in the Round, and Lakeshore Players. I am sure there are other companies that will rent from their prop/costume storage. (Companies that have an established theater space will be more likely to have storage space for costume rental.)

Costume Rentals—a combined project of the Guthrie Theater and Children's Theatre.
612-375-8722
costumerentals.org
855 East Hennepin Avenue
Minneapolis, Minnesota 55414

Theatrical Costume Company
612-339-4144
theatricalcostumeco.com
1226 Linden Avenue, Suite 122
Minneapolis, Minnesota 55403

Norcostco--Northwestern Costume—
costumes, make-up and technical theater supplies
763-546-9644
norcostco.com
815 Highway 169 N.
Plymouth, Minnesota 55441

Consignment stores

When searching for wardrobe and costumes, do not forget to check consignment stores for less expensive options.

Professional costumers and stylists

I once had a difficult costuming challenge. I struck out at my usual sources. I called a local professional costumer, and after a short phone conversation, I had the name of a store that had exactly what I needed. I offered to pay her for her time, but because it was such a quick call, she refused. If you are faced with a particular challenge, you may wish to consider hiring a talented local costumer stylists. *The Minnesota Film and TV Board Guide* lists several. Find the on-line guide at mnfilmtv.org.

Make-up sources.

Norcostco--Northwestern Costume—
costumes, make-up and technical theater supplies
763-546-9644
norcostco.com
815 Highway 169 N.
Plymouth, Minnesota 55441

Professional makeup artists.

The Minnesota Film and TV Board Guide lists several professional make-up artists. I am certain many of them would be happy to be hired to help you learn make-up techniques. Find the on-line guide at mnfilmtv.org. I have worked with all of the following talented professionals: Jen Santoro Rotty, Andrea DuCane, Sharon Davis, Natalie Hale, Teri Demarest, Cyndy Rae, Tessie Bundick, Crist Ballas, Cara Tollefson. Love them all. If they are busy with commercial, corporate, or film clients, they may turn you down. If you catch them at a slow time, I am sure they will consider teaching you for a modest hourly rate.

Essential wardrobe accessories.

Hollywood Fashion Tape, "The stars' secret to preventing wardrobe malfunctions" (hollywoodfashiontape.com).

Double-stick tape for wardrobe, bra hook-ups, and accessories, along with many other treasures to fix or prevent wardrobe and costume issues. Check the website; you will be glad you did!

Ear Prompters:
Equipment and Training

Consult Chapter 3 for more information about the uses for ear prompters. Ear prompters are not for everyone. In fact, a very small percentage of actors in town do "ear prompted" work. Do not rush out and spend the money on this equipment until you know you have an agent who will send you for such work.

The following may seem confusing unless you have an ear prompter coach who can show you the equipment. You may also go to ear-prompter.com to see pictures of some of the pieces.

You have a choice between wired and wireless.

- The wired model has a clear tube attached to the earpiece that goes behind your ear along your hairline, connecting to a wire that plugs into your recorder.

- The wireless model looks like a hearing aid, and is sold with an induction neck loop that plugs into the recorder. You wear the neck loop under your clothing, and it broadcasts the sound to your earpiece. It is a little easier to hide from the camera, but it is also much more expensive than the wired earpiece.

The wired model has four components:
- earpiece connected to a clear tube.
- micro cassette recorder or digital recorder
- wire connector
- Telex driver or transducer to boost the sound.

The wireless model has three components:
- earpiece
- induction neck loop (sends the sound from the audio source to the ear piece)
- micro cassette recorder or digital recorder.

Unfortunately, few places sell ear prompters as a set. Most folks have to go to three different places around town to get the full set-up. Your alternative is to order an ear prompter on-line, but this will be more expensive. The prices given below are estimates; contact the supplier to get actual prices.

Earpieces.

First, get the earpiece. The earpiece should be custom molded to your ear. Many places sell the generic fit models, but you will occasionally have problems with them. The sound from the earpiece will often "leak out" of the generic models, as the earpiece does not fit snugly into your ear. The audio engineer on the shoot will then complain that your prompter is too loud; you will have to constantly turn down the volume and you will struggle to hear during the entire shoot. The custom-molded earpieces fit so snugly that no sound leaks out. I used a generic fit wireless earpiece for a couple of years; it was workable, but occasionally frustrating. One generic fit model is now sold with a foam "sleeve" to help seal the sound. See Instant-Memory below.

Ear Level Technologies, Inc.—Ron Bloomgren
612-721-5711
3424 E. Lake Street,
Minneapolis. Minnesota. 55406

Call to schedule an appointment to have an earpiece custom made. They may also stock the optional Telex driver. You need one of the following:

- Wired earpiece with clear tube ($50 per ear)
- Wireless earpiece ($300—you need only one ear)

I suggest you start out with the less expensive option—the earpiece with tube. You can get by with only one ear, but you may wish to get both for more flexibility. (Having both ears may be helpful if they are showing you from the side or if your hair is quite short and it is difficult to hide the tube.) If you go with the wireless earpiece, you need only one. You choose which is most comfortable for you, right or left ear.

Recorders.

Most any type and brand of digital or micro-cassette recorder will work; however, it must have very clear sound. I used a basic Sony recorder for years which cost $30 to $40. A better quality recorder may produce better sound.

The recorder you purchase must have an ear jack. A pause switch is nice to have, and most recorders have this. A remote pause jack is really nice to have, but nearly impossible to find except through the mail order sources listed below. You may purchase recorders just about anywhere: Target, Walgreen's, office supply stores, and electronics stores. (Prices vary from as low as $20 on sale to as much as several hundred dollars.)

I have always used the old-fashioned micro-cassette recorder, though I know some actors who happily use digital models. The only drawback to a digital recorder is that it is more difficult to rewind or fast forward to the middle of a "take." This would be only an occasional inconvenience on a shoot.

Please note: Recorders have different sized jacks: some are 1/8 inch; others are 3/32 inch. Be sure you purchase a recorder that actually works with your wire connection, and vice versa. You can buy adapters to make it work, but the sound will be more consistent with the proper fit.

Wire connectors and induction neck loops.

Once you have an earpiece, you will need to connect it to your recorder.

- For the wireless model you will need an "induction neck loop." Fortunately, these are sold with the wireless earpiece, so you will not have to go searching for them.

- For the wired model, you will need a wire and connector (driver/transducer) that connects the clear tube to the recorder. When you get your earpiece molded, ask your earpiece seller to show you exactly what you will need. Ear Level Technologies may carry the driver or transducer, saving you a trip to one of the places below.

Telex driver/transducer.

AEI Master Distributors
612-338-4754
6020 Olson Memorial Highway
Minneapolis, Minnesota 55422

A Telex driver or transducer gives clearer sound to the wired earpiece. It connects the tube to the wire that plugs into your recorder. Tell them you need a "Telex RTR-04 and a Telex CMT-98 with a 5"cord and straight mini-connector." (If you just show up and tell them you need ear prompter equipment, most personnel will have no idea what you are talking about.) Total cost is about $40; a special order may take a week or two.

Full ear prompting systems.

I have found three businesses that sell ear prompter components and full systems. I have purchased products from two of these businesses. Another actor recommended the third. The products have different features and prices, but all appear to be good systems.

Instant Memory™ Ear Prompting Systems
770-828-0337
ear-prompter.com
1360 Martina Drive
Atlanta, Georgia 30338

A husband-wife team of actors in Atlanta started this business out of their home office. They have great equipment. You can get a wireless earpiece that is not custom molded, but they sell it with a tiny sponge "sleeve" that helps seal the sound. Or, you can acquire your own impression of your ear canal, send it to them, and they will produce the molded earpiece. Also, they have come up with a digital recorder with a remote pause switch. This is the best equipment I have found. See the website options and prices.

The Ear-Talk System
800-828-1990
manlytoys.com
Holmes Osborne, Bates City, MO 64011

Ovation!
earprompter.com
Brian Collins, San Diego

Ear prompter training.

The Talent Center: Don Cosgrove
651-306-9670
www.thetalentcenter.com

Don is great. I have taken other classes with him, and I am sure he teaches ear prompting quite well.

Marie Mathay
763-546-8216
mariemathay@comcast.net

Marie (AEA, SAG, AFTRA) has extensive professional stage, camera, and ear prompting experience. She used to teach on-camera and ear prompter at the Academy for Film and TV. She may now be willing to teach you ear prompter individually, particularly if you are a union actor. Contact her to ask.

Beth Chaplin

I teach ear prompter classes from time to time. I primarily teach students who have been referred to me by local agencies. (Prior on-camera experience or training, or extensive stage experience preferred.) If an agent recommends that you learn to ear prompt, they will put you in touch with me; or you may send an e-mail to beth@actingbiztc.com.

Bill Cooper
612-616-3159
billcooper.info

Bill offers one-on-one training, including ear-prompting. See complete listing in Appendix F.

Related Organizations

You will not interact with all of these organizations, but depending upon your interests, you will want to know about many of them!

Center for Independent Artists
612-724-8392
c4ia.org
4137 Bloomington Avenue S.
Minneapolis, Minnesota 55407

From the website: "Center for Independent Artists exists as a producing, convening and service organization for artists from diverse physical, cultural, and aesthetic perspectives – offering a place for visibility, intersection, conversation and career support. Celebrates the role of the independent artist as visionary in society. The Center nurtures independent artistic vision, fosters diverse cultural perspectives and seeks to build an educated, enlightened citizenry."

The Drama Book Shop, New York
212-944-0595
www.dramabookshop.com

A great resource for all things theater and acting. You can get books and scripts mail ordered quickly and easily with fast delivery. If you visit New York, it is fun to take an hour or so to check them out. They will likely have any business-related books or scripts that you cannot find here in Minnesota.

Hennepin Center for the Arts
612-332-4478
528 Hennepin Avenue
Minneapolis, Minnesota 55403

Hennepin Center for the Arts provides affordable office, studio, and performance space for more than seventeen Twin Cities arts organizations." Tenants include Ballet Arts Minnesota, James Sewell Ballet, Minnesota Dance Theatre, Zenon Dance Company, Illusion Theater, Minnesota Chorale, and VSA Arts Minnesota.

"In Fall of 2010, Hennepin Center will become part of the Minnesota Shubert Performing Arts and Education Center, a three-building complex that will also include the renovated Shubert Theater and a new glass-walled atrium connection the two historic buildings and serving them both as a common lobby" (from the website, artspace. org/properties/hennepincenter/).

IFP Minnesota Center for Media Arts
651-644-1912
Ifpmn.org
2446 University Avenue W., Suite 100
St. Paul, Minnesota 55114

IFP is a national organization that supports independent filmmakers. The Minnesota chapter offers classes, rental equipment (for members), and information. IFP Minnesota is an organization that "promotes and supports the work of artists who create screenplays, film, video, and photography in the Upper Midwest." They provide classes, access to facilities and equipment, film exhibitions, and events, etc. Many events and exhibitions are open to the public, while access to equipment is for members only. Members receive discounts on classes. While this organization is not a resource for actors, if you have ideas about becoming a film-maker, you will want to check them out.

Intermedia Arts
612-871-4444
intermediaarts.org
2822 Lyndale Avenue S.
Minneapolis, Minnesota 55408

"Our mission is to be a catalyst that builds understanding among people through art." Intermedia Arts' programming includes media arts, visual arts, performing arts, and literary arts. See the website for more details.

Media Communications Association International of Minnesota (MCAI)
www.mcai-mn.org

Many local companies who produce commercials and industrials (and more) are members of this organization. It is not an organization for actors, but you may want to check it out. If you do much commercial and industrial work, you will work with many MCAI members.

mnartists.org

From the website: "mnartists.org is an online database of Minnesota artists from all disciplines. It offers to Minnesota-based artists a central gathering place on the web, and will grow to become a marketplace and community hub. It offers the public a new way to explore art and get to know artists. In addition to providing artists with a web page containing images and information, Minnesotaartists.org will soon provide news and features about the local arts scent from a variety of sources. Minnesotaartists.org was developed as the result of a survey of Minnesota artists conducted by the McKnight Foundation. The survey revealed the survival struggles of individual artists. The McKnight foundation partnered with the Walker Art Center's New Media Initiatives group to develop Minnesotaartists.org."

Minnesota Film Arts
mnfilmarts.org

From the website: "Minnesota Film Arts is a non-profit organization dedicated to fostering an active and living appreciation of the film arts in the Twin Cities and greater Minnesota. We pursue our mission through numerous programs in the areas of presentation, production, and advocacy." Especially if you enjoy film festivals, check out the website.

Minnesota Women in Film and Television
www.mnwift.org

Promoting and supporting women in the film and TV production business (not an organization for actors).

The Playwrights' Center
612-332-7481
pwcenter.org
2301 Franklin Avenue E.
Minneapolis, Minnesota 55306

From the website: "The Playwrights' Center champions playwrights and plays to build upon a living theater that demands new and innovative works." "The Playwrights' Center is nationally recognized as the undisputed leader in the cultivation and promotion of playwrights and their work." The Playwrights' Center is at the heart of the Twin Cities' theater community.

Play by Play Theater Bookstore and Opening Night Gifts
1771 Selby Avenue
St. Paul, MN 55104
www.playbyplaybooks.com

A brand new resource for the Twin Cities theater community, Play by Play will have a callboard in the store with auditions, classes and jobs, and will allow theatres to leave "sides" for auditions. Play by Play will offer a large selection of new and used books related to the performing arts —theatre, film, dance, and opera. Free coffee, loads of theatre related events, along with artsy greeting cards and unique gift items await actors, dancers, students, educators, and audience members

Screenwriter's Workshop

612-659-8292
screenwritersworkshop.org
528 Hennepin Avenue S., Suite 507
Minneapolis, Minnesota 55403

From the website: "Screenwriters Workshop is an all volunteer organization which provides aspiring and practicing Minnesota screenwriters a setting for interaction and exchange of information. Since 1987 Screenwriters Workshop has promoted the development of Minnesota screenwriters. As members of Screenwriters Workshop, screenwriters, producers, directors, playwrights, and allied partners in filmmaking express their commitment to improving the quality of movie storytelling." If you are an aspiring screenwriter, be sure to see their website for more information.

Shoot in Minnesota

shootinminnesota.org

From the website: "Bringing major motion picture production to Minnesota through legislated incentives." A lobbying organization seeking to "educate the public, the legislature, the media and the press about the economic benefits major motion picture production brings in terms of jobs and revenue for local businesses and municipalities."

Springboard for the Arts

651-292-4381
springboardforthearts.org
308 Prince Street, Suite 270
St. Paul, Minnesota 55101

"A non-profit artist service organization. Springboard for the Arts' mission is to cultivate a vibrant arts community by connecting artists with the skills, contacts, information and services they need to make a living and a life."

Visit the website to sign up for their e-mail list. They offer workshops and all kinds of support for the business side of your art. Their services are too numerous to mention here.

Theater Communications Group

tcg.org

National organization for theater professionals across the country. TCG publishes *American Theater* magazine. See the website for details about membership.

Theater Space Project

theaterspaceproject.org

From the website: "Theater Space Project is a non-profit organization dedicated to providing quality space for live theater because it enlightens, inspires, and entertains in a totally unique way. Our mission is to support live theater by providing and managing performance space. The space will serve the needs of Minnesota's growing theater community."

Walker Art Center

walkerart.org

There's always something interesting happening at the Walker Art Center. On the website you can browse categories including theater, film, dance, classes and workshops, lectures, etc.

Resources for Artists with Disabilities

Interact Center for the Visual and Performing Arts
612-339-5145
interactcenter.com
212 Third Avenue N., Suite 140
Minneapolis, Minnesota 55401

From the website: "Founded in 1992 as a professional theater company that included actors with disabilities, Interact expanded its vision in 1996 to become a recognized center for both the performing and visual arts. Interact is a nonprofit 501c3 organization and a licensed day care facility."

"Today, Interact Center is the only center nationally that offers professional-level training, performances and exhibitions in multiple artistic disciplines, for artists with a wide range of disabilities, from physical to developmental to mental to behavioral. At Interact, adult artists with disabilities explore and expand their creativity as actors, writers, painters, sculptors and musicians."

See the website for more.

National Arts and Disability Center
http://nadc.ucla.edu/

This is not a local organization, but the website contains a tremendous number of resources and information about arts and disability. From the website: "Our mission is to promote the full inclusion of audiences and artists with disabilities into all facets of the arts community."

The website includes a link to "US and International theatre companies for performers with disabilities."

VSA arts of Minnesota
612-332-3888
vsarts.org
528 Hennepin Avenue, Suite 305
Minneapolis Minnesota 55403

From the website: "VSA arts of Minnesota makes the arts available and accessible to people with all types of disabilities throughout the state."

Bibliography

This is a short list of some of my favorite books (and resources) about the biz—particularly those that may be helpful to newer actors. New books are coming out all the time; visit Play by Play to find many more.

There are hundreds of books about various acting methods. I have included only a few that cover the basics. If you search for key names, you will find many more: Stanislavski, Hagen, Adler, Meisner and Strasberg, among others.

Play by Play Theater Bookstore and Opening Night Gifts
1771 Selby Avenue
St. Paul, MN 55104
www.playbyplaybooks.com

A brand new resource for the Twin Cities theater community, Play by Play will have a callboard in the store with auditions, classes and jobs, and will allow theatres to leave "sides" for auditions. Play by Play will offer a large selection of new and used books related to the performing arts - theatre, film, dance and opera. Free coffee, loads of theatre related events, along with artsy greeting cards and unique gift items await actors, dancers, students, educators, and audience members

The business of acting.

Callan, K. *How to Sell Yourself as an Actor* (Sweden Press, 2008).

This is one of my favorite books about the business. It is well-written and easy to read, with practical advice about the business side of being an actor—from New York to L.A. and everywhere in between. It is very motivating.

Henry, Mari Lyn and Lynne Rogers. *How to be a Working Actor: The Insider's*

Guide to Finding Jobs in Theater, Film and Television (Back Stage Books, 2008).

This book is another great resource about the world of acting, written by professionals in the biz.

Alterman, Glenn. *What to Get Your Agent For Christmas, and 100 Other Tips for the Working Actor* (Smith and Kraus, Inc., 1995).

A quick, funny read, but do not let the comedy fool you. It contains lots of practical advice about many aspects of the biz.

Acting concepts.

Brestoff, Richard. *The Great Acting Teachers and Their Methods* (Smith and Kraus, 1995).

Good history of the evolution of acting in America and a good overview of the most famous teachers in the western world. This book really helped me to understand the different schools of acting and their origins.

Shurtleff, Michael. *Audition* (Bantam Books, 1979).

I have read it a few times. This book discusses auditions, but you will learn far more about acting than just auditioning. Shurtleff's twelve guideposts are excellent.

Moston, Doug. *Coming to Terms with Acting—An Instructive Glossary: What You Need To Know To Understand It, Discuss It, Deal With It And Do It* (Drama Book Publishers, New York, 1993).

I wish I had this book twenty-five years ago. It helps to clarify the many terms that acting teachers toss out frequently in class. Entries in this book contain detailed descriptions and background information about almost every acting term you will ever hear.

Bruder, Cohn, Olnek, Pollack, Previto, and Zigler. *A Practical Handbook for the Actor* (Vintage Books, 1986).

The book is just what the title says: a simple, quick read, written by students of David Mamet. It de-mystifies the acting process. When you begin to be overwhelmed, thinking that you have to master every method of acting that ever was, read this book. It will ground you again.

Jory, Jon. *Tips: Ideas For Actors* (Smith and Kraus, 2000).

Very concise and easy to read, it is a reference book of tips and concepts as well as a reminder of many different acting concepts.

Guskin, Harold. *How To Stop Acting* (Faber and Faber, Inc. 2003).

This is my latest favorite acting book. From the book cover: "Guskin offers a strategy based on a radically simple and refreshing idea: that the actor's work is not to 'create a character' but rather to be continually, *personally* responsive to the text, wherever his impulse takes him." His students include Glenn Close, Christopher Reeve, and James Gandolfini.

Camera work.

Taub, Eric. *Gaffers, Grips and Best Boys: A behind the scenes look at who does what in the making of a motion picture* (St. Martin's Press, 1995).

Caine, Michael. *Acting in Film: An Actor's Take on Movie Making* (Applause Theatre Book Publishers, 1997).

Moshansky, Tim. *A to Z Guide to Film Terms* (First Wave Publishing, Vancouver B.C., 2007).

This is a tiny little book that contains an alphabetical guide to the lingo you will commonly hear at a video or film shoot.

Voice-overs.

Hogan, Harlan and Jeffrey Fisher. *The Voice Actor's Guide to Home Recording:* A money and time-saving non-technical guide to making your own voiceover demos and auditioning from home or on location (Thomson Course Technology, 2005).

Hogan and Fisher cover all aspects of the biz: technical needs, internet voice-over sources, auditioning, and reaching clients.

Hogan, Harlan. *VO: Tales and Techniques of a Voice-Over Actor* (Allworth Press, 2002).

Twenty-five years of voice-over experience and advice are packed into this fun read.

Baker, Joan. *Secrets of Voice-Over Success: Top Voice-Over Actors Reveal How They Did It* (Sentient Publications, 2005).

Each chapter is by a different successful voice-over artist; you have heard all of them!

Related topics.

Field, Syd. *Screenplay; The Foundations of Screenwriting* (Dell Publishing, 1994).

This was required reading for Jane Brody's film and TV class. The chapters on character are particularly interesting for actors.

Cameron, Julia with Mark Bryan. *The Artist's Way: A Spiritual Path to Higher Creativity* (G. P. Putnam's Sons, 1992).

"A Course in Discovering and Recovering Your Creative Self." Nurture your inner artist and let him or her come out to play.

Acting Related Jobs

Theme parks/festivals.

Nickelodeon Universe at Mall of America
mallofamerica.com (click on "Jobs")
Nickelodeonuniverse.com/employment
Bloomington, Minnesota

Auditions for costumed characters and/or performers have been advertised in the Sunday *Star Tribune* classifieds (performing arts section).

Renaissance Festival
Renaissancefest.com
Shakopee, Minnesota

The Ren Fest is held from August through early October each year. See the website for details. Auditions for performers have been advertised in the *Star Tribune* classifieds.

Valley Fair
Valleyfair.com
Shakopee, Minnesota

Auditions are usually held in February for summer positions (eighteen and older). The following positions have been listed in the past: singers/dancers, instrumentalists, technicians, costumed characters, street performers, magician's assistants.

Tours to schools.

The following companies produce shows that travel to schools in the area and around the country. Actors become part of a performing cast or a teaching cast. Positions are paid and usually include travel expenses. See the websites for more detail.

Climb Theatre
climb.org
National Theatre for Children
nationaltheatre.com

GTC Dramatic Dialogues
gtcdrama.com
(workshops and tours to colleges and universities)

Miscellaneous.

Minnesota History Center—Museum guide, interpreter, history player
mnhs.org

Positions may be listed on the website or advertised in the *Star Tribune* Sunday classifieds or minnesotaplaylist.com.

Crisis Company
crisiscompany.com

"Professional Role-Play Services." The Crisis Company hires actors to role-play in various situations for crisis intervention professionals such as police officers, dispatchers, hospital staff, etc. See the website for more information.

Puppetry

Kathee Foran (executive director of In the Heart of the Beast Puppet and Mask Theatre) suggested that I include a special section devoted to puppetry. Prior to researching this book, I was only vaguely aware of this art form in the Twin Cities. A few years ago, I was fortunate to work on an industrial shoot with a professional puppeteer. It was pure, delightful magic. I was fascinated. I look forward to attending the following theaters and events in the near future.

Barebones Productions

From bedlamtheatre.org: "Barebones Productions is a non-profit arts group focused on puppets and pageantry, producing events year-round, hosting workshops, traveling to schools and groups." "Barebones Productions is a Minneapolis-based collective of visual and performing artists that create spirited and spectacular parades, installations, and performances, the grandest of which is our Annual Halloween Show." "For three years now, we have also hosted an annual Dumpster Duel, challenging other area puppet groups to build performances out of found materials over the course of a weekend."

More detail about Barebones can be found at bedlamtheatre.org.

Bedlam Theatre Company
bedlamtheatre.org
1501 S. Sixth Street
Minneapolis, Minnesota

From the website: "To produce radical works of theater with a focus on collaboration and a unique blend of professional and community art." "Bedlam provides a steady diet of original, avant-garde for Minneapolis and regional audiences." "As a venue, Bedlam supports a year-round calendar of local, national and international artists, in theater, dance, music, puppetry, performance art and more."

In the Heart of the Beast Puppet and Mask Theatre
hobt.org
1500 E. Lake Street
Minneapolis, Minnesota

According to Executive Director Kathee Foran: "We employ more of an 'apprentice' type of model. Most people enter as unpaid interns or volunteers and then work up to being paid. We are always interested in meeting new puppeteers and encourage those interested in the field to contact us." (For more details, see the website or the listing in Appendix G.)

Open Eye Figure Theater
openeyetheatre.org
506 E. 24th Street
Minneapolis, Minnesota

Mixing screen projections, figures, music, human actors and shadow puppetry. For more detail see the website.

Twin Cities Puppeteers Guild

tcpuppet.org

A membership-based organization, it is a chartered guild of the Puppeteers of America, Inc. Meetings are open to anyone interested in puppetry. Be sure to see the website for details.

UNIMA–USA

unima-usa.org

This is the USA chapter of the Union Internationale de la Marionette, "promoting international friendship through the art of puppetry." According to the website, UNIMA is the oldest international theatre organization in the world.

"The organization's mission is to link puppeteers nationally and internationally, publish information on and for the field, offer support and technical assistance for professional puppeteers through seminars, conferences and symposia; stimulate the general public's interest in the art of puppetry; and promote the visibility of American puppeteers all over the world."

VEE Corporation

VEE.com

For-profit corporation that produces the Sesame Street Live shows and much more. Visit the website to see photos of their work.

Index